MW00452759

Gem and Lapidary

MATERIALS

For Cutters, Collectors, and Jewelers

Gem and Lapidary
MATERIALS
For Cutters, Collectors, and Jewelers

JUNE CULP ZEITNER

GEOSCIENCE PRESS, INC.
TUCSON, ARIZONA

Copyright © 1996 by June Culp Zeitner

Library of Congress Number: 96-75730

Published by Geoscience Press, Inc.
P.O. Box 42948, Tucson, AZ 85733-2948

All rights reserved. No part of this work may be reproduced by any
mechanical, photographic, or electronic process, or in the form of a
phonographic recording, nor may it be stored in a retrieval system,
transmitted, or otherwise copied for public or private use, without written
permission of the publisher.

Printed in Hong Kong

Cover design by Dianne Borneman

10 9 8 7 6 5 4 3 2 1

Distributed by Mountain Press Publishing Company
P.O. Box 2399, Missoula, MT 59806
1-800-234-5308

Publisher's Cataloging-in-Publication Data
(Prepared by Quality Books Inc.)

Zeitner, June Culp.
        Gem and lapidary materials: for cutters, collectors, and
        jewelers / June Culp Zeitner.
        p. cm.
        Includes bibliographical references and index.
        ISBN 0-945005-18-0

        1. Precious stones   I. Title.
        QE392.Z45 1996   553.8
                                                QBI96-20196

CONTENTS

Acknowledgements   vii

Preface   ix

I.   INTRODUCTION TO GEM AND LAPIDARY MATERIALS   1

II.   THE GEMS OF HISTORY   17

III.   TRANSPARENT FACETING MATERIALS   43

IV.   CRYSTALLINE QUARTZ   63

V.   CRYPTOCRYSTALLINE QUARTZ; THE AGATE FAMILY   85

VI.   QUARTZ: OPAQUE, BUT COLORFUL   127

VII.   QUARTZ: STRANGE AND WONDERFUL PSEUDOMORPHS   145

VIII.   CABOCHON FAVORITES OF YESTERDAY AND TODAY   169

IX.   CABOCHON AND CARVING MATERIALS   185

X.   ORNAMENTAL AND DECORATIVE GEM MATERIALS   205

XI.   PHENOMENAL GEMS: STARS AND STRIPES   235

XII.   METALLIC GEM MATERIALS   247

XIII.   ORGANIC GEM MATERIALS: GEMS FROM LIFE   259

XIV.   RARE, LITTLE KNOWN AND UNUSUAL GEM MATERIALS ·   273

XV.   GEMS FROM THE LABORATORY AND FACTORY   305

Appendix A: Refractive Index and Dispersion of Gemstones   323

Appendix B: Educational Associations   327

Appendix C: Publications   329

Bibliography   331

Index   339

Dedication

This book is dedicated with love and gratitude
to the memory of
my late husband Albert Zeitner,
who opened up the wonderful world
of gems and lapidary to me,
so many years ago.

PREFACE

ROCKS, MINERALS, AND GEMS are the foundation of an important field of science, but they are something else too — they are the materials of timeless art. This book is about minerals and gems which are used by lapidary and jewelry artists for beautiful objects which enrich the cultures of the world. It is hoped this book will help lapidaries expand their horizons by trying more of wonderful materials of this earth — and inspire jewelers to take another look at colored stones.

Science and art use materials differently and study them with different points of view, but the artist must base his work on certain scientific principles. The primary concern of the lapidary is to produce something beautiful. The primary concern of the jeweler is to use the products of the lapidary in the best possible way to please his customers.

Lapidary as an art is ageless, classless, and without national boundaries. It is unique in many ways. It has contributed to social and religious beliefs, to customs, rites, superstitions, and trade. Furthermore, the expert lapidary does not necessarily have a college degree, is not necessarily a professional cutter, and may even be self-taught. The expert lapidary does not have to use state-of-the-art machines. What a true lapidary artist needs is an eye for beauty, originality, and excellent craftsmanship. Equipment helps, of course, but the advances in lapidary art have come about, largely, through the talent and perseverance of people throughout the ages who chose stones as the medium of their art.

There are often discussions about whether lapidary is an art or a craft. Like oil or watercolor paintings, it is both. Every painting is not art. Artists must know their craft and be able to use it well to convey their feelings to others. The true artist not only knows the basics, scale, proportion rhythm, focus, perspective, harmony, unity and color, but he knows how to use these tools to present an original emotion or observation to draw the ultimate viewer into the picture. Certainly, the best lapidary work is as much art as the best paintings. A cutter of highly polished domed oval cabochons, is not an artist, but neither are thousands of "Sunday painters" artists, who dab watercolor, oil, or acrylic on paper or canvas. Conversely, if a lapidary's work is fresh, original, and done with skilled craftsmanship, and if it conveys a feeling of awe, wonder, understanding, or curiosity to the viewer, it is every bit as much art as when a painter is successful with his work on canvas.

We have today, the best craftsmen ever in the lapidary field. Many of our cutters are innovators and will be copied for generations. That is *art*. Our carvers are producing meaningful works in hard material, which are the equal of many master-works in hard material, and which are the equal of many masterpieces of the past done in marble or other soft material.

The standards of what is art have changed so that the National Endowment for the Arts calls experimentation *art*, even if it is ugly or biased, or absurd.

Lapidaries are naturally ahead of much of what passes for art, because their medium is gem materials, the most colorful and beautiful bits of this earth. With love and imagination, lapidaries through the ages have made their craft an art, and that art has never flourished as much as in the second half of the 20th century.

For some reason, art galleries have been slow to accept lapidary work as art — which may be because lapidaries are outnumbered so greatly by those who work with paper, glass, or clay. This is changing now. Gem engraver, Ute Bernhardt, for example, has been invited by several galleries to have "one person shows."

As people become more familiar with stones other than diamond, ruby, sapphire, and emerald, and with cuts other than brilliant, oval, and pear, the appreciation and acceptance of lapidary as an art will grow, and may well become a leading art form in the next century.

This book then, is about minerals and rocks as lapidary materials. The descriptions stress how the material looks to a lapidary artist, or jeweler, or connoisseur. It is not a book about *mineralogy*, nor a book about how to cut stones — it is about the *materials of lapidary*, the art of the ages.

June Culp Zeitner

ACKNOWLEDGEMENTS

Thanks to the Lapidary Journal for being a voice of the lapidary world, and for giving me a chance to be part of that voice. Thanks to Geoscience Press for seeing the need for a book on lapidary materials. I am grateful beyond words to the cutters, collectors, gemologists, miners, jewelers, and dealers who willingly shared their information, and to the photographers who have captured the beauty of gems on film.

I am especially grateful to Cathy Kjar-Schwafel, The Lizzadro Museum of Lapidary Arts, Russell and Doris Kemp, The Lora Robbins Gallery, Dr. Willie Reams, Gerhard Becker, Dr. Bob Mallas, Hing Wa Lee, Art Grant, Jerry Call, Michael Dyber, Herbert Duke, Harold and Erica Van Pelt, David Phelps, and Cecilia Gaston.

Others who have helped in so many ways have my heartfelt thanks. They include:

Vernon Korstad, John Bradshaw, Jane Perham, Mildred Beckwith, Mark Bielenburg, Frank Sykes, Keith Proctor, Dale Huett, David Smith, Reijo Nenonen, Joan Millton, Patrick Murphy, Horst Windisch, Rob Smith, Nancy Topp, Keith Hodson, Martin Colbaugh, Ed Nazelrod, Rocky Byrom, Rene Vandervelde, Lita Smith-Gharet, Anna Sabina, Leonid Prikazchikov, Lawrance Beebe, Anthony Karup, Kitty Starbuck, Lee Hammons, Eugene Mueller, Jim Manganella, Miles Smith, Scott Wolter, John Miller, Willis Smith, Larry and Virginia Kribs, Paul and Bette Peterson, Bernice Hallam, Bill Nicks, Susan Zalkind, Olive Sain, June McKenzie, Joe Carlton, Bruce Deter, Mark Smith, Delores Martin, Henry Hunt, Betty Crawford, John Kemmerer, Roland Rasmussen, John De Marco, Bob Miller, Steve Walters, Frank Jeckel, Dr. Ian Reban, Dr. Peter Bancroft, Terry Hicks, David Ratoike, Jefferson Kunisaki, Eduardo Olbes, John Watkins, Lloyd Nye, David Olson, Gene Hamm, Ed Schultz, Debbie Barlow, Dr. Jean Marr, Richard Whiteman, Fred Dorward, Hank Van Twuyver, F. Muller Bastos, Henri Louis Jacob, Eduardo Loli, Kirk Makepeace, Stan Leaming, John Snook, DonWobber, Ken Boulier, Susan Black, Peter Marino, Reuel Janson, C.R.Smith, Claude Atkin, Bill Edward, Tania Feigal, Dr. Robert Woodward, Roy Ploudre, Jorge Saadi, Jean Hollings, Olga Game, Francis Villamagne, Terry Power, Betty Warrington, Winona Favorite, Willis Leaf, Willow Wight, Herb Obodda, Walt Rubeck, W.C. Dansie, Sam Tsubota, Størk Halstensen, Jan Baumeister, Ute Bernhardt, Jim Kaufman, Eleanor Anderson, Joyce Foster, Amy Fulcher, Addison Saunders, Luis Rivera, Michael Taterka, Gorman Boen, Wesley Koerner, Fred Alteen, Saul Borak, Dr. John Sinkankas, Sy and Ann Frazier, Cal and Kerith Graeber, Robert and Sara Dowell, Pansy Kraus.

CHAPTER I

Introduction to Gem and Lapidary Materials

WHAT ARE GEM AND LAPIDARY MATERIALS?

FEW THINGS IN THIS WORLD are as universally treasured and admired as much as a brightly colored gemstone. Cultures have been influenced, battles have been fought, history has been changed by man's love of these precious bits of our rocky Earth. The lure of gems has been a magnet for adventurers and explorers, a status symbol for emperors and kings, a challenge for artists, and an objective of thieves. The history of mankind's involvement with gemstones is rich with exciting tales that are true but read like fiction, and conversely with folklore and myths that sound like facts.

In the distant days of prehistory, men chose stones that were prettier than average for their favorite weapon or tool, and probably soon noticed that eligible women coveted the attractive stones. Those who found and worked with the best stones soon occupied privileged positions in their tribes. Gradually the work of these primitive lapidaries became more and more complex, and lapidary became a true art. Even today people stand in lines in museums to gaze at the masterpieces of early lapidaries, and wonder how the raw stones could become objects of such beauty, with the limited technology of early man.

With our state-of-the-art technology, lapidary materials can be used in countless ways and cut with previously impossible perfection. With new cuts, new materials, new treatments, machines and tools, we are on the threshold of the greatest period of lapidary advancement ever seen.

LAPIDARY MATERIALS

Although people may have different perceptions of gem materials, most agree that these materials are rocks and minerals (including minerals of organic origin) having the following qualities: beauty, durability, and rarity. However, there are exceptions. In some countries a gem material is treasured even if it is not particularly beautiful. For example, in China ancient pieces of nephrite with dull or muddy colors may be regarded as fine gem materials. Turquoise is seldom durable. It is often too porous or chalky and the robin's egg blue fades to a dingy green, but to some cultures turquoise is an esteemed gemstone. Jasper is far from rare, but along with other cryptocrystalline quartzes, it has become one of the most popular gem materials.

Beauty in gemstones depends on several factors, especially color. Other things being equal, the better the color the more valuable the gem. Color tastes are extremely individual, but each color has several dimensions: hue, tone or value (value here is an artist's term meaning the same as tone), and intensity or saturation. Hue refers to a specific color such as red or blue. Connoisseurs prefer hues which are pure and clear and values which are not extreme. (In this case tone means the amount of lightness or darkness of the hue.) Those with a critical eye look for a degree of saturation as full as possible, with no hint of grayness or dullness. The apparent color of a gemstone is affected by many things, but this will be discussed later. Intensity is the amount of brightness or vivid chromatic purity of a hue.

A skilled lapidary can cut a gem so as to enhance the color. On the other hand, a careless lapidary, by incorrect cutting, can make a potentially good color look mediocre, which is one of the reasons lapidaries should make a careful study of any lapidary material.

Luster and texture are important aspects of lapidary materials. A satin or matte finished stone is dull compared with a stone having a mirror polish, but contrast often adds drama. The new "fantasy cuts" use contrasting textures and finishes to advantage.

Durability is the quality of stone that enables it to endure the physical and chemical hardships of the attacks by machines and compounds used in the cutting and polishing while still withstanding the abuses of time. Both the hardness and toughness of a stone contribute to its durability. Correct cutting can increase or destroy the durability of a stone. A few stones lack durability and are really quite fragile, but are so beautiful they are classed as desirable gems. Examples are opal and kunzite.

Rarity is possibly the least important attribute of a gemstone. In a way, all gem materials are rare because they are the most beautiful bits of a rocky globe where most of the components are neutral in color and fractured and marred by natural forces. What seems rare in one place may be common in another. A collector may look for unusual pictures in agates and call them rare, while the next collector may disregard the pictures and call the agates common. Some diamonds are rare, but not all diamonds. Some beryl is rare, but not all beryl. An agate with perfect color and pattern may be just as rare as some of the gem feldspars or garnets.

Because the economy of the mining industry governs the supply of gem materials, and current fashions govern the demand, some stones may be rare during some time periods, but not during previous or subsequent periods. An anachronism is that a truly rare gemstone is often not sufficiently known to have a ready

Coral is one of the ancient lapidary and jewelry materials.
Still popular, it comes in many colors and forms.
Photo by Dr. Willie Reams. Courtesy of Lora Robins Gallery, Richmond, Virginia.

market with prices that would reflect its rarity. A fine faceted benitoite may be just as exquisite as a diamond of the same size and cut, but the price will not show that.

All of these variables have made the old terms *precious* and *semiprecious* obsolete. The arbitrary terms were used to distinguish the big four—diamonds, rubies, sapphires, and emeralds—from all others. Many people also believed that faceted stones were inherently better—more precious than cabochons. In fact, an aquamarine with a dazzling eye or a garnet with a brilliant star can be more costly than many transparent faceted stones. So old beliefs about the monetary values of gemstones are fading.

In the twentieth century many gemstones have been synthesized in the laboratory with the high-tech products often rivaling the natural for beauty and durability. This has caused much controversy among purists who insist that since synthetics can be made in quantity, they lack rarity and cannot be true gems. Because the purpose of gem materials is to adorn, to embellish, and to decorate, it makes little difference to many people whether the gems are grown underground or in a lab. The truth is that nature's gems are usually treated or enhanced in some way before reaching the market. Most trusted as natural are the many varieties of agate, chalcedony, jasper, and other quartzes as well as aesthetic calcites and feldspars.

Some gem materials are becoming scarce. Major fields have been known and mined for centuries and most of these wonderful localities are worked out. In some cases where there may still be considerable material, mining has been halted because of political upheaval, economy, or unfortunate natural events such as floods, fires, or earthquakes. Some deposits can be mined only by hand. The gem fields may be dangerous and it is a huge gamble for the miners who may not find enough to pay for their efforts.

The Earth is by no means depleted of gem material. New materials such as tanzanite, charoite, and sugilite are discovered with regularity, and materials previously neglected are being found to have decorative uses as new lapidary techniques are worked out. To the innovative lapidary, rocks and minerals are the media for their art, so they are constantly initiating new uses of old materials, and making them look better than ever. Cutters look for materials that can be successfully worked to yield durable, artistic, and valuable products.

For this book, then, lapidary materials are defined as natural or man-made minerals, rocks, or certain organics, that have the beauty and durability to be treated by lapidaries for decorative and ornamental purposes. A lapidary is defined as a person who cuts or shapes gem materials. Lapidary is also the "art" of preparing gemstones. A lapidary's usual workplace is a lapidary shop. ("Lapidarist" and "lapidarian" are incorrect.)

LAPIDARY ROCKS

While most gem materials are minerals, some of them are rocks. When rock is taken apart, the separate entities are minerals. Granite is an example of a rock, and huge mountains are composed of it. However, that rock is made up of quartz, feldspar, mica, and perhaps tourmaline, epidote, and more, all of which at times are gem materials. Granite itself, for example, unakite, can be a lapidary material.

Rock can also be a massive formation such as obsidian. Massive organic deposits, such as coal, are also classified as rock. Obsidian has been used as a lapidary material by many cultures for eons, and coal has been used for carvings.

Rocks are not necessarily inferior gem materials just because they are more abun-

Artists of long ago left records in the rocks for contemporary lapidaries to contemplate. This photo was taken in northern Mexico.

dant than the minerals that are gem materials. Rocks chosen as lapidary materials must be carefully selected, but that is true of minerals as well. Lapis lazuli, a rock, is among the elite gem materials. Another rock, larvikite, is one of the most glamorous ornamental materials.

A rock that is a gem material is one with good color, exceptional pattern or other optical quality, and cutability. If a rock is beautiful, a skilled lapidary will find some way to use it, even if he or she has to stabilize it, fill in cracks, or make it into a doublet or triplet. Most rocks are opaque, muted in color, and somewhat more difficult to work with than other gemstones.

LAPIDARY MINERALS

Most gems are minerals, but only diamond is a single element, carbon. The others are made up of often complex combinations of the basic elements, which number over a hundred.

Unlike rocks, minerals belong to crystal systems. The study of the crystal of a mineral tells lapidaries much about how to cut it. The crystal may have cleavage planes that must be avoided, or it might have differential hardness. Color may be zoned or concentrated in the termination.

Each mineral is assigned a hardness on the Mohs scale, which rates talc as 1 and diamond as 10. This is of special interest to the lapidary because minerals that are too soft are polished only with extra care, and then do not hold the polish well, while minerals which are 8½ and 9 in hardness are considered difficult to polish with standard equipment.

Each mineral is also tested for density or specific gravity. This measurement compares the weight and volume of a solid with something of known density, in most cases water. Lapidaries soon learn that a 2-inch (5.08 cm) square of rhodonite is heavier than a 2-inch (5.08 cm) square of pink jasper.

Another characteristic of minerals that is important for lapidaries to understand is that a crystal may have any of a number of inclusions. A liquid inclusion may make the mineral unstable for cutting. Hairlike

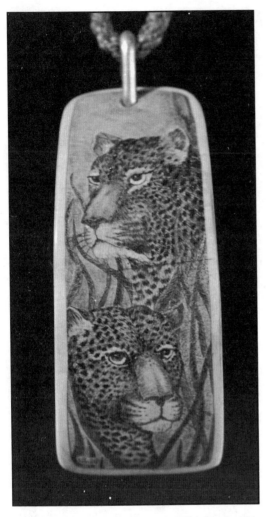

Lita Smith-Gharet used mammoth ivory for this lifelike scrimshaw.

defined eyes and stars is a considerable challenge to the lapidary.

The lapidary should have a knowledge of refraction, or how light is reflected from a cut stone. Light is bent when entering a stone, and it is the lapidary's objective to cut the stone so that it is as brilliant as possible. Whether a stone is singly or doubly refractive also helps in identifying the material. Each gem material has its own refractive index. Diamond, at 2.42, is one of the highest.

ORGANIC GEM MATERIALS

Another group of gem materials has some connection with living species, such as oysters, elephants, and pine trees. Some of these have become mineral. Pearls are mostly aragonite. Other organics—amber and jet—have undergone extensive metamorphosis. Having originated many eons ago, such materials are classed as fossils, but lapidaries are more likely to work with them than with pearls.

Organic gem materials are softer than most of the more common gemstones such as agate, feldspar, and jade. However, they have other qualities such as toughness or elasticity that make them quite durable. Lapidaries must learn the special qualities of these materials. Most are heat sensitive and several are toxic when being cut and shaped. Beginning lapidaries, especially those interested in carving, often try organic materials before working with harder gem materials, because ivory, bone, horn, shell, and others can be worked by hand with kitchen or workshop tools.

inclusions of rutile or tourmaline may pull and leave hollows. Some inclusions may spoil the appearance of a finished stone, whereas others, if properly oriented, may result in a superb gem.

Examples of how inclusions produce dramatic stones are rutilated quartz, tigereye, and star garnet. Eyes and stars are inherent in some pieces of gem material because the needlelike or hairlike inclusions are aligned according to a specific crystal system. Learning to cut well-

LABORATORY PRODUCTS

Synthetic gems are man-made duplicates of natural minerals. They have the same chemistry, the same physical characteristics, and they are beautiful and durable. Some synthetics can be easily produced in quantity and are therefore inexpensive. Lower in price than natural stones, synthetics vary greatly in price according to the processes used in their production. A top synthetic, such as the Gilson emerald or the Chatham ruby, can be enjoyed by the lapidary who cannot afford natural stones of high quality. Purchasers of fine synthetics are often those who keep their natural stones in vaults.

Synthetics are somewhat easier for the lapidary to work with because the vugs, fractures, large inclusions, and off-color spots have not been reproduced. A lapidary can get a large square of synthetic lapis lazuli or a boule of synthetic spinel and be able to plan the stones with a minimum of waste.

The synthesis of gem materials began in the late nineteenth century and reached a high point with the production of the General Electric synthetic diamonds in 1951. Some synthetic diamonds have been cut, but most synthetic diamond goes to industry. Recently many new synthetics have appeared. The variety includes colorful cabochon materials as well as faceting materials. Efforts are constantly underway to develop new synthetics, and also new laboratory materials that have exceptional gemstone qualities, but that may have no duplicate in nature.

HOW TO SELECT AND ACQUIRE THE RIGHT MATERIALS

Lapidaries have their own ideas about what they want to cut and their preferred areas of specialization. If a lapidary wants to make cabochons, he should read books about gem cutting. If he wants to carve, there are books specifically about carving.

Leonard Sires carved this three-dimensional picture of roses from onyx and serpentine. Photo courtesy of Lapidary Journal.

If faceting is the objective, several books give detailed information and instructions for this art. There are also books about specific gem materials such as beryl, turquoise, and garnets for the lapidary's needs. Some books are listed at the end of this chapter.

The big problem for lapidaries is to get quality material at the right price. First they must learn to evaluate the rough and then compare quality and price. Rough material should have good color and possibly pattern, uniform texture, freedom from large fractures, vugs, stains, or unwanted inclusions, and be large enough in every dimension to complete the project for which it is intended. In nearly every large city there is a lapidary or mineral store,

Award-winning amateur carver Bob Miller carved "Moses and the Burning Bush" in coal.

often called a "gem shop" or a "rock shop." Most such shops carry a number of kinds of rough material and are able to order others. Such shops are advertised in trade periodicals or in the yellow pages of the phone book.

A second source is to order materials by mail or telephone to individuals or companies who advertise rough gem materials in magazines or catalogs. Expensive materials, such as facet rough, usually sell by the gram. Most other materials sell by the pound, or if slabbed, by the square inch.

Sometimes ads will list material according to grades with the top grade designated "AA," "number one," "select," or some other term indicating best quality. Mixed grades are often called "mine run." Grading is done according to color, freedom from major flaws, scarcity of the material, and size. Customers should order the best grade they can afford, because they will get exactly what they pay for.

Some companies sell only to licensed retail dealers at wholesale price. Other companies will lower prices for an individual according to the size of the order. There may be a $200 minimum, a hundred-pound minimum, or the lower prices may be offered to those who order unopened bags or crates of imported materials, such as Brazilian agates.

Most mail order companies are reliable, but it pays to compare ads, to see how long a company has been in business, and to talk to others who order by mail. The customer who orders by mail should know as much as possible about the material he is ordering, and should learn to describe in exact terms what he wants. If he orders a pound of material, he should state if he expects one or two large pieces or several small ones. In many cases he should say what he wants to do with the material. If he wants to make a sphere, or a carving, several small pieces would not be suitable, but smaller pieces might be ideal for cabochons.

Look for the advertiser's policies. Sometimes materials cannot be returned unless the whole parcel is returned. If the material has been altered it cannot be returned. The dealer wants to be fair so he can stay in business, so he tries to interpret the customer's wishes. For those who intend to order lots of lapidary materials, it is helpful to get acquainted with the dealers who stock the wanted materials.

A third source of rough and slabbed lapidary materials is gem and lapidary shows that are held in most major cities, sometimes several times a year. These shows are advertised monthly in gem and mineral periodicals, and locally in newspapers, on radio, and television. Commercially sponsored shows often have little in the way of rough materials, but shows sponsored by gem and lapidary clubs often invite dealers who carry slabs, rough gem materials, and blanks and preforms.

At shows sponsored by clubs there is usually a "swap" area, which is another way to acquire material. A man from Wyoming could swap a piece of jade for a

Chinese artists are noted for elaborate ivory carvings. This Hing Wa Lee carving is topped by a series of movable nested balls.

piece of opal from Idaho, or a plume agate from Texas. Some state associations of gem clubs host annual swaps. The swap sessions work very well for those who know materials and values.

The final alternative is finding your own material in the field. There are hundreds of sites where a field collector may find gem material for cabochons, carvings, novelties, and sometimes faceting. Some of these sites are on public land administered by the government. Sites on private land, often owned by mining companies, are sometimes open to collectors. Other privately owned sites open for collecting may be fee areas, where visitors either pay a flat daily fee or pay a moderate price per pound for what they find. Some of these fee spots even furnish such equipment as pans and screens. Information about rock, mineral, and gem localities can be found in magazines and books. Many locality books are about one state or area and are illustrated with detailed maps.

With a few exceptions the self-found material is not of as high quality as what is available on the market, and if the cost of gas and other supplies is figured in, self-

Joseph Phetteplace created a life-size intarsia portrait of Abraham Lincoln with 2,700 pieces of jade, datolite, agate, catlinite, and petrified wood.
Photo by Russell Kamp.

held up for three years in Mexico because an unknown insect was on top of one of the bags.

THE MANY USES OF LAPIDARY MATERIALS

A person on a fishing or hiking trip finds some pretty stones, perhaps in a creek bottom. When dry, they lose color and he takes them to a rock shop to find out how to bring back their beauty. He is advised to buy a tumbler. Inexpensive and easy to run, the tumbler finishes the stones beyond his wildest dreams, and he is hooked.

There are many things to do with tumbled stones. They can be used with artistry for place cards, greeting cards, and note paper. Made into glittering gem trees with twisted gold wire, they are reminiscent of miniature Oriental Ming trees. A retired florist uses assorted tumbled stones for elegant floral pictures, plaques, and patio and garden decorations. Children make "critters" with tumbled stones that inspire their imaginations. Professionals may use their tumblers for cabochons or beads.

The beginner's next step is probably a diamond saw to cut the bigger rocks he found in the field into slabs just to see what's in them. After the slabs he will cut cabochons, mostly domed and oval. But the beginner should avoid the hazard of looking at lapidary as a narrow world of tumbled stones and cabochons. There are literally dozens of interesting and rewarding ways to use lapidary materials.

To start, cabochons do not have to be oval. They can be square, pear-shaped, round, hearts, crosses, stars, scarabs, scrimshaw, freeform, or fleur-de-lys. The lapidary learns materials by working with them and the materials beg to be tried with new techniques.

found material is not cheap. The exceptions are materials found by knowledgeable and experienced prospectors, those who spend lots of time and hard work in a field, those who may lease a productive area, and those lucky few with sharp eyesight who occasionally have incredible luck. There are few thrills equal to finding your own gemstones.

Professionals sometimes import a large percentage of their material. This is fine if they know what the material is like and know with whom they are dealing. Customs laws are interpreted differently, according to where the material comes in and whether the material is enhanced or not. A ton of fire agate, for example, was

Jewelry is an ancient use of gem materials. Bright stones have been used for ornaments and other purposes for thousands of years. Gemstones have been used for amulets, charms, talismans, fetishes, seals, cylinders, items of trade, religious and state uses, insignia, status symbols, and investments. Meant to be worn, the jewelry items often expressed emotions, for example, the mourning jewelry of the Victorian period.

Orbs, gem-encrusted swords, and magnificent crowns became state and empire jewelry. Rosaries are known as jewelry of religious significance. In more recent times, jewelry has been used as social statements such as class rings, lodge pins, and company logos. Now the main purpose of most jewelry is to adorn: to attract attention, to look fashionable and well dressed, and in a way, to impart self-confidence.

In previous times men wore as much jewelry as women. Today most jewelry is designed for women, although there are complete lines for men, often using the more durable materials. Of course, there is plenty of jewelry for children, especially teenagers.

A particular kind of jewelry is *beads*. Lapidaries can use bead mills or make the beads by hand. Beads can be made in a multitude of shapes, and may employ such lapidary skills as faceting, carving, and engraving. From beads it is only a short step to spheres, another lapidary specialty. *Spheres* and *eggs* of rock crystal, rutilated quartz, opal, and other materials are aesthetic objects that challenge the imagination and craftsmanship of the experienced lapidaries. Some of the more complicated spheres may have engraved designs or colorful inlaid accents.

As we dissolve the mists of prehistory, we find that humans have always used stones for some type of *carving*. Carvings in gem materials have helped record the history of many ancient cultures. Known as one of the highest forms of art, gemstone carving includes cameos, intaglios, bas-relief friezes, high relief, and carvings in the round. Other carvings are useful as well as ornamental, including such items as candlesticks, incense burners, bowls, vases, and teapots.

One prominent lapidary, Whitaker Freegard, specializes in carving hauntingly beautiful melodic flutes from gem materials. Meerschaum, ivory, and amber have been used for elaborate tobacco pipes. Sioux Indian lapidaries carve peace pipes and such tribal symbols as turtles, buffalo, and eagles from their sacred red pipestone. Gemstone carvings can be as small as a ringstone or as large as "Thunder," a jade figure weighing almost 500 pounds carved by Donal Hord and located in the San Diego Fine Arts Gallery. (A stone carving can also be as large as Mount Rushmore.)

Book ends, paperweights, pen bases, and *clock faces* can be made from lapidary materials. Some lapidaries make jade knife blades or handles, letter openers, or gavels. Others make boxes from vivid stones such as lapis lazuli, malachite, rhodochrosite, and sugilite. Some take on projects like gemstone lamp shades, floor tiles, countertops, tabletops, or fireplace fronts. Just name an item that should be more beautiful and there will be some lapidary to try it in gemstone.

Thin polished slabs of gem materials can be used like stained glass, in the manner of the jade church window made by cheese tycoon James Kraft. Thin slabs are also mounted to be used as breathtaking colored slides. Newly popular are the transparent stained glass–style gem ornaments called sun catchers.

Lapidary stones can be used to build *miniatures* and *models*. The Minnesota Valley Gem and Mineral Club built a replica of a historic grist mill. The Tulip City Gem and Mineral Club built a small replica of a Dutch windmill. Innovative lapidary Doris

Carefully selected tumbled stones were used to build this miniature replica of Holland, Michigan's windmill, a project of the local gem club.

Kemp built a miniature rock shop and a tiny florist's shop. Bill Dahlberg, award-winning Minnesota lapidary, built a miniature barnyard scene of pioneer days, complete with petrified wood ladder leading to the hay loft. There have also been miniature churches, carousels, and even small cities like Arizona faceter Jerry Muchna's delightful crystal village.

Mosaics are an archaic use of stones. Pebbles and broken stones shaped the realistic pictures on the walls and walks of Pompeii and other archeological digs. An advanced mosaic technique is intarsia or Florentine mosaic. Small pieces of gem material are individually shaped so that they fit together precisely forming a picture or design that from a little distance resembles an oil painting in color and detail. Intarsias may be very intricate and may take hundreds of hours of skilled lapidary work and hundreds of pieces of stone.

Exactly shaped pieces of stone can be inlaid in metal. Shell inlay is a special technique that has been used to inlay designs in wood, as in banjos, guitars, and other musical instruments. A particular type of inlay is called channel work. The parts of the inlay are separated by thin strips of metal.

Lapidary material *projects* are not necessarily small. A cemetery gate in Sioux Falls, South Dakota, is made of petrified wood from Arizona. Bok Tower in Florida is built of pink marble with elaborately carved details. Huge statues are carved of marble. Gravestones, cornerstones, memorials, and monuments are made of lapidary materials. In Czarist Russia whole walls were built of polished malachite. Stone can also be etched with acid to yield an incised pattern, or matte-finished words or patterns can result from sandblasting .

Lapidary materials can be used for making or decorating almost any object where beauty and durability are among the prime objectives. All these things made from lapidary materials involve basic lapidary techniques: cutting, grinding, sanding, and polishing. These techniques can be accomplished by hand, by home-made machines and tools, or by high-tech machines that include vibratory tumblers, diamond polishing wheels, gem lathes, flexible shaft machines, and many more.

Manufacturers of lapidary equipment regularly advertise in gem and lapidary magazines, and will send catalogs and names of local suppliers upon request. Lapidary machines are demonstrated at major shows. Clubs, schools, and recreational departments offer lapidary courses. It is also possible for a person with mechanical abilities to make his own equipment, and with the aid of a good book, be his own teacher. Eventually many lapidaries invent or modify machines or tools of their own.

THE PROFESSIONAL AND THE AMATEUR CUTTERS

The greatest percentage of lapidary products seen on the market are produced in cutting centers such as Idar-Oberstein, Germany, or Hong Kong. Often lapidary work is a tradition handed down through many generations. In addition to the well-known centers that provide stones for the world market, there are smaller regional centers for professional lapidaries. The turquoise cutters of the American Southwest are a case in point.

The variety and quality of work seen in a place like Idar-Oberstein is staggering. There are intricate carvings in the Fabergé manner, bowls, trays, beads, and cabochons. One of the revolutionary gem treatments to come from this premier cutting center is Bernd Munsteiner's "fantasy cuts."

Many professionals specialize in faceting and even narrow that specialty into cutting one type of material. Mexican natives near the calcite onyx mines of Puebla devote their lives to making carvings of that material.

Besides the work of professional cutters, the work of amateur cutters is also seen in gift shops, gem shops and shows, craft shows, art galleries, and museums. Amateur does not denote an inferior craftsman in any way. Quite the contrary, an amateur may be more selective of his material and spend infinitely more time in studying and cutting it. He works for the love of it and self-satisfaction, and not to meet a production quota. Some of the world's best cutting is done by dedicated, skilled amateurs.

COLOR

Color is one of the most important attributes of lapidary materials, but many lapidaries, gem collectors, and dealers are unable to correctly describe or name the colors they like. Any orange or brown stone is likely to be called red, and a purple agate is often called blue. Some of this confusion is because people see colors differently, and some people are blind to certain colors. A greater cause of confusion is the proliferation of fancy and inexact names given to colors such as tangerine, sand, sage, plum, flame, citron, and many more. Misleading to the public are color names such as jade or garnet because those names tend to confirm the common assumption that jade is always green and garnet is always red.

Color in a lapidary material is the result of the kind of light rays that are absorbed or reflected. A piece of red tourmaline, for example, will absorb most of the rays that produce yellow or blue; however, its red appearance will not be the pure hue as in a rainbow.

The perception of color for lapidary material is influenced by texture, luster, transparency, or opacity, size, irregularities (patterns, zoning, inclusions), surroundings, and source and type of light. A transparent piece of rose quartz will seem less pink than an opaque one; a thick piece will appear pinker than a thin one; and if a piece is placed beside a red vase, some of the red will be reflected on it. (That is why rose quartz beads are sometimes knotted with red cord.)

The easiest way to learn color is to study the artists' color wheel and memorize the relationship the colors or hues have to one another. In addition to the exact or pure hue, each color can be modified by its tone, or the amount of light and dark, and its saturation or intensity, the amount of brightness or dullness.

To the eye, the lightest color is yellow and the darkest is violet. Yellow, blue, and red are the primary colors. The Munsell color system includes green as a primary color. When an artist mixes two primary colors, the secondary colors—green, violet, and orange—result. When a primary color is mixed with a secondary color, a tertiary color is produced. Most colors are not the vivid intense pure hues, but are some mixture of light waves that to the eye seem to be tertiary or quaternary colors. Examples of tertiary colors are blue-green, red-violet, and yellow-orange. Quaternary colors are modified again— blue blue-green, red red-violet, and yellow yellow-orange (sometimes referred to as yellowish yellow-orange).

Most colors are either lighter or darker than the original hue. If they are lighter they reflect more white light; if they are darker they absorb the light. Lighter colors are tints and darker colors are shades. It is incorrect to say that pink is a shade of red.

Very few gem materials are full intensity—that is, as bright or saturated as it is possible for the hue to be. As light rays other than the dominant one act on the material, it becomes duller or "grayed," as the artists call it. Colors that are opposite on the color wheel, such as red and green, are complements, so if a piece of red jasper appears muddy in color it is because inclusions cause light rays of the complement to be reflected. Theoretically, if the three primary colors are mixed, the result should be black. Actually, when several colors are mixed in equal amounts, the result is gray, a noncolor.

Artist supply shops have color wheels or charts for sale or sample cards with the pure hues of the spectrum, and also books with color wheels and explanations of various aspects of color. If a person refers often to the color chart, it will soon be easy to see if a green leans toward blue or

yellow, or if a violet has more red in it than blue. Then, studying the original hue, a person can decide if the stone he is looking at is a shade or a tint, and if it is slightly less than full intensity or a very muted color.

If a customer studies color and then writes to a dealer who also knows color, specifying a piece of red red-orange jasper of only slightly reduced intensity and a piece of a light tint of yellow-green nephrite of more than medium intensity, he should get just what he wants. How much better this is than just ordering "red jasper and green jade." The component rays of a prism of light—red, orange, yellow, green, blue, and violet—are seldom pure on any object, but one reason for people's love of gemstones is that the colors of fine gems are nearer to perfection than most other natural objects.

A beam of white light includes the colors of the rainbow. The long waves, red, are at the top; the short waves, violet, are at the bottom. The components of white light are the dispersion and "fire" of the gemstones. In physics, the explanation of color is represented by a cone with white light at the top and black at the bottom. The primary colors include red, blue, green, and yellow. Tints top the double cone and shades are below with maximum saturation in the center. The ideal white light is the sun, but strong incandescent light is close enough to appreciate the true color of many gem materials. Neon or vapor-type lamps distort the colors.

An artist can produce the exact color wanted by mixing pigments, but the pigments of gem materials have been assembled by nature. However, those who prepare gemstones for market have learned how to improve the colors by various treatments such as heat, radiation, chemicals, dyes, oils, resins, and waxes. They can strengthen the dominant color, change the color, or eliminate detracting colors.

Cabochons are more important in jewelry now than for many decades, and are often seen in fine jewelry combined with faceted stones.

There are several color systems available to gemologists and jewelers, among them the GIA ColorMaster, the Gem Color Manual by Kuehn, Precise Color Communication by Minolta, and others. GIA has introduced a precise color communication system, GemSet, that classes 324 variations of 31 basic hues showing tone and saturation on gemlike color comparators—master "stones" in book form, counter display, or portable set. GemSet is cross-referenced with Color-Master.

Color is used with abandon now in comparison with the past. Colors formerly called "clash" colors, such as red, green, and purple, or pink, orange, and blue, often show up together in interesting jewelry. A profusion of color heightens people's interest in gems and, of course, heightens the pleasure of the lapidary.

RECOMMENDED READING

In addition to the books listed below, see the Bibliography for regional books and periodicals.

Arem, Joel, *Rocks and Minerals*. Phoenix: Geoscience Press, 1991.

Cox, Jack, *Cabochon Cutting*. Pico Rivera, CA: Gem Guides Books, 1974.

Desautels, Paul, *The Gem Kingdom*. New York: Random House, 1971.

Kennedy, Gordon, et al., *Fundamentals of Gemstone Carving*. San Diego: Lapidary Journal, 1977.

Kraus, Pansy, *An Introduction to Lapidary*. Radnor, PA: Chilton, 1987.

O'Neil, Paul, Planet Earth. Gemstones. Alexandria, VA: Time-Life, 1983.

Sinkankas, John, *Field Collecting Gemstones and Minerals*. Tucson: Geoscience Press, 1988.

Walter, Martin, *Gemstone Carving*. Radnor, PA: Chilton, 1977.

CHAPTER II

The Gems of History

Beryl	**Diamond**
Aquamarine	**Garnet**
Emerald	Almandine
Golden beryl	Andradite
Morganite	Grossular
Red beryl	Pyrope
Chrysoberyl	Spessartine
Alexandrite	Uvarovite
Catseye	**Peridot**
Corundum	**Spinel**
Ruby	**Topaz**
Sapphire	**Zircon**

COLORFUL AND SHINING GEMSTONES reach far back into the history and traditions of every culture. The ancients did not know anything about mineralogy or gemology, but they did know what was bright and beautiful. Excavations in Egypt and Colombia have helped reveal the universal love of gems. The King James version of the Bible refers to 124 different gems and minerals. India has a 5,000-year tradition of involvement with gems.

Many of the 12 sacred gems worn by Aaron, brother of Moses, are identical to the 9 sacred gems of the Hindu Navaratna. It is not just coincidence that these peoples of long ago admired the same gemstones.

Three aquamarines cut by Michael Dyber, 13.10, 31.50, and 17.10 carats, are examples of new cuts that make every stone unique.

The gemstones they liked were vivid in color, they were durable, and they were found as lustrous crystals which needed very little shaping or polishing.

By the time of the early Roman Empire, lapidaries were highly skilled at engraving gems. Fine gems were collected by rulers, nobility, and religious leaders. Wealthy families like the Borgias had an entire suite of precious gems for each month of the year. Thieves, murderers, and pirates also yearned for gems, so the course of history was changed in many places because of the lust for gems.

Scholars are not certain about some of the specific gems referred to in history, since early gem descriptions referred to color, not to other physical characteristics, and not to the chemical makeup. What is known is that reds, blues, and greens,—called rubies, sapphires, and emeralds—

were valued extremely highly. Hard color-less stones were known thousands of years ago—some may have been diamonds, and some may have been something else, but they were called diamonds.

Those four stones eventually became known as precious and all others were called semiprecious. The importance of color is illustrated by the fact that garnets were at one time considered equal to rubies, and spinels were mistaken for rubies in many countries. Cleopatra's emeralds may have been peridots.

Many of the important gems of history were brought back to Europe by Jean Baptiste Tavernier, who made six long voyages to the Orient in the seventeenth century. Tavernier brought to Louis XIV, of France, and other regal customers great diamonds, rubies, emeralds, and pearls. His journals describe the wonderful turquoise of Persia, the balas rubies (spinels), topaz, and sapphires of the Great Mogul. Tavernier visited the great mines of India and the Orient and purchased important diamonds, among them the blue "Hope."

The Spaniards came to the New World in search of gold—their real bonanza was emeralds. Pizzaro, Cortez, and other conquistadors took great quantities of shimmering green gems from the Indian tribes of Colombia, Ecuador, Peru, and Central American countries.

The important gem mines of Russia's Ural Mountains were first opened in 1517 after nomads paid their taxes to the city of Novgorod in small diamonds. The mines produced emerald, topaz, and beryl, but the location of the diamonds was not found for centuries.

Another historic gem, garnet, was mined by the Lake Dwellers in prehistoric Europe. These primitive people knew how to drill holes in the handsome crystals so they could wear them for adornment. The garnet mines of Bohemia produced the dark, rich red stones that reminded ancients of pomegranate seeds, from which the garnet group derives its name. Many mines were operating in the sixteenth and seventeenth centuries, and by the nineteenth century there was a huge cutting industry in Bohemia, employing thousands of lapidaries and goldsmiths.

All of the crown jewels of Europe boast priceless examples of historic gems. All of the great gem collections in museums have specimens from the mines of history and prehistory. It is remarkable that now at the end of the twentieth century many of these ancient localities are still producing. There are still rubies and sapphires in the Orient, emeralds in Colombia, and garnets in Bohemia.

The gems in this chapter are not necessarily the best, the most beautiful, or the most precious, but they are gems of history.

BERYL
Beryllium aluminum silicate
H. 7½–8   D. 2.62–2.90
Pleochroic   Hexagonal

Beryl has been divided into color groups since early history when emerald was a green stone, not particularly green beryl. Aquamarine was known as a blue stone but not recognized as being the same mineral as emerald.

Beryl has a wide color range, but since the colors in one group can vary so much, the varieties are not named for color as much as in the past. Here are some of the color divisions, with colors derived from traces of chromium, iron, manganese, vanadium, and others:

Emerald—green, colored by chromium
Aquamarine—blue, blue-green, green-blue
Heliodor—yellow, golden, yellow-orange
Morganite—pinkish orange, orangy pink, pink, rose, orange, peach
Goshenite—colorless
Bixbite or red beryl—red

Beryls of colors that do not fit the above categories are merely called beryl. An example is the brown beryl of Governador Valdares, Brazil, or the black star beryl of Mozambique. To improve the color or to produce a stable color, beryl is sometimes heat treated or irradiated. It has also been dyed, used with foil, or made into doublets or other layered stones. Beryl is found in granite pegmatites, schists, and metamorphic rock. Enormous crystals of beryl are found in pegmatites. Opaque, translucent, and transparent, beryl can also qualify as a phenomenal stone.

In addition to the emerald localities in this chapter, there are deposits in Norway, Austria, Zambia, Zaire, South Africa, Tanzania, Madagascar, Pakistan, India, and Australia.

Keith Proctor, jeweler and gem dealer of Colorado Springs, has some of the world's most aesthetic gem beryls in his collection. Many of his crystals are matched with a faceted stone of the same color. An exotic specimen is a 2½-inch (6.35 cm) twinned morganite crystal attached to a 5-inch (12.70 cm) rubellite.

The Lizzadro Museum of Elmhurst, Illinois, has a rectangular emerald cut green beryl weighing 975 carats. The California Academy of Science has a superb collection of 22 carved beryls, transparent to translucent, ranging from a few grams in weight to 110.63 grams. An 86,136-carat emerald carving by R. Chan of Hong Kong is thought to be a record.

The dispersion of beryl, .014, is only medium, but the appearance of a stone is improved by some of the newer cuts with more facets. Cleavage and heat sensitivity are not problems with beryl. Tin oxide or Linde A or 50,000 diamond are good polishes for beryl.

Most lapidaries never get a chance to cut a really fine emerald. Commercial-quality emeralds may be heavily included, so rough should be carefully examined under magnification. Emeralds should be cold dopped and handled more carefully than other beryls, then polished with cerium, tin, or chrome oxide. Pol-A-Gem, a lap permanently charged with cerium oxide, is a good choice.

Aquamarine

Blue beryl is an excellent lapidary and jewelry material. Aquamarine is one of several beryls known for its dominant color, originally, in this case, the color of a calm tropical sea—a tint of greenish blue. Iron is the main coloring agent. The color range includes pale blue, medium blue, bright blue, blue-green, and light green. Recent crystals found in Pakistan are a rare powder blue. Many of the bluer and more intense colors are achieved by heat treatment. Some aquamarine is silky and can be cut into lovely cat's-eye cabochons. A particular type of striking deep blue beryl is called Maxixe. It has been irradiated and the color is not stable.

Aquamarine is not as heavily included as emerald and is found as much larger crystals. A gem-quality aquamarine crystal from Brazil weighs 243 pounds. The Smithsonian has a handsome richly colored prism from Brazil that measures 9½ x 3½ inches (24.13 x 8.89 cm). The American Museum of Natural History has a 13-pound aquamarine crystal. The Field Museum has a faceted aquamarine from Maine weighing 137 carats. New Deal Minerals of Denver has a Brazilian crystal weighing 2,300 grams in a dark blue-green color. An unusual 129-carat aquamarine crystal has a distinct 6-point fixed Star of David, caused by preferential etching.

Green and light blue-green beryl crystals of well over a ton have been mined in the Black Hills of South Dakota, but most of the material is opaque. (It has been used for cabochons and tumbled baroques.) Small transparent crystals have been found and cut from mines near Keystone. Other aquamarine locations are Russia, Madagascar, Namibia, Nigeria, Zambia, Kenya, Zimbabwe, Afghanistan, India, Burma, and Sri Lanka. In the United States, California, Idaho, Colorado, Maine, and North Carolina have cuttable beryl.

Aquamarine has been used for engravings, carvings, cabochons, faceted stones, fantasy cuts, beads, and ornamental objects such as eggs and spheres. Some years ago, aquamarine of good quality was tumbled as large baroques by Craftstones. Some of these stones were chatoyant.

Cutters enjoy working with aquamarine. It is available in excellent sizes, has very few inclusions, and is tough and heat resistant. The outer skin seems to have more color so the table should be parallel to the crystal axis.

The green hue can be removed, according to professional cutter Jerry Call, by putting the stone in a burnout oven at 300 degrees C. The temperature can be pushed up by 50 degrees until the desired color is reached. (Stones must always be allowed to cool slowly.)

Emerald

An emerald of top color and quality weighing several carats is far more rare than a gem-quality diamond, and can be priced considerably higher. Very fine emeralds of large size may sell for $80,000 a carat. The superb color of the best emeralds is so desirable that the synthesis of emerald has been a top priority with creative gem scientists.

Emerald is green beryl colored by chromium. Although 8 in hardness, it is brittle, full of inclusions (most of the time), and suffers from internal stress.

Emeralds have been considered elite gems since the time of Cleopatra and perhaps much earlier. The Inca's rulers had great treasuries of emeralds, many of which were sent by Pizzaro to the queen of Spain. The Czars had impressive emeralds among their crown jewels. The imperial jewels of Iran gleamed with fine emeralds, among them Empress Farah's spectacular emerald crown. The 217-carat Mogul is engraved on both sides.

Emeralds have been engraved, carved, cut into cabochons, or faceted, and made into beads. (A lady from Illinois bought a green native cut bead necklace for a few dollars at a flea market and found that it was made of emeralds from India.) Emeralds are also polished in nugget shapes or natural crystal shapes as in the collection of Iran.

A 2.5-carat Columbian emerald is set with diamonds in white gold.

The most famous emerald mines in the world for several centuries have been those of Colombia. Generations of miners have endured deprivation, primitive conditions, bandits, and risk of life to search for these truly precious gems. At present, Colombia mine operators are planning a cartel.

Emeralds from various localities are recognized by their inclusions. Emeralds are treated with oils, resins, plastic, or dye to hide imperfection or improve colors. Emerald substitutes include green corundum, green garnet, green spinel, green quartz, and green glass.

The value of an emerald is determined by the depth of color, the clarity, the size and weight, the cut, and to some degree the origin. Material should be selected for the best color and for inclusions (jardin) that do not detract.

Brazil

An emerald location in Brazil is Santa Terezinha, 150 miles northwest of Brazilia. These emeralds, found in all shades and hues of green, often have distinct color zoning. In the crystals with the most intense colors, chromite crystals are common inclusions. Other inclusions are pyrite, limonite, talc, and calcite. The finest crystals are remarkably clean. The emerald crystals are found as stubby hexagonal prisms in talc schist with beryl-bearing pegmatites including mica, feldspar, tourmaline, and zircon. The mining is done by hand in pits and trenches. Sizes range from minute to half an inch and more. Occasionally crystal clusters are found. Brazilian cutters sometimes use Opticon as a fracture sealer.

Colombia

Colombia is number one in production and quality of emeralds. Most of the world-famous emeralds have come from the mines of Colombia. It is said that the Incas wore mammoth emeralds and their Temple of Manta displayed an emerald the size of an ostrich egg.

At one time 30,000 people lived and worked in the city of Muzo, at one of the most notable mines. The other leading mine is the Chivor. Both mines have been worked intermittently for centuries and have changed status many times. Recently the mines have been strictly regulated and controlled, with most of the emeralds winding up at the Banco de la Republica of Bogotá.

The emeralds of the Muzo Mine are mostly short prismatic crystals occurring in calcite in limestone veins, while those of Chivor occur in metamorphic shale. Other notable mines are at Gachalá and Coscuez.

The Los Angeles County Museum exhibited two remarkable emeralds in 1989. The largest crystal weighs 682 carats. The other is an aesthetic matrix specimen. Both are from the Muzo Mine. Dr. Peter Keller, museum consultant, says both exceed the quality of the Patricia

Trapiche emerald crystals from Colombia are unusual for cabochons.
Photo by Dick Thomas,
courtesy of Lapidary Journal.

emerald (632 carats) of the American Museum of Natural History and the Gachalá (858 carats) of the Smithsonian. A crystal called the Muzo weighs 16,020 carats and is said to be the world's largest high-quality emerald.

An unusual kind of emerald, the trapiche, has a natural six-sectioned pattern formed by the crystal's natural hexagonal growth. Some of the starlike or flowerlike patterns are separated by a white albite filling or a black carbonaceous shale. Trapiche emeralds are found at both the Muzo and the Chivor mines. Although some are clear enough to facet, the gems are better suited to cabochons. The first trapiche crystals outside of Colombia are now coming from Brazil. The coloring is the reverse of the Colombian occurrences. Chrome oxide is a good polish for these stones that should be selected for color, pattern, and contrast.

*Right:
The metamorphosed
shell of extinct
ammonites
furnishes this vivid
material called
ammolite.
Photo courtesy of
Korite.*

*Above: Jim Kaufmann wins gem-cutting
awards with his mastery of the art of inlay.
Photo by A. B. Kohler, Co.*

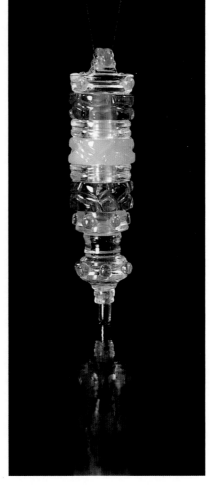

*Right: Henry Hunt experiments with
colored gems like other artists experiment with
paints. Here he stacks tourmaline,
amethyst, chrysoprase, and peridot.
Photo courtesy of Henry Hunt.*

Left: A gemstone swallow sits on the edge of a quartz bowl, carved by E. Bank of Idar-Oberstein (4 ¾ inches high). Courtesy of Lora Robins Gallery. Photo by Dr. Willie Reams.

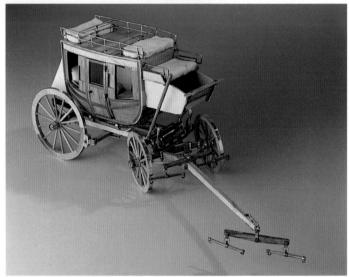

Right: Melvin Maier made this replica of a Wells Fargo stagecoach of petrified wood. Scale ⅜ inch = 1 inch. Courtesy of Kalamazoo Geological and Mineral Society.

Left: A faceted tanzanite of 14.43 carats accompanies this fine 1¾-inch tanzanite crystal that was stolen from Keith Proctor collection and never recovered. Photo by Harold and Erica Van Pelt.

Quartz replacements of the three kingdoms of Earth are interesting lapidary materials. This is a pseudomorph after coral from Tampa, Florida. Zeitner collection.

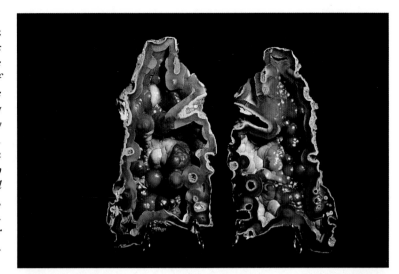

The mysteries of agate geodes keep many people interested in lapidary as a hobby.

Agates are among the most beautiful and fascinating of natural objects. This one is from Oregon.

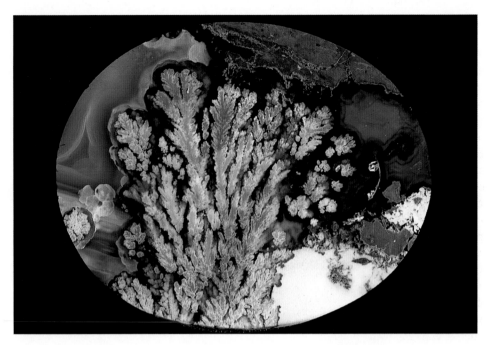

Above: Priday plume agate cut from a thunderegg proves the lapidary and jewelry qualities of cryptocrystalline quartz.
Below: Tourmaline flamingos show off the excellence of tourmaline as well as the artistry of Gerhard Becker. Courtesy of Gerhard Becker, Idar-Oberstein, Germany.

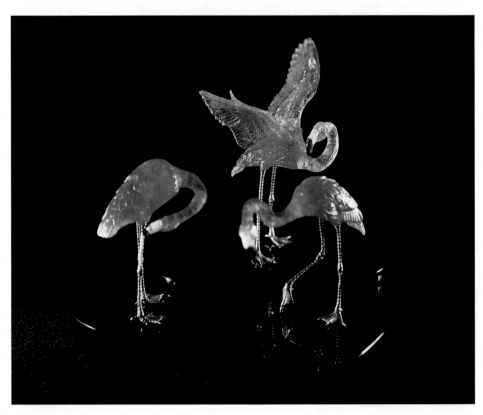

North Carolina

Emeralds were discovered in 1875 and finds seem to be getting bigger and better as time goes on. A 934.90-carat aesthetic cluster of bright green crystals was found by collector Glenn Bolick at the Hiddenite and Emeralds Mine. Glenn also had a magnificent single crystal of 722.70 carats. Professional cutter Arthur Grant faceted a 15.46 stone of rich green color, the June Culp Zeitner emerald, and a near flawless square cut emerald with blue-green/green dichroism, said to be the finest quality ever found and cut in the United States, from other crystals in the Bolick collection. The Carolina emerald faceted by Jerry Call, faceting instructor, is 13.14 carats.

Other locations for North Carolina emeralds are the Rist Mine, the Ellis Mine, the Crabtree Mine, the Old Plantation Mine, and the Turner Mine. An elegant cutting material is emerald matrix from the Crabtree Mine. Emerald matrix is now being mined for jewelry. Small bright green emerald crystals with acicular black tourmaline in a matrix of white albite have been cut by amateurs into excellent cabochons.

Russia

Gem-bearing pegmatites with superb emeralds were discovered in the Ural Mountains well over a century ago, and for many years provided beautiful stones for the Fabergé artists and the Czars. Emeralds were found in alluvial gravels and in situ. The emeralds of the Urals are of mixed qualities, but the best are a rich green color and compare well with other fine emeralds. Exceptionally large crystals have been found, but not entirely of gem quality. A record crystal is over 15 inches (38.10 cm).

Zambia

Zambia is currently the major African producer with blue-green and saturated green stones of high quality and usually only minor inclusions of biotite, magnetite, or muscovite. The emeralds occur in schists in mines at Hiku, Kofabu, and Kitwe. Some of these stones have pronounced pleochroism, changing from blue-green to yellow-green when turned in the light.

Zimbabwe

Emeralds were discovered at Sandawana, Zimbabwe, in 1957. Saturated green crystals, mostly small in size, occur in granitic pegmatites in an area of metamorphic schists. Small faceted stones are splendid for melee and jewelry set with clusters of stones.

In most cases, Sandawana emeralds can be recognized by their inclusions of acicular tremolite and minute platelets of biotite. A few other locations in Zimbabwe also produce beryl.

Golden Beryl

An appealing color of beryl is golden beryl or heliodor. The tints vary from pale yellow to muted yellow-orange (golden) to yellow-green. The coloring agent is iron and sometimes titanium. Well-colored crystals of golden beryl are not as plentiful as crystals of aquamarine. Some of the better localities are Madagascar, Brazil, Namibia, and Ukraine. Crystals occur in pegmatites and in metamorphic rock.

In the United States golden and yellow beryl crystals have been found in South Dakota, Maine, Connecticut, and North Carolina.

A magnificent step cut golden beryl weighing 2,054 carats was cut from Brazilian material by John Sinkankas and is in the Smithsonian gem collection. A 314-gram crystal from Ukraine has cutters waiting for a chance to work with large yellow beryls.

There are also cat's-eye golden beryls, with the chatoyance resulting from tubular inclusions. Numerous cat's-eye cabochons were shown in Tucson recently, but the color may have been produced by irradiation.

Golden beryl does not have many inclusions and is easily polished with cerium oxide; however, cuttable sizes are seldom available.

Morganite

This lovely beryl, named for American financier and gem connoisseur, J. P. Morgan, is predominantly pink in color, although the pinks may vary from blush to rose, to peach and pinkish orange. Since morganite colors, caused by manganese, tend to bleach out when exposed to sunlight for long periods, most of the material is routinely heat treated for stability.

Some of the early morganites from Madagascar were a deep pink with a hint of blue or violet. Morganite crystals from Pala, California, are aesthetic museum specimens. The California morganite is usually a pastel peach color. Brazilian morganite now dominates the market, also with pale stones, although dark orange stones found there have also been called morganite.

The Royal Ontario Museum of Toronto has a 1,625-carat morganite. A museum in St. Petersburg, Russia, has a 598.7 step cut rose-pink stone from Madagascar. An 11,000-carat pinkish-orange morganite carving by Chinese artist Hing Wa Lee was made for Herb Obodda in 1981 from Afghanistan rough. The largest cut morganite, from Maine, is 184.2 carats and is in the state museum. A remarkable discovery of morganite was made in Maine in 1989.

Morganite color can be improved in a burnout oven starting at 200 degrees C,

according to Jerry Call. Temperature can be increased by 50-degree increments if desired.

For cutters, larger stones will accent the color. Intricate facet cuts make the stones appear livelier. Morganite takes a brilliant polish with cerium oxide, which makes the stone glow.

Red Beryl

Exciting beryl crystals, intense red and raspberry red, occur in the Wah Wah Mountains of Utah. The location at the south end of the range is at an elevation of 7,500 feet. The mine has been developed as open pits by the Harris brothers, of Delta, Utah, who introduced their stunning crystals at Tucson in 1977.

The small hexagonal prisms occur in resistant gray rhyolite or in veins of kaolinite. Beautiful as specimens, crystals large enough to facet have also been found.

Red beryl also occurs in Utah's Thomas Range, but so far the crystals are very small. The dichroism is from yellowish-red to purplish-red. Resembling fine rubies, the faceted red beryls are remarkably clean.

CHRYSOBERYL
Beryllium aluminum oxide
H. 8½   D. 3.68
Pleochroic   Orthorhombic

Alexandrite and Catseye

Alexandrite, a color-change chrysoberyl, was discovered in the Ural Mountains in 1830. So contrasting is the red/green color change of the Russian gems that the description "alexandrite-like" became an

Headdresses of the Rajahs of India often combined diamonds, emeralds, rubies, and sapphires with pearls. Photo courtesy of International Gem and Jewelry Shows.

adjective for defining color change in other gem species.

The color change is from green or bluish green in the daylight to red or violet-red in incandescent light. Chromium is the agent of color. Alexandrite occurs as unusual crystals, often cyclic twins called trillings or sixlings for their pseudohexagonal habit. Found in granite pegmatites, gneiss, mica schist, or as rolled pebbles in gravels, most gem-quality alexandrites are small, seldom providing stones of more than 5 carats. Cat's-eye alexandrite and star alexandrite are also known. Sometimes cat's-eye cabochons are in the 20-carat range and over.

Other sources of alexandrite are Sri Lanka, Burma, Tanzania, Zimbabwe, and Brazil. A 73-carat alexandrite crystal from Brazil yielded an 18.5-carat cat's-eye with a good color change. The color change of the Brazilian stones is from bluish green to raspberry red. Fine alexandrites of over 6 carats are so rare that they rank among the most expensive of stones, some of them topping $40,000 per carat.

Just as alexandrite is the king of color change, cat's-eye chrysoberyl sets the pace for phenomenal stones. In fact, the stones are usually simply called catseyes. With gem qualities that live up to their beauty, chrysoberyl cabochons are hard, tough, and durable. The aesthetic stones can be colorless, honey yellow, yellow, greenish yellow, pastel green, or a tint of yellow-brown. Honey-colored stones with bluish white chatoyance are especially aesthetic.

A primary source of chrysoberyl has been the gem gravels of Sri Lanka. Other sources are Brazil, Zimbabwe, India, Burma, Australia, and New Zealand. An enormous chrysoberyl crystal from Brazil was shown by Amsterdam Sauer of Rio de Janeiro at Tucson. Catseye crystals in the 300-carat range have been recorded.

In addition to oval or round cabochons with well-centered eyes, chatoyant material is also used for carvings. A cat's-eye carving of a horse head, pale yellowish brown in color and weighing 31.11 carats, was carved in Idar-Oberstein. The cat's-eye phenomenon is caused by exceptionally dense parallel needles and tubes. Proper orientation with the ultrafine fibers crossways of the length of the eye in the cabochon is the first and major problem for the lapidary. Only small to medium pieces are marketed from time to time. Chrysoberyl polishes slowly and should be worked with diamond. Linde A on a tin lap, 14,000 diamond on tin, or diamond on copper all work well.

Chrysoberyl does not always have color change or cat's-eyes. Some is transparent faceting material which yields excellent stones for jewelry in a variety of colors including yellow, colorless, green, gold, and brown. For cat's-eyes, Jerry Call uses a drop of star oil or even honey on the rough held under a bright light source to locate the strongest ray.

CORUNDUM
Aluminum oxide
H. 9   D. 4.0
Pleochroic   Hexagonal

Ruby

Vivid red rubies, hard and durable, are among the most admired gemstones. around the world. Well-cut rubies of fine color are among the most expensive of gemstones in the 3-carat and over range. With hardness next to diamond, rubies are used for engagement rings and other jewelry which may be exposed to daily wear. Rubies are used for beads, cabochons, carved or engraved stones, and faceted stones, and are equally popular with men and women.

Rubies are shaped and polished with diamond after cold dopping. A tin lap and ½- or ¼-micron diamond will bring a good polish.

Burma

The best-known ruby locality is the Mogok Stone Tract of Upper Burma (now Myanmar), an area known for magnificent rubies since the sixteenth century. For many years the British controlled the production of the ruby mines, but since their withdrawal in 1931, mining has been sporadic and is now strictly controlled by the communist government. Although the government holds an annual auction, it is said the best stones come to the market through Thailand.

Rubies and other fine gems, such as spinels, are found in pegmatites, metamorphic schists, white marble, and granite intrusives, with most of the mining being done by natives in pits and quarries. Pigeon-blood color, a saturated purplish red, is the choice color, but dozens of tints and shades of red are found. Some star rubies also occur in the Stone Tract.

The rubies vary in size, but fine ones in the 5 carats and over range are extremely rare. The British Museum has a Burmese ruby crystal weighing 690 grams. The Los Angeles County Museum has an excellent bright crystal of 196 carats. A 15.97-carat ruby from Burma sold recently at a Sotheby auction for $3.63 million, making it the highest price ever paid for a single ruby.

Macedonia

One of the rarest of all rubies is the Macedonian ruby, which has a unique color, a combination of rose-red, fuchsia, and lavender. Dr. Aris Mallas, gem distributor and writer, who has made an extensive study of these rubies, does not know why this color cannot be found elsewhere, but he notes that once a gemologist becomes familiar with this color, he can always spot a Macedonian stone. These stones were known in Greece at the time of Alexander the Great. Although the historic deposits were considered worked out centuries ago, a few of these rubies are still seen today.

Sri Lanka

The rubies of the Sri Lanka gem gravels often lean more toward pink than saturated red. In fact, Sri Lanka also mines exquisite pink sapphires, and sometimes the difference between a pink ruby and a pink sapphire is a matter of controversy.

Tanzania

Very large opaque rubies are found in green chrome zoisite in the Matabuto Mountains of Tanzania. Some of the crystals have translucent and transparent sections. The rubies have a bright chrome rich color.

Large ruby carvings have been made from crystals of exceptional size and color. Bob Harvill, Texas gem carver, created a gem carving "The Good Samaritan" from a 5-inch (12.70 cm)-diameter crystal. Other famous ruby carvings are "Ecce Homo" by Harry Derian, the "Mercy Ruby" by Lincoln Borglum and Marvin Wilson, and the "Liberty Ruby" by Alfonso de Vivanco. A magnificent ruby eagle was carved by Eberhard Bank of Idar-Oberstein. The carving weighing 890 grams was cut from a 15-pound crystal. Some of the Tanzanian crystals are 8 inches (20.32 cm) in diameter.

Thailand

Thailand is of major importance in the production of rubies. Deposits of Chantabun and Battambang are alluvial and are being worked by placer methods. The color of these rubies is generally darker and less intense than the rubies of Burma.

Others

Rubies have also been found in Vietnam, Pakistan, China, Milawai, Kenya, Afghanistan, and India. Many of the rubies from India are star rubies. Rubies have also been recovered from the Cowee

Ruby beads from the Orient are enhanced with textured gold and baroque pearls.

Creek area near Franklin, North Carolina, and from several locations in Montana in the United States.

Most rubies are heat treated to improve the color, remove minor silk, or develop enough silk to produce a star. Famous rubies are the 43-carat Peace Ruby, the 167-carat Edwardes Ruby of the British Museum, and the 138.7-carat Rosser Reeves Ruby of the Smithsonian. Rubies are historic stones mentioned in the Bible and in the literature of many countries; however, several thousand years ago ruby merely referred to a red stone, and even a century ago spinels were mistaken for rubies.

Sapphire

Sapphires come in every color except red and are among the finest of gems. Blue sapphire is better known than the other colors; in fact, the word sapphire means blue, but other colors are sometimes sensational and are gaining in popularity in this age of colored stones: yellow, gold, orange, pink, mauve, violet, green, brown, black, and colorless.

Found in metamorphic rock and placer deposits, sapphires can be transparent, translucent, or opaque, as in the case of black star sapphires. Sapphires are colored by iron, titanium, and sometimes chromium. Like rubies, most sapphires are heated for color improvement.

Sapphire has been known since Biblical times, but scholars are not sure whether the sapphire of those times was really corundum. Sapphires appeared in the crown jewelry of Europe at the time of the Holy Roman Empire.

Famous sapphires are the 330-carat Star of Asia in the Smithsonian, the 337.10-carat Catherine the Great sapphire in the Winston collection, the 423-carat Logan of the Smithsonian, the 536-carat Star of India in the American Museum of Natural History, and the 1,444-carat Blue Star of Queensland. A cushion-shaped sapphire of 337. 66 carats in a Cartier brooch sold at Christie's auction for $2.3 million. A sapphire cabochon of 191.58 carats is in the crown jewel collection of Iran. A faceted yellow sapphire weighing 185.14 carats may be the world record for this color.

Most lapidaries do not work often with material of 9 in hardness. Facet-quality rubies are expensive, but sapphire rough may be available, especially in other colors than top blues. More lapidaries may become involved in cutting star sapphires. The cabochon should be oriented in one direct light source and one arm of the star should be crossways of the center of the oval. High-domed cabochons are the best. Many amateur cutters learned to cut star stones through show demonstrations and a book by Ernest Michaud and David Miller entitled *Steps to the Stars*.

Jerry Call reminds faceters to place the darkest color to the culet of the stone. Star stones are oriented with a drop of star oil on the stone held under direct light. Diamond is the best polish for corundum and water is the preferred carrier. Some cutters prefer diamond on ceramic; others use diamond on copper or wood.

Asia

Asian mines have produced sapphires for many centuries and are still important producers. Unique stones of a wonderful cornflower blue from *Kashmir, India*, set the goal for blue sapphire color. A velvety or sleepy appearance is distinctive for these sapphires which are found in pegmatites or placer deposits. Sapphire production has been from the Old Mine and the New Mine, with the material from the New Mine not equal to the older, but little is on the market from any source at present. A spectacular Kashmir sapphire of about 75 carats is an oval brilliant cut stone in the crown jewel collection of Iran.

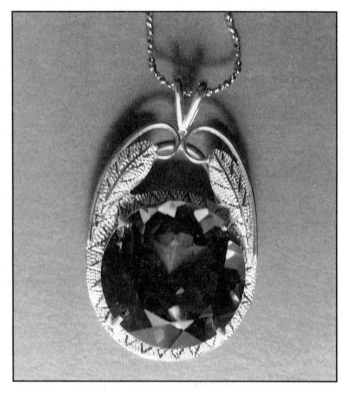

Roland Rasmussen set this faceted gem in hand-engraved gold.

The sapphires from *Thailand* are found in gem gravels in Kanchanabui. Mines have been operating in this area for over 30 years. The material is routinely heat treated. The sapphires mostly have hues that are more grayed than the stones of Sri Lanka or Burma and the blues are much darker. Star stones have been found in a volcanic area at Khao Ploi Waen.

The yellow sapphires and occasional orange stones (padparadscha) from *Sri Lanka* are especially beautiful. A recent find near Ratnapura was a bypyramid orange crystal of over 1,100 carats. Another distinctive sapphire is a pinkish orange or orangy pink *padparadscha*. The word is not used as much now as in years past, but since the color is so beautiful and rare, the price is also upscale. Connoisseurs of fine gems often ask for these stones by that unusual Sinhalese name. The classic locality for vivid padparadschas is Sri Lanka, although others have been found in Burma, Thailand, and recently in East Africa. A 1,126-carat crystal from Sri Lanka yielded a number of showy gems, the largest of which was 47 carats.

Padparadschas do not occur in as large sizes as sapphires of other colors. Faceted stones of 10 carats or more are rare. The American Museum of Natural History has a faceted oval golden orange stone of 100 carats, the finest large padparadscha on public display and a great favorite with the public.

Almost every color of sapphire is found in Sri Lanka's gem gravels, including fancy pinks, blues, greens, and violets. A fine gem-quality colorless sapphire of 42.05 carats was recently faceted.

More attention has been focused lately on the dramatic color-change sapphires from several locations. A striking 21.55-carat star sapphire from Sri Lanka has a color change from rich bluish purple to pale blue. Star sapphires of all colors come from Sri Lanka mines. A rare doubly terminated blue crystal of large size was a recent find.

A large part of the sapphire industry in Sri Lanka is the geuda trade that started in the late 1970s. Geuda sapphire is milky and almost colorless. The gem industry of Thailand discovered that heat treating these near worthless stones turned them into valuable blue sapphires with desirable permanent color. Millions of carats have been sent from Ratnapura to Thailand for treatment.

Heating colorless sapphires in powdered titanium and iron (color agents for natural sapphire) causes them to acquire a fused layer of good blue color about 0.4 mm in thickness. This diffusion-treated sapphire is so far meeting some resistance because of the retailers' obligation to disclose treatments and the public's misunderstanding of the permanence of such processes. Diffusion is quickly identified by the use of a portable immersion cell Mini-cube II invented by gem-testing instruments supplier Dr. W. Hanneman of Castro Valley, California.

Australia

Sapphires have been found in many parts of Australia. A notable deposit is in New South Wales, while a major deposit is in Queensland, near Anakie. Beautiful yellow sapphires are the premier product of this field, although some of the blues are of excellent color. Other colors include green and purple as well as particolored stones. Black and bronze sapphires from the area are cut as star stones.

Joan Millton, gem dealer from Brisbane, says that many of the Australian darker blue stones have been heat treated in Thailand. She also feels optimistic because Australia is gaining better control of its sapphire industry by doing more of its own heat treating. The Japanese have gained a sizable foothold in the industry in Australia.

The Black Star of Queensland is a record from Australia, weighing 733 carats. The Kingsley sapphire is a yellow and green particolor stone of 162.26 carats.

Tanzania and Others

Sapphires of a myriad of colors occur in the Umba River region of Tanzania. The oranges, violets, and color-change stones are of particular interest. Corundum gems occur in pegamatite veins in a large area of serpentine and limestone, and in alluvial deposits. Heavily mined, the sapphires include a high percentage of facetable material. Color agents are manganese, iron, nickel, vanadium, and titanium.

Sapphires are also found in Zimbabwe, Kenya, Afghanistan, Madagascar, Russia, and Brazil. Star sapphires from Kenya have acicular inclusions of hematite and rutile.

United States

Montana. Montana has a number of important sapphire deposits. They are found in Missouri River bars and gravels, and in place. The finest blue color, cornflower blue, comes from Yogo Gulch in the Judith Basin. Amazingly free from flaws and transparent, the crystals occur in an igneous dike. The deposit was discovered in the late nineteenth century and has been worked off and on ever since. The only thing that has kept the Yogo sapphires from being world leaders is their small size. About 25 years ago the area was promoted as Sapphire Village, a second home or retirement home for those interested in gems and lapidary and wanting a chance to dig their own stones.

Several different companies took turns at trying to operate the Yogo mines at a profit. A Colorado company, Intergem, marketed the sapphires as cut stones and finished jewelry, promoting them as Royal American Sapphires. The present owner is Roncor, Incorporated, of Los Angeles. Jefferson Kunisaki of Roncor says that fine sapphires are still being produced. Geologists estimate that sapphires may exist as deep as 7,000 feet. Mines have only reached depths of a few hundred feet. Amax Explorations recently took a lease on the main dike at Yogo to intensify mining operations.

Dry Cottonwood Creek is a potential big producer. Over a million carats of sapphires have already come from this area. In addition to the blues (which are now being heat treated), there are pinks, violets, greens, and yellows. Mark Bielenburg, who has the mineral rights to the Dry Cottonwood Creek deposit, thinks this deposit may rival great deposits worldwide. He feels the Rock Creek stones may have a different origin than other deposits. Some of the stones look as if they had been melted, showing no growth lines under a microscope, Bielenburg says.

Gem Mountain has been mined for many years, sometimes as a fee-basis mine for amateur prospectors. Most collectors have found sapphires with little trouble and also an occasional ruby. The enormous deposit has been sold and will now be operated commercially.

Eldorado Bar is another sapphire-bearing area that has been worked extensively and has produced many fine stones. An 18.85-carat natural blue sapphire was a recent find. Particolored sapphires have also come from here.

The Big Sky sapphire came from a dredging operation on the Missouri River. A rich blue faceted stone of 12.54 carats was cut from the 24-carat crystal.

Other Montana locations are the French Bar, Mings Bar, Spokane Bar, Emerald Bar, Magpie Gulch, American Bar, Danas Bar, and Camp Creek. The state of Montana is now starting to promote its sapphire industry as well as its other gemstones. There is a feeling that Montana may become a world leader in sapphire production.

North Carolina. Sapphires also occur in several counties of North Carolina. Colors include pink, blue, lavender, green, violet, and yellow—all in pastel and muted shades and tints. Carolina corundum occurs as water-worn pebbles, crystals, crystal clusters (rare), and massive material. Most of the massive material is only specimen or industrial grade. However, some is translucent and silky so that star cabochons can be cut. Facet-grade material is uncommon.

Corundum Hill and the mines near the Cullasaja River produced many tons of corundum years ago, and the Department of Interior estimated that many more tons remain. Cowee Valley in Macon County has been producing sapphires for many years. Most of them are found by tourists and "rockhounds." Other sapphire-producing areas are Buck Creek, Whitewater, Chrysler Hill, and "Chunky Gal" Mountain.

Most North Carolina sapphires are better adapted to cabochons than faceted stones. Some very large pieces of cuttable massive sapphire have been found, so some of the cabochons have been in the 25-carat range and over.

DIAMOND
Carbon
H. 10   D. 3.51
Cubic

If someone would define diamonds as being the only stone hard enough to scratch glass, as white stones that are everlasting, as the traditional engagement stone of the ages, or as the most valuable and rare of all stones, he would be wrong in every instance.

Although worn as talismans ages ago, the true beauty of diamonds could not be revealed until technology found ways to facet them to bring out their hypnotic fire. But even in the times of Mogul rulers, when cuts were primitive, heads and kingdoms were lost over diamonds.

Diamond cutting has evolved from a simple table cut, grinding off the top point of an octahedral crystal, to elaborate faceted miniature carvings such as a horse head, a star, or a sail boat, made possible by laser technology. There are also sensational new cuts such as the Barion and trilliant. Diamonds have been made into step cut beads. They are now cut by highly trained professionals (rarely has an amateur been known to cut a diamond) in several cutting centers. The equipment used for diamond cutting and polishing is not the same as the equipment used for colored stones.

Diamonds are found in alluvial gravels or in kimberlite pipes. The pipes penetrate deeply beneath the Earth's crust. Of igneous origin, kimberlite is not a lava. Kimberlites are of great age and often of great size. They are related to peridotite and an ultrabasic rock, eclogite. Kimberlite is yellowish on the surface and blue farther down. Other gems found in kimberlite are garnet, spinel, zircon, diopside, and enstatite.

Diamonds at 10 are the hardest of all gems, far harder than the first runner up, corundum, but they are not indestructible. A severe shock can break a diamond because of the perfect cleavage. High dispersion (fire), at 0.044, is diamond's other greatest asset in addition to its hardness. Diamond, the only gem which is just one element, is colorless and flawless if pure, but many important gem diamonds have

been colored. People remember the "bewitched" Hope diamond, but they may forget that it is blue. Diamond "fancies" can also be many shades of yellow, green, champagne, sherry, red, mauve, and pink. Marvelous pink diamonds are now coming from Kimberley, Australia. A gray-violet diamond recently found at Argyle was discovered to be colored by hydrogen.

The diamonds the great gem merchant Tavernier brought back to Europe from his adventures were from India. When the fabled mines of Golconda began to play out, diamonds were discovered in Brazil. Then the vast pipes of South Africa were discovered. Later discoveries were in other African nations, among them Botswana, Ghana, Zaire, and Sierra Leone. In recent years discoveries were made in Venezuela, Guyana, China, Australia, and Siberia. Russia is now a major producer, as is Australia. Canada has several diamond pipes that are being tested. Currently there is a diamond rush in the Northwest Territories. Testing and exploration are also proceeding along the Colorado/Wyoming border and in upper Michigan in the United States.

A pipe at Murfreesboro, Arkansas, in the United States has yielded many cuttable crystals to tourists and rockhounds who dig in the Crater of Diamonds State Park for a fee. Commercial mining there is again being considered. Alluvial diamonds have been found in the Appalachian and Great Lakes states and in California and Montana.

Large and important diamonds are still being found. The 3,106-carat Cullinan was found in the early twentieth century; the 616-carat Kimberley octahedron (1974); the Star of Sierra Leone 968.9 carats (1972); and the 890-carat Zale diamond, which became famous in the mid-1980s. A recently cut brown diamond is 545.67 carats.

A historic Austro-Hungarian crown is set with sapphires, diamonds, and pearls.
Courtesy of International Gem and Jewelry Shows.

Aside from the fact that diamond is the lapidary's best cutting tool, the most involvement with diamonds by lapidaries has been cutting replicas of the world's greatest diamonds in glass, quartz, or recently in cubic zirconia. Such sets of diamond replicas are used for shows, museums, and educational purposes.

Diamonds are judged for color, clarity, cut, and carat weight. A top-grade diamond should be a pure colorless white (or a fancy color) free from visible inclusions, cut to exact proportions to bring out the ultimate brilliance, and should be at least a carat in weight to be an investment stone. "D Flawless" is a rare top stone.

As are most gems, diamonds are frequently enhanced by various treatments. They may be heated, irradiated, coated, drilled by laser, or filled.

GARNET
Almandine
Iron aluminum silicate
H. 7½   D. 4.05
Cubic

Almandine, a member of the garnet family with excellent lapidary qualities, is widespread in contact zones of metamorphic rock. It often has constituents of other garnets, so there is an array of desirable colors: red, red-orange, orange, red-violet, brownish red, wine, and purple. If the almandine is admixed with pyrope, the colors tend toward the purplish reds, while if the other principal constituent is spessartite, the reds favor the oranges.

Large gem-quality almandines come from Burma, Sri Lanka, India, and Brazil. Cabochons and beads are made from these garnets. Cat's-eye and star garnet cabochons are among the phenomenal stones. Most of the commercial garnet jewelry is on the dark side, with the color derived from ferrous iron. Lapidaries often buy native cut garnets from Asia and recut them for striking results.

The world's largest garnet mine for many years was the Barton Mine on Gore Mountain, New York. The brownish-red almandine was quarried here for abrasives, but gem-quality material was also found and cut.

Almandine is also the star garnet of Idaho. The branches of Emerald Creek have yielded great quantities of large water-worn garnets in several shades of red, many with dazzling four- and six-rayed stars. Some of the almandines weigh several pounds, and a few weigh up to 60 and 70 pounds. Pink and orange garnets have been found, and purple garnets come from the Dinnerbucket Mine.

Another almandine location in the United States is the Black Hills of South Dakota where transparent crystals up to ¾ of an inch (1.90 cm) have been found and cut. Crystals occur in contact zones of quartz and mica schist near Custer.

Showy crystals 1 or 2 inches (2.54–5.08 cm) in diameter or more occur in schist near Wrangell, Alaska. Many of these well-formed crystals are better as specimens than lapidary material. Garnets of the almandine type are found in California, Colorado, Michigan, and Connecticut.

Garnets were known as carbuncles in the ancient past. The Greeks and the Romans cut and engraved almandines. Garnet crystals have been found in the medicine bags of American Indians.

Small garnets are brilliant cut, while larger ones may be step cut or carved. Some cutters prefer shallow pavilions for dark almandine to lighten the color. Star stones are cut in high round or oval cabochons, or used for small spheres or beads or for tumbled stones for a variety of projects. A hollow almandine garnet egg, 70 millimeters in diameter, carved by Manfred Wild of Idar-Oberstein, was pictured in the Lapidary Journal's special garnet issue.

Garnets have ranked high in the bead market in the last few years. Small drilled garnets have been braided, woven, and twisted into multistrand necklaces. Round garnet beads up to 10 millimeters in diameter have been strung with pearls, rock crystal, rose quartz, and amethyst. Multistone rings and bracelets use garnets of several colors.

Andradite
Calcium iron silicate
H. 6½   D. 3.70
Cubic

Andradite is brittle and less hard than some of the other garnets, but the green variety is possessed of splendid dispersion—0.057, which is greater than diamond. The colors of andradite are usually greens, yellows, browns, and near black.

Perhaps the most precious of garnets is the chrome green andradite *demantoid* which was discovered in a placer gold mine in the Ural Mountains in the nineteenth century. Later in-situ deposits were found in serpentinite. Russian gem importer, Leonid Prikazchikov, reports a new demantoid find in the Kamchatka Peninsula of Russia. The lovely tints and shades of green come from trace amounts of chromium, titanium, and manganese. Most demantoids are small, but a dark green crystal from the well-known locality of Piedmont, Italy, weighs 144 carats. (The Italian location of the Ala Valley also has a yellow andradite that has been called topazolite.)

Demantoid has also been reported from San Benito County, California, along with other colors of andradite. Some unusual stones from the California locality are chatoyant yellow brown on the surface and green at the core. Cat's-eye stones heavily included with byssolite have been cut from these crystals.

Other demantoid localities are Czechoslovakia, Zaire, China, and Korea. Good demantoids are rare and seldom seen outside of major collections.

Black andradite, schorlomite, and melanite were used for mourning jewelry in Europe in the nineteenth century. Melanite is titanium rich and is found in Italy. Schorlomite, also colored by titanium, is found in California, Scotland, Israel, and Japan. Both are rich in magnesium and iron as well.

Yellow-green andradite from Stanley Butte, Arizona, has been faceted. Crystals up to 2 inches (5.08 cm) in diameter have been found there, and also massive material.

An interesting type of andradite (now said to be an andradite-grossular combination) was recently shown at Tucson. Brownish yellow and olive green stones with bright iridescence from Hermasillo, Mexico, were shown both rough and faceted. The blue, green, and yellow iridescence seemed to be confined to the surface layer and was said to be caused by diffraction. Most of the stones were small.

Darker tones of andradite will appear more fiery if the cut is shallow. Chrome oxide gives a good polish.

Grossular
Calcium aluminum silicate
H. 7   D. 3.60
Cubic

Long ago grossular garnet was known as hyacinth; however, the same name was used for zircon. The name cinnamon stone was applied to grossular garnets found in Sri Lanka. Grossular garnets are colored by iron, manganese, vanadium, or chromium or combinations of these elements.

Grossular has a color range dominated by yellows and greens, although colorless, red, and pink also occur. Garnet species are not determined by their color. The various species have individual physical and chemical characteristics. Most grossulars are 7 in hardness, but some are slightly above or below.

Hessonite is a variety of grossular. Sri Lanka has been the most important source of these cinnamon-brown and yellow stones. Several locations in Italy have produced hessonite in a variety of colors. Siberia, Tanzania, and Australia are other sources. Fine orange stones have been coming from Mexico lately. An exceptional location is the Jeffrey Mine of Quebec, Canada. Locations in the United States are California, North Carolina, New Hampshire, Maine, and Vermont.

A spectacular discovery of green grossular garnet, since named *tsavorite*, was made by mining engineer Campbell Bridges in the late 1960s. These green garnets were discovered in Kenya and Tanzania. Similar crystals have been found in Pakistan. The green colors, due to vanadium and chromium, vary from light greens to rich greens and yellow-green. The top color is an intense pure green, which has become popular as an emerald substitute because of its superior lapidary qualities. It is quite free of inclusions, over 7 in hardness, and has a dispersion of 0.027 as opposed to 0.014 for emerald.

Ivory elephants are heavily ornamented with gold and gems of Sri Lanka—ruby, sapphire, zircon, chrysoberyl, and more. This herd was presented to the Lora Robins Gallery by Herbert Duke of International Gem and Jewelry Shows.

Tsavorite has been described as occurring in potato-shaped nodules. Faceted stones are excellent for jewelry.

Fractures commonly occur in tsavorite rough, so many of the faceted stones are small; however, crystals of about 50 carats occur. Lapidaries need to study each piece with care. Intense color is of prime importance.

Jalostoc, Morelos, Mexico, has pink grossular garnets (called rosolite) embedded in white marble. Some of these are almost opaque.

Massive grossular garnet is an interesting variation. One occurrence from South Africa has been called Transvaal jade for its resemblance to nephrite. The translucent material is used for carvings, cabochons, and beads. This cryptocrystalline material has shades and tints of green due to chromium. The supply of this material has been limited by the intense recent activity of platinum mines in the region.

White massive grossular from China has been used for carvings and beads. Califor-nite is an attractive green native material which is partly grossular and partly idocrase. Massive garnet containing hydro-grossular has been found in Idaho. Massive grossular has excellent lapidary qualities and can be used for jewelry and carvings. With no cleavage or heat sensitivity problems, garnets are easily worked with silicon carbide or diamond and polished with Linde A on leather for cabochons or 14,000 diamond on Lucite for faceted stones.

Pyrope
Magnesium aluminum silicate
H. 7–7½   D. 3.65
Cubic

Admired for many centuries, pyrope garnets vary from red-orange to red-purple, with a rich dark red being the most common color. Well-cut pyropes are fiery and bright. Garnet jewelry has been found in Bronze Age excavations. The most important ancient source of gem pyrope garnets was the former Czechoslovakia, where Bohemian carbuncles were thought to be equal to rubies. Tavernier was said to have carried a basket of fine, large garnets from Teplitz to the king of France. Bohemia became a cutting center, reaching its heights during the Victorian period when small pyropes were set closely together in distinctive jewelry. Similar garnet jewelry keeps recurring in the fashion world.

Chrome-rich pyropes have especially good red color as compared to other red garnets. Most are colored by iron and are relatively free of inclusions. While the majority of pyrope crystals are small, fine large stones do exist. A pyrope weighing 468 carats is said to be in the Green Vaults of Dresden.

Pyropes from the kimberlites of Africa and Russia succeeded the Bohemian stones in popularity. A pyrope location was discovered in Australia around the turn of the twentieth century.

A rose-red to purple-red variety of pyrope with almandine was discovered in Macon County, North Carolina, in the late nineteenth century and was given the name *rhodolite*. Later, these intermediate garnets were found in Sri Lanka, Tanzania, and Zimbabwe. The African stones have been considerably larger than those from North Carolina. Tanzania has violet-red and raspberry red star rhodolite garnets. Some cut stones are in the 16-carat range.

From Tanzania and East Africa come color-change pyropes which are blue-green in the daylight and red-violet or wine-red in incandescent light. When admixed with spessartine, the Tanzanian pyropes have a pronounced alexandrite effect. Pyrope-spessartines from East Africa occasionally appear purple in daylight. Pink and peach-colored pyrope also occurs in East Africa. A record pink faceted stone is 63.06 carats.

A recent discovery in Kenya and Tanzania is a mixture of pyrope and spessartine called *malaya* (malaia) which ranges through a number of tints from yellow-orange to red-orange with the best stones being a vivid orange with a slight pink overtone. A vibrant 49.62-carat faceted malaya garnet is in a private collection.

A garnet field in Apache County, Arizona, has drawn considerable attention. The dark red pyropes occur in igneous rock at Garnet Ridge. A similar occurrence is in nearby Utah. Indians spotted the bright red pebbles on ant hills and took them to trading posts or sold them to visitors. The Fort Defiance pyrope locality is on the Navajo Reservation.

Spessartine
Manganese aluminum silicate
H. 7½   D. 4.20
Cubic

Spessartine garnets with a dispersion of 0.027 and a cheerful array of sunny colors are among the most exquisite members of the garnet group. Colors include yellow-orange, orange, red-orange, and orange-red. Few orange gems can rival an intense orange spessartine. Colors are attributed to manganese and iron.

A famous locality for spessartine is the Rutherford Mine at Amelia, Virginia. An exceptionally large piece found at this location weighed 1,675 carats; however, most stones are 10 carats or less. A second notable location for spessartine is in San Diego County, California. Mines near Ramona and near Pala have produced bright gem-quality spessartines in the form of trapezohedral crystals occurring in pegmatites. A new find in 1987 was made at the Little Three Mine near Ramona. A large spessartine from Ramona is 39.5 carats. Fine spessartines come from Madagascar and Brazil, and collector Knut Morland found an 8-inch-diameter spessartine while blasting feldspar near Evje, Norway. Intense orange spessartine is a new discovery in Namibia.

Spessartines do not have the usual faceted marble shape of other garnets. They are lustrous, etched, striated crystals with complex shallow pyramid-shaped terminations on the surface. Cutters should be aware of small voids.

Uvarovite (and other garnets)
Calcium chromium silicate
H. 7½   D. 3.71
Cubic

Uvarovite is a green garnet which occurs in massive form or as small transparent to translucent crystals occurring in metamorphosed limestone and serpentine in chromite deposits. Besides chrome, uvarovite contains traces of titanium and iron. The crystals are rare and small in size. With good hardness and a high refractive index (1.87) it would furnish sensational stones if larger crystals were to be found.

The best uvarovite has come from Finland and Russia. Other locations are Norway, South Africa, Quebec, Canada, and California. Some Russian uvarovite is now available.

There are several other rare garnets belonging to the calcium division, among them *kimzeyite*, a dark calcium zirconium garnet from Magnet Cove, Arkansas, and *goldmanite*, a green calcium vanadium garnet. Drusy uvarovite on chromite is exciting for jewelry.

PERIDOT
Magnesium iron silicate
H. 6½   D. 3.40
Orthorhombic

A lovely green gem was admired by the Pharaohs and their courts thousands of years ago. The source of Egypt's ancient gems was the Red Sea Island once called Topazios and the gem was the one now called peridot. The island (now Zabargad) is still a source of fine peridot crystals. Some faceted stones from this historic location are over 300 carats. A crystal section measuring 2½ x 2 x 1 inch, (6.35 x 5.08 x 2.54 cm) is in the British Museum.

Peridot occurs in basalt, peridotite, and other igneous rocks and in metamorphic limestones. Always green, peridot can be lime green, greenish yellow, yellowish green, light, medium, or dark saturated green, or brownish green. The color of darker stones is sometimes lightened by heat treatment. In addition to tabular crystals, peridot occurs as embedded grains, small rounded nodules, or in clusters called bombs. Peridots of choice green color come from Egypt, Burma, and Norway. Other locations are Finland, Ethiopia, Antarctica, Australia, Canada, Mexico, and the United States.

A large proportion of the commercial peridot now on the market comes from the San Carlos Indian Reservation, Gila County, Arizona. Most of the yellow-green stones are small, but faceted stones of several carats are cut regularly. A cut stone known as Geronimo's Secret weighs 100 carats. New Mexico also has peridots in eroding volcanic rock near the Mexican border. Stones up to 50 carats are reported there.

Pallasite meteorites are another source. Attractive faceted stones up to 1.39 carats were recently cut by German artist Andreas Becker from an Argentinian pallasite.

The exceptionally clean Norwegian material is a favorite of European faceters. Small beads are also made of peridot and uncut stones are tumbled for necklaces, mosaics, gem trees, and other gemstone uses.

One of the largest faceted peridots is an oval stone of 430.47 carats in the Colorado School of Mines Museum. A 280.65-carat Burmese peridot was recently offered at Ed Tripp's auction in Tucson. Chatoyant peridot is occasionally cut into cat's-eyes.

Peridot is easy to cut and difficult to polish. Adding a few drops of muriatic acid to polish slurry is one solution, but it is better to use 14,000 diamond. Peridot is tough and not heat sensitive. Lapidaries should examine the rough for small platelets, discs, or needles.

SPINEL
Magnesium aluminum oxide
H. 8   D. 3.58
Cubic

Red spinel is such a beautiful gem that it has often been mistaken for high-quality ruby. The Black Prince's ruby and the Timur ruby of England's crown jewels are both spinels. Huge red spinels are in the collection of the former shahs of Iran. The largest of these is an enormous 500-carat stone polished in its natural water-worn shape. Large baroque-shaped polished spinels also appear in the crowns and jewels of the Russian czars.

In the early 1980s a large number of dealers in Tucson featured faceted red spinels from Sri Lanka. Most of the stones were brilliant cut and under 10 carats with intense color. Spinel can also be blue, green, violet, colorless, and black. Although iron is a common coloring agent for spinels, some of the fine blue stones are colored by cobalt.

Spinel is part of a group that includes chromite, franklinite, ghanite, hercynite, and magnetite. Some blue and green spinels are ghanite. Dark green spinel has been called ceylonite or pleonaste. Galaxite is dark red.

Spinel is a common metamorphic mineral found in crystalline limestones, serpentines, and contact zones of basic igneous rock. Black spinels are found in the ejecta of Mt. Vesuvius, Italy. Well-shaped, lustrous spinel crystals are usually octahedral. There can also be massive veins and water-worn pebbles in alluvial gravels.

Magnificent red spinels occur in Sri Lanka and Burma. Purple-pink spinels are new finds in Tanzania. Blue spinel is from Nigeria and Brazil. Thailand has blue and violet crystals. Other localities for excellent material are Pakistan, Thailand, Cambodia, India, and Tadzhikistan. The sensational find in the Pamir Mountains of Tadzhikistan has produced lovely bright pink gems.

Color-change spinels are known which change from purplish pink to pinkish purple or from gray-purple to dark rich purple. Many spinel crystals or rolled pebbles are relatively free of inclusions, but a few have silky parallel inclusions which make them suitable for cat's-eye cabochons or occasionally four- or six-rayed stars.

Spinel has been found in the United States in California, Washington, Arizona, Montana, Colorado, New York, New Jersey, Virginia, and North Carolina. A very desirable gemstone, spinel has a toughness in addition to excellent hardness. It is suitable for traditional and innovative new cuts and for fine jewelry.

Not heat sensitive and with no cleavage problems, it can be cut with normal procedures. Linde A on leather will bring a mirror polish to cabochons, and Linde A or alumina on tin is recommended for faceted stones. Larger pieces can be carved or engraved.

TOPAZ
Aluminum fluosilicate
H. 8   D. 3.51
Pleochroic Orthorhombic

Although topaz was formerly thought of as a yellow, orange, or golden-colored

The Virginia Reel cut was designed by Lapidary Hall of Fame faceter Edith Strout, who used the new cut for this 80-carat topaz.

stone, it is now commonly thought of as a bright blue stone. Actually the natural crystals can be many different colors, including pink, red, green, brown, and colorless, in addition to the golds and blues. The assorted blues now flooding the market are irradiated and heat treated. Natural blues are not as intense.

Topaz is found as stubby prismatic crystals in granite, granitic pegmatites, rhyolite, and in alluvial gravels. Extremely large crystals have been found, some weighing hundreds of pounds. Brazil is the leader in production of gem topaz. Yellow, orange, colorless, and sherry-tinted crystals come from Minas Gerais. Light brownish stones are heated to a desirable pink. Natural pink crystals are now on the market from Pakistan. Blue and green crystals come from Russia; blue and colorless from Mogok, Burma; colorless and brown from Australia; and brown and sherry-colored crystals from Tepetate, Mexico. (Crystal clusters in matrix from this locality are superb.)

In the United States topaz is the state gem of Texas and Utah. The Texas topaz from Mason County is blue or colorless. The Utah crystals from the Thomas Range are sherry colored. Other states

having topaz are California, Idaho, Colorado, New Hampshire, and South Carolina.

During the years when yellow to orange topaz was the most frequently seen, citrine—or yellow quartz—was often sold as topaz, leading to real topaz being offered as "precious topaz."

The San Diego Natural History Museum has a fine blue topaz crystal from Ramona 3½ x 3½ x 2½ inches (8.89 x 8.89 x 6.35 cm) A faceted 36,853-carat champagne-colored topaz from Brazil was cut by professional cutters Elvis Gray and Alan Pobanz. The Smithsonian's American Golden cut by Leon Agee is 22, 892 carats. Master

At 90.5 carats, this faceted topaz from Brazil is one of the many exceptional faceted gems in the Lora Robins Gallery in Richmond. Photo by Dr. Willie Reams, director.

cutters Glenn Lehrer and Lawrence Stoller cut a 34,650-carat stone from a 79-pound crystal that Ed Swoboda acquired in Brazil. The 21,327-carat Brazilian Princess was cut from the same crystal. A chameleon carving by Alfred Zimmerman weighs 13,720 carats.

Leonid Prikazchikov, specialist in Russian gems, says a Russian topaz record is a crystal weighing 248.6 pounds. The Lizzadro Museum has a brilliant-cut 675-carat natural blue topaz from Brazil.

Lapidaries may find the perfect cleavage of topaz a problem. Topaz is brittle but not particularly heat sensitive. It is sometimes chatoyant and suitable for cat's-eye cabochons.

Faceting instructor Jerry Call says topaz has the best color down the crystal axis and should have the table parallel to the axis. However, the cleavage is also parallel to the axis, so the table may have to be cut a couple of degrees away from the axis. Suitable polishes are Linde A, alumina, cerium oxide, or 14,000 diamond.

ZIRCON
Zirconium silicate
H. 7½   D. 4.65
Pleochroic   Tetragonal

Zircon is a popular jewelry stone. It has high refraction, good dispersion, and an assortment of wonderful colors, including shades and tints of red, orange, yellow, blue, and green.

A complex mineral, zircon is affected by traces of the radioactive elements uranium and thorium. The nearly amorphous damaged crystals are known as low zircon, while the normal crystalline examples are called high zircon. Sleepy-looking damaged stones are called metamict, and are less dense than the normal crystals.

Zircon has a wide distribution as an accessory mineral of igneous rocks such as granite. It is sometimes found in contact metamorphic rock and also in alluvial gem gravels. It is present in meteorites as well as in rocks from the moon.

Most cutting material comes from Asia—Sri Lanka, Burma, Cambodia, and Thailand. A recent discovery of gem-quality crystals is in Tanzania. Other localities are Quebec and Ontario, Canada, Norway, and Australia. In the United States zircon is found in Arizona, Colorado, South Dakota, Oklahoma, Texas, Maine, Massachusetts, New York, and North Carolina.

Low-type zircons are mixtures of greens, grays, yellows, and browns. They have fine parallel lines, much like diffraction grating. Green metamict zircons from Sri Lanka can be weirdly iridescent.

Cat's-eye zircons are usually 8 carats or less in size, but they are translucent, lively stones. A record is a gray-green round cat's-eye cabochon weighing 125.47 carats. A unique pinkish purple zircon is a recent find in India. A late discovery of varicolored zircons in Australia is in the Harts Range of the Northern Territory. The crystals are found in colors of red, yellow, brown, pink, and purple. The occurrence on Zircon Hill produces crystals up to 5½ pounds in weight. None of these stones appear to be metamict. Only small areas of the large crystals are suitable for cutting. Crystals and fragments are also found in a creek bed draining the area. A 35-carat brownish purple stone was faceted from this locality.

Undesirable colors of zircon, such as brown, are customarily heat treated to alter the color. Zircons with very little radiation damage can be restored to high zircon by heat. The color of treated stones may alter with time, but most treated stones are not marketed until their stability is tested.

Zircon crystals often help form the flowerlike patterns of porphyry, such as the "chrysanthemum stone" of Vancouver, British Columbia. A suite of 17 Harts Range zircons was cut from colorless to dark red crystals for the Australian Museum of Earth Sciences. The American Museum of Natural History has a brilliant cut greenish blue zircon from Thailand which weighs 208.65 carats.

Promoted 50 years ago as a diamond substitute, zircon is now an alternate birthstone for December. High zircon is brittle and prone to chipping; however, it is not heat sensitive and does not have a strong cleavage, so it is considered easy to cut. Linde A on tin is a popular polish. Superior results come from polishing with diamond. Metamict zircon is unpredictable to work with.

RECOMMENDED READING

Bancroft, P., *Gem and Crystal Treasures.* Fallbrook, CA: Western Enterprises, 1984.

Desautels, P., *The Gem Kingdom.* New York: Random House, 1986.

Federman, D., *Gem Profile: The First 60.* Shawnee Mission, KS: Modern Jeweler, 1988.

Keller, P., *Gemstones and Their Origins.* New York: Van Nostrand Reinhold, 1990.

Webster, R., Gems, 5th ed. London: Butterworth-Heinemann, 1994.

SPECIFIC GEMS

Hughes, R., *Corundum.* London: Butterworths, 1990.

Newman, R., *The Ruby and Sapphire Buying Guide.* Los Angeles: International Jewelry, 1991.

Rouse, J., *Garnet.* London: Butterworths, 1986.

Sinkankas, J., *Emeralds and Other Beryls.* Radnor, PA: Chilton, 1981.

CHAPTER III

Colorful Faceting Material

Amblygonite
Andalusite
Apatite
Axinite
Benitoite
Brazilianite
Chrome diopside
Danburite
Diaspore
Epidote
Euclase
Feldspar
    Heliolite
    Orthoclase

Iolite
Scheelite
Siderite
Sinhalite
Sphalerite
Sphene
Spodumene
    Hiddenite
    Kunzite
    Triphane
Tanzanite
Tektite
Tourmaline

FACETING MATERIAL IS FAR MORE RARE than material for cabochons, carvings, or ornamental purposes. The beauty of faceted stones comes from the way the stone reacts to the light. One of the measurements is the refractive index that gives the angle produced by the bending of the light rays in a transparent stone. Another measurement is dispersion that results from the faceted stone or prism separating the white light into the colors of the spectrum. This property is also called fire.

Birefringence also has an effect on the appearance of a faceted stone. It is the strength of the breakup of a light ray into two rays when the stone is doubly refractive.

Although translucent and even opaque stones can be faceted, it is the transparent minerals which are best adapted to this lapidary technique. The clarity of top-quality faceting material is of prime importance.

Faceting materials should have good color, and for jewelry use they should have a hardness of 6 or over, although some faceted stones of around 5 in hardness can be used for jewelry that is not exposed to hard wear, for example, pendants or earrings. Some stones of 5 or 6 hardness have a toughness which compensates for less than desirable hardness.

Fluorite is an example of a transparent stone which can be faceted, which has low refractive index (1.434) and low dispersion (.007) but often has good clarity and color. Benitoite is an example of a gem with high refractive index (1.80) and excellent dispersion (.046). Somewhere in the middle is spodumene, which has a refractive index of 1.66–1.67 and dispersion of .017, but when well chosen and properly cut, it will yield beautiful stones. Gems of average refraction and dispersion can be splendid if they have great clarity.

Faceting has come a long way since the days of the jamb peg. State-of-the-art machines make it possible to facet many more materials than previously and some machines have been especially adapted to facet giant sizes of transparent materials so that previous size records are constantly being broken. The OMF (optically magnified facets) is capable of precision cutting of curved facets. Great improvements are seen in the laps as well as the machines themselves. Gemologists know more about more materials than ever before, and this information is used by lapidaries to cut more beautiful stones.

Faceting used to be just for professionals, and their techniques were tightly kept secrets, but in this century amateurs have learned the art of faceting and some have become as good as any professional faceter in the world. The amateurs have more time for experimenting and have developed many new cuts. Top amateurs are never satisfied with a stone that is almost right but demand that each stone be as near perfection as possible. Although amateurs may sometimes be persuaded to sell a record stone, the stone was cut for love, not money. Many professional faceters have backgrounds as amateurs rather than apprentices. Faceting is not used only for cut stones for jewelry— it is used for ornamental objects of art such as eggs, spheres, pyramids, crystal models, and even carvings.

Cutters learn the characteristics of each stone and study a piece of rough under magnification to determine the best way to deal with inclusions, flaws, color zoning, cleavage, and other individual qualities. The objective of a good cutter is to produce the most beautiful stone possible, not necessarily the largest. If good faceting material is difficult to acquire, cutters often purchase poorly cut or native cut faceted stones and recut them with surprising results. Expert cutting accents the color, enhances the liveliness, and makes the stone beautiful and desirable.

Traditionally the most popular cuts have been brilliant cut and step cut; now combination cuts are often used. Well-known shapes are oval, marquise, pear, square, and briolette. Bernd Munsteiner's fantasy cuts have resulted in creative cuts that combine flat facets with concave cuts and elements of cabochons and carvings.

Facet-quality material is also used by creative lapidaries for cabochons and art objects. Most faceting material comes from transparent crystals which are among the most aesthetic objects in nature. Magnificent crystals of rare minerals, or of unique characteristics, should not be cut just to give the world another faceted stone. To some lapidaries a marvelous piece of natural material can only be enhanced by human artistry.

AMBLYGONITE
Lithium aluminum fluophosphate
H. 6   D. 3.11
Triclinic

Yellow amblygonite crystals suitable for faceting come from Brazil. Burma has also produced facet-quality crystals. Small gems have been faceted from lilac crystals from Namibia, and pegmatites of New Mexico and California have provided faceting material. Cabochons have been cut from translucent white massive amblygonite from the Beecher Lode, Custer County, South Dakota, from pink masses west of Custer and white crystals from the Corky claim near Custer. Other locations are France, Germany, Sweden, Namibia, and Australia.

Faceted stones over 10 carats are scarce, except from Brazil where 100-carat yellow stones are possible. Cabochons of 40 x 30 mm are known, and are also quite rare. Pale colors are tints of yellow, green, lilac, and blue.

Occurring in granite pegmatites, amblygonite is a part of a group of similar phosphates including montebrasite, natromontebrasite, and tavorite. Most cut gems are montebrasite. Cleavage, perfect in one direction, could be a problem. Work wet at slow speed and polish with Linde A on tin. Dealers in rough sometimes have the material, which should be selected primarily for color.

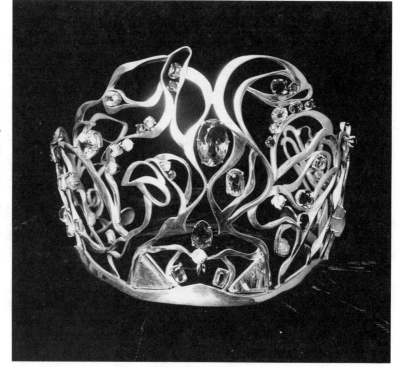

The "Crown of Brazil" by Michael Schwartz includes andalusite, tourmaline, euclase, and kunzite. Courtesy of International Gem and Jewelry Shows.

ANDALUSITE
Aluminum silicate
H. 6½–7½   D. 3.17
Pleochroic   Orthorhombic

Andalusite has the same chemical composition as sillimanite and kyanite. First found in Andalusia, Spain, andalusite comes in a suite of delicate colors: pink, gray, light to medium olive green, and a muted shade of reddish brown. Most facetable rough comes from Sri Lanka and Brazil. Strongly dichroic, andalusite yields extremely aesthetic gems when cut by a skilled lapidary. The color change of a well-cut stone is quite remarkable. The material is tough and well suited to jewelry.

The blocky orthorhombic crystals are found in metamorphic worn pebbles from alluvial gravels. Most pebbles will cut small stones, usually less than 5 carats; however stones of 100 carats have been cut. Cushion cuts are good, and fantasy cuts are sensational, although dispersion and refraction are only medium. Cabochons can also be cut from colorful material.

Cat's-eyes are also known but scarce. A green-yellow cat's-eye from Brazil weighs 7.34 carats. Rarely, Brazilian brownish green stones may be in the 30-carat range. The Smithsonian has a faceted brown stone from Brazil of over 28 carats.

When carefully oriented and cut to bring out the pleochroic colors, the stones are very elegant. The material has perfect cleavage in one direction, which is easily avoided by experts. It is not heat sensitive. Emerald cuts are preferred. Tin oxide on tin will bring a high polish. Stones should be selected for attractive color change and are often available.

APATITE
Calcium phosphate
H. 5   D. 3.20
Pleochroic Hexagonal

Apatite comes in a wonderful suite of colors, tints, and shades of blue, violet, green, yellow, and pink, plus brown, white, and colorless. It can be transparent, translucent, or opaque. Apatite is a group name and fluorapatite is the most common variety. Occurring in igneous rocks, hydrothermal veins, and metamorphic rock, apatite is found as prismatic or tabular crystals, massive, stalactitic, or as concretions.

A facetable blue-green apatite from Ontario, Canada, has been named Trilliumite. Yellow-green apatite from Bancroft will facet stones up to 10 carats. Transparent yellow apatite from Durango, Mexico, is abundant. Called amarillas by the miners, the crystals will yield faceted stones of up to 25 carats. Large green crystals come from Brazil. Individual crystals may be up to 4 inches (10.16 cm) long. Regal blue-violet crystals of fluorapatite from Mount Apatite, Maine, are among the most aesthetic of apatite specimens. Small gem-quality purple and blue apatite crystals are also found in South Dakota, in the pegmatites of Pennington County.

Recently, bright blue-green apatite of facet quality has come from Madagascar. Bright green crystals from Kenya and distinctive pink crystals from Pakistan also look promising. Colorless apatite comes from Bolivia. Other apatite locations include Norway, Germany, Spain, Italy, South Africa, Madagascar, India, Sri Lanka, and Burma, and California, Idaho, New York, and Georgia in the United States.

Apatite is also used for cabochons, particularly cat's-eyes. The green cat's-eyes from Brazil or yellow-green chatoyant stones from Kenya, Sri Lanka, or Tanzania are fine examples. Some of the cat's-eyes from Tanzania are reddish brown from inclusions of hairlike goethite. Light yellow apatite cat's-eyes can be so sharp that they could be mistaken for chrysoberyl at first glance. Recent appearances in Tucson were blue-green cat's-eye cabochons the rich color of Paraiba tourmaline. A blue cabochon quality apatite from Siberia is called lazurapatite. The largest known faceted apatite is a 186-carat green gem from Brazil.

Apatite is exceedingly heat sensitive and should be cold dopped. Crystals may be remarkably free from flaws. Apatite is brittle, but cleavage is not a problem. It should be cut with a thin saw blade and ground only with fine grinding wheels. For faceted stones an alumina charged Pol-A-Gem lap brings excellent results. Cabochons may need extended fine sanding. Tin oxide brings a good polish. Dealers of facet rough often advertise apatite at reasonable prices.

AXINITE
Calcium aluminum borosilicate
H. 6½–7   D. 3.26
Pleochroic   Triclinic

Cut axinites are uncommon but quite distinctive with strongly pleochroic colors of purple, yellow, red, blue, or variations. Found in contact metamorphic areas and in alluvial deposits, gem-quality crystals come from Baja California, Sri Lanka, and Tanzania. Cut stones over 5 carats are extremely rare, but stones from Mexico

have been 20 carats. Other localities are Brazil, England, France, Germany, Norway, and Finland. U.S. locations are California, Nevada, and New Jersey. Well-cut stones can be interesting with good color and dispersion.

A notable find was made in the 1970s during the construction of the New Melones Dam in Calaveras County, California. In the albite-axinite-quartz veins were vugs of purple-brown axinite crystals up to 4 inches (10.16 cm). Stones were faceted from about 2 to 5 carats. A 24-carat step cut stone from Baja California, Mexico, is in the Smithsonian. An especially large crystal from Brazil is 9 inches (22.86 cm) in length.

The axe-shaped crystals are extremely included, which may cause some orientation problems for lapidaries. Although brittle, axinite is not heat sensitive, and can be cut with little difficulty and polished with Linde A on tin. Bright pleochroic material with few flaws is hard to find.

BENITOITE
Barium titanosilicate
H. 6½   D. 3.64
Pleochroic   Hexagonal

A truly unique and exquisite gem is the California original named for the location near San Benito River in San Benito County. Although known as a blue gem, benitoite has also been found as small pink crystals in Santa Cruz County. Colorless crystals have also been found. The discovery of these triangular crystals filled a gap in crystallography as well as provided a splendid U.S. gem. With a refractive index of near 1.8 and a diamondlike dispersion of 0.047, cut gems resemble blue diamonds. Birefringence is strong.

Crystals, sometimes almost 2 inches across, occur in a snowy natrolite matrix, often with shiny dark crystals of neptunite. Larger benitoite crystals are usually flawed or included. Cut gems of over 3 carats are exceedingly rare, but the Smithsonian has a faceted stone of 7.6 carats. This distinctive stone is the state gem of California. A magnificent 4½-inch (11.43-cm) crystal is in the gem collection of the California Federation of Mineralogical Societies.

Masses of natrolite with benitoite crystals occurring as a low-temperature deposit in serpentine veins were discovered in 1906 near the headwaters of the San Benito River. The mine has been worked off and on ever since, along with another mine discovered nearby at a later date. The current size record is a 15.42-carat cushioned triangular step cut faceted by professional faceter Mike Gray.

Benitoite is rare, but many faceters and collectors in the United States have small cut stones. There is little difficulty in cutting the stones since they are not heat sensitive and do not have problem cleavage. Polishing, even with the preferred cerium oxide, may come up quickly and overtiming presents problems. Small facetable stones can sometimes be acquired, but production is limited and the demand is great.

BRAZILIANITE
Sodium aluminum phosphate
H. 5½   D. 2.98
Monoclinic

Brazilianite is essentially a one-locality lapidary mineral and is named for the country of its discovery. The spectacular yellow-green crystals were discovered in 1944 in pegmatites in the state of Minas Gerais. First described by Dr. Frederick Pough, the new species was deemed too soft for lapidary uses except for collectors' stones. Well-protected stones can be used for pendants and earrings. For some time there were fake matrix specimens on the market because the splendid new species proved so attractive to crystal collectors.

The crystals occur in pegmatite cavities as a hydrothermal mineral. A number of large stones have been cut—Pough says up to 20 carats. Many museums and private collections have faceted brazilianite. Cranbrook Institute of Science, Bloomfield Hills, Michigan, has a crystal of exceptional clarity and bright apple-green color that is 4¾ x 4 x 3 inches (12.06 x 10.16 x 7.62 cm).

Bright yellow, clean gems are seldom over 15 carats in weight, although clouded crystals are sometimes hundreds of carats in weight. Moderately heat sensitive, and with perfect cleavage in one direction, the material can be cut and polished with no difficulty using alumina on a tin lap. Brazilianite is not commonly available.

CHROME DIOPSIDE
Calcium magnesium silicate
H. 5½–6 ½   D. 3.29
Pleochroic   Monoclinic

Since diopside is used for splendid cat's-eye stones, it is discussed in that chapter; nevertheless, a very special chrome green occurrence deserves additional attention. Emerald green chrome diopside from Russia's Ural Mountains had been known since the early 1970s when it was advertised in the *Lapidary Journal*. Reijo Nenonen, a Finnish gem cutter, writes that another excellent source is the uvarovite garnet mine of Finland. Massive chrome diopside for cabo-

Mary Supplee used 800 gems of Russia in this Fabergé-style egg clock. Courtesy of International Gem and Jewelry Shows.

tery about some of the Russian material is that vanadium and no chrome content are shown by the Chelsea filter according to writers and gem dealers Sy and Ann Frazier, who imported a quantity of excellent material.

Cut stones are imposing, and thus, quite expensive. Emerald cuts are best and are appropriate for pendants, earrings, and custom-made jewelry. The material is difficult to work with because of a tendency to glaze. Extra fine laps and slow speed are used for faceted stones, and cabochons are polished with chrome oxide on leather. Fine-colored material is available from time to time.

DANBURITE
Calcium borosilicate
H. 7   D. 2.97
Orthorhombic

The remarkably clear colorless crystals of danburite from Charcas, Mexico, resemble topaz crystals. A 5½-inch (13.97-cm) crystal from Charcas is in a private collection. Crystals of over 6 inches (15.24 cm) have been among the fine crystal groups mined near San Luis Potosi. The smaller crystals have more brilliant faces and the terminations of the larger crystals are of excellent facet quality. Some of the crystals are yellowish, greenish, or light brown, but they are not as clean as the colorless ones. Yellow and clear, colorless crystals up to 6 inches (15.24 cm) long have been mined in Baja California. Etched yellow and peach-colored crystals occur in Burma. Golden yellow stones of superior color have recently come from Sri Lanka. Orangy-brown material originates in Madagascar. Other occurrences are in Japan and Russia.

Danburite occurs in metamorphic rock. Cut gems are usually less than 5 carats,

chons is quite common in Finland. It is somewhat lighter in color than the Russian material.

Faceted stones and small cabochons shown in Tucson have been under 3 or 4 carats. The large stones are only in the 15-carat range. A recent find is in Xing Jiang, China; bright green crystals of over 50 grams have been reported.

Chrome diopside occurs in kimberlites and in calcium-rich metamorphic rock. It is a member of the pyroxene group, which also includes jadeite, a species also sometimes colored by chrome. A curious mys-

Danburite is a light yellow faceting material from Mexico.

from the brown material discovered in Turkey in the 1980s. One stone is a step cut stone of 157.66 carats. An unusual stone is a 26.97-carat color-change stone that has a pink/green change. Other color-change stones, such as yellow-green to yellow-brown, are known in this strongly pleochroic species. One- and two-inch (2.54 and 5.08 cm) crystals have been shown in Tucson.

Colorless crystals have been found in Newlin, Pennsylvania, blue and violet crystals in Chester, Massachusetts, and red mangandiaspore in South Africa. The South African material has been used for cabochons. Other locations are Greenland, Norway, Switzerland, Greece, and China.

Diaspore is a constituent of pisolitic bauxite. The diaspore group also includes goethite. It occurs in metamorphic schists, limestones, and corundum deposits.

With good hardness, diaspore makes attractive stones suitable for jewelry. It is very brittle and prone to splintering or fraying at the edges. The table should be cut almost perpendicular to the strong cleavage plane. Cold dopped stones achieve a prepolish with a 1,200 lap and a polish with Linde A on tin or plastic.

although professional cutter Art Grant recently cut a 37-carat stone from Russian rough, a record stone at the time.

Danburite is easy for lapidaries to cut. Brilliant cut stones are the most aesthetic. Clean stones make attractive and durable gems suitable for jewelry. They can be polished with alumina or Linde A. Clean crystals are on the market sporadically.

DIASPORE
Aluminum oxide
H 6½–7   D. 3.30
Pleochroic   Orthorhombic

Diaspore occurs in metamorphic limestones in massive, stalactitic, and crystal forms in colors of yellow, green, lilac, pink, rose, and greenish brown as well as colorless. The largest cut stones have been

EPIDOTE
Calcium iron aluminum silicate
H. 6-7   D. 3.38
Pleochoric   Monoclinic

Epidote is a complex group of minerals found as a low-temperature deposit in metamorphic rock. Massive epidote is a constituent of many rocks; however, facetable crystals of good quality and large size are not common. The distinctive colors of epidote are pistachio green, dark forest green, yellowish green, and brownish green.

Epidote is a member of the epidote group, which includes clinozoisite, piedmontite, hancockite, allanite, thulite, and zoisite (tanzanite), a group of minerals that wraps around the color wheel.

Transparent pistachio green epidote comes from Norway, but is rarely large enough to facet. A fine deep green crystal from Austria measures 10 x 1 inch (25.40 x 2.54 cm). Austria is a major source of facet rough. Brazil and Alaska are other sources of facet-quality crystals. More epidote locations are California, Michigan, Massachusetts, Mexico, Finland, France, Italy, Japan, Korea, Australia, Burma, and Pakistan. Most faceted stones are dark and small. The best materials are yellow-green crystals from Brazil. Rich green stones have also been cut from the Green Monster Mountain on Prince of Wales Island, Alaska. The University of Alaska Museum has an elegant crystal cluster measuring 5 x 8 inches (12.70 x 20.32 cm). Some epidote includes golden needles of iron minerals. Epidote

Iolite, enstatite, andalusite, and spinel adorn the crowns of India as well as rubies, sapphires, and emeralds. Courtesy of International Gem and Jewelry Shows.

can be used for small carvings such as fantasy cuts, which do not need to be as clean as faceted stones. The lighter-colored crystals produce the most appealing gems. Darker stones look better if cuts are shallow.

Piemontite is the member of this group that is mostly a tint or shade of red, due to manganese, and hancockite, containing lead, is brown or black. Clinozoisite—brown, yellow, or green—is sometimes faceted. Cutting-quality piemontite comes from Baja California, Mexico. Super-rare hancockite is from New Jersey.

Perfect cleavage in two directions may be a problem, as is a strong twinning plane in many specimens. There is also some heat sensitivity. Epidote is often cold dopped and polished with Linde A, or cerium oxide on tin or plastic. Available material is often small and dark.

EUCLASE
Beryllium aluminum silicate
H. 7½   D. 3.10
Pleochroic   Monoclinic

Euclase is a facetable mineral of good hardness which is found in transparent crystals of beautiful pastel blues, yellows, and violets. Many crystals used for cutting are colorless. Faceter Jerry Call has a 43-carat yellow-green euclase that he faceted from rough from Minas Gerais, Brazil. He also faceted an 18.29-carat blue-green Brazilian stone. Not many euclase gems weigh over 15 carats; however, a record may be the 145-carat stone faceted by professional faceter Mike Gray. Optical qualities are medium, but well-cut stones are splendid.

Gemmy euclase occurs in weathered pegmatites and schists near Ouro Prato, Brazil, as prismatic crystals several inches long. Other locations for euclase are the Ural Mountains of Russia, Austria, Norway, Tanzania, Guyana, and Zimbabwe. Intense blue cuttable crystals come from the Miami district of Zimbabwe.

Faceters should avoid the cleavage, but otherwise the material presents few problems because it is not heat sensitive and takes a rapid polish with ease with Linde A on tin after cutting on a fine lap. It is hard enough for jewelry, well suited for fantasy cuts, and particularly attractive if the color is light blue-green. Good pieces are occasionally available.

FELDSPAR
Heliolite (and facetable labradorite)
Sodium aluminum silicate
H. 6–6½   **D 2.70**
Pleochroic   **Triclinic**

Heliolite is a proposed name for the bright facet-quality labradorite from Lake County, Oregon. Bob and Barbara Rodgers, pioneer miners at the site, advanced the name heliolite as their transparent material was quite distinctive and was easily differentiated from the heavily included straw-colored sunstone from the same area. The use of the word heliolite in this context has been endorsed by Dr. Frederick Pough, author and editor. The vibrant heliolite has a remarkable array of colors—yellow, orange, red-orange, green, and violet. The color range may be due to the traces of colloidal copper or possibly an iron mineral.

Bob Rodgers had a gorgeous collection of faceted stones of rainbow colors, including a record pleochroic lemon-yellow stone of 86½ carats cut by Buzz Gray, professional cutter, and several unique bicolored stones. A few of the transparent stones show some

This well-cut 10-carat light green euclase is from Brazil.

schiller, but most are remarkably clear. Transparent highly colored heliolites in the 10-carat range are not uncommon. The Rodgers mine was sold a few years ago. There are several other claims in the area near Plush on BLM land. A 54.78-carat faceted sunstone from Oregon shows considerable schiller. The production of heliolite has been fairly steady for some years now and the stone is becoming better known.

Facet-quality labradorite also occurs in Chihuahua, Mexico. A 92-carat golden-colored faceted stone is from this locality. The Los Angeles County Museum has a yellow faceted stone from Mexico which weighs 129 carats. Labradorite is also found in California, Utah, South Dakota, Greenland, Labrador, Norway, Sweden, Finland, Madagascar, and South Africa.

Labradorite occurs with basic igneous and metamorphic rocks. Only a portion of labradorite has the phenomenal quality called labradorescence. It can be translucent or nearly opaque as well as transparent. It is found as tabular crystals, compact massive material, or granular material. It belongs to the plagioclase feldspar series.

Massive labradorite or large crystals are often badly fractured so material must be selected and oriented with care. Rough should be examined both wet and dry with a loupe. If there is schiller in the stone it should be oriented so that the reflections are the most visible from the table. Labradorite is not especially heat sensitive. The perfect cleavage presents no difficulty during cutting, but the material may scratch during polishing (with cerium oxide on plastic) if care is not taken. Cabochons are cut from labradorite. It is also suitable for carvings, tiles, and ornamental uses.

The Ponderosa Mine is now producing facet-quality labradorite in a new Oregon location north of Burns. Some of the crystals weigh nearly a pound each. The colors are generally yellows and reds, many with coppery schiller. Ponderosa gems are marketed as sunstone. Ponderosa Mine crystals can be faceted with 600 and 1,200 diamond followed by cerium oxide on felt. Rough is usually available, although the choice colors are uncommon.

Orthoclase
Potassium aluminum silicate
H. 6–6½   D. 2.55
Monoclinic

Orthoclase is a common feldspar found in abundance in worldwide localities. It is a constituent of igneous rocks, where large crystals occur in pegmatites. Colors are white, yellow, red, green, and sometimes colorless. (Orthoclase with special optical effects such as moonstone is discussed in the phenomenal gem chapter.)

When transparent, orthoclase is used for faceted stones. Yellow transparent orthoclase, rich in iron, comes from pegmatites in Madagascar. Facetable pieces are sometimes in the 500-gram range and

sunny faceted stones are in the 100-carat range. The Smithsonian has a showy faceted yellow stone of 249.5 carats from Madagascar. Other worldwide sources are Mexico, Greenland, Switzerland, Zimbabwe, Burma, and Sri Lanka. Some of the Sri Lankan stones will cut stars. The Mexican material is pale yellow and varies from transparent to opaque.

In the United States, orthoclase comes from California, Nevada, Idaho, Arizona, New Mexico, South Dakota, Arkansas, New York, Virginia, and North Carolina. The New Mexico orthoclase is the sanidine variety. An interesting type here is smoky gray in color, similar to smoky quartz, but the smoky color fades when exposed to sunlight. Much of the New Mexico material is adularescent and used for cabochons; however, some is faceted.

Orthoclase is used for cabochons in South Dakota. Light red and flesh-colored crystals suitable for cutting are found in Pennington and Custer counties in the Black Hills. Phenocrysts of orthoclase also occur in porphyritic rock. Some of these colorless phenocrysts are clear, but not large enough to facet.

Step cut stones are best adapted to this material. Faceters need to be aware of perfect cleavage and heat sensitivity. The toughness is poor and scratching may be a problem. Faceted stones can be finished with diamond on wood. Transparent orthoclase of good color and size is not easy to locate.

IOLITE (CORDIERITE)
Magnesium aluminum silicate
H. 7–7½   D. 2.55
Pleochroic   Orthorhombic

This stone is noted for its pleasing blue color, but not all crystals are blue. Colorless, yellow, gray, and brown crystals also occur, as well as several colors of massive and granular material.

When chatoyant, iolite is used for cat's-eye cabochons. Strongly pleochroic, iolite is found in pegmatites, gneisses, and schists, usually as nodules in a metamorphic matrix. Most gem material now comes from India, Tanzania, Namibia, and Brazil.

Blue cordierite in schist from Custer County, South Dakota, has been cut into cabochons. Small transparent sections are not big enough to facet; however, facet-quality blue material has been found in the Laramie Range of Wyoming. Iolite also comes from California, New York, New Hampshire, Connecticut; Ontario and Quebec, Canada; and Sri Lanka and Madagascar.

Dark blue star iolite comes from Kuruvesi, Finland, and is used for striking cabochons. Facet-quality iolite and chatoyant blue-gray rough comes from a large deposit at Orissa, India. Several colors come from Harts Range, Northern Territory, Australia, among them a white crystal of 6.6 pounds. A cat's-eye cabochon from here weighs 23.65 carats. Four-rayed star stones come from Tanzania, Sri Lanka, and Brazil. An odd variety of iolite from Sri Lanka has been called bloodshot iolite because of inclusions of small flat platelets of reddish hematite or goethite.

Flattened blue oval-shaped iolite beads and faceted beads of excellent blue are recent additions to the jewelry market. The material is probably from India. Most iolite has flaws and inclusions, so clean cut stones over 10 carats are uncommon. Gem dealer Anil Dholakia obtained a 111.02-carat faceted stone from India.

Rough should be oriented so that the blue color predominates. Jerry Call tells his students to place the table parallel to the blue direction of the pleochroic stone. Faceted stones are more colorful if step cut. Polish with tin oxide on hard leather for cabochons or cerium oxide on plastic for faceted stones. Supplies of iolite are adequate.

SCHEELITE
Calcium tungstate
H. 4½–5   D. 6.10
Tetragonal

Colorless, yellow, yellow-green, green, and brown crystals of scheelite will cut exceptionally lively and brilliant gems because of the diamondlike (0.038) dispersion. Although large crystals occur, clear areas and cut stones are usually small; however, California locations have yielded crystals for cut stones in the 20-carat range. Most of the faceted stones are colorless or yellow, but some are orange, green, red, or brown. A gemmy light green crystal from Sri Lanka was faceted for a 12.20-carat stone.

Scheelite occurs in contact metamorphic deposits, pegmatites, and placer deposits commonly associated with wolframite. It also occurs as masses intergrown with wolframite, pyrite, and quartz. In addition to the California location, scheelite of cuttable quality has been found in Arizona, Utah, South Dakota, Colorado, and Montana. Fine yellow crystals have come from Sonora, Mexico. Crystals up to 13 inches (33.02 cm) in length have come from Japan and Korea. Australia and Sri Lanka have marketed a quantity of cuttable material. Other localities are Canada, Brazil, Finland, France, Italy, Germany, Malaysia, Siberia, and Burma. Bright orange scheelite has been discovered in Hunan, China. Large crystals have been found in Korea in recent years.

Faceted stones have been used for jewelry in protected items like earrings or

Above, Left: A Becker original is a colorful tourmaline parrot perched on sculptured quartz. courtesy of Gerhard Becker, Idar-Oberstein, Germany. Above, Right: Quartz owls are comfortable on their amethyst branch. Carved by Gerhard Becker, Idar-Oberstein, Germany. Below: This splendid iris agate was cut by V-Rock of Canton, Ohio.

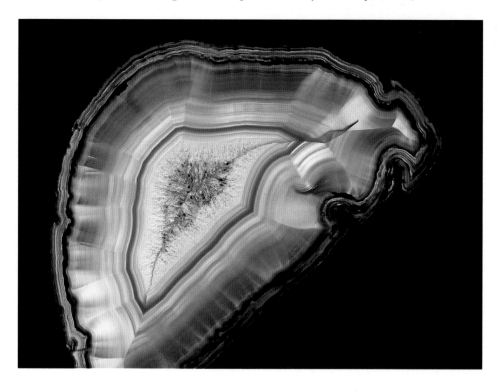

Above: Russian crowns of the czarist era accented religious motifs with rubies, emeralds, and pearls.
Photo courtesy of International Gem and Jewelry Shows.

Right: Ivory carvings studded with native gems are historic products of Sri Lanka. Courtesy of International Gem and Jewelry Shows.

Above: The Dan Bakers of Garland, Texas, created this replica of the Crown of Charlemagne for the International Gem and Jewelry Show.

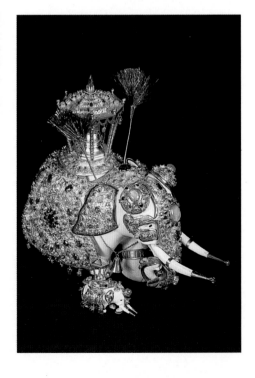

Above, Left: Ivory, coral, and tourmaline have been transformed to art objects by Hing Wa Lee of Los Angeles. The tourmaline pendant is 2½ x 1½ inches.
Above, Right: Lapis lazuli from Afghanistan becomes a multidimensional Oriental mountain under the skilled hands of Hing Wa Lee.
Below: Betty Crawford, channelwork artist, cut malachite, goldstone, and mother-of-pearl for these charming hummingbirds.

Carved from Alaska jade, these vases are 9 ½ inches high. Courtesy of Lizzadro Museum of Lapidary Arts, Elmhurst, Illinois. Photo by Russell Kemp.

Fabergé-style raspberries, 8 inches in height, were carved in Idar-Oberstein for the Lizzadro Museum of Lapidary Arts. Lizzadro photo by Russell Kemp.

This pietra dura portrait of Joseph Lizzadro, founder of the Lizzadro Museum, was made in Florence, Italy. It measures 16 x 20 inches. Photo by Russell Kemp.

pins, but usually these stones are shown in collections, where amateurs often take them for diamonds. A 45-carat faceted scheelite from Sonora, Mexico, is displayed at the Arizona Sonora Desert Museum in Tucson.

Scheelite is not heat sensitive, but it is brittle and has distinct cleavage, which is not a serious problem. It can be polished with Linde A on wax or chrome oxide on Ultralap. Brilliant cuts are especially lively.

SIDERITE
Iron carbonate
H. 3½   **D. 3.83**
Hexagonal

Siderite is a common carbonate but is not often transparent enough to facet; however, pieces suitable for cabochons are occasionally cut, particularly when mixed with calcite and rhodochrosite.

Siderite has strong dispersion, so if the yellow or green tint is acceptable, the resulting stones are beautiful. Cabochon material may be brown or brownish yellow.

Siderite occurs as crystals or massive material in pegmatites, ore veins, or sedimentary deposits. The colors are due to iron minerals. Botryoidal iridescent specimens are aesthetic. Locations in the United States are Colorado, South Dakota, and Idaho.

In the early 1950s, iridescent botryoidal siderite, reported to be from Arizona, was used for interesting cabochons. Large rhombs from Brazil have been used for cabochons. Other locations are Bolivia, England, Germany, Austria, Italy, and Australia. Transparent brown crystals from Portugal have provided most of the facet material, but similar material occurs in Spain, Greenland, and at Mont Ste. Hilaire, Quebec.

Stones are usually step cut and worked with some difficulty because of the perfect cleavage in three directions. Slow speeds are recommended. Polish cabochons with tin oxide on leather with a few crystals of oxalic acid added to the slurry. Facet with Linde A on tin. Facet-quality siderite is not common. The material is too soft for jewelry.

SINHALITE
Magnesium aluminum iron borate
H. 6½–7   **D. 3.50**
Pleochroic   **Orthorhombic**

Named for the Sanskrit word for Ceylon, sinhalite was discovered as rolled pebbles in Sri Lanka's gem gravels in 1952. At first it was thought to be a brown peridot, an iron-rich olivine gem. Gemologists B. W. Anderson and C. J. Payne suggested that the stones were too pale to have a high iron content. Then Dr. Switzer at the Smithsonian examined a specimen and determined the gem was not olivine, and W. F. Foshag reexamined the so-called brown olivine of the British Museum. It was soon determined to be a new species.

Sinhalite is a metamorphic mineral that occurs in limestone/granite contact zones as well as alluvial deposits. The color of sinhalite varies from yellow-brown to orange or golden brown and greenish brown and occasionally pink. Crystals have come from upper Burma. Another location for cuttable sinhalite is Tanzania, where the stones have a pinkish cast. The Sri Lankan stones are quite large—a record is a faceted stone of 158 carats. Sri Lanka is presently the major producer.

Mark Smith, a professional cutter from Thailand, has seen clean rough in Sri Lanka in the 150-carat range, but these larger pieces tend to be dark. He prefers the lighter-colored material that is in the 30-carat range.

John Sinkankas says in *Gem Cutting* that the material cuts more like tourmaline than peridot. It is not heat sensitive and is easy to work up to a final polish, which can best be achieved by Linde A on tin. Gem dealers do not often have it in stock.

SPHALERITE
Zinc sulfide
H. 3½–4   **D. 4.10**
Pleochroic   **Isometric**

Faceted sphalerite gems, too soft for wear, are nevertheless sensational stones. Facetable sphalerite may be yellow-green, yellow, orange, red, brownish red, brownish green, or colorless. Material from Spain is red, while green from Mexico yields fiery gems. Bright green occurs in Zaire. Large gems in the 100-carat range have been cut from the Spanish material and gems in the 50-carat and over range come form Mexico, Utah, and New Jersey. GIA examined a 55.62-carat olive-green faceted stone from Mont Ste. Hilaire, Quebec. Light-colored stones are more fiery than diamonds because of 0.056 dispersion.

Translucent sphalerite can be used for cabochons. The Sy and Ann Frazier gem newsletter featured a yellow and red sphalerite egg. The Arizona Sonora Desert Museum has three faceted sphalerites of great brilliancy and large size, two from Baja California Norte, and one from Pima County, Arizona. The largest is 18 x 11 mm. The California Academy of Science has a red-brown 150.38-carat oval faceted sphalerite from Spain. These are eclipsed by the record 1,269-carat faceted stone in the Colorado School of Mines Museum.

Sphalerite is an abundant mineral in zinc deposits. It is found in hydrothermal ore veins and in contact zones of metamorphic deposits and in limestones and dolomites with galena and other sulfides. Other important deposits are in Missouri, Oklahoma, Kansas (tristate area), Arizona, Wisconsin, Tennessee, Canada, Mexico, England, Scotland, Germany, Italy, Namibia, Zaire, and Australia. In England sphalerite is called zinc blende.

Sphalerite has perfect cleavage, but is not brittle or heat sensitive. If it were not for the low hardness it would be one of the most desirable jewelry stones. Once the sawing is oriented so that the table is not parallel to a cleavage plane, the stone is shaped and polished with little trouble. It takes a brilliant polish with alumina on tin and makes a lively stone for any collection; however, it is not easy to come by.

SPHENE
Calcium titanosilicate
H. 5–5½   **D. 3.45**
Monoclinic

With a high refractive index, strong birefringence, and excellent dispersion, sphene makes a dazzling gem. The colors are yellow, green, and brown. High-quality faceting material has come from Brazil, Mexico, and Madagascar. Easy to cut into sensational stones, sphene's popularity is only dimmed by its inferior hardness. Lapidaries may prefer the contemporary name titanite. The occurrence of sphene is widespread as an accessory mineral in igneous rock, metamorphic rock, and schists. It occurs as compact masses or in wedge-shaped or prismatic crystals colored by chromium.

Intense green crystals colored by chromium have come from Baja California, Mexico. Gem-quality yellow-green sphene comes from Sri Lanka. Cuttable orange sphene comes from Burma and honey yellow crystals come from New South Wales, Australia. Well-formed yellow-green gem crystals come from the Harts Range of Central Australia. Stones up to 20 carats have been cut by faceters able to get good rough. Other localities for sphene are Crestmore, California; Magnet Cove, Arkansas; Franklin, New Jersey; South Dakota; Pennsylvania; Quebec and Ontario, Canada; Greenland; Norway; France; Finland; Switzerland; Austria; Pakistan; and New Zealand.

Most crystals are twinned, but after correct orientation with the twinning plane parallel to the table, cutting is easy. Experts suggest polishing with Linde A on tin. Large clean pieces of rough are seldom seen.

SPODUMENE
Lithium aluminum silicate
H. 6½–7½   D. 3.18
Pleochroic   Monoclinic

Spodumene, a major source of lithium, appears in granite pegmatites in many countries, and in a few of these a small amount is gem quality. The chief spodumene gems are kunzite and hiddenite while some gems (colorless or yellow) are called triphane.

Hiddenite

Hiddenite is the rich green variety of spodumene colored by chromium discovered during the emerald prospecting days of the nineteenth century in North Carolina. The emerald green hiddenite crystals were small, elongated, and color zoned, with the terminations being the best areas for faceting. A 9.9-carat stone is in the American Museum of Natural History. Few cut stones weigh 5 carats.

Unlike kunzite, the color of hiddenite is stable. Like kunzite, it occurs in pegmatite pockets. Green spodumene occurs in Afghanistan, Sri Lanka, and Brazil, but because of the lack of chromium, it is not hiddenite. North Carolina hiddenite is scarce.

Kunzite

Kunzite, named for American gem pioneer G. F. Kunz, comes in delightful tints of pink, peach, lilac, orchid, and sometimes blue. The colors are due to manganese and small amounts of iron. Bicolor and tricolor crystals as well as cat's-eye material have been mined. Heat treatment can deepen the delicate tints. Kunzite is subject to fading and should be kept away from sunlight.

Excellent kunzite comes from the gem pockets of San Diego County's Pala district. Afghanistan and Brazil are the main suppliers of cutting-quality crystals. Madagascar and Burma also have gem-quality crystals and recently crystals similar to those from Pala have been found in Sri Lanka. Small kunzites have been cut from giant "logs" of spodumene from Pennington County, South Dakota.

Found as etched, flattened prismatic crystals, kunzites from Afghanistan and Brazil can weigh 16 pounds or so. A rare doubly terminated crystal from Afghanistan is 6 inches (15.24 cm) long. Although a spectacular gem, kunzite is fragile. It should not be subjected to hard wear, sudden shocks, or bright lights.

Kunzite is sometimes used for carvings besides cut stones. A kunzite carving, lilac in color and superb in quality, is a Buddha 5½ x 3½ x 2½ inches (13.97 x 8.89 x 6.35

cm) carved by Hing Wa Lee of Los Angeles from Afghanistan material. A record 1,267-carat faceted pink kunzite is in the Los Angeles County Museum. The San Diego Museum of Natural History has a California crystal 12 x 7 x 2½ inches (30.48 x 17.78 x 6.35 cm). The Lizzadro Museum has a 550-carat faceted lilac stone. A marquis cut blue kunzite from Afghanistan is 290.87 carats. An aesthetic crystal in the Houston Museum of Science is 12 inches (30.48 cm) tall. Professional faceter John Ramsey supervised the faceting of three fine Brazilian stones weighing 725, 514, and 145 carats.

Kunzite is one of the most difficult minerals to cut. With exceptionally easy cleavage and parting planes, kunzite must be sawed at exactly the right angle, with a sharp new blade. Cabochons are polished with tin oxide. The best color is parallel to the length of the crystal. Grinding wheels should not be used. Only fine grits should be employed for sanding. A good polish results from tin oxide on tin, 50,000 mesh diamond, or Linde A on tin. A blue kunzite of 290.87 carats took a month to cut. This material is a challenge to cutters and is presently easily available.

Triphane

Yellow triphane and other colors of spodumene have yielded larger stones than the green hiddenite or the lilac kunzite. Canada's Royal Ontario Museum in Toronto has a yellow-green stone cut by John Sinkankas that weighs 1,800 carats. A yellow stone from Afghanistan material weighing 1,240 carats, cut by Mike Gray, is the largest faceted yellow triphane.

Giant crystals "logs" of spodumene are often found. A crystal from the Etta Mine in South Dakota was 42 feet in length. Colorless triphane from near Keystone,

Pennington County, has been faceted as well as yellow-green spodumene. Excellent cat's-eye cabochons have been cut from Pennington County spodumene. Cabochons, including a few snow-white chatoyant stones, have been cut from the South Dakota spodumenes from the Etta Mine.

Spodumene has perfect cleavage and frays on edges. Preforms should be made by hand. Facets are cut with 600 grit. Leave a natural face on the culet until last. Tin oxide will bring a bright polish. Suitable for jewelry, spodumene will not take hard wear. Many dealers have at least some colors of spodumene.

TANZANITE
Calcium aluminum silicate
H. 6–6½   D. 3.38
Pleochroic   Orthorhombic

In 1966 a native of Arusha, Tanzania, made an astonishing discovery, a beautiful, rich blue crystal. Soon others were looking for the blue crystals thinking they might be sapphires of exceptional color. (Early laboratory tests were for dumortierite). Testing proved that the stones were zoisite, a mineral never before found in this color or quality. Tiffany and Company named the blue stone tanzanite and vigorously promoted that name. Tanzanite was named, of course, for the country of origin, since Tiffany felt that zoisite was not an appropriate name for so exquisite a gem.

The terminated prismatic crystals occur in a tough metamorphic rock in a remote mountain area. Trichroic, they belong to the epidote group of which zoisite is a member. Since the initial discovery, several mines in the region have produced the gems, and now it is reported that gems on the market are coming from a new area. The newer material is said to have more inclusions and color of less intensity.

Faceted stones became an immediate success because of the gorgeous sapphire blue color. At first, prices were quite moderate, so amateur cutters had a chance to buy and cut the rough, but prices have gradually risen. One of the largest cut stones is a faceted gem of 122.7 carats in the Smithsonian collection. Stones of about 20 carats were not unusual in the early days of the mining operation, but are scarce at present. Rarely tanzanite will cut a cat's-eye cabochon. A few color-change tanzanites change from daylight blue to bright purple in incandescent light.

The intense blue color is achieved by heat treating selected rough to drive out the less desirable trichroic colors, which may be reddish brown or grayish orange. Credible heat treatment can be accomplished at less than 500 degrees C. Blue and yellow directions will give a pure blue after heating, while the blues and reds will yield a purplish blue. Jerry Call says the material that came out earlier was easier to heat than the present material.

Creative German cutter Bernd Munsteiner carved and faceted a 57-carat fantasy cut from nearly flawless tanzanite. A recent find in Tanzania is gem-quality transparent chrome green zoisite, which after some discussion has been named chrome tanzanite or green tanzanite.

Tanzanite is brittle and abrades easily. To orient tanzanite for the best blue, cutters use a Polaroid filter and rotate the stone. Cutters say tanzanite presents little difficulty in cutting and polishing. Most prefer round or oval brilliants. Cleavage, perfect in one direction, is not a problem, but the material is somewhat heat sensitive. Cerium oxide and chrome oxide are polish choices, used on plastic laps. There seems to be a fairly steady supply of rough.

TEKTITE (MOLDAVITE)
Natural glass
H. 5½ –6   D. 2.60–3.40

Tektites occur in many parts of the world, but of all the occurrences, the transparent bottle green tektites of the former Czechoslovakia are best known among lapidaries. These odd-shaped sculptured-appearing objects have long been thought to have extraterrestrial origin, but this theory is now the subject of controversy. Many scientists believe that the amorphous forms have a more earthly beginning. High among the new studies is the impact theory.

Found near the Moldau River in Bohemia and Moravia, the moldavites have been prized as far back as Paleolithic times. A huge moldavite collection is in the National Museum in Prague. The age of the moldavites has been determined at over 14 million years.

Moldavites are high in silica and are colored by iron. Some moldavites have aesthetic splash patterns. The etched shapes are used as found in innovative jewelry. Transparent light green specimens are faceted as oval or round brilliants or other shapes, and are carved into pyramid or crystal shapes for New Age adherents. Cabochons and small carvings are also made from moldavites.

Moldavites vary in size from less than a gram to well over 200 grams. According to Dr. Ian Reban of Czechoslovakia, the average weight is 6 to 7 grams; faceted stones exceeding 15 carats are rare. Moldavites are used for many kinds of jewelry, although they are too soft for daily wear. In Czechoslovakia, moldavites are often combined with Bohemian garnets.

Other tektites from worldwide localities are mostly used for scientific study or collectors' items. Some of the localities are

Australia, Tasmania, Philippines, Java, Indochina, Georgia, and Texas. Some of the Texas tektites, bediasites, have been cut as curiosities.

Moldavites are worked the same as obsidian or glass. There is no cleavage, but like obsidian the material is brittle. Cerium oxide on plastic brings a bright polish for faceted stone, and cerium oxide on leather does the same for cabochons. For jewelry, moldavites should not be subjected to hard wear. Currently, rough should be available from several dealers. The lighter colors should be selected for best results.

TOURMALINE
Sodium aluminum borosilicate
H. 7–7½   D. 3.05
Pleochroic   Hexagonal

A marvelous group of related minerals provides a great color choice for faceters. The major gem species are *dravite*, which is usually black or brown; *schorl*, which is usually black; *uvite*, which is green or brown; *elbaite*, which can be green, pink, rose, blue, or violet; *liddicoatite*, variegated rich tertiary colors; and chrome-dravite, which is emerald green. Many elbaite crystals exhibit several beautiful colors, the most interesting of which may be the so called "watermelon" crystals, an appropriate mix of red and green, with a red-ripe center and green "rind." Particolored crystals may exhibit three or more colors in succession lengthwise, such as red, white, and green.

Tourmaline crystals are common occurrences in granite pegmatites and in schists and contact metamorphics around the world. The handsome vitreous crystals are prismatic, vertically striated, and color zoned. Most of the gem crystals are transparent, although some with silk inclusions or parallel tubes are translucent and can be cut into cat's-eye stones.

Tourmaline colors come from iron, manganese, vanadium, and chromium, and probably copper as in the recent discovery at Paraiba, Brazil. The rainbow of colors makes tourmaline one of the most important contemporary gems. Color names once used for tourmaline are rubellite for red, indicolite for blue, and achroite for colorless. Rubellite is the only one of these terms still used to any great extent by the jewelry industry.

Most of the faceting rough now comes from Brazil, although excellent gem-quality material also comes from Maine, California, Afghanistan, Pakistan, Namibia, Zimbabwe, Tanzania, Mozambique, Madagascar, Kenya, and Nepal. Tourmaline has been treated by heat, irradiation, and acid, but many cut stones are natural.

A 23.61-carat rich red oval liddicoatite may be the present record for this recently identified gem tourmaline species. This stone is said to be from Brazil, although the variety was first found as large dramatic crystals in Madagascar.

Chrome dravite from Karelia, Russia, is a relatively new find. Rich green crystals colored by chrome occur in micaceous carbonate rock. Chrome-green cat's-eye tourmaline has been discovered in Tanzania. Intense yellow crystals come from Zaire and golden yellow from Kenya.

Green and yellow tourmaline high in manganese come from Zambia. They are heat treated from red brown. Raspberry red tourmaline also comes from Zambia. It belongs to the schorl-dravite series. Cut stones from Zambia are in the 40-carat range.

A superb tourmaline color from Brazil was an eye-stopper at Tucson a few years ago. It was a remarkable cranberry-red crystal from the Jonas Mine in Minas Gerais, Brazil. One crystal from this pocket weighed 300 pounds (1363 kilo-

Tourmaline is a top-colored stone, often called the rainbow gem. Saturated pink is a popular color choice.

grams) and a broken crystal when pieced together was 42 inches (106.68 cm) long. Amazing crystals were exhibited by crystal connoisseur-jeweler, Keith Proctor, who has a remarkable collection of rainbow-colored tourmalines.

Fine blue crystals of the tourmaline known as indicolite are a recent discovery in Pakistan. Some of the most elegant tourmaline comes from San Diego County, California. Tourmaline authority Bill Larson notes that the Himalaya Mine has produced flawless bicolor stones up to 50 carats. A remarkable gem pocket of pink and bicolored tourmaline was discovered in the Himalaya in 1989. Large crystals from the Himalaya are used for carvings, and some for cabochons and fantasy cuts. Larson says only about 1 percent are top faceting quality. This mine was the

world's leader in the production of gem tourmaline in the early twentieth century. The pink elbaite from the Himalaya is superb. Other great California mines are the Tourmaline Queen, the Pala Chief, and the Stewart Lithia.

Huge cut stones of tourmaline are possible, but many crystals are so magnificent that even enthusiastic cutters decide to leave them in their natural state. Unusual specimens are named, such as the Steamboat, or Rabbit Ears, or the Rose of Itatiaia.

Nevertheless, numerous stones have been cut weighing over 100 or even 200 carats. Most major museums and prestigious private collections have conspicuous specimens of tourmaline. Tourmaline, as a multicolored gem group, is a relative newcomer to the gem world.

Educator/author Peter Bancroft designed and constructed a magnificent and complex gem pocket for the Josephine Scripps Mineral Hall at the San Diego Natural History Museum, featuring over 30 impressive California tourmaline crystals along with fine crystals of kunzite, morganite, topaz, garnet, feldspar, and quartz.

The Maine State Museum has several cut tourmalines of pink, green, and tricolor from the notable Plumbago discovery, each weighing over 20 carats. Maine jewelers presented the "Maine Tourmaline Necklace" to the state in 1977. Made by Addison Saunders, it highlights some of the most sensational colors from the great strike of the early 1970s. A graceful blue tourmaline falcon carved by Eberhart Bank of Idar-Oberstein, Germany, measures 12 inches (30.48 cm). A bicolor pink and green tourmaline carving from Afghanistan material, a Hing Wa Lee masterpiece, weighs 6,000 carats. Lee considers his spectacular Afghanistan rubellite pendant of 200 carats one of his best carvings.

Gerhard Becker of Idar-Oberstein made a series of delightful composite carvings of colorful birds from tourmaline from the United States. The Herbert Klein workshop produces flowers of tourmaline in the Fabergé tradition. Some Idar-Oberstein cutters make small birds and other carvings from tourmaline for jewelry use. American carver Ute Klein Bernhardt uses tourmaline for creative gem cameos and engravings.

Tourmaline crystals are used uncut in some designer jewelry. Thin polished slices of watermelon tourmaline make striking sets of earrings and pendants. Tourmaline can be tumbled for ornamental objects like gem trees. It can be made into beads, chip, round, oval, or carved. Small eggs and spheres are exquisite. Stones can be faceted in imaginative cuts. Dazzling cat's-eye cabochons can be cut from chatoyant tourmaline. Examination of chatoyant tourmalines by GIA has shown growth tubes to be the most frequent cause of this phenomenon in green tourmaline, while needlelike inclusions are more numerous in red and blue varieties.

Tourmaline is slightly tough and heat resistant, a durable stone for jewelry. Faceted stones of dark color should be oriented with the table parallel to the long axis of the crystal. Thermal shock should be avoided. Polish with Linde A or tin oxide on tin, or use diamond all the way. For carving, flexible shaft tools and silicon carbide and diamond points bring intricate detail. In darker stones, ends are undercut for improved color appearance. The brownish color of some rubellite will disappear if gently heated in a test tube. Tourmaline rough of many colors can be found on the market quite readily at this time.

RECOMMENDED READING

Arem, J., Color *Encyclopedia of Gemstones.* New York: Van Nostrand Reinhold, 2d ed., 1987.

Kunz, G., *Gems and Precious Stones of North America.* New York: Dover, 1968.

O'Donoghue, M., *Gemstones.* London: Chapman & Hall, 1988.

Parsons, C., *Practical Gem Knowledge for the Amateur.* San Diego: Lapidary Journal, 1961.

Sauer, J., *Brazil: Paradise of Gemstones.* Rio de Janeiro: Private, 1982.

Schumann, W., *Gemstones of the World.* New York: Sterling, 1977.

Sinkankas, J., *Gem Cutting: A Lapidary's Manual.* New York: Van Nostrand Reinhold, 3d ed., 1984.

Vargas, G., and M. Vargas, *Faceting for Amateurs.* Thermal, CA: Private, 1977.

SPECIFIC GEMS

Dietrich, R., *The Tourmaline Group.* New York: Van Nostrand Reinhold, 1985.

CHAPTER IV

Crystalline Quartz

Amethyst	Milky quartz
Ametrine	Phantom quartz
Aventurine	Rock crystal
Binghamite and Silkstone	Rose quartz
Blue quartz	Orchid star quartz
Citrine	Sagenitic quartz
Dumortierite quartz	Sioux quartzite
Ferruginous quartz	Smoky quartz
Gold in quartz	Strawberry quartz
Green quartz	Tigereye

Silicon dioxide
H. 7   D. 2.65
Hexagonal

QUARTZ IS THE MOST REMARKABLE of lapidary materials. It is abundant, available in large pieces, has a good hardness, and comes in all the primary and secondary colors and hundreds of shades and tints and mixtures in between. It can be transparent, translucent, or opaque. It may possess such fascinating qualities as asterism, aventurescence, chatoyancy, iridescence, or iris structure. It may have wonderful patterns and dramatic inclusions. As a replacement mineral it has no peer, because quartz replaces animal and plant fossils, and other minerals.

The wonderful properties of quartz have been known since prehistoric times when early man used quartz for weapons, tools, and fire, as well as for amulets, charms, and fetishes. Quartz was used for the development of tinderboxes, the flint-lock rifle, grist mills, and grindstones. It is a major building material as building blocks, glass, and a constituent of concrete. Quartz is used for roads, transportation, communication, electronics, and to geologists it is sometimes the mother lode of gold or the sign of a gem pocket.

A third of the birthstones or alternates are quartz and probably half of the stones of Aaron's breastplate were quartz. Myths of antiquity—amethyst, bloodstone, and carnelian—are based on quartz. Quartz has been a major material in ancient Rome, Greece, India, and China. From the cameo cutters of classical times to the fantasy cuts of Bernd Munsteiner, there is hardly a lapidary who has not tried quartz.

Crystalline quartz is silicon dioxide, hardness 7, density 2.65, which occurs in coarse grains, masses, or in distinct crystals in all rock types. It belongs to the hexagonal crystal system. It is weakly pleochroic, and has a dispersion of 0.013 and a refractive index of 1.544–1.553. It is doubly refractive, uniaxial, and optically positive. Most quartz does not show cleavage, but does show a conchoidal (shell-like) fracture. Although quartz is acidic, it is chemically passive.

Quartz can be colored by traces of numerous elements, including iron, manganese, nickel, copper, and chromium. Its appearance is also altered by inclusions of water, gases, pyrite, marcasite, chlorite, goethite, hematite, limonite, rutile, tourmaline, muscovite, fuchsite, actinolite, chrysocolla, hornblende, crocidolite, dumortierite, and others.

Descriptions of the qualities of quartz almost make it sound like a living thing. For example, crystals occur as twins and show growth lines. Perfect crystals grow slowly where there is sufficient space. Some crystals are left handed and some are right handed. They may be twisted or deformed or capped. To top it off, quartz has a piezoelectric quality that keeps quartz clocks ticking as regular as a pulse. It is no wonder that people have become curious about quartz and have often attributed magic or supernatural powers to it.

Natural quartz has several look-alikes, including synthetic quartz, which has become a necessity due to the huge oscillator plate industry. High lead glass is often called "crystal" and is used for beads, cut crystal ware, and other items which resemble quartz when finished.

Quartz crystals are artistic masterpieces, occurring in a variety of aesthetic habits, some of which are much too beautiful to cut, even if they are gem quality. Examples of these are skeletal crystals, crystals with showy phantoms or scenic sagenite, doubly terminated crystals, or scepter crystals. Handsome crystals may be color zoned, or show striations or etched faces. Tiny sparkling drusy quartz crystals are used for creative high-fashion jewelry. Drusy quartz is dramatic when the crystals form a translucent "icing" over blue chrysocolla, black agate, or red petrified wood.

As a constituent of granite, high quartz has been formed at high temperatures, but the large crystals of low quartz have formed at lower temperatures and have cooled slowly. Quartz crystals can be formed from supersaturated solutions at temperatures less than 573 degrees C.

Much crystalline quartz for lapidary use is from crystals. This includes rock crystal, amethyst, smoky quartz, rutilated quartz, and citrine; however, rose quartz crystals are very rare so faceting material usually comes from clear areas of massive rose quartz. There are also some crystalline quartzes such as tigereye or dumortierite quartz which are massive in occurrence. Quartzite is a metamorphic quartz and an example of lapidary-quality quartzite is aventurine.

When sawing quartz with a diamond blade low on coolant, lapidaries may notice an odd bright glow. This is known as triboluminescence. Most granular and fibrous quartzes do not fluoresce.

Heat treating quartz alters the color and this is a common practice for some varieties. (Details are under the specific headings.) Quartz has also been dyed, sometimes after being crackled. A new treatment that alters the color on rock crystal is called Aqua Aura. It consists of a thin gold plating on rock crystal faces which produces an aqua color. A development in the Southwest is a red-purple dyed quartz used as a sugilite substitute for inlaid and channel-style Indian and western jewelry.

Quartz is found in most parts of the world. Lapidaries may acquire pieces at shows, in shops, stone yards, or through mail order. One thing which has kept interest in the lapidary hobby is that lapidaries can have the thrill of finding their own quartz gem material without going too far from home. Another thing is the endless variety of quartz that keeps every prospector hoping that his or hers will be the next great quartz discovery.

TREATMENT OF QUARTZ

Quartz is not a difficult material for lapidaries. Since it is readily available, and relatively inexpensive, it should be used for learning new techniques and creative experiments.

Cutters should examine rough under a bright light with magnification to avoid fractures and undesirable inclusions. They should buy the best color and quality rough they can afford. Some quartz will have orientation problems, for example, color-zoned amethyst. The color bands should be parallel to the table for faceted stones. For cabochons, the varied color can make an interesting pattern. Chatoyant quartz should be oriented with care. For cat's-eyes, the fibers must be flat on the base of the cabochon and must be at right angles to the length of an oval cabochon. For stars, the crossed legs should be located under a single incandescent light.

Colorful quartz for faceting can be oriented by putting the rough in an immersion liquid or oil under strong light to locate the color zones. The shape of the cut is then planned according to the shape and size of the best color.

Crystals of amethyst, smoky quartz, and rock crystal are brittle, so the quartz will chip if too much heat develops during grinding or sanding. Keeping it very cool in every step, including dopping, prevents trouble. Quartz has a tendency to acquire scratches, which can only be eliminated by extensive wet sanding. Most quartz will attain a prepolish with 600-grit silicon carbide and a bright polish with cerium oxide. Alternatives are diamond paste on wood laps or using silicon carbide up to the final sanding stage and then finishing with 1,200 through 50,000 diamond. Faceted stones are often worked on a Lucite lap. Alternate polishes are Linde A, alumina, and tin oxide.

Flexible shaft tools can be used for quartz carvings. A wide variety of carborundum and diamond points and wheels are made. Professional carvers prefer fixed arbor carving machines. A Jacobs chuck on a rigid carving machine can hold commercial tools or tools the lapidary makes himself for specific purposes. The advantage of the fixed shaft machine is that both hands are free to hold the work, thus giving greater control. Gem lathes and drill presses are also used for quartz objects.

Quartz can be easily tumbled in rotary or vibrating tumblers using silicon carbide abrasives. Better stones result if the stones are preformed before tumbling. Grits of 100 through 600 bring the material to a prepolish. Fillers are used as the volume of the stones is reduced and also as carrying agents for polish slurries. Alumina, tin oxide, or the manufacturer's compound are used for glassy polishes. A final run in a dry detergent like Tide has been successful for some lapidaries in producing a superior polish.

Texturized stone and matte finishes are used on quartz gemstones. Sometimes the originality and intricacy of a cut show up better with a matte finish or a mixed finish. Smooth, fine sanding in one direction will give a frosted finish on quartz. Air abrasive techniques have been used on large lapidary items.

Quartz is used in sphere machines and bead mills, and for automatic cutting machines. Many quartz items appear mass produced, but innovative lapidaries will always find a way to make exceptional one-of-a-kind masterpieces from crystalline quartz.

Binghamite, silkstone, tigereye, and aventurine are composed of fibrous quartz, or in the case of aventurine, granular aggregates. They have the quality of toughness, so they do not fracture under stress like brittle materials, but they may split or break into grainy bits. Prolonged sanding with new wet sanding cloth in the sequence of 220, 400, 600, or 1,200, 3,000, 8,000, grit diamond should bring a prepolish. Polish with cerium oxide is lustrous. Tigereye is not heat sensitive.

To orient tigereye, the stone is turned slowly under a single light source and the plane of the best chatoyancy is marked. Fibrous inclusions should be at right angles to the long axis of an oval cabochon.

Binghamite and tigereye should be selected for color, chatoyancy, and minimum flaws, such as too much jaspery iron. Aventurine is selected for color, uniform fine grain, and appearance of spangled inclusions.

AMETHYST

Amethyst is purple or violet crystalline quartz. A prized and sometimes revered historic stone, amethyst is high in popularity not only for quartz gems, but among all cutting materials, and may be the most cherished of hardness 7 gems. From pale lilac color to the glamorous red-violet Siberian color, all tints and shades of amethyst have been cut for rings, beads, pins, bracelets, and earrings, and have been mounted in gold and combined with diamonds or pearls for high-fashion jewelry. The Siberian color is considered most valuable.

Amethyst occurs in all rock forms with crystals varying from tiny sparkling drusy coatings to tapered prisms. It can occur as uniform terminations lining geodes, or in veins in ores. Amethyst crystals are often color zoned and striated. It is interesting that many deposits of amethyst are so unique that they can immediately be identified as to their source. For example, the handsome dark crystals from Guerrero, Mexico, have colorless or slightly milky terminations while those from Vera Cruz are lighter toward the base and darker at the tips. The amethyst from Thunder Bay, Canada, occurs in uniform aggregate crusts and is often coated with red enamel-like iron oxide. The royal Ontario Museum exhibits a 22-carat faceted stone from Thunder Bay with fine Siberian color.

"Day Break" is the name of this original cut by Edith Strout, shown here in quartz. Photo couresty of Lapidary Journal.

Amethyst has been the chosen stone of kings and popes and is the birthstone of February. Although various translations of the Bible differ on the names of gems, all versions use the word amethyst as one of the 12 foundation stones. Catherine the Great of Russia was a collector of amethyst. Her regal gems came from the Ural Mountains. England's St. Edwards crown is adorned with a large amethyst.

The color of amethyst is attributed to ferric iron and in some cases manganese and titanium, but the color is also affected by natural irradiation. The specific hue, intensity, and tone of each occurrence varies with the locality. Repeated or polysynthetic twinning is common in amethyst. Each band is the reverse of the bands above and below. The cutting characteristics are different and so is the color. The color may be developed according to the position of layers (lamellae) of right- and left-handed twins with alternate pigmentation. Heat and bright light will fade amethyst. For example, a crystal cluster of fine amethyst from Vera Cruz is now clear "rock crystal" after 10 years in a glass case facing east. Crystals from Madagascar are bluish violet, while those from Bahia, Brazil, lean toward the red side of the color wheel. Amethyst is sometimes banded alternately with smoky quartz or clear quartz. Amethyst also occurs in Afghanistan, Namibia, South Africa, Malawi, India, Australia, and Sri Lanka.

In the United States amethyst is the state gem of South Carolina. Dark violet crystals have been found in North Carolina, Georgia, and Maine. In the west there are locations for amethyst in California, Montana, Wyoming, and Colorado. The Four Peaks amethyst location in Arizona has been mined for dark attractive crystals. Stunning violet scepter crystals several inches long have been found on the Nevada/California line.

Adularescence in the minor rhombohedral faces of amethyst crystals from Artigas, Uruguay, is a newly observed phenomenon called the Lowell effect. According to *Gems and Gemology,* it is being studied by the GIA. Jack Lowell, gemologist, who first observed the phenomenon, saw blue or white sheets of light under crystal terminations. He believes this may be due to polysynthetic twinning. This same effect has been observed in colorless quartz from Poona, India.

Amethyst forms at low temperatures and pressures in crystals that seldom exceed 5 inches. Crystals weighing 50 pounds or more have been found in Brazil, but are usually not of high quality. Brazil is the major producer of amethyst currently, with several colors and grades of amethyst. Milky material may be tumbled, intermediate material can be used for cabochons, beads, or carvings, and the best material is faceted for jewelry. Professional cutter David Epstein wrote in *Colored Stone* that stones in the 50-carat range are not uncommon at Maraba, where fine red-violet crystals occur. Epstein says brilliant cuts are best.

A record amethyst occurrence is a geo-delike cavity from Serro do Mar, Rio Grande do Sul, Brazil, 33 feet long, 5½ feet wide, and 3 feet high. Dark richly colored amethyst crystals lined the entire cavity. A 660-pound geode from Minas Gerais stands guard in the foyer of the Houston Museum of Natural History. Such geodes form in amygdaloidal cavities in host basalt. Open pit mining yields the large geodes (often 4 feet long or over) which must be carefully chipped from the matrix.

Amethyst with chevron bands of white or lavender-white alternating with medium to dark purple comes from Namibia and is often used for beads and cabochons. The amethyst crystals from Thunder Bay, Ontario, are small and uniform in size and are used for electroformed points and clusters for novelty jewelry. The crystals from Guerrero, Mexico, are facet quality.

Contemporary jewelry designers make creative use of the flowerlike agate and amethyst stalactite sections from Rio Grande do Sul, Brazil. Concentrically ringed agate centers are surrounded by radiating amethyst crystal petals of transparent purple.

Fine amethyst is often set in gold, its complementary color, and enhanced with diamonds or seed pearls. Faceted or smoothly polished amethyst beads and intricately carved pendants are fashion favorites. In some contemporary jewelry, amethyst is combined with other faceted stones such as rubellite, rose quartz, or peridot.

Several cuts are used for amethyst, with step cut stones being especially popular. Amethyst may have directional differences in cutting, due to its structure. It is brittle and somewhat heat sensitive. If kept cool and thoroughly sanded, it should produce no major problem for cutters. Cerium

oxide on Lucite will give a glassy polish; so will 50,000 diamond. The best-quality rough is not always available.

AMETRINE

Ametrine is a trade name for a bicolor violet and yellow quartz coming from Bolivia, which presents the ultimate in contrast. The bicolor gem was introduced in Tucson in 1979. This interesting color combination has been produced in the laboratory by Dr. Kurt Nassau, but the original material from Bolivia was natural. The iron mineral goethite may be a chief coloring agent of both amethyst and citrine. Polysynthetic twinning is noted only in the amethyst areas. The association of amethyst and citrine has been known for many years and the material has been known by several other names, among them trystine and golden amethyst.

Quantities of ametrine were exported from Brazil during the 1980s. The mine at La Gaiba, Bolivia, is said to be no longer active; however, the government is encouraging a resumption of mining.

This unique quartz variety won immediate acceptance among faceters, carvers, and cutters of Munsteiner-like fantasy cuts. These stones are excellent for advanced lapidaries because they challenge the imagination.

The amethyst shows banding, but not the citrine. The amethyst is purple with a hint of blue and the wedges of citrine are a bright, clear yellow.

Glenn and Martha Vargas suggest emerald cuts for ametrine to bring out the desired bicolors. If cut so that the colors appear to mix, the result is a uniform orchid appearance, not nearly as eye catching as the contrast of distinct purple and gold.

AVENTURINE

Aventurine is a granular quartz, similar to quartzite, which is spangled with minute flakes or platelets of muscovite or other mica, or goethite or hematite. It occurs in several desirable colors in veins and massive deposits. The colors are shades of green, blue, tangerine red, red brown, and golden brown.

The best-known aventurine to the lapidary has been the intense green material which has come from India for many years. Used for beggar beads and other native jewelry, it has also been exported in the rough for lapidaries in Europe and America. The green color is due to fuchsite mica. Some of the material shows several variations of green. Aventurine also comes from the eastern Transvaal in Africa. A green aventurine in China is highly valued because the color resembles jade.

A discover near Ennis, Montana, has the potential of supplying large quantities of lapidary-quality aventurine to cutters. Bernice Hallam and her husband saw a flagstone walk of fine aventurine in Ennis and tracked down a large local deposit. A red-brown aventurine is found in Washington, Wisconsin, and Vermont. Platelets of hematite may contribute to this color.

The so called "tangerine aventurine" now on the market is a tint of orangy red, a color resembling bright carnelian or coral. It is less translucent than carnelian and more grainy. The localities of this material have been variously given at shows as Brazil or South Africa. Russia also has red aventurine, as does Spain, Chile, and Australia.

Aventurine is a useful lapidary material because it comes in large-size pieces. It is tough, compact, and has good color. Lapidaries polish it with tin oxide on felt, or carve it with gem lathes or fixed shaft or flexible shaft carving machines.

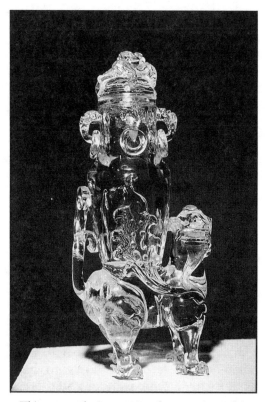

This unusual quartz wine decanter, carved in China, is an attention getter in this Lizzadro Museum of Lapidary Arts, Elmhurst, Illinois. Photo by Russell Kemp.

BINGHAMITE AND SILKSTONE

Very similar to tigereye, binghamite is fibrous quartz found near Crosby in the Cayuna iron range of northern Minnesota in which the replaced fibers are a red hematite and yellow goethite rather than crocidolite. Bill Bingham, an amateur lapidary from St. Paul, discovered the colorful quartz on the mine dumps in 1936 and found it to be an excellent material for polished slabs, ornamental objects, and jewelry. The finest material was soon collected by enthusiastic gem cutters.

Binghamite has parallel fibers of warm colors—reds, yellows, and golds—interspersed with opaque white quartz and often black metallic hematite. Some specimens also have small white areas with fibers at right angles to streaks of hematite. Some interesting pieces are brecciated.

John Kemmerer of Minnesota assembled a remarkable collection of variations of this material and the similar silkstone, which he made into polished slabs. Rarely the two materials are intermixed, resulting in complex patterns.

Silkstone is virtually the same material as binghamite and probably one name should serve them both. Silkstone has fibers which are more random, shorter, twisted, and with a greater color variation. There is blue and green silkstone in addition to the reds and golds of binghamite. Silkstone also seems less likely to have white quartz inclusions. Both materials are suitable to a multitude of lapidary uses and take and hold good polish if handled like other materials of more than one hardness. Both materials are now hard to get, except in Minnesota.

BLUE QUARTZ

Several East Coast and southern states of the United States have blue quartz that is chatoyant and often shows asterism. This quartz is found in pegmatites or as float. The phenomenal effect is due to the inclusion of finely disseminated rutile needles. Pieces of blue quartz are usually small in comparison with other massive jewelry-quality quartzes. Abundant needles of rutile give the quartz a chatoyant and milky look.

Colors of this quartz range from a faint grayish or whitish blue, smoky blue, light sky blue, and lavender-blue to medium blue-violet and gray-blue. The depth of color has been found to be unrelated to the apparent amount of rutile needle inclusions. The blue color is due to selective scattering of light waves.

Gem-quality blue quartz was found in a significant deposit in the Starfel Mine in Chamber County, Alabama, by "Lucky" McDaniel, a Georgia prospector. The stars are silvery and distinct with many pieces of material showing multiple six-rayed stars. Pieces of star blue quartz from this locality weigh up to 8 to 9 pounds, which is exceptional for this type of material. The color is a pale, slightly grayed blue, varying to a light milky blue. Besides being cut into sensational cabochons, the material is used for breathtaking spheres. The most transparent material has been faceted.

Blue quartz also comes from Fairfax, Madison, Hanover, and Amelia counties, Virginia, from Rutherford County, North Carolina, and from South Carolina, Georgia, and Vermont.

A recent find of multiple-star quartz in Sri Lanka was compared to the Alabama occurrence. The Sri Lanka material was grayer and included pink. Other locations for blue quartz are Norway, Finland, India, Australia, and Madagascar.

This type of quartz should be cold dopped and treated to prolonged fine sanding, then polished with cerium oxide on felt or leather. High-domed cabs or small spheres have the best stars. Good rough is not easy to locate.

CITRINE

Yellow crystalline quartz is citrine. It is transparent or slightly milky and comes in a suite of sunny colors including lemon yellow, canary yellow, honey color, yellow-orange, golden yellow, and yellow-brown. Colors come from ferric iron. Natural citrine is not common, so most, if not all, of the citrine on the gem market is heat-treated amethyst or smoky quartz. Heat-treated amethyst from some localities results in bright citrine which may have a reddish highlight seldom seen in natural citrine.

Natural citrine is colored by iron oxide. The lighter colors are faintly dichroic. Citrine which is of amethyst origin can be identified by the polysynthetic Brazil twinning. Ripple marks on surfaces, due to the polysynthetic twinning of the amethyst, also distinguish the Brazilian citrine. Heating smoky quartz produces a greenish yellow or yellow-gold color. Smoky quartz from Cordoba, Spain, makes excellent yellow citrine.

Citrine is a desirable gemstone, but not well known because it has masqueraded for so many years as topaz. Some natural citrine resembles some topaz in color only. Citrine crystals of good color come from Crystalina, Goias, Brazil. Minas Gerais supplies much of the citrine on the market. Other locations for citrine are Mexico, Scotland, France, Russia, Madagascar, Australia, and New Zealand. Smoky quartz with a warm yellow-brown tone (instead of cool gray) is close to citrine. In the United States, citrine is found in California, Colorado, New Mexico, and New York.

A 19,548-carat marquise cut citrine faceted by Michael Gray is in a private collection. The Smithsonian has a 120-pound smoky citrine specimen from Brazil.

Citrine is a bright and inexpensive faceting material and can be used for large and stunning faceted stones, cabochons, and fantasy cuts. It is also used for beads and small carvings. Small pieces are tumbled for chip beads and gem trees. Faceted citrine is polished with tin oxide on plastic. Dealers of faceting material usually have citrine or can obtain it.

Quartz beads in tints of yellow orange and smoky brown combine with a carved oval in mixed colors of yellows and browns.

DUMORTIERITE QUARTZ

Slim needles of blue, violet, or pink dumortierite massed in quartz or quartzite make a desirable cutting material in one of the less common color sequences for quartz. When polished, the material resembles lapis lazuli except that the blue is not saturated and there are no pyrite or calcite inclusions.

Dumortierite is a complex borosilicate which has been used in the manufacture of porcelain. It is so dense in the quartz that the material appears entirely blue with some mottling of lighter or darker hues. Hardness of dumortierite is a little higher than quartz and differential hardness causes cutting problems.

California's Cargo Muchacho Mountains north and east of El Centro, Imperial County, have produced countless chunks and boulders through the years of high-grade blue dumortierite quartz. San Diego County had violet material. Boulders have also come from Yuma County, Arizona, and Luna, New Mexico. Idaho and Nevada also have blue dumortierite. A large quantity of dark blue and violet material has come from mines in the Humboldt Range near Oreana in Pershing County, Nevada. A rare occurrence of pink dumortierite is in the same county. Canada, Mexico, Brazil, and Madagascar also have dumortierite quartz.

Dumortierite is used for bowls, carvings, cabochons, and beads. The source of the beads on the market is probably Brazil. The color is an interesting smoky blue and the material is practically flawless. After shaping with fine grinders, dumortierite quartz should be sanded and polished with diamond. If needles pull, Opticon can be used as a filler.

FERRUGINOUS QUARTZ

Quartz colored red or yellow by iron minerals is occasionally used for lapidary purposes. Such quartz is usually opaque. Crystals of ferruginous quartz are often distorted. Massive ferruginous quartz occurs in iron mines and sometimes has inclusions of metallic hematite.

Red quartz colored by hematite may have a superficial resemblance to rose quartz, but the color is due to finely divided particles. An interesting variation occurs near Prague, Czechoslovakia, with a starlike red and yellow ferruginous pattern. The yellow coloring is goethite. Ger-

many and England also have ferruginous quartz. Ferruginous quartz is found in Ontario, Canada, in connection with the vast amethyst deposits there.

Pecos diamonds are ferruginous quartz crystals found in Eddy County, New Mexico, on both sides of the Pecos River. Most of these small crystals are doubly terminated and of a uniform smoky red color, although some are yellow, green, or brown. Interesting crystals are pseudocubic in form. Occasionally bicolored crystals are found. The largest crystals may be 1½ inches (3.81 cm). The smallest crystals are very brilliant and those over ½ inch (1.27 cm) less so. These quartz crystals have been used as found for jewelry. Small cabochons have been cut from the bicolor crystals.

Ferruginous massive quartz, resembling rose quartz, is common in the pegmatites of the Black Hills of South Dakota, particularly in the Harney Range. This quartz is used for ornamental objects such as bookends, clock faces, and interior and exterior decoration. This type of quartz may have inclusions which make it difficult to work. If it is translucent, the densest color should be at the base of the cabochon. Many ferruginous quartzes are available.

GOLD IN QUARTZ

A cherished lapidary material in California is native gold in quartz. White quartz with lacy patterns of shining yellow crystallized gold was often found in the bonanza days of California's gold rush. In the late nineteenth century, lapidaries and jewelers were paying $20 to $30 per ounce for the quartz if the pattern was aesthetic, the gold bright, and the quartz white. Large quantities of gold in quartz were sold to California lapidaries and jewelers. Much of

Arkansas is the major source of quartz crystal sin the United States.

the cutting was done in Oakland according to Kunz. In the late nineteenth century, jewelry set with California's popular cutting material reached fad proportions in the eastern states. Some black quartz with native gold was found in Calaveras and Amador counties.

Gold in quartz was used for other things besides jewelry. There were cane handles, paper weights, perfume bottles, fan holders, and even inlay in furniture. Kunz reported that a large design in the Notre Dame cathedral in Paris is made of California gold in white quartz.

Gold is known to occur in amethystine quartz in Hungary. It has been observed in milky quartz, "bull" quartz, and jasper. Locations for gold in various types of quartz in the United States are Oregon, Idaho, Colorado, Montana, and South Dakota.

The price of the California rough was governed by the amount of gold judged by the specific gravity of both quartz and gold, by the then current price of gold, and most of all by the beauty of the specimen. If the quartz was translucent and of good size with few flaws, and the gold lacy or picturesque, the price was higher.

Little of this material is available now. Some pieces in private collections are occasionally cut. The cuts are usually oval cabochons with the gold well centered and near to the surface, maybe covered by a polished layer of quartz. The material needs to be carefully analyzed before cutting. Cabochons should be thicker than usual. Since massive quartz may be fractured, the material should be worked slowly with great care; also, this type of quartz may have many inclusions. After meticulous wet sanding, cerium oxide on leather or 8,000, 14,000, and 50,000 diamond will produce the polish.

GREEN QUARTZ

Green quartz can be colored by several elements and minerals but is not present in mineable deposits in many places, so much of the green quartz in the past was amethyst from Montezuma, Minas Gerais, Brazil, which turned green upon being heated to 510 degrees C. It is variously called prasiolite or vermarine. This material is gray green to grass green and transparent. Quartz from Ceara, Brazil, Four Peaks, Arizona, and Vinton, California, also turns green when treated. Cut stones were usually less than 15 carats.

Natural green quartz can be colored by iron, nickel, copper, or chlorite. There is green quartz colored by copper in northern Michigan. Bruce Deter describes the quartz as nearly opaque and medium grayish green in color, not unlike "spinach nephrite." Green quartz has also been found in Arizona, Utah, and Idaho. Quartz with dense green actinolite inclusions has been found in Pennsylvania, and some Arkansas quartz looks green from inclusions of chlorite. Green quartz also comes from South Africa, India, and Australia. Størk Halstensen reports a large deposit of green quartzite near Finnmark, Norway, that is used for many ornamental purposes. Particolored green and violet quartz has been found in Zimbabwe.

Stunning light yellowish green quartz crystals come from Naica, Chihuahua, Mexico. The color may be from chlorite. The crystals are exceptionally lustrous and can be used for jewelry.

Green quartz is used with amethyst, citrine, rock crystal, and other quartzes for all quartz suites in jewelry. Orient the green quartz by immersion, then sand carefully, finishing the sanding with 8,000 diamond, followed by Linde A or cerium oxide on tin. Diamond will produce the polish.

MILKY QUARTZ (WHITE QUARTZ)

One might think that white quartz is the most common of all quartz varieties. For the lapidary this is certainly not true. Most white quartz is not truly white, but leans toward the grays or tints of dirty yellow. In fact, most quartz that could conceivably be called white at first glance is poor quality and highly flawed. It is full of cavities, solid, liquid, and gas inclusions, and has coarse grains and uneven distribution of color, resulting in gray, translucent areas interspersed with opaque white areas.

When white quartz is fine grained, pure white, with uniform color, it is an excellent lapidary material, especially for intarsias, composite carvings, and wherever a hard, white material is needed. Some material is best obtained from broken white quartz crystals, but some pegmatites also have small veins of massive white quartz that are cuttable. The finer the grain, the whiter the appearance. Translucent white quartz can also be used at times for cat's-eyes.

If white quartz has aesthetic inclusions such as gold, streaks of green or blue caused by copper minerals, or streaks of red caused by iron or cinnabar, it can also be used as a lapidary material. Recently, white quartz with realgar was used for vivid cabochons.

Good-grade milky quartz alternates with rose quartz in some of the South Dakota mines and milky quartz occurs near Custer. Water-worn nodules of white quartz from badland areas of South Dakota, Wyoming, and Montana are cuttable. Other locations for milky quartz are California, Arizona, Texas, Arkansas, North Carolina, and New Hampshire. Lapidary-quality white quartz crystals occur in New South Wales and Queensland, Australia.

A number of years ago white or partially clear quartz was "crackled" by heating and quenching and then dyed in an assortment of rather gaudy colors for beads, tumbled stone jewelry, and lapidary compositions which called for plenty of color. White quartz is used for beads, cabochons, clock faces, bowls, and carvings. It is usually heavily included and should be shaped and sanded with great care.

PHANTOM QUARTZ

Phantom quartz crystals make such sensational display items that they are seldom cut for jewelry except if the phantom crystals are small or damaged, or if there is a large deposit of phantom material. Sometimes faces showing the phantoms most distinctly are polished to accent the crystal growth pattern. Phantoms occur in groups, clusters, or singles.

Phantom quartz crystals are those which exhibit ghostlike growth patterns within the crystal. The ghost crystals, especially the terminations or caps, are often strongly outlined by a mineral of a contrasting color, such as chlorite, actinolite, or a clay, mica, or iron mineral. Other phantom faces are often distinct as well, but it is seldom that entire ghost crystals are plainly outlined. The phantoms on a single crystal may be multiple and shadowy. Quartz crystals from Brazil have exhibited as many as 20 distinct terminations of growth stages of the crystal. Red phantom crystals from Bahai, Brazil, with colorless outer surfaces and almost opaque interiors, have yielded sensational cabochons.

The overall color of phantom crystals may be smoky, water clear, or amethyst. Amethyst phantoms may be cut into unique faceted stones. Phantoms may be gray, yellow, green, red, or violet.

Major quartz crystal deposits often have some phantom crystals. Brazil is the major source currently, but aesthetic phantoms also come from Canada, Mexico, the Alps, the Urals, Africa, and in the United States from Arkansas and California.

When the phantom inclusions are white-capped pyramids, the crystals are cut into spheres or large cabochons or ornamental items. Frosty white phantoms in clear colorless quartz are polished as New Age metaphysical objects.

Binghamite from Minnesota is quartz with fibrous iron inclusions, resulting in a chatoyant appearance.

Elegant cabochons can be made from phantom quartz, if the caps are cleverly oriented. The material is also tumbled and carved.

ROCK CRYSTAL

Rock crystal, the ice turned to stone of the ancients, is clear transparent quartz, usually found as handsome, well-developed developed crystals. So important to industry is pure clear quartz that synthetic quartz had to be developed.

Clear quartz crystals can be as small as the tiny drusy crystals that may line geodes, vugs, and cavities, or they can be as large as a Brazilian crystal that weighed an estimated 44 tons. A crystal from Madagascar was reported to be 25 feet in circumference. Thirty tons of clear quartz crystals came from a single cavity in Arkansas. One lustrous Coleman Mine crystal was 1,200 pounds.

Quartz crystals are found in sedimentary, metamorphic, or volcanic rock formations. The crystals may be in geodes, loose in clay, associated with ores, or in gem pockets. They are often associated with other gem minerals such as tourmaline or beryl. The appearance of clear colorless quartz can be changed by inclusions, phantoms, healed fractures, growth lines, etching, and other natural processes.

Colorless transparent quartz has been mined and used by early civilizations, and before that by primitive cultures in various parts of the world. Quartz objects have been excavated in China, India, and Mexico, among other places. The University of Pennsylvania Museum has a 55-pound rock crystal sphere which once belonged to the empress of China.

Lapidaries do wonderful things with quartz. It is faceted, cabbed, used for doublets and triplets, carved, turned on a lathe, hand lapped, tumbled, and polished in its natural shape. Beads, spheres, eggs, vases, candlesticks, goblets, and bowls of sparkling quartz are beautiful lapidary masterpieces. Many fine artists have chosen quartz as their prime material. Harold and Erica Van Pelt make superbly crafted and artistic vases, candlesticks, and other items of quartz. A 7,500-carat faceted quartz stone by Michael Gray is in a private collection. The Smithsonian has an elegant 7,000-carat faceted rock crystal egg cut by John Sinkankas and a large limpid quartz sphere. The National Museum of Melbourne has a faceted oval brilliant of 8,512 carats cut by Alex Amess. Idar-Oberstein artists Gerhard

Gwen Swanson, AFMS jewelry trophy winner, created this stunning rutilated quartz pendant. Photo by Russell Kemp.

Becker, Erwin Pauley, Peter Gerber, and Arthur Veek worked together on a 15½-inch fine quartz figure of Atlas bearing the weight of the lapis lazuli earth on his shoulders. The colorless quartz was from a near flawless 22-pound piece from Madagascar. Glenn Lehrer and Lawrence Stoller carved the "Empress of Lemura," a 42½-pound sculpture of optical-grade quartz, finished by hand by electric sanders.

Creative cutter Kevin Lane Smith sets pieces of colorful materials such as lapis lazuli, chrysoprase, and sugilite into the top of quartz jewelry and cuts the facets to reflect the colors. A century ago lapidaries working for Peter Carl Fabergé were carving quartz vases filled with natural-looking gem flowers, and apparently thriving in fresh water.

Canadian carver Tom McPhee uses rock crystal for sensitive relief carvings. Jerry Muchna uses clear quartz to make faceted carvings such as "The Minute Man" and "Iwo Jima."

For collectors, there are quartz stars, elephants, snuff bottles, faceted ring boxes, and Buddhas. A quartz object of mystery is a carved human skull of amazing accuracy that was found in Mexico and is now in the British Museum.

In addition to the countries mentioned, Switzerland, Russia, Burma, and Australia have clear quartz. Several localities in the United States are eclipsed by the Hot Springs area of Arkansas. They are California, Arizona, Montana, North Carolina, Georgia, and Maine. The limpid doubly terminated quartz crystals from Herkimer, New York, are in a class by themselves for sheer natural beauty. Their double terminations, clarity, and gleaming faces make them so elegant they are called "Herkimer diamonds" and used for jewelry just as they are. Veritable textbooks for the study of quartz, these small crystals make up in perfection what they lack in size.

The public should be wary of the word crystal. Most commercial "crystal" objects are lead glass, not quartz. Many New Age crystals are not true crystals, but are cut in crystal shapes.

Rock crystals are often interpenetrating twins. There is limited double refraction and an internal spiral arrangement. Rock crystal is slightly brittle and has no cleavage, but it does have directional differences in hardness. Cold dopping works well. Sanding must be cool, slow, and careful. Cerium oxide on felt or leather is usually successful. If the rough is troublesome, fine sanding with 800, 1,200, and 3,000 diamond will help.

ROSE QUARTZ

The rose quartz of the lapidary is a massive material occurring in pegmatites in many parts of the world. Magnificent rose quartz crystals come from the Sapicaia Mine and Lavra da Ilha, Minas Gerais, Brazil, but these are museum specimens and are not used for cutting.

Pale pink, rose pink, lavender pink, smoky rose, and rose red are some of the many lovely tints of this variety of quartz. Most rose quartz is translucent rather than transparent and some milky pink quartz is almost opaque. Rose quartz is faintly dichroic. The variation of color in rose quartz is due to trace inclusions of iron, manganese, and titanium. Immense dikes of rose quartz yield large blocks for carvers, decorators, architects, and artists. It has been used as a decorative material in the Orient for centuries.

Some rose quartz shows distinct asterism when heavily included with rutile needles. Silvery six-rayed stars on rose-pink quartz are gems with great feminine appeal.

Rose quartz is often highly fractured, with the most fractured material coming from northern climates. Fractures are compounded when the material is mined by blasting. There is also a rumor that rose quartz is subject to fading, and this has been proven to be true for quartz of only some deposits.

Excellent-quality rose quartz for lapidaries comes from Rio Grande do Norte, Brazil, and also from Mexico, Canada, Russia, Namibia, Australia, and New Zealand. Faceted stones in the 100-carat range have been cut from transparent Brazilian rose quartz.

Rose quartz is found at numerous locations in the United States. Several deposits in Maine have been mined for many years.

La Grange, Georgia, has asterated rose quartz. Colorado, Arizona, California, and Virginia have rose quartz localities.

The greatest producer in the United States for over 100 years has been South Dakota where 18 mines are known to have rose quartz. The Scott Mine southeast of Custer is quarried only for rose quartz and has yielded tons and tons of high-quality material which has been sent to the Orient and to Germany for cutting and carving.

The quartz varies from building quality (a mansion in Rapid City, South Dakota, is built of rose quartz) to facet quality and starstone quality. The colors range from peach to rose, to pinkish lavender. A quantity of the material is banded with white probably due to liquid inclusions. Some of the many Pennington and Custer County deposits have inclusions of black tourmaline while others are known for their black pyrolusite dendrites. Water-worn rose quartz nodules are common in the badlands.

Rose quartz is currently one of the most popular bead materials. It is also used for pendants, cabochons, spheres, eggs, bookends, tiles, and carvings. The Field Museum in Chicago has a 10½-inch bowl turned from South Dakota rose quartz. The South Dakota Museum of Geology in Rapid City has excellent specimens of South Dakota rose quartz. A new discovery of pink banded quartz in Brazil has not been classed as rose quartz. It is highly transparent in part and colored by iron in distinct areas.

The color of rose quartz cabochons shows up better if the material is cut a little thicker than usual and if the bottom is rough sanded but not polished. A cabochon of rose and white layered quartz could have a white base. For faceted stones deeper pavilions help the color. Rough should be examined in a brilliant light using magnification to locate fractures and inclusions. When working it, wet sanding must be thorough. A polish with cerium oxide on leather or felt is bright.

Orchid Star Quartz

A California locality has a pink quartz variation with pink color bordering on lilac or lavender. Named orchid star quartz, it was discovered by uranium prospectors after World War II. After off and on digging by area hobbyists, the mine was reopened in 1989. Most of the quartz at the location is white, but the rare seams of translucent to transparent or slightly milky orchid-colored quartz are carefully removed as gem rough. The less transparent material has multistar asterism.

Judson Darling and other local cutters feel that the orchid quartz has opal in its composition, because its cutting qualities differ considerably from the usual white or pink quartz. The white quartz is in a large dike with the orchid variety lying in a band no more than several feet wide, horizontal to the vertical dike. The mine is located in a granite area in northeast California at an elevation of 7,500 feet. Biotite mica is associated with the quartz deposit. This quartz has been used for elegant star stones, small multistar spheres, slabs, carvings, and faceted stones.

SAGENITIC QUARTZ AND QUARTZ WITH INCLUSIONS

Crystalline quartz is sometimes penetrated by slender needles of various minerals such as rutile, actinolite, epidote, goethite, and others, creating astonishingly exotic patterns. Chlorite and montmorillonite create gardens, clouds, and fans. The colors of inclusions in quartz are like a painter's palette.

The needlelike inclusions are called sagenite or fleches d' amour or Thetis hair-stone. Specific designations such as rutilated quartz or tourmalinated quartz are also used. Other inclusions may be platelets, gas or liquid-filled tubes, clumps of inorganic material, or well-developed crystals, for example, garnets or pyrite.

Among the inclusions of crystalline quartz are actinolite, ajoite, byssolite, carbon dioxide, chlorite, crocidolite, chrysocolla, cuprite, dumortierite, epidote, fuchsite, garnet, gold, goethite, helvite, hematite, hornblende, limonite, marcasite, montmorillonite, muscovite, pyrite, rutile, tourmaline, and water.

Currently the lapidary favorite is a brilliant golden rutilated quartz from Minas Gerais, Brazil, with three sheaves of shining golden needles making a fixed six-pointed star at 60-degree angles. This quartz is a marvelous cutting material for creative lapidaries who use it for cabochons, fantasy cuts, and carvings.

Sagenitic quartz crystals may have extremely fine needles or rather wide tabular needles, or the inclusions may be pencil-like as in the case of tourmaline. The quartz is usually rock crystal, but it may be smoky quartz, amethyst, or slightly yellowish or milky. The needles may be red, gold, black, white, brown, green, yellow, blue, pink, or white. Sometimes inclusions are so dense that they seem to give the quartz the actual color of the inclusions. The needles may have a splendid metallic luster. Divergent fine sprays of elongated needles in clear, transparent quartz make a striking contrast. The jackstrawlike hit or miss patterns are excellent for cabochons, bowls, or candlesticks.

Historically, Madagascar, Switzerland, and Russia have produced handsome sagenitic crystals. Currently Brazil is the major source. Mexico and Namibia also have sagenitic quartz. The occurrences of Australia are known as grass stone.

An almost black quartz from Mexico is heavily included with pyrite, marcasite, chalcopyrite, and silver. It has been used for beads and ornamental objects. Mined from Solaverna Mine of Zacatecas, it is referred to as solavernaite. In the United States, crystals with attractive inclusions have been found in California, Arizona, New Mexico, Montana, Colorado, Arkansas, Rhode Island, Pennsylvania, and North Carolina.

Quartz with inclusions is exciting for ornamental objects. A human hand of fine rutilated quartz was carved in amazing detail by Harold and Erica Van Pelt. Michael Dyber's rutilated quartz "Moonrise" won him a prestigious award in an Idar-Oberstein competition. Munsteiner's "Metamorphose" is a rutilated quartz sculpture weighing 214.3 pounds, carefully carved to bring out all the shimmer and sparkle of the remarkable inclusions.

Susan Allen has used included quartz to carve internal scenes of natural history. Inclusions such as dendrites, phantoms, needles, and clouds are part of the scene. Gerhard Becker recently exhibited a number of striking cabochons and carvings of sagenitic quartz with golden needles shaped like fixed six-ray stars.

A recent sensation in Tucson was turquoise blue ajoite in quartz crystals shown by Rob Smith. In a private collection is a relief carving with a gardenlike background from Pala, California, quartz. Lovely jewelry has been made from cabochons of quartz with chlorite from Arkansas.

Sagenitic quartz and quartz with other inclusions have been used for snuff bottles, containers, bowls, carvings, beads, pendants, brooches, rings, and many other items. The material is so varied that it should be carefully selected with the pattern in the right scale for the intended use.

Faceted quartz with inclusions of dendrites and phantoms usually has wide

Roland Rasmussen cut Brazilian rutilated quartz for this pendant and set it in hand-fabricated gold.

tables with well-centered features near the girdle. Such stones are cut from Brazilian material.

There are two main problems in working with included quartz. The first is to attain the correct orientation, and the second is to protect the inclusions. For example, if not handled with care, the needles could pull and leave hollow canals. Some lapidaries fill any needle entrances with Opticon before final polishing. Crystalline quartz is brittle and should be worked wet and kept cool to avoid flaking and chipping.

SIOUX QUARTZITE

Sometimes called Sioux Falls jasper in the past, this red quartzite is used for many exterior and interior decorating projects, as well as for lapidary work on a smaller scale. In tints and shades of pink and red, the metamorphic rock is exposed at Sioux Falls, Dell Rapids, Alexandria, and Garretson, South Dakota. It forms part of the gorge of the palisades of the Big Sioux River. Seven hundred twenty state border markers of pink Sioux quartzite weighing 800 pounds each mark the North Dakota/South Dakota line.

Hard and compact, the quartzite has been used for building materials, monuments and memorials, carvings, decorative objects, and jewelry. Area lapidary artists often produce logos, insignia, and elaborate designs on slabs of quartzite with a sandblaster. Select material is also used for carvings, clocks, bookends, and cabochons. The material is fine grained, hard, tough and easy to work with.

SMOKY QUARTZ

Crystalline quartz that is some tint or shade of gray or brown is called smoky quartz. The gray can be a pale, nearly colorless, transparent tint, or it can be a grayed yellow-brown, or a dark charcoal shade, or almost black and nearly opaque. Smoky quartz crystals are color zoned and sometimes grade toward either amethyst or citrine colors. Smoky quartz can accompany water-clear quartz or amethyst.

Smoky quartz contains aluminum, lithium, calcium, or magnesium and not the traditional coloring elements of amethyst, rose quartz, and blue quartz-iron, manganese, and titanium. Irradiation is thought to be a contributor to the smoky color. There are also liquid inclusions in smoky quartz.

Occurring in crystals or masses, smoky quartz is common in pegmatites in high-temperature deposits. Crystals may be thin drusy crusts or giants weighing nearly half a ton. The crystals are often highly modified.

Dark, lustrous, smoky quartz crystals from Switzerland's Alps are among the most aesthetic specimens. The depth of the color is said to increase with the altitude at which the crystals are found. Alpine smoky quartz crystals are displayed in most gem and mineral museum collections.

Smoky quartz is the beloved "cairngorm" of Scotland, used for some of the finest antique Scottish jewelry. The color of the cairngorm is yellow-gray and often verges on citrine. The darkest and most opaque of this smoky quartz is known as morion. Other fine smoky quartz comes from Brazil, Russia, and Madagascar.

In the United States a particularly richly colored smoky quartz is found in the pegmatites of the Pikes Peak area of Colorado. The superb crystals have a tinge of warm brown but are very transparent. Shining crystals with dark terminations occur in splendid groups with amazonite, topaz, goethite, and other minerals, furnishing dramatic cabinet specimens as well as excellent faceting material. Faceted stones in the 800-carat range have been cut.

New on the market are striking amethyst-tipped smoky quartz crystals from Powell County, Montana. Smoky quartz from Hot Springs, Arkansas, is usually a pale gray in color, however it has often been treated to darken the color. Recently, magnificent crystals have come from western Montana. They weigh up to 27 pounds and vary from nearly clear to nearly black. Large crystals and handsome clusters were shown at Tucson. A recent discovery of excellent smoky quartz crystals is in Inyo County, California. Smoky brown in color, the crystals have fascinating inclusions of starlike rutile sprays, hematite, chlorite and more. The crystals can be used for faceted stones, cabochons, or fantasy cuts. Other locations are Utah, Maine, and North Carolina.

The Smithsonian has a faceted smoky quartz egg weighing 3,000 carats cut by John Sinkankas. The GIA collection has a faceted stone of 8,580 carats. Michael Dyber carved "The Eternal Flame" from an 18½-pound piece of smoky quartz from Brazil. The finished 12-pound sculpture was done with 45-, 30-, and 15-micron diamond and polished with cerium on felt.

Gerhard Becker's majestic "Skyline Reflection" consists of rearrangable geometric forms of textured and highly polished clear and smoky quartz, resembling the skyline of New York City. Some of the flawless abstract buildings are 3 inches (7.62 cm) tall. One of the most exquisite items in the Lizzadro Museum of Lapidary Arts is a graceful smoky quartz Madonna rising from a magnificent cluster of natural smoky quartz crystals.

For jewelry, transparent smoky quartz with a hint of yellow or brown is preferred for faceted stones or beads. More opaque colors are used for cabochons. Smoky quartz with rutile inclusions makes striking cabochons. It is worked with silicon carbide or diamond. Polish with cerium oxide is preferred.

STRAWBERRY QUARTZ

Some absolutely sensational quartz crystals came from Mexico in the late 1950s. The shining and sparkling crystals were vivid strawberry red. The quartz was excellent-quality rock crystal colored red by myriads of platy inclusions that were determined to be hematite oriented in line with the structure of the crystal.

Some of the crystals were deeply striated and etched; a few were eroded or deformed. Many were excellent for specimens and all were wonderful for cabochons for jewelry. The crystals came from

Fascinating rutilated quartz spheres from Idar Oberstein's F. A. Becker Studio are popular with decorators. Photo courtesy of Gerhard Becker.

southern Chihuahua pegmatites and pegmatites near Arizpe, Sonora. A few of the crystals were over 2 inches (5.08 cm) in diameter, and clusters measured up to 6 inches (15.24 cm) across.

Several lapidaries used the red quartz for large heart-shaped cabochons. The most beautiful cabochons used material cut parallel to the reddest hexagonal face of the crystal using the part next to the crystal face for the top of the cabochon. Cabochons cut from cross sections of terminations of smaller crystals sometimes showed a fixed star effect. Heavily included quartz requires plenty of water and careful sanding.

TIGEREYE

Tigereye is silicified crocidolite, a blue asbestos mineral, a variety of the amphibole riebeckite. Because of the silky acicular structure of the crocidolite, the quartz which has replaced it is chatoyant. Colored by iron minerals, the material shows alternating bands of yellow golds and golden browns, which makes it suitable for cameos and intaglios as well as a multitude of lapidary products.

Some of the tigereye retains blue crocidolite inclusions in which case the basic color is dark blue. Many pieces are bicolored, providing a unique blue and gold color combination admired by creative lapidaries. A greenish hue results when blue and yellow fibers are evenly mixed. Heat treating of tigereye turns it to a rich, dark red, while bleaching with commercial bleach results in a pleasing honey color.

For many years the major source of tigereye has been Griqualand West in South Africa from Prieska to Griquatown. There is a ban in the exportation of rough tigereye, but South Africa Gem and Mineral Society leader, Horst Windisch, says small amounts can legally be exported by tourists who fill out application forms and get the proper permits. The reason for the ban was to promote a local gem-cutting industry. In the 1940s and 1950s

An exciting new find of chatoyant blue quartz in California has been named Mojave Blue. Photo courtesy of Bill Nicks. Photo by Art Arlington.

tigereye rough was exported in great quantities at extremely low prices. Now the solid thick pieces of rough are difficult to obtain.

Tigereye is semiopaque to semitranslucent. Tough and hard, it can be oriented so that lively and lustrous bands of light seem to move across the surface. Boxes, carvings, tiles, and other large objects have been made from tigereye, but its chief use has been for jewelry, particularly men's jewelry.

A particular variation of tigereye from Namibia was named Pietersite by its discoverer. Quite translucent, the fibers are not straight and parallel as in most tigereye, but are distributed in irregular brecciated masses in the quartz. The inclusions are red, red-gold, and dark blue with stunning brecciated patterns. A superb cabochon material, pietersite is now very scarce. South African authority Windisch says it is all mined out and only rarely available from old stock.

A newer locality for tigereye is Australia. In the 1970s large quantities of red tigereye were exported from Western Australia. Some of this bright material was streaked with metallic hematite and sold under the name "tiger-iron." Tigereye also occurs in South Australia. The Australian tigereye was popular for jewelry and ornaments for several years, but there is little on the market now. A small quantity of tigereye was found near Globe, Arizona, and later a mine in Placer County, California, produced some yellow and red tigereye with twisted fibers.

For the lapidary the tricky problem is correct orientation, so that the base of the slabs is parallel to the plane of chatoyancy. Also the material is not uniform, showing distinct differences between the dark and the light bands. Low-domed cabochons will give wide bands of chatoyancy, while high-domed cabochons will give narrow eyes. Rough tigereye can usually be purchased.

RECOMMENDED READING

Hunt, H., Lapidary *Carving for Creative Jewelry*. Phoenix: Geoscience Press, 1993.

Kunz, G., *The Curious Lore of Precious Stones*. New York: Dover, 1968.

Sinkankas, J., *Gemstones of North America*, 2d ed. New York: Van Nostrand Reinhold, 1976.

Webster, R., *Gems*, 5th ed. London: Butterworth-Heinemann, 1994.

SPECIFIC GEM MATERIALS

Dake, H., et al., *Quartz Family Minerals*. New York: Whittlesy, 1938.

Frondel, C., *The System of Mineralogy, The Silica Minerals*. New York: Wiley, 1962.

O'Donoghue, M., *Quartz*. London: Butterworths, 1986.

CHAPTER V

Cryptocrystalline Quartz: The Agate Family

Agate
    Banded and fortification agate
    Brecciated agate
    Eye agate and dot agate
    Fire agate
    Iris agate
    Lace agate
    Moss agate
    Plume agate
    Sagenitic agate
    Thundereggs
Chalcedony
    Black chalcedony
    Blue chalcedony
    Carnelian
    Chrome chalcedony

    Chrysocolla
    Chrysoprase
    Damsonite
    Mojave blue
    Myrickite
    Pink chalcedony
    Prase and plasma
    Psilomelane chalcedony
    Sard
Geodes
    Bolinos oil agates
    Coconut geodes
    Dugway geodes
    Enhydros
    Polyhedroids

CRYPTOCRYSTALLINE QUARTZ or microscopically crystalline quartz is far and away the most abundant, most used, and most popular of lapidary materials for the amateur lapidary and for many commercial lapidary enterprises, such as manufacturers of beads or bookends, bowls, and other decorative objects.

Cryptocrystalline quartz has a lot going for it. It has a suitable hardness, near 7, and often a toughness; it is available in large sizes;

it is easy to work with, takes a good polish, and comes in every imaginable color and pattern.

The premier gem-cutting center, Idar-Oberstein, Germany, was born in 1437 when residents started cutting the beautiful local agates. Delightful and imaginative quartz objets d' art are still produced there. A love affair with agate started the growth following World War II and subsequent explosion of the amateur gem-cutting hobby, which has been important in the advancement of lapidary techniques and uses of many different lapidary materials.

Although there is great variation in this type of quartz, the chemical composition of the many individual kinds is identical—that is, silicon dioxide. It is the physical and optical properties that make the difference. Chalcedony, a major variety of cryptocrystalline quartz, consists of minute interlocking crystals or uneven fibers and thus is tougher than most crystalline quartz. Chalcedony is layered with fibers perpendicular to layering. Pure chalcedony is translucent, colorless, or pale bluish white. It is porous, so traces and inclusions of other minerals bring color and pattern to otherwise ordinary-appearing material. The porosity varies with the layers. Chalcedony often forms waxy, botryoidal coatings over other minerals. The outer shell of many geodes is chalcedony. It is the filling of thundereggs, the cementing agent of breccias and conglomerates, and a replacement mineral for plant and animal fossils and for other minerals. It forms as veins and as nodules.

When chalcedony has distinctive bands, colors, and patterns, it is known as agate. The ancient Sumerians drilled agate beads. The Romans and Greeks used agate for their cameos, which have become classical examples of lapidary art. The early American tribes made their finest projectile points of carefully selected agate.

When chalcedony is so impure that it is opaque or nearly so, and also when it lacks the distinctive banding of agate, it is called jasper. Sometimes earthy in texture, jasper forms large masses in igneous rock. So close are agate and jasper at times that one grades into the other in a mixture called jasp-agate. A favorite rockhound definition is "If I find it, it's agate! If you find it, it's jasper."

Similar to jasper are the silica-rich sedimentary rocks, chert and flint. Chert occurs in massive lenses in limestone, dolomite, or sandstone, often replacing the fossils that formed the limestone. Infiltrations of iron and manganese minerals and several others have brought high color to some cherts, making them durable and attractive cutting materials. Flint more often occurs as hard nodules in the softer limestones. Nodules may be oddly shaped and have smooth exteriors. When flint is colorful it can also be used for lapidary work.

Names are often confusing among cryptocrystalline quartzes. Ohio flint, for example, is chert. Some so-called agate, for instance, the prairie agate of South Dakota, is generally classed as jasper by lapidaries, but the alluvial pieces may have originated as chert. Some of the jasper of the West Coast is silicified ash or mud.

Capital letters for agates and jaspers indicate place names, or trade or industry names given specific materials by their discoverers, miners, or distributors. Such names are not accepted mineral names.

Chalcedony or agate can grade into jasper and opal. For some reason the name designation in these silica materials is often more important than the appearance of the material. Agate is thought of as being very desirable, while flint and chert, no matter how bright their pattern or color, are thought to be the least desirable. A creative and skillful lapidary can make just as original and beautiful cabochons and carvings from well-selected chert as he can from jasper or agate.

The sheer abundance of cryptocrystalline quartz, even after nearly a century of concentrated hunting in the United States, is heartening. Fairburn agates, Lake Superior agates, agate-filled thundereggs, picture jaspers, Texas petrified wood, Ohio flint, and many, many more are still found with regularity and cut with dexterity.

Lapidaries can acquire excellent gem chalcedony at shows, by mail order, at shops, or by finding it themselves. The latter is a major reason for the popularity of many of these materials. Lapidaries learn to love the materials close at hand and those they find themselves. They patiently experiment with these materials to find the best uses and get the best polish possible. In the following states lapidaries were so proud of their native cryptocrystalline quartzes that they were successful in having them named as official state gems or stones: Florida, agatized coral; Louisiana, agate; Minnesota, Lake Superior agate; Mississippi, petrified wood; Missouri, mozarkite; Montana, moss agate; Nebraska, blue agate and prairie agate; Ohio, flint; Oregon, thunderegg; South Dakota, Fairburn agate; Tennessee, agate; Texas, petrified palm wood; Washington, petrified wood.

Proof of the great popularity of these quartz gems is that J. C. Penney and other department stores not only sell agate and jasper jewelry but also plastic imitations. Upscale jewelers often have jewelry featuring carnelian, chrysoprase, or black onyx. Every gem show brings new examples of cryptocrystalline quartz variations and new ways to work them.

Most of the fine-grained quartzes if carefully selected are easy to cut and polish. Select the material for the desired use, looking at color, pattern, fractures, vugs and flaws, size, and uniformity of texture.

Agate and other chalcedony cabochons should have excess material removed with a trimsaw. Grinding goes fast with 100 grit followed by 220, with the stones and machines kept wet. Wet sanding starts with 220 and moves to 320 and 400 or 600. Tin oxide or cerium oxide slurries on felt or leather produce a high polish.

AGATE

Agate is translucent chalcedony, cryptocrystalline silicon dioxide, often showing layered concentric growth, and usually exhibiting definite color contrasts and/or distinctive patterns.

Agate can occur as masses, veins, nodules, or fillings and is present in every rock type. With a hardness of near 7 and a density of 2.65, agate is slightly tough, has a conchoidal fracture, and a waxy or vitreous luster. Agates are found in most parts of the world and have been a lapidary material for many centuries. Agates and items made of agate dating from prehistoric times are found in most major museums.

The colors of agate cover the spectrum and the patterns of agate know no limits. In size, agates may be small water-worn pebbles such as the Sweetwater moss agates of Wyoming, or they can be as massive as a car, such as one in the agate fields of Rodeo, Durango, Mexico.

Besides being mixed with jasper or opal, agate can be intermixed with crystalline quartz, hematite, marcasite, pyrite, or other minerals. It may be a replacement for wood, bone, coral, or shell.

Most of the studies of agate involve banded agate or fortification agate, and not the agates distinguished by sagenitic or other inclusions. The German chemist, Liesegang, because of his laboratory experiments, concluded that agates were

South Dakota's colorful Fairburn agates typify the fortification variety of agate.

formed from silica gel and that the regular banding resulted from absorption of mineral salts. Clifford Frondel, author of Volume III of *Dana's System of Mineralogy*, explains that the rhythmic flows of silica deposited hydrothermically formed the agates. He did not believe the silica originated from surrounding rock.

Max Bauer felt that successive flows of magmatic silica–laden waters built up agates layer by layer. He also placed great importance on ducts. John Sinkankas, in *Agates of North America*, points out that chalcedony forms at low temperature and that the silica-bearing water can seep in through the cavity walls because of the porosity of the surrounding rock.

Although there is considerable disagreement about how agates formed, most scientists now accept that agate forms near the surface from silica deposited at relatively low temperatures between 100 degrees C and 300 degrees C (212–636 degrees F). Many feel that the concentric patterns must be the result of magmatic waters with mineral salts penetrating the gel-filled cavity.

Some of the most beautiful agates have exceptionally delicate and fragile inclusions, which gives some credence to a theory that

they grew in a silica solution rather than semirigid gel. These older theories are epigenetic, meaning the agate filled the existing gas pockets in igneous rock after the surrounding rock was solid. A newer theory is that of scientist and author, Benjamin Shaub, who says that agates are syngenetic, that is, they formed contemporaneously with the surrounding rock from jelly-like accumulations of silica.

There are many puzzles about agate that have not fully been explained by any single theory. There is no reason to believe that all agates formed in the same way. Just as three chefs might have three different recipes for the same cake, nature could have had several forces at work creating what we now call agate. In geodes with chalcedony or agate exteriors, the quartz crystals inside point toward the center, yet in some agate nodules there are bands of agate alternating with crystals which point to the exterior.

Ducts and tubes, which are obvious in some agates and missing in others, have often been debated. They have been called entrance or exit canals. According to the Shaub theory, they are caused by a developing pressure which forces any remaining semiliquid to the point of lowest pressure, where it at last hardens. In a few of these ducts there is a miniature banded agate pattern, or some may have a hollow space. Ducts are common in Brazilian banded agate, but lacking in moss agate and agate with acicular inclusions.

John Sinkankas made a study of the types of inclusions that lend distinction to agates. These are delicate needles or filaments, or lacy plantlike growths, minute black platelets, or small curds—dots of mineral matter.

Among the most interesting are the agate with hairlike mineral inclusions called *crystallites*. Spherical aggregates of needles which radiate are called *globulites* or margarites. A hodge-podge of criss-

A prime use of sardonyx, onyx, and other banded agate is for cameos. This classic masterpiece is by Gerhard Becker of Idar-Oberstein, Germany.

cross lines is *reticulated*. Fan shapes are *divergent*. Exotic patterns are formed from needles of hornblende, goethite, gypsum, rutile, or zeolites. Such agates are called *sagenitic*.

Examples of agates with hairlike inclusions are the pom-pom and thistle agates of Brewster County, Texas, and agates from Nipomo and Horse Canyon, California. An agate from Chihuahua , Mexico, is commonly called sagenite.

In agates found in younger volcanic flows, such as many of the Mexican agates, the inclusions are fine crystals of the actual mineral. These agates, because of the tendency of the inclusions to undercut or pull, present problems for the lapidary, but skilled craftsmen make sensational cabochons from stones with interesting inclusions.

In some agates, probably of earlier origin, the mineral forming the pattern is entirely gone, replaced by chalcedony, but retaining the appearance of the former mineral. In some agates part of the inclusions appear to be pseudomorphic and others appear to be true mineral inclusions.

Sinkankas points out that plumelike inclusions are surrounded by haloes of clear chalcedony. Some of these haloes appear blue and are closely parallel to the edges of the plume, but very narrow in width. Small fortifications seen in otherwise opaque quartz materials are also blue.

Shapes of agate are fully as varied as the colors and patterns. Some agates are round geodes, potato-shaped thundereggs, bottle-shaped pseudomorphs, egg-shaped nodules, flat sandwich-like seams, grape-shaped, stalactitic, or strange polygons like the polyhedroids of Brazil.

Agates are colored by traces or inclusions of iron, or manganese minerals, or chlorite, clay, copper, or nickel. Patterns are created when the minerals enter the silica gel in rhythmic sequence. The color may also be a result of radiation, as shown in partially buried agates, which have exposed surfaces brighter or darker than those that were below ground. The color of the agate may also be affected by tiny tubes or cavities, or variation of silica growth, which results in a milky appearance.

The colors of agate when examined closely are not the same as they seem to be at first. A striking black dendrite is really dark brown. When one band appears red in a Mexican agate and the next band pink, both bands have the same coloring dots, but they are denser in the red band. If the next band is orange, it may be a mixture of yellow and red dots.

An agate of high-grade chalcedony with a "turtleback" pattern may appear to have no color unless it is cut into thin slabs, which when held up to the light, reveal the pure colors of the rainbow. This phenomenon is due to diffraction grating— thousands of ultrafine concentric layers packed closely together.

Besides the many natural colors of agate, artificial colors are prevalent. Agates may be heat treated or dyed to change or improve the color. Results from heating may look quite natural as this process mimics nature, but dyed agate often looks too intense, or has a color seldom seen in natural stone.

The many names of agate are often associated with the area of occurrence, such as Montana moss agate, or they refer to the pattern, such as lace agate, or the color, such as carnelian. Rarely the name refers to a person, such as myrickite. When the name of the locality, description, or person has an "ite" ending, this indicates a trade name, pseudonym, or nickname, not a distinct species. To be official, names ending in "ite" must be accepted by the International New Minerals and Mineral Names Commission, which does not consider new agate names, because agates are all one mineral, quartz.

Most of the agates on the market now are from Brazil, Uruguay, Australia, Mexico, and South Africa. In the United States many fine, brightly colored agates are found and cut by amateurs. The locally found material may be some of the most spectacular ever found, but there is seldom enough of it in any one place to support a major mining or cutting industry. Cutting industries in addition to Germany are Brazil, Israel, Hong Kong, Taiwan, Thailand, China, and India.

Agate is the favorite lapidary material of thousands, because there are no two alike, and because it is easy to cut and polish, or to carve, or to adapt to dozens of lapidary techniques. The fact that agates are so widespread has led many people to enter the lapidary hobby or industry.

Agate can be shaped and sanded with diamond or silicon carbide. A normal procedure is shaping with 100 and 220 grit, sanding with 220, 320, 400, and 600 grit, and polishing with tin oxide or cerium oxide on felt or leather. Agates are always available, but the best American agates may be sold only in the state or region where they occur. Following is a look at some of the many variations of agate. New ones are constantly being found and the end is not in sight.

Banded and Fortification Agate

When the banding in agates is straight, it is called onyx; when it is rounded and parallel, it is merely banded agate; when the banding is sharply curved with irregular deep scallops resembling ancient forts, it is known as fortification agate.

Banded agate patterns may be among the most complex and fascinating of any lapidary material. The layers of chalcedony in a good fortification agate are distinctly delineated and often with considerable color contrast. The best fortification agates are fine grained, uniform, translucent, and aesthetic.

Banded and fortification agates are found in basalts, metamorphic rock, or in alluvial rock fields. Agate nodules and veins are widespread. The most common colors of banded agates are browns, whites, tans, grays, muted reds, and oranges, but the real prizes have more intense hues of red, pink, yellow, violet, coral, blue, and green.

Various agate fields tend to have individual characteristics such as the width of the bands, the complexity of the patterns, the translucency, skin color, texture, inclusions, size, and other attributes which make it possible for some experts to distinguish most agates from different locations at a glance.

Sometimes the entire agate has one type of banding, but at other times a straight banded portion is at the bottom of a circular or oval banded pattern. In some cases, banding is the only pattern on a nodule, but often there is sagenite in the outer agate layer, or the banding may by accompanied by eyes and other patterns.

Agate Creek, Australia

A renowned agate deposit called Agate Creek is located near the Robertson River in North Queensland, Australia. Fine banded and fortification agates have come from this rugged area for more than half a century.

These colorful agates include reds, blues, yellows, oranges, and neutrals such as brown, black, and white. Some of the agates have crystalline or crystal-lined centers, while many are filled with white and gray straight onyx banding. Many of the agates have extremely closely spaced bands similar to Lake Superior agates. Iris agate is an occasional treasure. The bands are usually monochromatic or analogous in color, rather than contrasting as in the case of the Chihuahua Mexican nodules. There is also some moss agate.

The agates are widely used for tabletops, display slabs, wall panels, desk ornaments, and jewelry. They appear to be under extreme tension, resulting in cracks developing after the slabs have been sawn. These fine agates are not nearly as common as they were 10 or 20 years ago. Polishing presents no problems. Most are polished for display rather than jewelry.

Balmorhea Agate, Texas

Some of the showiest agates for collectors of polished nodules or slabs come from Lake Balmorhea, Reeves County, Texas. The agates are large fortification nodules of high-grade chalcedony with distinct and contrasting wide bands of various tints and shades of blue with gray, black, and white. Some of the agates have hollow centers with white or colorless quartz crystal linings. One of the record Balmorhea agates weighs 320 pounds.

The agates have been found near the lake after heavy rains. They have seldom been used for jewelry, although the blue colors are very tempting, but the nodules are so striking that they are usually cut in half or in slabs and polished for specimens. These agates are high-quality chalcedony and are easily polished. They are seldom sold.

Botswana Agate

Among the agates imported from the African continent are the banded and fortification agates of Botswana. Some of these agates are quite opaque and seem closer to being jasper than agate. Only about 2½ inches (6.35–10.16 cm) in diameter, they have concentric bands, varied in width and not as deeply fluted as other fortification agates.

The colors are mostly neutrals— browns, tans, grays, light yellows, creams, and off white—but the duller colors are occasionally enlivened by wide bands of pink, rose, peach, coral, or orange. Imported in the rough, the agates are used for slabs, cabochons, and decorative items.

Brazilian Agate

The most important source of agate today is Rio Grande do Sul, Brazil. These large, high-quality agates have been exported by the ton ever since the cutters of Idar-Oberstein discovered that walls

Brazilian agates form the butterflies and flowers of this stained-glass lamp shade by John De Marco.

and fences of that part of Brazil were built of agate nodules. At first the agate was shipped to Germany as ballast, destined for the cutting industry, which had fallen on hard times because of the depletion of the local agate supply. Now the agate is shipped all over the world as rough and as finished gemstone objects.

Most of the Brazilian agates are banded, although some very novel patterns also occur. Bulls-eye patterns are distinctive. The chalcedony is translucent, compact, and uniform, with few fractures. Nodules vary in size from 1 or 2 inches (2.54 or 5.08 cm) in diameter to 9 or 10 inches (22.8 or 25.4 cm) or more. Geodes and enhydros are common in some locations.

Years ago a large proportion of Brazilian agate was dyed. The colors, though somewhat gaudy, were well accepted. Now, for the most part, heat treating has been the successor to dyes. Heat treating can be done in a conventional kitchen oven. Slabs are layered in pans of sand and put into the oven, which is then set for 200 degrees F. The temperature is increased every hour by 50 degrees F until 500 degrees F is reached. After ½ to 1 hour, the oven is turned off and allowed to cool unopened for 12 hours. The heat treatment brings out reds, oranges, yellows, and contrasting darker colors. Heat-treated banded agate is excellent for cameos, beads, and art objects.

A John De Marco window uses agates and other gemstones in the manner of stained glass.

Some companies and many lapidaries have specialized in Brazilian agate slabs. Flawless complete rounds of fancy agates are favorites. Tons of fine slabs of Brazilian agate are sold at Tucson. In the l920s and l930s "aggie" marbles from Brazil were coveted by every child. The large dyed "shooters" from Brazil are now collectors' items. A few amateurs now make agate marbles using bead mills.

One of the popular agates of Brazil is *rainbow* agate, which has excellent natural coloring. *Blackskin* agate is noted for its fine quality and beautiful patterns. *Piranha* agate nodules are large and richly colored with fine, concentric bands.

Richard Hahn of Idar-Oberstein made a 7¾-inch (19.68-cm) red agate cameo bowl showing seven classical figures. The bowl takes the natural shape of the agate, and clearly shows the exit channel or duct. A strange agate has recently been reported from the Brazil/Guyana border. It has a criss-cross lattice of quartz crystals with banded agate filling the cavities of the lattice.

The *Journal of Gemology* reports that the pattern scale is too large for the material to be considered for jewelry. Such agate is used for display specimens and could possibly be adapted to large lapidary items.

Brazilian agate is one of the easiest lapidary materials to work with. It can be successfully tumbled, worked with silicon carbide or diamond wheels or discs, or with flexible shaft or rigid carving machines. It is also worked with lathes and automatic cabbing machines. Brazilian agate can be bought by the piece or ton.

Chihuahua Agate, Mexico

Agua nuevo nodules run to pleasing blues and greens. The agates, 2 to 3 inches (5.08–7.62 cm) in diameter, usually have analogous color combinations. They have broad concentric bands with white for contrast. These agates were found in a small area and did not become as well known as some of the nodules of nearby ranches. They were used for jewelry and polished specimens, and are now reported to be scarce.

Apache and *Apache flame* agates have been admired for their intense reds. The Apache nodules are small, only a couple of inches in diameter, with vivid red banding, contrasting with white, yellow, and colorless bands of variable width.

Apache flame is an extraordinary agate with large-scale bold patterns and splashes of intense clash colors such as red, orange, and purple in basic clear, bluish, high-quality chalcedony. The agates are rather oblong in shape and filled with ornate and puzzling patterns. This is a unique fortification agate. A wonderful pattern showing sharp parallel layers will suddenly fade into clear chalcedony with watercolor-like streaks of saturated reds and yellows. The patterns are usually too large for jewelry.

Aztec purple is loved for its rare, bright purple colors, as implied by the name. It is essentially a fortification agate with white and blue-gray bands enhancing the shades of violet, lilac, orchid, and lavender. The overall effect is often that of rich amethystine chalcedony. A similar purple agate is found in the Mexican state of Durango, but it is not clear whether this is also classed as Aztec purple.

Bird of Paradise agate is an unusual Chihuahua agate that has been used for jewelry and decorative objects. While not strictly a banded agate, it has areas of bands or fortifications with lavish feathery patterns in red, pink, and purple with a groundmass of light-colored chalcedony, which has numerous small vugs or sugary areas. The bright feathery patterns are outlined with blue haloes.

Casas grandes nodules are small, rounded, and rather pale in color. There is very little contrast in the bands of lavender, pinkish lilac, gray, and white. The nodules are similar in size and shape. They have been used for jewelry, particularly earrings and pendants.

Coyomito agates are among the finest of the Chihuahua agate with their excellent patterns and beautiful colors. They are quite similar to the Lagunas, which many consider the top of the line, but are somewhat smaller on average. Colors are often intense, sometimes pastel. Aragonite pseudomorphs are seen in some of the larger Coyomitos. Eye patterns and flowerlike patterns are well developed between the exaggerated fortifications. A Coyomito of 3 or 4 inches (7.62 or 10.16 cm) in diameter may have several small fortification patterns in addition to a larger one. Thin slabs of Coyomitos about 1–1½ inches (2.54–3.81 cm) in diameter are wonderful for earrings.

Gallegos agates are found as large handsome nodules, some of which are hollow. Rare iris agate of superior quality is found in Gallegos agate more often than in many other Chihuahua agates. The chalcedony of these agates is uniform, high quality, and seldom flawed. Nodules are banded in reds, pinks, yellows, or purples, with each nodule particularly rich in a specific hue. Hollow centers are lined with sparkling drusy quartz crystals. These agates make splendid display pieces when cut in half or in slabs and polished by hand or with a vibralap.

Laguna agate just may be the world's best fortification agate. It is certainly the favorite agate of the many varieties that have come from the ranches of northern Mexico. These nodules of high-quality chalcedony have ornate, fluted, holly leaf-shaped fortifications of gorgeous colors, sometimes with many colors in a single nodule. Many of the colors are tertiary colors such as blue-violet, red-violet, or yellow-orange. With these are tints of pink, peach, rose, gold, and lavender and sometimes a muted shade of red such as cranberry or raspberry.

Each broad band is made up of dozens of ultrafine bands, as many as 30 fine bands of a single hue making up one wide band. The variations of color are due to the concentrations of color dots. Between the intricate fortification patterns are areas with patterns resembling targets, sunsets, flowers, or clouds.

The average size of a Laguna nodule is between 2½ and 6 inches (6.35 and 15.24 cm) in diameter, but a few are known in sizes of 8 or 9 inches (20.32 or 22.86 cm) across. Record sizes are 50 to 60 pounds. The agates are in an immense deposit of iron-rich rhyolite on the vast Ojo Laguna ranch. More or less potato shaped, the agates have irregular pock-marked skins. When cut, the outer edges of about ½ inch (1.27 cm) or so may have sagenite, moss, or plume. This will be outlined by a blue halo containing the fortification patterns.

Lagunas are certainly jewelry quality, but connoisseurs of fine agate usually cut the nodules in halves or slabs for display purposes. A top-quality polished Laguna nodule may sell for about $1,000 dollars and a large well-cut cabochon could sell for $100 dollars or more. Lapidary trophies have been won for hand-polished Laguna slabs, done in a flat glass pan with appropriate grits.

Loma Pinta nodules have wide bands with uncomplicated fortifications. Each of the color bands is made up of 12 or more extremely fine bands. With an average size of 2–4 inches (5.08–10.16 cm) in diameter, these agates are quite round and regular in shape. Predominant colors are tan, beige, yellow, ivory, and flesh pink, accented by a wonderfully bright coral color. Although well suited to jewelry, these are again the type of agate that lapidaries prefer to use for display. Now and then a rare sphere or egg cut from Loma Pinta is seen in a shop or at a show.

Moctezuma agates are small, round banded, or fortified nodules with rather wide bands and contrasting colors of pinks, yellows, and blues. Usually an entire nodule is filled with one elaborate pattern. Moctezumas may also have circular patterns. Colors are not as intense as some of the Chihuahua nodules. These agates have been used for jewelry. Chihuahua agates are still sold, but lapidaries will do better if they can locate old stock.

Dryhead Agate, Montana

A rugged area in the Big Horn River country of the Montana/Wyoming border has elaborately patterned and vibrantly colored fortification agates known as dryheads. With clash colors of red, orange, yellow, and violet, the dryheads resemble the Tepee Canyon agates of South Dakota. Like Tepees, they are found in limestone. Dryheads have less matrix and more complicated patterns than Tepees, plus finer lines and more similarity in color. The dominant color is red; the bands are mostly narrow and distinctly fluted. The ornate auxiliary patterns cover most parts not covered by the fortifications.

Dryheads are handsome collectors' specimens when surface polished. They have also been cut for showy cabochons, and recently, bright dryhead beads were a market success. Rough is occasionally sold.

Durango Agate, Mexico

There are huge agate fields in several areas of the state of Durango. Two of the most beautiful varieties are purple. One of these is purple lace agate with numerous small monochromatic fortifications and the other is a vein-type fortification agate with well-developed fortification patterns in tints and shades of violet from the slightest tint of lavender to rich reddish purple.

An agate field near Rodeo has banded agates of every imaginable color, averaging in size from about 3 to 6 inches (7.62 to 15.24 cm) in diameter. However, some of the agates here are immense and would easily weigh a ton.

Another field nearer to the city of Durango yielded great quantities of an agate called *High Fidelity* or Hi Fi. This was mined by an American and sent to the United States and other countries in large lots.

Hi Fi is a seam-type or vein-type agate with various colors and sizes of fortifications, but tending to have more blacks and whites and fewer bright colors than the agates of Chihuahua. This agate was available in large pieces and was used for many types of lapidary projects over 30 years ago. Some is still available when old collections are sold.

Fairburn Agate

Fairburns are found in southwestern South Dakota over a large area of badlands dotted with alluvial rock beds consisting primarily of quartz materials. Fairburns have fortification patterns that are bold and sharp in the best agates. Colors may be distinct contrasts instead of tints and shades of one color as in the typical Lake Superior agate. The best colors are red, a coral tint of red-orange, peach-pink, yellow, rust, maroon, brown, blue-gray, black, and white. The color pigments are so dense that parts of the deeply convoluted fortification bands seem opaque. Centers are often quartzy.

The sizes vary from 1 inch to 10 inches (2.54 to 25.4 cm) across, but the average size is less than 3 inches (7.62 cm) in diameter. If there are small fortification patterns on jasper, the stone is not classed as a Fairburn. The agates may have weathered out of an ancient formation on the edge of the Black Hills.

On the exterior Fairburns are irregular and pock marked. Broken parts are often found. A large complete Fairburn is rare. Most Fairburns show some patterns and color on the exterior, but the exterior has usually weathered so that it is predominantly brown, tan, gray, or black. Agates with vivid full-face patterns, or fortifications that cover the entire agate, are the most highly prized.

The South Dakota School of Mines and Technology in Rapid City has an excellent Fairburn exhibit highlighted by a rare 14-pound agate. Several others 12 pounds and over are in private collections. Fairburns are used for jewelry, spheres, eggs, and other lapidary work, but usually they are surface polished, cut in half, and polished or left as found. Some are sold in South Dakota shops, but seldom the best.

Kentucky Agate

Fortification agates of beautiful patterns and colors come from the Cumberland Mountain foothills of Kentucky. Intense reds with yellows, oranges, blues, and blacks make surprisingly aesthetic polished nodules or nodule halves. The red and black nodules are rarest. Heat treating the red and yellow agates will produce the desirable red and black. The nodules are mostly geodes and only a small percentage are filled with bright agate; the rest have quartz crystals.

The agates were discovered in the early 1970s and were abundant at that time. Large agates weighing from 35 to 100 pounds were found at first, but now a 5-pound one is difficult to come by. Cutters say fractures are the main defect of these agates but that even fractured nodules can be used for colorful cabochons.

Keswick Agate

In the limestone quarries near Keswick and Ollie, Iowa, banded agates are found; they are known as coldwater agates. The most attractive of these are called Keswick agates for the location. Coldwater agates are intricately banded and patterned agates similar to lace agate. Most coldwater agate occurs in muted neutral tones, but Keswick agate has bands of red, yellow, blue-gray, black, and white. The banding is irregular and fine with circles, clouds, and eyes and many complex outlines. Favorite patterns are elaborate eyes accented by red, rose, or coral. The heart of large pieces of quartz material contains the best-quality agate. The material takes a high luster.

Lake Superior Agate

Many of the Lake Superior agates are banded or fortification agates. The agates occur in the basalts of Lake Superior or weathered out in streams, fields, along lake shores, in mine dumps, gravel piles, and excavations in the states of Minnesota, Indiana, Wisconsin, Iowa, Illinois, Michigan, Missouri, and to some extent in North and South Dakota, Nebraska, and Kansas.

The agates are nodules ranging in size from about an inch (2.54 cm) to monsters near the 100-pound mark; however, an average good "laker," as the agates are affectionately called, is about 3–5 inches (7.62–12.7 cm). An agate weighing a pound or more is considered large. The record is a 108-pound agate from Moose Lake.

The bands of the Lake Superior agates are extremely fine and faithfully parallel. The principal hue is red and all the shades and tints of this vibrant color. Other colors with the reds are yellows, oranges, browns, tans, grays, and whites. Iron minerals are responsible for the colors. The agates are translucent, fine grained, tough, and vitreous or waxy in appearance.

Variations in the patterns are eyes, tubes, bands of crystalline quartz, and onyx bands. Some of the agates are carnelian, some sardonyx. Interesting inclusions are native copper, pyrite, chalcopyrite, hematite, limonite, goethite, and sagenite needles. As in many fortification agates, the tiny pigment dots of the color bands are clearly visible.

A particular kind of Lake Superior agate is called *painted agate* or paintstone, in reference to its bright opaque color which appears to be painted on, due to the heavy concentration of pigments. It might be technically termed jasp-agate because it is not translucent.

A distinctive kind of painted agate is called *Paradise Beach agate* for the location near Grand Marais. The nodules are mostly brilliant orange with visible inclusions of native copper. Tube agate and ruin agate are among the rare types of Lake Superior agate. Eye agate, with perfectly round concentric bands, is most popular locally.

Lake Superior agate is the state gem of Minnesota. The agates are popular for jewelry, for display as polished nodules or slabs, and for collections of "as found" agates. They can be purchased throughout the Midwest.

Laramides

A large area near Laramie, Wyoming, has agate nodules that have been named "laramides," for the Laramie Range of the Rocky Mountains, by John Miller, who has collected and studied them for years. Although the agates are quite individual and distinctive, many resemble the Montana moss agate when cut. The chalcedony is high quality and the colors are mostly muted or neutral, including black, brown, gray, white, tan, rust, brick, yellow, and red. Banded agates are numerous. Some of the better agates have bluish chalcedony. Tube agates, iris agate, and geodes are among the many variations. The agates fluoresce green under short wave.

Laramides are usually irregular on the surface and often have elongated shapes. Botryoidal chalcedony coats some of the agates. Fortification patterns are often mixed with tubes, eyes, and straight banded onyx.

The many types of agate found near Glendo, Wyoming, are considered part of the laramide family of agates. Some of the Glendo agate has been dyed and shipped in quantity to Europe. These are versatile agates suitable for jewelry and many lapidary techniques.

Luna and Apache Creek Agate, New Mexico

Luna and Apache Creek agates are similar fortification agates from western New Mexico. The Apache Creek agates have fortification banding or onyx banding in good-quality chalcedony but with generally pale colors, light blue, blue-gray, white, colorless, and sometimes black.

Found in a rhyolite formation, the Apache Creek agates vary from 1 inch (2.5 cm) in diameter to 8 inches (20.32 cm) in diameter. The rind of these agates often shows imprints of calcite crystals.

Luna agates are gray, blue-gray, ivory, and colorless and often have hollow centers with drusy quartz. Very large Lunas have been found. Care must be taken in examining the agates after the first thin cut, because some of them have exceedingly fine lines, with turtleback patterns, and will yield glamorous iris agate. Like many agates, the New Mexico varieties are usually sold near where they occur.

Onyx Agate

Agate consisting of straight parallel bands of alternate colors, such as black and white, blue-gray and white, orange and white, or brown and white, is correctly called onyx agate. The name is doubly confusing because banded calcite is also called onyx, as is the dyed black chalcedony of the jewelry market. When the straight banded agate is reddish brown with white it is called sardonyx.

Good banded onyx is translucent in the lighter colors and almost opaque in the darker browns and blacks. Sometimes the straight parallel banded part of an agate covers only one section of the stone. Most onyx agates feature two contrasting colors and the remainder of the agate will have the same colors as the straight banded portion. If the contrast of color bands in onyx agate is not strong enough, the agate can be heated.

Onyx agates are found in most major agate deposits, but are not as common as the circular banded agates or the fortification agates. Brazil is the major producer of onyx banded agate. Onyx banded agates have been hunted for years in the Lake Superior agate deposits of Minnesota, Wisconsin, Iowa, Illinois, and Michigan. Some of them are true sardonyx. Many of the Oregon thundereggs have onyx banding with warm dark tones contrasting sharply with stark white. Horse Canyon agate of California often has straight bands. The Rio Grande Valley and the Needle Peak areas of Texas have examples of onyx agate.

The chief use of onyx agate is for cameos, intaglios, and decorative additions to useful items such as onyx handles for knives or letter openers. There are also onyx beads, eggs, rings, and other jewelry items.

In the process of engraving a two-layered stone the lapidary chooses the layer he wishes for the carving and the one he wants to keep as a background. If the cameo face or figure is cut in a red layer, the lapidary carves close to the white layer when he wants a lighter color. The process of carving cameos or intaglios is exacting and challenging. Idar-Oberstein–trained Midwest artist, Ute Klein Bernhardt, has produced most of the portrait cameos being done in the United States. Bernhardt uses a fixed shaft machine and makes her own tools. A fixed shaft machine has a chuck that holds various tools. This

Purple agate grapes center this gemstone picture by Anders Oxehufwud.

method of carving has the advantage of freeing both hands to hold the work.

Sowbelly Agate

This gorgeous agate of southwestern Colorado deserves a better name, but those who are familiar with it don't let the name bother them, because the amethyst color and the unusual pattern make the material one they just have to try. It is striking for display specimens, small decorative objects, and appealing cabochons.

Parallel bands of crystalline amethyst alternate with gray-white chalcedony, which also fills most of the spaces between the crystals. The amethystine agate occurs in silver veins near the town of Creede in Mineral County at a 9,000-foot elevation.

The amethyst terminations are small and uniform and of a light to medium bluish violet color. The points face inward toward the center of the vein in a "comb structure." In the best material the chalcedony is white and the amethyst is a medium lilac hue. Inclusions of native silver add luster to some specimens. Other inclusions are sphalerite and galena. Heaps of discarded amethyst from the overburden of the silver mines were collected during the 1940s and 1950s.

Drusy white quartz and drusy amethystine quartz line cavities and vugs in the center of the sandwich-like vein material. The material can be polished to a gleaming finish with high-tech diamond methods. Some pieces may need Opticon as a filler. Inclusions of drusy quartz and native silver can be turned to assets by imaginative lapidaries. It is seldom advertised.

Tepee Canyon Agate

Tepee Canyon agates are fortification agates in large silicified limestone nodules found in Tepee Canyon in the Black Hills of South Dakota. The predominate colors of the intricate patterns are a muted red and red-orange, coral, yellow, rust, brown, cream, purple, and pink. The bands are narrow, numerous and contrasting. The gray-brown matrix is polishable. The irregularly shaped nodules are large, 6–10 inches (15.24–25.40 cm) in diameter. Some nodules are mostly the jasper, but many have an agate center surrounded by

the polishable matrix. Drusy amethyst vugs are a feature of some of the finest agates.

The agates have been mined by commercial miners and amateurs for many years, and since they are more numerous than the Fairburns, they have been cut for jewelry more than Fairburns. Large, brightly colored cabochons are possible. Frequent fractures keep the larger agates from being used very often for display; however, when flaws are minor a large polished slab of Tepee is a real showpiece. Such slabs are polished on vibrating laps. Lapidaries can buy the agates in South Dakota.

Brecciated Agate

Sometimes just called breccia, this type of agate is fascinating. The history of the agate can be speculated with fair accuracy upon close examination of a brecciated nodule. The agate was originally a finely patterned whole nodule. A natural calamity broke the exquisite nodule to jagged fragments. Perhaps eons later a repentant nature glued the angular pieces back together with her healing chalcedony. But the fragments were not glued together with any particular order as in a jigsaw, but rather the mended agate became a hodgepodge, with some of the original exterior patterns and colors in the center, and the colors splashed hit or miss.

Many agate-rich areas have some brecciated agate, but the brecciated pieces are often scarce. Some agates from Brazil and Mexico are brecciated. Stone Canyon agate (or jasper) of Monterey County, California, is an unusual brecciated material in autumnlike colors of orange and black, yellow and red. Brecciated agate is found on the Arizona desert near Burro Creek. Another location is between

Glendo and Guernsey, Wyoming. If the agate is compact and homogeneous, cutting presents no problems.

Butterfly Agate

Sometimes called butterfly stone, a brecciated agate from Mexico is found as thunдеregg-shaped nodules, often the rounded type of nodules with irregular joined sections. Nodules weighing up to 10 pounds are found with jigsawlike patterns in many colors, mostly earth tones and muted reds, violets, yellows, oranges, and greens.

Patterns are best toward the exterior of these agates. Many nodules have been severely fractured and then fully or partially healed. The agates are opaque except for small sections and should probably be classed as jasp-agate. There are only minor inclusions of translucent chalcedony. Some of the jaspery sections appear coarse and porous while others are as compact, fine-grained, and solid as flint.

Butterfly agates make interesting cabinet and display specimens if cut in half or slabbed. Skillful lapidaries have made highly unusual cabochons from select pieces of complex brecciated patterns. The small-scale patterns with color contrast between the patches are best for cabochons. It may be necessary to use Opticon to fill in porous areas or unhealed fractures before polishing.

Youngite

Near Gurnsey, Wyoming, is an interesting deposit of brecciated pastel-colored agate called Youngite. The agate is stalactitic with white or colorless groundmass decorated with stringers, tubes, and growths of pink, rose, and pale yellow. The highly brecciated patterns are the most unusual. There are many botryoidal portions lined with sparkling drusy quartz throughout the material. Large and showy pieces of the material have been cut and

polished for bookends and decorative objects, with the drusy cavelike vugs only adding to the interest. Cabochons with feminine appeal can be cut from the white on white material with small patterns of flowery pinks. Youngite is still sold in Wyoming.

Eye Agate and Dot Agate

Concentric round rings of contrasting colors can form "eyes" in some agates, either as the main pattern or as auxiliary patterns. Colors vary a lot, but if the eyes are black and white or dark brown with white, the patterns are indeed eye catching! Eye agates, well known in history under the old name Aleppo stone, were credited with magic powers by their superstitious owners.

Some of the eyes are more or less oval or even tear drop shaped. There may be numerous eyes in one agate, or a large agate may have one enormous bull's-eye target. Eye agates differ from dot agates by concentric rings instead of color spots.

Eye agates can be found wherever there are large and varied agate beds. Brazil has dramatic eye agates. Some of the most interesting Lake Superior agates have multiple eyes. Some Fairburn agates have eyes as auxiliary patterns. Many of the agates of south and west Texas, Arizona, and northern Mexico also have distinct eye patterns. Eye agates make showy display pieces and are sometimes used for surprisingly lifelike jewelry. A single black and white eye mounted as a ring is a sure attention getter.

Dot agates are found in many agate areas, differing from other agates of a particular formation only in the patterns which are formed by round dots of varying size and color. These dots are larger than the tiny dots which make up the bands of some fortification agate, and they

*Colorful agate cabochons create this springtime
picture by Anders Oxehufwud.
Picture is 10 × 16 inches.*

are not arranged in bands or any other particular pattern, but are randomly scattered throughout each stone.

Bloodstone

Bloodstone is translucent green chalcedony with bright red spots. An old name for bloodstone is heliotrope. It was once so popular that it was named the birthstone for March. It was popular in Scottish and Victorian jewelry. The ordinary quality is heavily included dark green with minor areas of red, but the best quality is a translucent rich green with well-distributed true red spots. The green is due to chlorite and iron, and sometimes has a dense mossy effect. The red is also due to an iron mineral. Bloodstone has been described as a jasper, but it is translucent enough to be called agate.

Bloodstone occurs as nodules in agate deposits and sometimes as veins in metamorphic deposits. Often it is among the rare varieties in a prolific agate location, for example, excellent nodules of bloodstone are found on occasion in Montana where most of the agate is neutral in color. Scarce nodules occur in the multicolored chalcedonies of the Rio Grande Valley in Texas. Other U.S. occurrences are California, Oregon, Wyoming, and Colorado. Other sources are India, Brazil, and Australia .

Suitable to be used for jewelry or carvings, bloodstone should be carefully selected so that the unique color combination will be an asset to the cabochon or carving. It can be polished by ordinary methods used for chalcedony and is usually available in the rough.

Fish-egg Agate

In the rock beds near Scenic, Pennington County, South Dakota, nodules of a material similar to polka-dot agate occur, except that in this case the round red and yellow spots are much smaller, only $\frac{1}{8}$ inch (3.1 mm) in diameter or less. The small dots are also packed more closely together in the white, creamy, or colorless groundmass of translucent chalcedony.

These agates were first found and named fish-egg agate in the 1930s. The nodules are water-worn and seldom over 2½ inches (6.35 cm) in diameter.

Fisheye Agate

An area near Villa Ahumada, Chihuahua, Mexico, produces an agate called fisheye agate by the natives. Clusters of brightly colored spots are scattered in translucent colorless chalcedony. The material is in a wide vein in volcanic rock. Exported to distributors in El Paso, Texas, fisheye was popular in the 1960s for unusual cabochons. Some is still seen in shops.

Pigeon Blood Agate

This highly prized red agate from Utah is a white chalcedony with drops, blobs, and swirls of vivid reds, making it a bright and intriguing material. It is found on Pigeon Blood Hill in the Orchio Hills, Emerson County, Utah. Eye-catching cabochons result when the material is snowy white and the red inclusions are evenly or artistically spaced. Some of the pigeon blood agate has a red groundmass decorated with patterns of even brighter red.

In this same area, orchid and purple agate is found. Unique among the area agates is *green olive* agate, featuring edible-appearing slices of Spanish olives filled with red pimiento.

Polka Dot Agate

This type of agate, named for the original location near Madras, Oregon, has an appropriately descriptive name. The round spots are concentric circles of variegated shades of brown, red, and yellow in a pure white or more translucent gray-white stone. Other dots are opaque white on translucent off-white. The spots seldom exceed ½ inch (1.27 cm). The smallest dots are less than a pinpoint.

Scenic patterns result when there are opaque brown and yellow mountains, hills, winding country roads, and terraced fields. These brown areas are opaque. Exceptionally realistic scenes occur when the lapidary orients a dark landscape against a white sky with one orange-brown spot representing the sun. This agate also makes stunning cabochons.

The vein of this material is found in rhyolite. Editor Lelande Quick suggested that the material should be called polka dot jasper, but the material is too translucent for jasper. Polka dot agate is still collected at the Richardson Ranch in Oregon. Similar agate has been found in Wyoming, Texas, and a few other places, but the Oregon material is immediately identifiable.

A lighted agate panel for this Tulsa library was made by the Tulsa Rock and Mineral Society.

Texas Orbicular Agate

Another variation of agate with decorations of round spots is found south of Marfa, Texas. The chalcedony is translucent and excellent in quality. The round inclusions are close together and multicolored red, yellow, orange, and tan with a greater size range than the previous "dot" agates. The agates occur in pockets in the rhyolite flows of west Texas.

This agate and most other "dot" agates are well suited to jewelry; however, a strange western Texas agate that at first glance appears to be a "dot" agate is not used for jewelry. Instead it becomes an exotic specimen when slabbed and polished for display. It is a brightly colored material with rather evenly sized dots apparently well lined up in a carefully planned pattern. On closer inspection each dot turns out to be a tiny geode or agate nodule all cemented with a multitude of

Above: Fabergé-style Russian Coachman and Balalaika player are carved from chalcedony, labradorite, sodalite, jasper, and obsidian (both 4 ½ inches high). Courtesy of the Lizzadro Museum of Lapidary Arts.
Photo by Russell Kemp.

Above: Showy faceted stones in the Lizzadro Museum are a 675-carat topaz, a 228-carat citrine, a 460-carat kunzite, a 67-carat aquamarine, and a 190-carat amethyst.
Photo by Russell Kemp.

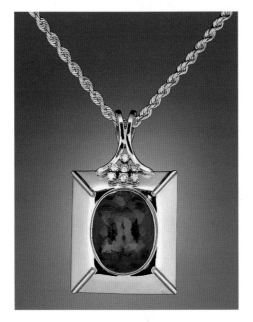

Left: A faceted 18.5-carat Brazilian rubellite makes a sensational pendant in the Keith Proctor Master Jewelers collection of Colorado Springs.
Photo by Tino Hammid.

This record calcite, 1,072 carats, faceted by Art Grant, shows the beauty an expert cutter can achieve with a soft lapidary material. Photo courtesy of Art Grant.

Art Grant's fabulous fluorite weighs 3,965 carats and was cut from rough from Illinois. Photo by Brad Walker.

Susan Zalkind and Paul Hawkins chose American alabasters for a line of innovative work.

Above: Intricately textured black onyx and jasper are examples of Steve Walter's innovative work. Photo by Steve Walter.

Below: A cross section of watermelon tourmaline was used by Idar-Oberstein–trained artist Ute Bernhardt for this motion-filled gem engraving.

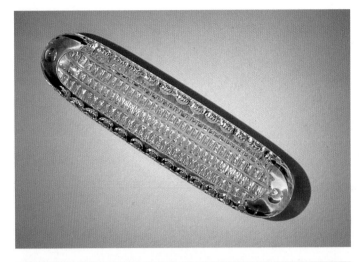

Michael Dyber's carved aquamarine weighs 71.05 carats. Photo by Larry Croes.

Beryl and tourmalines were Michael Dyber's choices for these imaginative carvings. Beryl (top is 37 carats, tourmalines are 16 and 12 carats). Photo by Larry Croes.

Imperial jade from Burma is a glamorous material for cabochons, carvings, and jewelry. Courtesy of Hing Wa Lee.

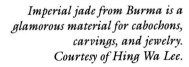

others to a homogeneous mass by chalcedony. Some of the tiny round geodes have crystalline quartz–lined cavities. Hollows can be filled with water-soluble wax topped with clay or a paste made of soap flakes. The nodule halves are then Vibrolapped or sanded on a wide belt sander.

Fire Agate

Fire agate, with its special phenomenal property, is iridescent, almost metallic appearing, and is one of the elite agates of the American Southwest and Mexico. In the late 1940s, iridescent chalcedony with botryoidal internal bands found in small irregular pieces was collected in southern California and Arizona and was named fire agate. The agate occurs in seams, pockets, and alluvial beds.

The really good fire agate with iridescent colors was scarce and few cutters knew how to handle it, so plenty of banded red and white chalcedony wound up being called fire agate. Material from the original find was identified and described by Dr. Frederick Pough who was then at the American Museum of Natural History.

Other discoveries in Arizona in the late 1940s and early 1950s led more people to recognize the elusive agate. Cutters had figured out by then that the agate should be slowly ground and not cut. By the late 1950s, lapidary artist Olive Colhour was skillfully carving figures from fire agate.

The great beauty of fire agates is caused by orderly hexagonal platelets of silica, coated by crystals of goethite arranged in numerous grapelike layers in the chalcedony. Colors caused by light interference are rich shades with metallic brilliance, red, green, yellow, bronze, gold, orange, blue, and purple. Browns and bronzes predominate in many specimens.

The patterns are bubbly and frequently

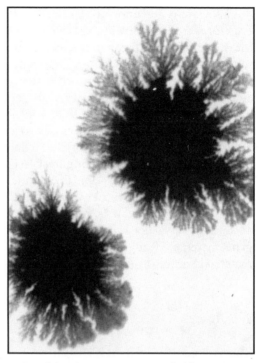

Dendrites in agate are remarkably intricate growths of trace manganese or iron minerals.

show multiple distinct segments at various levels and highlight several different colors within a single stone. Other patterns are stalactitic. The structure of the material combined with the goethite produces the opal-like optical effect.

Fire agate comes from California, Arizona, and New Mexico, but in recent years a large quantity of select material has been coming from several states in Mexico where it is found in fine-grained rhyolitic rock. Botryoidal masses often form crusts on rhyolite. Most of the chalcedony pieces in a given field are not fire agate but are cuttable reddish brown and white chalcedony.

Mexican mines are in Chihuahua, San Luis Potosi, Aguascalientes, and Jalisco. Fire agate may be difficult to recognize in the rough because in thick pieces of chalcedony the "fire" may be deeply buried and disguised by brownish carnelian layers.

Fire agate is a glamorous jewelry stone. Free-form stones following the contour of the stone and the fire patterns are more suitable than oval cabochons. The stones should be worked wet with much patience and deliberation. Working with diamond up to 50,000 with a flexible shaft tool is preferred by many, but others say diamond cuts too fast. A layer of clear chalcedony must be left on the brightest layer of iridescent fire. Many lapidaries prefer starting with grinding rather than cutting. If cut, only a thin cap is removed. Fire agate deserves wider recognition as a fine gem material. Rough and "windowed" material is readily available.

Iris Agate

This unique and sensational agate has a rainbow color spectrum because of its structure, instead of trace amounts of other minerals as in other agates. The ultrafine bands, like diffraction grating, produce the rainbow effect when seen at the proper angle with transmitted light. The ultrafine fibers are twisted and alternating bands have slight variations in refraction.

The iris agate in the rough or when first slabbed may seem ordinary and colorless. Lapidaries should look for very translucent agate with extremely fine parallel bands often in a turtleback-like pattern. Some iris agate, that of Montana, for instance, may have some brownish or reddish banding or near-black dendrites, but the narrow iris layer will be clear, and seemingly a better grade of chalcedony. Experts estimate that there may be up to 50,000 concentric bands per square inch in the iris layer.

A rough iris agate may be more translucent than others in a lot. When lapidaries have reason to suspect that their agate may be iris, they should first cut the slab ⅛ of an inch (3.17 mm) in thickness. A thin slab dipped in cutting fluid and held toward the light should reveal the iris effect if present.

Iris agate is found as nodules and occasionally veins wherever there are extensive agate beds; however, the iris agates are very scarce and often overlooked by cutters who fail to slab them because they appear colorless, or slab them too thick while looking for colors or patterns other than iris. Excellent iris agate has been found in Montana and west Texas. Antelope, Oregon, is the center of an area where showy iris agate has been found.

Spectacular iris agate has been found near Weiser, Idaho. Other states where iris agate occurs are California, New Mexico, Arizona, Washington, Wyoming, and Tennessee. Iris agate has also been noted from the Laguna, Moctezuma, Coyomito, Casas Grandes, and Gallegos nodules from Chihuahua, Mexico. Brazil and Uruguay are major sources as well as the Numinbah Valley of Southeast Australia.

Round concentric fine bands of twisted fibers that yield the rainbow effect may surround patterns of eye or tube agate and are occasionally seen in chalcedony limb casts, but the most magnificent specimens are the full-face fortification slabs of translucent to transparent agate showing the distinctive turtleback structure and exhibiting breathtaking spectral colors. Alternating bands have variations in refraction.

Iris agate slabs should be thin. For best results, hand lap and polish on both sides. Automatic laps have been successfully used with each slab carefully weighted and protected. For jewelry stones such as earrings, cold dopping is best.

Lace Agate

Lace agate is a generic term for a widespread type of agate with a fanciful pattern that resembles lace in some respects— except that lace usually has a very regular and predictable pattern, and lace agate is more or less hit or miss. Lace agate has bands, eyes, dots, tubes, zigzags, scallops, fortifications, picots, and pointelles. The complex and delicate patterns are random, intricate, and irregular, with no discernible sequence.

Lace agate is usually a vein agate, although water-worn pieces may resemble nodules. The patterns in lace agate may be so dense as to render the material opaque. This type of agate usually occurs by itself in specific areas and not in agate fields with other types of agate. There are occurrences in many places in a variety of hues and color combinations.

Blue Lace Agate

One of the best natural blue quartz gems is the blue lace agate from Namibia. It is a vein agate with wavy and convoluted, more or less horizontal, bands of several tints of blue with some of the patterns mixed with white or colorless chalcedony. The agate is translucent but slightly milky. Some areas are predominantly a uniform tint of blue that can be used for beautiful blue cabochons. The quality of this agate is excellent for such lapidary purposes as spheres, eggs, carvings, and ornamental and decorative items. Like other fine chalcedonies, it is easy to work. It is often advertised.

Crazy Lace Agate

An example of what most lapidaries think of when they ask for lace agate is the crazy lace agate of Chihuahua, Mexico. The bright and busy patterns are disoriented and closely packed, but the overall effect is lacy, perhaps more like many kinds of lace patched together.

Crazy lace agate has multiple colors which do not necessarily change when the pattern changes. Colors are red, orange, yellow, pink, brownish violet, gray-blue, brown, gray, black, cream, and white. Red and yellow, from iron oxides, are the dominant colors of this vein agate. Frequently there are vugs, crevices, or sugary and porous areas , or spots of calcite or kaolinite in the agate.

This agate was extremely popular with lapidaries for cabochons and other work in the 1950s and 1960s when there was a large quantity of colorful high-grade material on the market. Currently the agate called crazy lace does not approach in color or quality what was available in the past. Crazy lace agate may undercut and needs extended sanding with sharp, and then well-worn, wet sanding cloth.

Missouri Lace Agate

Missouri lace agate is found in Washington County on the spoil piles of old barite mines. A vein agate, it has intricate fortifications, eyes, clouds, flowery patterns, and zigzags. Some bands are tightly packed quartz crystals and there are often vugs and coatings of drusy quartz. Usually this highly patterned agate is dull in color with neutral tones of gray, beige, black, white, and colorless, but occasionally some will have vivid bands of red or yellow to contrast with the more somber colors. The colorful boulders are coated on the exterior with limonite. Missouri lace is still available. The brightest colored agate was dug out during the construction of a swimming pool in Washington State Park.

Missouri lace agate is used for cabochons and carvings. Polished with tin oxide on felt after fine sanding with 600, the agate is used for jewelry.

Moss Agate

Fragile and delicate mossy-appearing inclusions are found in many colors in clear or neutral-colored chalcedony. Since many of the contrasting patterns form mosslike designs, or dendritic clumps or streamers of graceful Spanish moss, the agate is called moss agate. Variations resemble seaweed, snowflakes, starbursts, or composite flowers. Moss agate has been called by many other names, among them tree agate, mocha stone, seaweed agate, amberine, medfordite, flower agate, bouquet agate, landscape agate, red top agate, Yellowstone agate, white moss agate, and variegated agate. Moss agate is found in many places along with other agates in igneous, metamorphic, or sedimentary deposits. Moss agate occurs as veins, as nodules in place in igneous rock, and commonly as water-worn nodules in alluvial gravels.

The colors of the mossy patterns are dark brown, reddish brown, red, yellow, orange, gold, green, and brownish green. Usually there are variations of a single color of moss in one nodule, but sometimes a nodule will have two or more colors of dendritic patterns.

Moss agate has a long history of many uses by lapidaries. The green moss agate of India has been used for amulets, beads, and other ornaments for centuries and is still available. Arrowheads and projectiles found in the western United States are often chipped from fine moss agate. Antique Scottish jewelry features moss agate.

The splendid patterns, in some cases, were formed by impurities present when the agate was first forming, and in other cases, the impurities may have been a secondary infiltration. The minerals creating the patterns are usually manganese or iron oxides, or chlorite. Following are a few variations of this important agate type.

Amethyst Sage Agate

A magnificent agate from Denio, Nevada, is called by the trade name amethyst sage in allusion to its smoky amethyst color with its black dendritic sage brush patterns. The chalcedony is translucent and high quality. The smoky amethyst color has a hint of rose. Dark dendrites are abundant and feathery. They are especially well developed along the edges of the agate where they resemble desert plants along a stream.

The exterior of the material is white and rough. This agate material is superb for jewelry as it is very distinctive with a good color and pattern. The agate is available at some shops in the Northwest.

Chimney Creek Dendritic Agate

A vein of dendritic agate in Nevada is mined in large chunks of intricately patterned colorless and white chalcedony with black dendrites. Resembling the star and snowflake patterns of the Wyoming Sweetwater agate, the Nevada material occurs in pieces up to 60 pounds. In the same area small nodules are found with similar but smaller black patterns.

India Moss Agate

Many variations of moss agate have been used for centuries in India for beads and a multitude of lapidary projects. Scenic agate, black and white moss agate, and pink, green, and yellow moss agate are just a few kinds of agate found in mountainous areas in place and in large alluvial fields.

Some of the material from India has milky background colors with graceful overall patterns of moss, and some is translucent and may have well-developed dendrites such as the historic tree agate. The green moss agate is exported in quantity and is also cut locally for beads and cabochons.

Indian moss agate was popular about a century ago in Europe, where it was called mocha stone. Several colors of moss agate are found in fields in the states of Gujarat, Bombay, and Mayurbhanj. Commercially important are the Kathiawar Peninsula and the Deccan Plateau. Agates of paler colors are heated. Bowls, beads, and other agate items are produced in India, but large quantities of rough agate are exported.

Montana Moss Agate

The best-known agate to American lapidaries may be Montana moss, a distinctive dendritic agate with dark brown, almost black, patterns in rather clear, milky, or grayish chalcedony.

The vast location is on both sides of the Yellowstone River and its tributaries from west of Billings, Montana, to the vicinity of Williston, North Dakota, a short distance from where the Yellowstone feeds into the Missouri. The total agate-producing area is about 350 miles in length, but most of the agates in recent years have come from small streams and gravel bars from about Miles City to Terry, Fallon, and Glendive.

Elaborate dendritic growths are prized, as well as pictures of pine trees or evergreen forests. The water-worn nodules are white on the exterior, smooth, rounded, and translucent. Possible areas for superb cabochons are found by holding wet nodules up to a bright light.

The average size of Montana agate nodules is from 2 to 4 inches (5.08 to 10.16 cm), but many have been found that are 5 and 6 inches (12.70 to 15.24 cm) in diameter or more.

Some of the bands are partially colored with reddish brown faded-looking streaks, but it is the moss, not the bands, that attracts the lapidary. The best of the moss is called red top. The dark dendritic growths topped with red are caused by manganese. Patterns may follow growth lines or healed fractures within the agate. Some of the patterns seem to have formed around a center and radiated from there in a pattern resembling an ink blot on a folded absorbent paper.

Montana moss agate has been a favorite of lapidaries for over 50 years. It is still found in the gravel bars of the Yellowstone, an area that is a field trip destination of thousands each year. Several shops in Montana use the native agate for slabs, cabochons, polished nodules, jewelry, carvings, and spheres. Cabochons or slabs with aesthetic scenes, or pictures that are like a photograph of another object, bring high prices.

Montana agate is now used for contemporary cuts such as tongue, blade, and bullet, for innovative gold jewelry. An astonishing number of early lapidaries in the United States learned their craft with Montana agate. Montana agate is sold throughout the Northwest.

Oregon Moss Agate

Oregon has an abundance of cryptocrystalline quartz gems, among them a marvelous variety of moss agates. Moss agate is found near Prineville. Dendritic limb casts with well-developed black radial-type patterns in pale translucent chalcedony are among the best. Colorful moss agate is found near Ashwood, Antelope, and Madras in central Oregon. Red moss agate from Antelope is a favorite. Another area for quality moss agate is in southwestern Oregon near Ashland, Medford, and Grants Pass. In eastern Oregon an old location that is still producing moss agate is Graveyard Point near the Idaho border. Colors of Oregon moss agate are red, green, orange, yellow, brown, black, and white. Enormous amounts of Oregon agate have been commercially mined or collected by amateurs and cut by lapidaries everywhere.

There is a bewildering variety of moss agate in Oregon, marketed under various trade names. Some of the agate is available in large enough pieces for lamp bases, book ends, desk sets, bowls, and similar large lapidary undertakings. Most is suitable for jewelry.

Rio Grande Agate

An area deserving of more attention for its wonderful moss agate is the Rio Grande Valley of Texas. Gravel deposits there have many large nodules in a better variety of color than almost anywhere else.

The water-worn nodules have few fractures or flaws. The agates are very common in the gravel pits and in ranch fields in Hidalgo and Starr counties. Agates may be caliche covered, so it is hard to tell the quality until cut. The fabulous array of colors includes red, gold, yellow, orange, black, brown, and green.

Occasionally a super agate of green with red turns up. Vivid green moss agate is the least common and the most desirable. The moss is in the form of threads, ribbons, and streamers instead of the tree-like patterns of Montana. Sometimes the mossy strings and patches are so dense that the material appears opaque until held up to a light or slabbed. In other nodules the streamers of moss are delicate, widely spread, and graceful.

Since the gravel is immediately crushed, it is likely that many south Texas roads are paved with Rio Grande agate. Texas dealers have adequate supplies of this easily worked agate.

Seaweed Agate

Seaweed agate is agate with wispy strings and webs of chlorite or some other mineral usually against colorless, gray or white groundmass. If translucent, the delicate green stringers almost look as if they were floating. Lapidaries should select pieces which are not too dense with inclusions. A few graceful streamers are more impressive than a tangle of them.

The seaweed agate of the Rio Grande Valley of Texas is typical of this type of material that occurs in many places but only in small quantities. The tangled green strands are as fine as if drawn with a fine penpoint and the varying grays and whites of the groundmass give the appearance of depth to the agate.

Seaweed agate is also found in Oregon near Antelope, Ashwood, and Richland. Some of the Horse Canyon agate of California qualifies as seaweed agate. Nevada and Idaho also have wispy green seaweed agate.

Sweetwater Agate

Along the Sweetwater River drainage area in Wyoming a myriad of small moss agates keep weathering out of the alluvial deposit. Noted for their green fluorescence in addition to their smoothly rounded shapes and fanciful dendrites, the little agates have been used for tumbled stones and cabochons for over 50 years.

Many of these agates, only an inch or so across, are white or gray-white in color with distinct dark gray starlike dendrites; others are gray in color so the dendrites do not show up as well. The chalcedony is good quality and virtually flawless. If the ground color is milky and the dendrites well centered, cabochons are very attractive. When tumbled, the agates are smooth enough when found to be tossed into the fine grind.

Plume Agate

Plume agate is sometimes grouped with dendritic or moss agate, and sometimes they do overlap, but the best plume agate is quite distinctive and deserves a special classification. The patterns in plume agate are usually not an overall pattern, but confined to one area, and perhaps to only one or two plumes. The plume growths are like graceful and fluffy ostrich feathers, or delicate newly emerging ferns, or Oriental floral arrangements.

A typical plume is a well-proportioned growth of microscopic crystals of a mineral such as pyrolusite or goethite enclosed in translucent chalcedony. The edges and tops of the crystal growth are flatter and thinner than the center of the growth, giving form and texture to the plume and varying the color.

The plume itself may be translucent or opaque or it may have a submetallic luster. The colors may be black, white, red, pink, yellow, orange, blue-gray, gray-green, or brown. Plumes are neatly framed by halos of clear or blue-white chalcedony. Usually the plume will be a dramatic contrast with the clear or milky groundmass, but the white on white plume is an exception.

Nebraska geologist Roger Pabian believes that in plume agate the plume formed first and in moss or dendritic agate the agate was first. There are several other theories. Plume agate is found in place in igneous formations, in veins in metamorphic rock, and in stream deposits .

Among the most exotic cabochon materials, high-quality plume agate cabochons bring premium prices. Colorful polished nodules or slabs may sell for several hundred dollars. One of the choice cabochon materials for the lapidary, plume agate cabochons are the most dramatic when the template is used with a flair, such as centering the best plume so that it is entirely outlined by clear chalcedony. The center of the plume should be near the center of the dome of the cabochon. The plume pattern itself should be left with a covering of chalcedony. The agate is kept cool and polished with tin oxide on felt.

Pabian tumbles the skin off of plume nodules first and then cuts the plume in the long direction. He blocks the end pieces in plaster to get all the possible plumes from each good agate. Lapidaries may prefer to buy slabs than trust their luck with rough nodules.

Bouquet Agate

Southwest Texas is blessed with a marvelous variety of agates, many of them fitting in the plume category. A type of plume agate found near Marfa is called bouquet agate. Pink, red, and yellow flowerlike growths, complete with leaves and stems, occur in high-grade chalcedony. A variation has white fluffy flowers similar to chrysanthemums in blue chalcedony. The reverse is also found: blue flowers in white chalcedony. This has been called *bluebonnet agate* for the Texas state flower. Undercutting could be a problem with some plume. A layer of translucent chalcedony should be left over the plume or floral growths.

Carey Plume

Carey plume is a splendid Oregon agate found near Prineville. The fiery red plumes often appear blurred, as if an attempt had been made to erase them. They have distinct dark reddish brown dendritic tips of more concentrated mineral, iron, or manganese, which must also be the source of the red color. The agate is recognizable at a glance. Collected for many years, it is often used for jewelry.

Graveyard Plume

Idaho/Oregon Graveyard Point plume is an old favorite of lapidaries in the United States. Exceptional plumes are snowy white against colorless or milky chalcedony. The plumes and the chalcedony may have tints of red or orange too. Yellow and golden-colored plumes also occur in this seam agate, with the plumes perpendicular to the edges of the seam. Milky or off-white chalcedony, with plumes of blue and orange, is considered best. Doublets have been made of thin domes of plume over a brightly colored material such as chrysoprase or red jasper.

Nova Scotia Plume

Plume and moss agate are found in the extensive basalts of Nova Scotia. Locations on some of the bays and coves yield an endless supply of agates because of marine erosion.

The plume agates occur over a wide area but are not predominant in any one place. The plumes are red, yellow, green, and brown and rarely bright green tipped with pink. The chalcedony is gray or white or nearly colorless and sometimes almost opaque.

Priday Plume

A superb plume agate is found in some of the thundereggs from the old Priday beds in Oregon. Many kinds of agates occur here, but excellent plume is scarce. The best examples look like miniature floral arrangements of summery tints of yellow, pink, or blue surrounded by pure chalcedony.

Priday plume makes cabochons that appear like bouquets under glass. Slabs of plume with well-centered designs make handsome cabinet specimens. Colorful Priday plume is among the most beautiful and most expensive of agates. It is superb for jewelry or for exhibits of polished specimens and an impressive addition to collections. Slabs or preforms may be a better buy than rough.

Woodward Ranch Plume

A west Texas agate from the Woodward Ranch near Alpine has striking black and red plumes. Beautiful and complicated plumes are found in rough biscuit-shaped nodules in the local igneous rock. The fancy plumes lie parallel to the flat face of the biscuit or to the top of the biscuit and are often very close to the surface. The nodules are too rough and irregular to see the plume before cutting, and of course not every nodule has a brilliant plume. The agates should be cut just like cutting the top off a biscuit.

In addition to the spectacular black and red plume, other plume and dendritic agates abound, among them patterns in

yellow, orange, coral, and brown. Most of the plume-bearing nodules are 3–4 inches long (7.62–10.16 cm), but occasionally a huge agate is found in the 50-pound range.

Sagenitic Agate

Some agates, besides being colored or patterned by small amounts of iron, manganese, chlorite, or other mineral, contain acicular or needlelike inclusions, or fine crystals of various minerals, all of which are usually called sagenite or sagenitic agate. Although the word sagenite often refers to needlelike rutile crystals, it can also mean inclusions of tourmaline, hornblende, actinolite, chlorite, marcasite, goethite, pyrite, or any of several zeolites.

Sometimes finer than hair, needles resemble broad and shining straws in other examples. The colors of the included needles may be golden yellow, red, red-orange, black, red-brown, white, dark blue, and green. The groundmass of sagenitic agates is usually colorless, pale gray, blue gray, or white. Good sagenite agate is highly translucent. The sagenite is often near the outer surface of one portion of the agate, although it is sometimes distributed all around the outer perimeter or even throughout the agate. The sagenite is usually a single mineral and one color in an individual agate. There is often a halo effect separating the sagenitic portion of the agate from the rest of the agate, which may have an altogether different color and pattern.

A set of templates will help cutters find unique patterns for cabochons. Sagenite must first be oriented so that the best pattern is surrounded by and covered with enough chalcedony to be stable. Next, undercutting may be a problem. Extra wet sanding with fine silicon carbide or diamond is recommended. If the needle tips

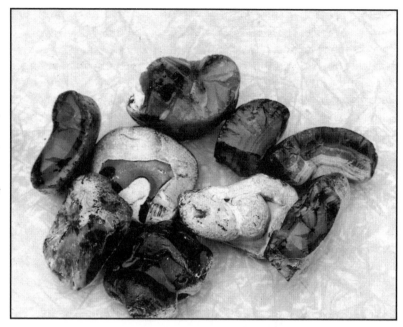

Montana's moss agates have been the choice material for many novice lapidaries. Photo by Larry Field. Courtesy of Lapidary Journal.

have left pits, the stone is cleaned thoroughly and the pits are filled with Opticon and repolished after curing. Some type of sagenite can usually be located.

Mexican Sagenitic Agate

Northern Mexico has often produced large quantities of sagenite. Some of the states are Chihuahua, Sonora, and Coahuila. The vast agate deposits near Rodeo, Durango, also have fine specimens of sagenite. Much of the Mexican sagenite is a black or brown edging on banded agate nodules, but some of it is vein agate patterned all over with fine, medium, or coarse needles of red, yellow, gold, or gray-blue.

Nipomo Agate

Nipomo, California, was once a prime site for marvelous sagenite agate. Needle-like sprays of black and brown crystals occur in clear or off-white agate, patterned in yellow, peach, red, and blue, with metallic marcasite adding to the glamour. Sometimes called bean field

agates for the location where they were found, the memorable sagenite was once abundant near San Luis Obispo. Moss patterns and bright fortifications often accompanied the luxurious sagenitic sprays. The agate was used for jewelry and for displays, but is now a collector's rarity. Inclusions may cause undercutting unless the agate is worked wet with fine grits.

Oregon Sagenite

Several localities in Oregon also have wonderful sagenite. Among these are beach agates from Yachats, Lincoln County, and some nodules at Agate Flat or Agate Desert. Beach agates from Lane and Curry counties often have sagenitic patterns. Sagenite borders can be found on banded agates. Oregon lapidaries exhibit extraordinary sagenitic specimens with sharply contrasting needles in translucent pale chalcedony.

Pom Pom and Thistle Agate

Spheres of radiating crystals decorate the exotic pom pom agate of Needle Peak,

Texas. The gala pom poms are usually golden yellow and the rest of the agate may be finely banded iris. A variation is the delicate wispy thistle agate. Sprays of exceedingly fine blue-gray needles resemble thistle blossoms. Several colors of sagenite have been found in the alluvial deposits of this semidesert area.

Most of the pom pom and thistle agates are small, usually highlighted by one outstanding pattern. These are rarely marketed.

Thundereggs

There is some confusion about geodes and thundereggs. They are not the same thing. Thundereggs are a special kind of spherical agate-filled nodule that occurs in the perlite or decomposed perlite beds of many of the western states. A popular theory is that the outer part of the thunderegg is siliceous ash that shrunk and broke apart while solidifying, leaving a more or less star-shaped or butterfly-shaped cavity which was then filled by subsequent silica gel and magmatic waters.

The "eggs" are entirely silicified, but the broken irregular outer portion is opaque and unpatterned, while the agate interior is translucent and may have banding or plume patterns. In color the opaque part matches the surrounding rock, while the agate center is usually colorless or white with pastel or bright patterns. The silicified rhyolite shell may take up half of the nodule. This silicified shell may be brown, gray, ivory, taupe, or bluish or yellowish.

Dr. Dave Mustart of San Francisco State University has investigated many thundereggs and decided that they are expanded and devitrified spherulites that occur in perlite, an obsidian with a high water content. He points out that they seem to be closely related to lithophysae,

hollow bubblelike spherulites with a concentric structure which occurs in certain obsidians and rhyolites.

Benjamin Shaub believes the siliceous nodules were formed directly from silica-rich magmas releasing nuggets of colloidal silica, which formed spheres that grew until the surrounding rhyolite solidified. The pure colloidal silica moved to the center, while bits of rhyolite and iron minerals mixed with the exterior.

The "eggs" are usually covered with protuberances on the exterior instead of being regularly shaped, but with rough surfaces as in the case of agate nodules in volcanic cavities. Varying greatly in size, thundereggs up to 6 feet (182 cm) in diameter have been found. Many specimens have been found of several eggs grown together, each with its distinct agate interior. The average size of thundereggs differs from one bed to another, but most are not under 2 inches or over 6 inches (5.08 or 15.24 cm) in diameter.

In each specific area the eggs tend to be very similar in both the starlike, butterfly-like, or oak-leaf–like enclosing pattern and the agate-filled interior. As in most gem material locations, the finest examples are rare. One has to cut dozens of Priday eggs before finding an exotic bouquet of pink and yellow flowers.

In many of the best agate-filled eggs the first agate band in the angular outline of the filling is of high-quality, translucent, bluish chalcedony, like an irregular halo around the rest of the agate. Thunderegg patterns include colorful plumes, moss, and bands. Jasper and opal are also found in thundereggs.

In some cases, such as the Butte Creek eggs, which have a creamy yellow and red exterior layer, the rhyolite makes more interesting cabochons than the agate. The patterns are sometimes brecciated and sometimes scenic. Lapidaries often cut cabochons that show both the exterior layer of the thunderegg and the filling. Various types of eggs can be bought in Oregon and other Western states, and many lapidaries dig their own.

California Thundereggs

The Chocolate Mountains of Imperial County, California, have produced banded agate–filled thundereggs, some of them onyx banded and some puzzling ones with the bands diverging at several angles.

Some exceptional thundereggs were once found in San Bernadino County northeast of Granite Wells at Lead Pipe Springs. With a true blue chalcedony filling, the eggs are sometimes enhanced by sagenite. This once productive area is now within the boundary of a military reservation, so these thundereggs are collectors' items from the past. They were usually sawed in half and lapped as specimens for display. Several other California localities have yielded showy eggs which are usually cut and lapped as display specimens.

Idaho Thundereggs

Thundereggs occur in several places in Idaho. One of the principal areas is Poison Creek, in western Owyhee County near the Oregon border. Extremely large thundereggs have been found in rugged canyons of the region. Succor Creek Canyon has thundereggs which may be filled with blue common opal or rarely precious opal.

Another location is south of Twin Falls near the Nevada border. Eggs of all sizes have been found here, mostly filled with fine agate and occasionally jasper. Others, almost hollow, may contain calcite or zeolite crystals.

Nevada Thundereggs

Humboldt County, Nevada, has a thunderegg location at Coyote Springs. Blue opal is the filling of some of these eggs. Another Nevada location is in Nye County where the thunderegg fillings are attractive red, orange, brown, or green moss agate. Thundereggs have also been found in the Trinity Range near Lovelock in Pershing County .

New Mexico Thundereggs

Large deposits of thundereggs are south of Deming, New Mexico. Mostly brown and round with rough surfaces, the agate interiors are often colorful fortification agate with tints and shades of red, orange, purple, and yellow, plus black, white, and neutrals.

The eggs are usually about 4–6 inches (10.16–15.24 cm) in diameter, but some are as large as one foot in diameter. Occasionally there are hollow centers that may be lined with small or drusy amethyst crystals.

Some of the thundereggs do not contain agate but have quartz crystals or jaspery rhyolite. The agate centers are sometimes straight banded onyx agate, and at other times mottled agate, often called cloud agate. These thundereggs are usually halved and polished for display, although some of the agate centers have been used for cabochons and jewelry.

Oregon Thundereggs

There are dozens of varieties of thunderegg in Oregon, usually named for the location of the particular bed, but trade names are also used since several kinds of eggs may occur at one area.

Eggs from the *Ochoco* beds sometimes have red agate. Others from the region have a greenish exterior and have moss agate fillings. *Succor Creek* eggs have a gray-brown exterior and are filled with quartz or chalcedony in pale colors, the best of which is pink. The area is also well known for agate nodules and seam agate.

Thundereggs from the *Pony Creek* dig have several variations. The *Priday surprise* eggs have blue banded or moss agate fillings and occasionally plume. They are often geodes. The *Friend* eggs have colorless and white dendritic agate similar to Montana moss agate. The *Smallwood* eggs have solid black fillings, sometimes with botryoidal centers.

Larry Kribs, collector, miner, and dealer from Bend, Oregon, has thundereggs from more than 50 beds. He says there are 30 beds near Madras, 20 in the Ochocos, 11 at Buchanan, 10 or more at Succor Creek, and also at Steens Mountain, 2 to 3 at Lakeview, 4 at Dry Creek, 3 at Crowley, 2 at Maupin, and 1 at Ironside.

Kribs says trace amounts of gold have been found at all four of his mines. He points out that Oregon geologist Gary Gray considers thundereggs a leading indicator of epithermal gold. Kribs feels that the Crowley beds are among the most interesting because they are filled with blue opal, sometimes with play of color. Oregon thundereggs are of great interest to specimen collectors, to students of quartz family occurrences, and to lapidaries. Lapidaries can only guess what is inside of a thunderegg, so dozens are sawed in half in search of an exquisite pattern and color.

Australian Thundereggs

An Australian location for thundereggs is in Queensland near the village of Tamborine south of Brisbane. The eggs are mostly round and range in size from 4 to 8 inches (10.16 to 20.32 cm) on the average. Colors are due to traces of iron oxide. Star-shaped patterns of silicified rhyolite similar to those of Oregon are common. Fillings include bands, moss, and cloud agate and crystals. A similar locality is north of Brisbane near Yandina.

British Columbia, Canada, Thundereggs

A large deposit of thundereggs was discovered in a remote area of British Columbia west of the Fraser River at Black Dome Mountain, an extinct volcano. Thousands of the eggs were cut by Cana-

dian and Northwestern U.S. lapidaries in the 1960s, revealing banded and fortification patterns, straight and concentric banding, and solid colors in tones of orange, amber, and green. Some had crystal centers and clear chalcedony.

COLORED CHALCEDONY

The next group of cryptocrystalline quartzes are mostly colored but not highly patterned silica materials, often referred to as chalcedony. Physically and chemically they are like agate, except that they usually lack the patterns of agate. The colors show variations, for example, blue chalcedony may have light and dark, bright and muted areas, but not in distinct bands, dendrites, or other contrasting patterns.

Colored chalcedony is found in the same types of deposits as agate, and both may be in the same deposit. Many occurrences of colored chalcedony are in veins rather than nodules. At times the surface material is a different color than the mined material. Chalcedony is often intermixed with chert, jasper, and other quartzes and may form coatings on other minerals.

Colorless and unpatterned chalcedony is often dyed to resemble chrysoprase, gem chrysocolla, blue chalcedony, or other variations. Jewelers' black onyx is dyed chalcedony. Among the many elements and minerals which add color and pattern to chalcedony are copper, chlorite, chrysocolla, goethite, hematite, nickel, chromium, manganese, rutile, titanium, malachite, azurite, lazulite, realgar, actinolite, chalcotrichite, cinnabar, psilomelane, and marcasite.

All of the variations of chalcedony have good hardness and toughness and are excellent lapidary materials, widely used since ancient times.

Black Chalcedony

Many writers and jewelers claim that there is no natural black chalcedony because the commercial black chalcedony called black onyx is all dyed. Nevertheless, black chalcedony does exist in numerous places, although most of it lacks some jewelry qualification. For instance, the amount in a given area is not great enough, or the pieces are too small, or the color is not uniform for commercial operations. Amateur lapidaries collect and use natural black chalcedony for cabochons, jewelry, intarsias and mosaics, small carvings, and polished display nodules and slabs.

Cuttable black chalcedony is dense black but translucent when held toward a light. Black chalcedony may be interspersed with some clear or white bands or marbling. It is found as veins or nodules and in alluvial gravels. The color may be due to finely distributed manganese or carbon, or irradiation.

Black chalcedony is found near Scenic and Interior, South Dakota. In the Scenic area black nodules weather out of clay banks, and in the Interior location veins of thick black and colorless chalcedony are found on the surface and sticking out of the ground as part of wide flat sheets.

Water-worn pieces of black chalcedony are found in the agate fields of Montana near the Yellowstone River and in Wyoming near the Sweetwater River. Occasional nodules of black chalcedony are found in the Rio Grande gravels of Hidalgo and Starr counties in Texas. Some of the chalcedony pseudomorphs after coral from Tampa Bay, Florida, are botryoidal black chalcedony. A lot of petrified wood in the West is replaced by black chalcedony. Other locations are southern California, Oregon, New Mexico, and Utah.

Black chalcedony has also been found in Mexico, Uruguay, and Brazil. Natural black chalcedony seldom furnishes material for flawless cabochons larger than 30 x 40 mm. High-quality material is polished with ease using tin oxide on leather.

Blue Chalcedony

Many chalcedonies are called blue, but most of these are more gray than blue. The few that are true tints or shades of blue are beautiful lapidary materials, and useful for jewelry, cameos, carvings, intarsias, and other lapidary work.

A large deposit of blue chalcedony is in Fog Basin on the Pine Ridge Indian Reservation of western South Dakota. The chalcedony occurs in sedimentary clays in veins and broken pieces in washes. The blue color varies from baby blue to a slightly muted sky blue. Some pieces are sugary and thin, but the good ones are waxy with a subconchoidal fracture, solid, and uniform and about ½–¾ inches (1.27–1.90 cm) in thickness. Upper and lower surfaces straight and parallel, but rough in texture. Most of the pieces which have been broken by weather conditions are about palm size or less. Occasional pieces have a sandwichlike effect with a strip of white, or rarely pink, between the two broad bands of blue.

Another American location for blue chalcedony is near Crawford, Nebraska, where blue chalcedony and blue and white, black, or colorless banded chalcedony occurs north of the city near Highway 2. Large pieces up to 100 pounds were found. The blue is of medium intensity with darker spots and lighter sky blue areas. The material was so unusual and attractive it was named the official state gem.

A location near Sweet Home, Oregon, is the site of the famous *Holley Blue* agate that has been popular for about 40 years.

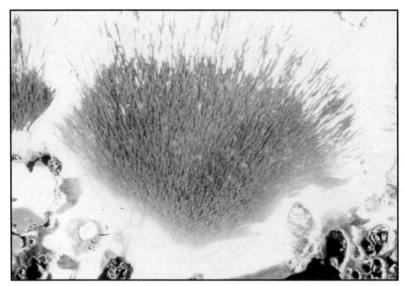

Sagenitic agates have inclusions of crystals of other minerals.

Superb robin's-egg blue chalcedony is found near Ellensburg, Washington. The true blue nodules weather out of the basalt in the Wenatchee National Forest.

A deposit of blue chalcedony near Deer Lodge, Montana, has been named *Glory Blue*. It is a vein deposit with seams up to several inches thick in rhyolite. The best color, according to mine operators Paul and Bette Peterson, is heavily coated with iron oxide and pyrite. Translucent or almost opaque, the chalcedony is a soft robin's-egg blue or a deeper blue with a hint of lavender. Large cabochons may be cut and polished with no trouble.

Other blue chalcedonies come from Lead Pipe Springs, California, the Florida Mountains of New Mexico, and Fiddler Canyon, Utah. Probably the best blue chalcedony was the lovely blue, hard, compact material that came from Hotchfield, Namibia, about 30 years ago, and is still occasionally seen.

Chalcedony can be blue in color from traces of iron, titanium, manganese, or copper. Apparently irradiation has some effect on the color also, as the chalcedony on the surface of the South Dakota deposits has a much superior color to that dug up from buried sections of the veins. The good blue chalcedonies are uncommon and fine lapidary materials. They have been used for cameos, Fabergé-style flowers, eggs, spheres, cabochons for jewelry and beads.

Carnelian

Carnelian, because of its warm bright colors, has been one of the most popular chalcedony gems for many centuries and in many cultures. It has been a favorite lapidary material in China, Italy, Greece, Scotland, Russia, France, and the United States. India has provided jewelry-grade carnelian since 500 B.C.. Most museums have magnificent works of art in carnelian, including Fabergé flowers, Oriental carvings, gem Ming trees, snuff bottles, Japanese netsuke, and Scottish jewelry.

Varying from light peach to vivid orange to red-orange and brownish red, carnelian is seldom a true red. Heat treating produces the brightest hues. Nodules found on the surface with red exteriors are often brownish inside.

Carnelian is found as nodules, crusts, geodes, and seams in igneous, metamorphic, and sedimentary rock. It is a low-temperature deposit, fibrous, translucent, and pigmented by iron oxide. Fossils or minerals are sometimes replaced by carnelian.

Among the carnelian localities in the United States are Cady Mountains, California; Lebanon, Oregon; Chehalis, Washington; Deming, New Mexico; Clifton, Arizona; Custer County, South Dakota; Crawford, Nebraska; Van Horn, Texas; Morris County, New Jersey; and Bedford County, Tennessee. Other locations are Mexico, Brazil, Uruguay, India, and Australia.

Carnelian is hard and tough, translucent, colorful, and durable, altogether an excellent lapidary material, suitable for fine carvings and designer jewelry. It is used for beads, pendants, spheres, bowls, knife handles, clocks, and almost anything else a lapidary can think of. What's more, it is easy to work by silicon carbide or diamond methods. The final glossy polish on carnelian can be achieved with tin oxide or cerium oxide on leather. Lapidaries can usually get good carnelian.

Chrome Chalcedony

An attractive bright green chalcedony colored by chromium instead of nickel, which colors chrysoprase, was discovered in the 1960s in what was then Rhodesia. It is translucent and compact with fairly even color distribution.

Found in a long narrow vein at an 8-foot depth, the occurrence is in altered serpentine in the Great Dike of Zimbabwe. Most of the cutting material is less than 2 inches (5.08 cm) in width. (Similar material has been reported from Russia.)

Named *mtorolite* for the location of Mtoroshanga, the material is sometimes mottled with white. Mossy-appearing patches occur in some areas in the rich green groundmass. Overall the color is not quite as intense as the best chrysoprase. A considerable amount of the material was shipped to Idar-Oberstein where it was cut into a variety of jewelry stones, including cameos. Cutting techniques are the same as for the other colored chalcedony. Dealers of fine materials sometimes have a little chrome chalcedony for sale.

Chrysocolla (Gem Chrysocolla, Chrysocolla Chalcedony)

One of the most sensational of all the chalcedonies is that which is colored a vibrant electric blue, greenish blue, or blue-green by the copper mineral chrysocolla. It is also a gem material so little known that sometimes even experienced lapidaries think it is an opaque mixture of blue and green copper minerals which includes some of the soft and crumbly mineral chrysocolla with fibrous malachite and other calcium carbonates.

Gem chrysocolla, or chrysocolla in chalcedony or quartz, is translucent high-quality cryptocrystalline or sometimes crystalline quartz. It has been called gem silica, which seems to be a meaningless name, since so many gemstones are silica. There is no consensus about what to call this material, but many opt for the misnomer "chrysocolla."

The gem-quality material is fine grained, uniform, compact, and quite evenly colored with lovely, intense blue. In appearance it is very similar to chrysoprase, which is colored green by nickel, except that copper has produced blue. Sometimes gem chrysocolla is similar to the best turquoise in color, but being harder, more translucent, and less porous than turquoise, as well as rarer, it is a better gem material.

Chrysocolla chalcedony occurs in the oxidized layers of copper mines in veins, often with other quartz. The combination of this blue gem material covered with sparkling drusy quartz makes a unique cutting material used for creative jewelry in the Southwest. Botryoidal chrysocolla with a vitreous or waxy luster is also used uncut for designer jewelry.

Occasional inclusions are green malachite, dark blue azurite, black tenorite, or red cuprite or chalcotrichite. Chrysocolla plumes in translucent chalcedony are exotic and rare.

One of the top locations in the world for gem chrysocolla is Arizona. Gila County produced bright, almost transparent chalcedony. Other locations are Bagdad, Bisbee, and Morencei. Much of the high-grade material was sent to China, Hong Kong, and Idar-Oberstein for cutting, where it has been made into beads, pendants, cameos, rings, bowls, spheres, eggs, carvings, art objects, and cabochons.

Exceptional examples of Arizona gem chrysocolla may also have sagenite or dendrites. Lapidary expert Martin Koning of Morristown, Arizona, had rare and magnificent large cabochons of intense translucent blue material with vivid inclusions of red, black, or green chalcotrichite, tenorite, or malachite. The Sonora Desert Museum of Tucson, Arizona, displays a 68-carat cabochon of highest-grade gem chrysocolla cut by Koning.

Excellent gem chrysocolla was found in the copper mines of Zacatecas, Mexico, 15 to 20 years ago. It is crystalline quartz colored by copper instead of chalcedony. The color is a little lighter than the deepest blue from Arizona, but the material has far fewer inclusions, and is harder and more translucent than most of the Arizona material. Some chrysocolla chalcedony is said to fade, but the material from Zacatecas is stable. Chrysocolla chalcedony from another Mexican location is now available.

Other worldwide locations are limited, but some fine material has come from Russia, Zaire, and Australia. Recently some showy gem chrysocolla with chalcotrichite and malachite has come from Peru.

Chrysocolla is cut and polished in the same manner as other cryptocrystalline quartz. Keep it cool as it is mildly heat sensitive. Tin oxide, cerium oxide, or Linde A on felt or leather will bring a good polish. Diamond is a good choice. Top chrysocolla is not easy to locate.

Chrysoprase

Chrysoprase is one of the most beautiful of all quartz gems and indeed there are few gems that have a more desirable color. Discovered in Silesia (Poland) in the eighteenth century, the microcrystalline gem material is quartz colored green by nickel. Later it was suggested the color came from the nickel clay mineral pimelite, a term which is seldom used. It forms a series with kerolite. Instead of a fibrous structure typical of chalcedony, chrysoprase is composed of tiny spherules similar to the structure of precious opal. Chrysoprase was used in classic times for cameos.

A remarkable discovery of high-quality chrysoprase was made in Queensland, Australia, in 1964. Chrysoprase, associated with nickel-bearing serpentine, was found in seams and nodules. The veins were sometimes up to 8 inches (20.32 cm) thick, but most of the material is between 2 and 4 inches (5.08 and 10.16 cm) thick. The color varies from a bright apple green, resembling fine jade, to a lovely pastel tint of true green to yellowish green. Most pieces are coated with white altered quartz. The host rock covers a wide area near Marlborough Creek.

Tons of the material were exported to gem cutting centers such as Idar-Ober-

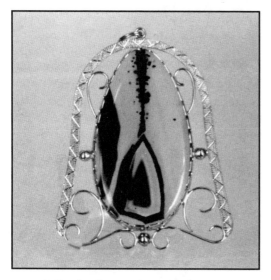

People often see pictures in agate. Roland Rasmussen saw a lute in this carefully cut cabochon.

stein, Hong Kong, and China, where it was processed for the market as cabochons, carvings, snuff bottles, beads, cameos, bowls, and other exquisite lapidary items. Rough material was also marketed in the United States.

Chrysoprase has also been found in Western Australia near Kalgoorlie and Kookynie. Veins and nodules of various tints of green, including apple green, occur in fields with jasper and other quartz minerals, and also common opal. Jowetts Well, Comet Vale, and Riverina are three locations.

In the late nineteenth century a seam of high-quality chrysoprase was discovered near Visalia, California. Translucent green material of apple-green color and nearly opaque lighter green veins was found associated with serpentine. There was active mining for about 30 years. Two other California locations are near Lindsay and Porterville, both in Tulare County, south of Visalia .

Chrysoprase from the state of Goias, Brazil, is darker and more opaque than the best of the Australia and California occurrences. A small amount of chrysoprase was mined in Russia and occasional occurrences have been noted in South Africa.

It has been said that chrysoprase fades, but there is little evidence of that in examples of Australian material that were mined 30 years ago. Colorless chalcedony is often dyed to imitate chrysoprase .

Chrysoprase is popular for jewelry and carvings. The translucency and the marvelous green color recommend it for many lapidary uses. Although it may be slightly more heat sensitive than other fine-grained quartzes, it is cut with ease and polished with chrome oxide. Fine chrysoprase is on the market occasionally.

Damsonite

A slightly grayed rose-violet variation of chalcedony was discovered in Arizona in 1980. Historians believe the material may have been mined by the Indians 200 years ago or more. The fine-grained, compact, almost opaque material has been mined and marketed under the trade name Damsonite. A small percentage of the deposit is considerably closer to jasper than chalcedony. The amethystine colors are from traces of manganese and iron. The developer, Dan Donaldson, had the material analyzed by the Colorado School of Mines, the University of Arizona, and tested by GIA. The material is found with other chalcedony varieties in the Burro Creek area north of Bagdad, and has evidently been collected by others who do not know it by that name. Similar material is sold as Royal plum.

Dendritic patterns have been noted in some of the material. Damsonite is tough and about 7 in hardness. The material was deposited at low temperatures in a hot springs area, so many pieces are crusted with snowy white.

Damsonite achieves a prepolish with a well-worn 400 silicon carbide belt and can be finished with the lapidary's choice of polish compound. It is a good material for jewelry, and the supply seems to be steady.

Mojave Blue

New on the market in the late 1980s is a gem-quality chalcedony from Kern County, California, called Mojave Blue. It is adularescent and semitranslucent to semi-transparent with colors of pastel baby blue, ice blue, powder blue, sky blue, and light violet-blue. The adularescence is a result of finely disseminated fibrous inclusions.

When polished, the cabochons resemble moonstone. Many lapidaries were introduced to Mojave Blue at a recent Tucson show where the color and chatoyancy attracted much attention.

The material occurs in basalt as a replacement after calcite, in clays following fracture of the basalt sheeting. Most rough material weighs only an ounce or less, so resulting cabochons are usually not large. This is a rare one-locality occurrence. Mine developer Bill Nicks of Woody, California, R & B Gems, has cut some remarkably clear cat's-eye cabochons from this material. Nicks says the stone is in demand by cutters of phenomenal gems. A limited amount of material is available. Milky rough makes the most chatoyant cabochons.

Myrickite

So bright that it looks like a modern neon dye, Myrickite is the most vivid chalcedony. The flame red-orange color comes from the mercury mineral, cinnabar. The original discovery, near Lead Pipe Springs, California, had red spots of cinnabar in clear chalcedony; however, a more recent discovery in a Homestake Mine in northern California was almost solid red-orange, an incredibly intense color for high-grade translucent chalcedony. Marketed as cut stones in Tucson by Roberts Minerals, the cabochons were immediately snapped up for fine jewelry. Idaho, Washington, Oregon, and Nevada have reported small amounts of myrickite.

An opal variation of this cinnabar-colored silica was found near Elko, Nevada, in the 1950s. While it was beautiful for specimens, it was too brittle and fragile to be cut for jewelry. In this case the fiery red color was in streaks on an off-white groundmass. Myrickite would be better known and rated more highly if only there were more of it.

Pink Chalcedony

True pink chalcedony may be the rarest color of this cryptocrystalline quartz group. Other pinks are also rare—peach pink, baby pink, or lavender or lilac pink, referred to as pinkish purple or purplish pink. Pink and lilac-colored chalcedony has been found in the Turtle Mountains of California. Peach-pink chalcedony was found near Nipomo. Pale pink and lavender desert roses have occasionally been found near Wickenburg, Arizona, and pink chalcedony nodules are found near Duncan and Wikieup, Arizona. Impure pink chalcedony from Burro Creek is called pastelite.

South Dakota has veins of layered chalcedony in Jackson and Pennington counties, some of which is a pink layer sandwiched between two blue or white layers, or two pink layers with a white center. The center layer of these sandwich chalcedonies is often sugary in texture, so only small cabochons of solid pink material have been cut.

A large deposit of lovely pink agate and jasper was discovered between Perkinsville and Jerome, Arizona, in the early 1940s. It is now said this discovery may have been bustamite. The pink material is translucent to almost opaque with patterns confined only to light mottling and streaking of color variations. The material is excellent for cabochons.

Probably the outstanding examples of pink chalcedony in the United States are the pink limb casts of Jackpot, Nevada. They are translucent, sometimes dendritic, and have exquisite delicate pinks. Pastel pink limb casts are also found near Prineville, Oregon. This is also an excellent quality of chalcedony and is sometimes further enhanced by lacy black dendrites. Some Oregon beach stones are also pink chalcedony.

Prase and Plasma

Prase is a green chalcedony colored by fibrous hornblende and chlorite. Usually translucent, some of it is so heavily included with fibers that it is almost opaque. The green is not a saturated color like chrysoprase, but a duller color sometimes called leek green.

Nodules or small veins in some varied chalcedony deposits have been called prase. They have been found in Washington, in Montana, in the iron ranges of Minnesota, in upper Michigan, in the Rio Grande River gravels, and in Vermont. The agate fields of Durango, Mexico, have prase, as do Uruguay, South Africa, and Australia. It can be handled in the same way as carnelian or sard.

Plasma is a microfibrous chalcedony which occurs in several shades of green, mostly rather dark or muted, although it sometimes verges on apple green. The color is said to be from dense needles of actinolite, but authorities disagree on this. Its inclusions and structure render it almost opaque, but it has the other qualities needed for good chalcedony: hardness, toughness, uniform structure, and polishability. Some older locations are Egypt, Madagascar, and India, and in the United States, Oregon, Washington, and Montana. However, locations are widely scattered with only minor occurrences in any locality.

Vibrant green plasma sometimes bordering on blue-green occurs in an old cinnabar mine in the Clear Creek area of California. The green plasma is rarely streaked with the intense red of cinnabar, making a contrasting material for superb cabochons.

Plasma and prase can be used for jewelry, spheres, mosaics, intarsias, carvings, and other projects. Currently the names seem interchangeable since few cutters bother to have cryptocrystalline quartz analyzed before cutting. In fact, most cutters classify both as green agate or green chalcedony.

Psilomelane Chalcedony

Dense black with an almost metallic luster and complicated malachitelike patterns, psilomelane, as it was called in the late 1950s and early 1960s, was examined by John Sinkankas and found to be chalcedony probably colored by the manganese mineral psilomelane.

There were large quantities on the market—rough, slabbed, and tumbled. The exact location was never confirmed, but it is thought the psilomelane chalcedony came from Durango.

Psilomelane is now a group name according to the International Commission on New Minerals and Mineral Names, and the accepted species name is

Green plasma was carved finto a realistic oak leaf by Donald Diller. Common flint was used for this acorn.

romanechite. It occurs as a secondary mineral by the weathering, in this case, of manganese in silica deposits.

This particular occurrence from Mexico was botryoidal and stalactitic. The material was rather dirty to work with, but was made into highly polished cabochons. It was marketed as Crown of Silver, and is now difficult to find.

Sard

Sard is virtually the same as carnelian except that the colors are less vivid, tending more to yellow and browns rather than oranges and reds, but sometimes the difference is in the eye of the beholder. Because sard contains trace amounts of iron minerals, it can be heat treated to richer colors the same as carnelian.

Sard is found in volcanic and metamorphic deposits and in alluvial gravels with chalcedony of other colors. It is found in California, New Mexico, Colorado, Wyoming, South Dakota, Texas, Brazil, and Australia, among other places. As a brownish material, its best use is for needed color areas in intarsia, mosaic, or inlay.

Sardonyx is reddish brown and banded so it is classed with agates. The red and white or cream layered material is popular for cameos and beads. Sard is quite common, but good sardonyx is not.

GEODES

Geodes are natural inorganic objects, most often chalcedony, which are or have been hollow. Geodes were first defined as rounded hollow stones, until odd shapes like the agatized coral geodes of Florida and the polyhedroids of Brazil became better known.

Geodes can occur in igneous, metamorphic, or sedimentary rock. The interior may be lined with botryoidal chalcedony or with crystals, usually quartz, pointing inward toward the center. Some of the geodes in many deposits such as the Warsaw formation of Iowa are solidly filled in with quartz. There is a possibility of many mineral inclusions in geodes, but few are of lapidary quality. The main exception is the amethyst geodes of Brazil and Uruguay, although many of these are used as specimens.

In addition to Florida, Iowa, and Brazil, other well-known geode localities are in California, Arizona, New Mexico, Utah, Missouri, Illinois, Indiana, Kentucky, Tennessee, Mexico, England, Czechoslovakia, Zimbabwe, and Australia. Geodes are often cut in half and lapped for display.

Bolinos Oil Agates

Strange agates indeed are these California beach agates that may be survivors of a prehistoric oil spill. Highly translucent to almost transparent, these agate nodules are dug from the sands of the Pacific by eager collectors. The black inclusions are a tarry substance.

Oil-filled quartz geodes are found in Illinois. Many agates and geodes are water filled, but those with considerable bitumen are unusual. Queensland, Australia, also reports oil-filled nodules. Careful choices have been polished as curiosities.

Coconut Geodes

These Chihuahua, Mexico, geodes from Ejido Esperanza are popular cabinet specimens when cut and polished by lapidaries. Some have a thick banded chalcedony shell, but the agate is usually dull or colorless, so the intriguing nodules are kept as specimens. The quartz geodes have other crystals including calcite, pyrolusite, siderite, opal, hematite, goethite, gypsum, or others. Thin-shelled specimens are more exciting. The geodes occur in volcanic tuff.

While colors are drab whites, blacks, grays, and browns, the inclusions are slim plates at odd angles, small spheres, sparkling rosettes, platy crystal growths, botryoidal structures, stalactites, and stalagmites. Interior crystals or structures may have drusy coatings. A portion of the geodes have dark smoky quartz or amethyst crystals as linings.

For lapidaries the thrill has been to accurately judge how to cut the geode in order to get the best-looking miniature cave and to avoid destroying the fascinating inclusions. Tens of thousands of "coconuts" were exported to the United States in the mid-1960s. Albert Zeitner, who cut many of these geodes when he was a gem and mineral dealer, had excellent luck cutting through the flattest area the long way, but avoiding the two or three other flattened eyelike areas. The specimens were Vibrolapped.

Many other varieties of geodes have come from northern Mexico and some of the small ones have been used for jewelry and ornamental items, often using the technique of electroforming and electroplating. There always seems to be some geodes on the market.

Dugway Geodes

Most western collectors have specimens of polished Dugway geodes in their collections. These large and interesting geodes have been dug from near the Dugway Proving Grounds of west central Utah since they were discovered some 50 years ago.

The geodes are mostly spherical. Dug from volcanic soil, many of the natural spheres are rhyolite, but lots of them contain blue and white banded agate or beautiful quartz crystals. The agate is in a layer of concentric bands and the centers are hollow. The crystals of quartz are clear, blue, white, blue-gray, or gray. Botryoidal linings are found in some of the geodes.

These geodes are mainly cut in half by lapidaries and polished for cabinet specimens or competitions.

Enhydros

Enhydros are among the most intriguing of all quartz objects. They are hollow cryptocrystalline and crystalline geodes containing water. The inner cavities are usually lined with quartz crystals while the rest of the geode is usually translucent chalcedony. The enhydros may be rounded nodules, such as those from Brazil, or they may be shaped like bottles or covered vases such as those from Tampa, Florida.

These water-filled agates make interesting specimens when ground and polished close enough to the water in the center that the movement of the water can clearly be seen as the enhydro is handled. The lapidary must work slowly and keep the enhydro cool.

Water-filled geodes form at low temperatures and pressures and contain air spaces as well as water. Most enhydros now on the market are quite small, only a few inches in diameter with less than ½ ounce of water, but some have been known to contain several cups of water.

Most of the enhydros currently are from Brazil or Uruguay. Italy and Australia also have noteworthy examples. In the United States, besides the agatized coral enhydros from Florida, there are enhydros on beach locations in California and Oregon.

Some enhydros found in Oregon and Washington are pseudomorphs of chalcedony after various species of pelecypods or gastropods. Among the most elegant are nautiloid shells replaced by translucent chalcedony. Fossil shells containing water are sometimes polished as specimens to reveal the liquid center.

Agate enhydros were found at Kalama, Washington. Hollow water-filled quartz casts were found in North Carolina. Small polished enhydros such as the finger corals from Florida have been used for conversation piece pendants.

Translucent gray and white agate enhydros from Brazil have sometimes been carved. Hing Wa Lee of California has carved Buddhas from Brazilian enhydros. Enhydros are usually available.

Polyhedroids

A surprising discovery in Brazil in the early 1970s defied the usual conception of agate as more or less rounded nodules possessing concentrically layered, gracefully curved patterns. These strange agates formed perfectly straight sides—hexahedrons, tetragons, pentagons, and other geometric forms. The polyhedroids, as they came to be called, were mined in a remote part of Paraiba, Brazil, for a few years until events closed the mine down.

The colors of the polyhedroids are gray, beige, buff, cream, white, blue-gray, and black. Sizes range from 2 to 10 inches (5.08 to 25.40 cm). The high-grade chalcedony bands follow the outline of the angled exterior in concentric lines sometimes slightly wavy and then again appearing as straight as if drawn with a ruler. Chalcedony bands may alternate with crystalline quartz bands. Most of the centers are hollow with smooth, low-relief botryoidal linings often in black or white. Larger hollows are lined with quartz crystals. Composite specimens were found of several distinct individual shapes cemented together on their similarly angled planes by silica. Thin sheets of silica adhere to many polyhedroid faces. The surfaces of some faces are as flat as if they had been lapped; others have light cross-hatched markings as if they need more sanding. There are 5 to 10 faces on each polyhedroid.

Polyhedroids are found loose in red clay. Several theories have been advanced as to the origin of these unique agates. Due to the lack of planes of symmetry they cannot be pseudomorphs. They may have started as flat thin sheets of silica in mudstone or limestone that allowed for boxwork-like joining, or they may have started as fillings of angle plated quartz.

These geometric geodes have been cut in half and polished with Vibrolaps for fascinating displays. Thin slabs have been made of smaller polyhedroids for sensational natural earrings or abstract pendants. Hollow geometric slabs have also been used as frames for a contrasting material. A few dealers still have a limited supply.

RECOMMENDED READING

See also list for Chapter 4.

Dake, H., *The Agate Book*. Portland, OR: Mineralogist, 1957.

Leiper, H. (Ed.), *Agates of North America*. San Diego: Lapidary Journal, 1966.

Quick, L., *The Book of Agates*. Philadelphia, PA: Chilton, 1963.

Shuab, B., *Origin of Agates, Thundereggs and Other Nodular Structures*. Northhampton, MA: Agate, 1989.

Wolters, S., *The Lake Superior Agate*. Minneapolis, MN: Burgess, 1994.

CHAPTER VI

Quartz: Opaque but Colorful

Chert and flint
- Alibates flint
- Basanite, touchstone, Lydian stone
- Mookaite
- Mozarkite
- Novaculite
- Ohio flint
- Pastelite

Jasper
- Algal jasper
- Apache red jasp-agate
- Biggs jasper
- Black Butte jasper
- Bruneau jasper
- Cave Creek jasper
- Chocolate rock jasper
- Christmas jasper
- Cripple Creek jasper
- Deschutes jasper
- Desert rose jasper
- Disaster Peak or Picture Rock
- Egyptian jasper
- Indian paint rock jasper
- Jasper conglomerate
- Keeganite
- Kindradite
- Lahontarite
- Lavic jasper
- Mohave jasper
- Morrisonite
- Owyhee jasper
- Poppy jasper
- Ribbonstone (ribbon jasper, banded jasper)
- Rocky Butte jasper
- Rose-eye
- Spiderweb jasper
- Spring Mountain jasper
- Stone Canyon jasper
- Stormy skies jasper
- Succor Creek jasper
- Three Finger Butte jasper
- Turkey tail
- Wild horse jasper

CHERT AND FLINT

Clifford Frondel, scientist and author, says there is no sharp distinction mineralogically between flint and chert. Most lapidaries think of chert as lighter in color than flint and occurring in large lenses and huge bedded deposits. Cutting-quality chert is almost opaque, fine grained, compact, and uniform and colored by iron oxides in bright hues of yellow, red, orange, blue, and brown. Such chert resembles jasper so closely that it is often called by that name. When cut and polished it is indistinguishable from jasper. In fact, a fine-grained chert is often superior to some jaspers as a cutting material.

The term flint has mainly been used for the dark siliceous nodules which occur in chalk and limestone. The grain of flint is said to be smaller than that of chert. The darker colors of flint may be due to included carbonaceous matter. Both flint and chert contain marine fossil remains. Both are tough as well as hard. Flint and chert in well-known lapidary quality deposits grade into chalcedony and sometimes common opal. Chert is coarser grained and more porous than flint.

Flint has been commercially important for centuries. Brandon, England, is a town built of flint and by flint. Residents were employed making tinderboxes before the coming of matches. Later they turned to the manufacture of gun flints.

Chert occurs in Great Britain also. France and Germany both have flint and chert. Other places with extensive chert include southern Africa and New Zealand.

Alibates Flint

Now a national monument, a 600-acre site north of Amarillo, Texas, is known for its distinctive flint (chert) which was quarried up to 12,000 years ago by early inhabitants who used the fine-grained colorful material for weapons, ceremonials, and ornaments. Expertly chipped Clovis points have been found many miles from the site where the quarries yielded abundant material. More than one ancient culture admired this tough, hard material and used it for their own purposes, which included barter for such materials as turquoise and catlinite. Evidence shows that the tribes were selective of the material, digging deeply to find the colors and patterns that pleased them most.

The stratum bearing the flint is spread over a zone of more than a mile and lies between areas of silicified dolomite. The predominant colors of the flint are red, red-brown, plum, purple, yellow, and orange. Some of the material is fibrous and translucent and would qualify as agate, especially material with dendrites or fortifications. Drusy quartz and rarely amethyst enhance choice pieces.

Flint also occurs outside the boundary of the national monument on private ranches where it is often revealed by erosion. Texas lapidaries have used Alibates flint for vivid cabochons and polished slabs. Flint is easy to cut and polish, following 400 sanding cloth (wet) with tin oxide on felt.

Basanite, Touchstone, or Lydian Stone

This compact very fine-grained black cherty jasper, known for centuries as the best material for a streak test for gold, has been known as touchstone or Lydian stone by the early metallurgists. Often described as velvety black, the material is uniform and dense and usually entirely opaque. Basanite is harder than some jaspers and also has a toughness which enhances it as a cutting material.

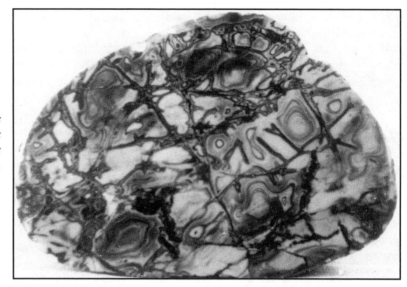

The mysterious patterns of jasper, chert, and flint are intriguing to lapidaries.

Small quantities of basanite are found in many jasper localities. Historically basanite has come from Asia Minor and India. The first touchstones to be widely recognized were water-worn pebbles from the Tmolos River. Kunz mentions an outcrop of black jasper near Cornwall, New York. Basanite is found as pebbles more often than in place. A current locality for cutting quality basanite is near Winnemucca, Nevada. Lapidaries find many uses for the material marketed as Black Beauty basanite.

Basanite is excellent for a backing material for opal doublets or triplets. It is also used for tabletops and other ornamental objects as a substitute for black marble or black jade. The material presents no problems to cutters. Follow 220, 320, 400, 600 sanding with tin oxide on felt or leather.

Mookaite

This is a local name for a decorative Australian chert which is dark red or gray in color with patterns in yellow, brick red, and purple. Patterns are patches, swirls, and spots. The rock is fossiliferous. Some of the chert grades into common opal and some into chalcedony. Both are paler in color than the cherty material.

The main outcrop is at Mooka Station, West Australia. The material has been exported in quantity.

Mozarkite

Mozarkite, a chert found near Lincoln in Benton County, Missouri, is brightly colored and aesthetically patterned. It is fine grained with many areas resembling agate more than chert. Colors that predominate are red, pink, rose, yellow, orange, plum, maroon, and blue-gray. The patterns are cloudlike, flamelike, and swirly bands, sometimes with small fortifications. Selected pieces are scenic. Drusy quartz coats some of the best pieces. Large masses and weathered boulders occur in road cuts, stream beds, and around dams and lakes in several regions in west central Missouri. Mozarkite is so popular with Missouri lapidaries that they were influential in having it named the state rock. It is available in large pieces and has been used for ornamental items, jewelry, and carvings. Well-cut cabochons of Mozarkite may be indistinguishable from many of the other cryptocrystalline quartzes from other areas. The material is exceptionally easy to work with.

Novaculite

Novaculite is a dense, even-textured, light-colored, cherty rock occurring in quantity in Arkansas's Ouachita Mountains. Novaculite is an important industrial stone because of its purity and consistent fine grains. Most of the material used for whetstones or Arkansas stones is white, but lapidaries are attracted to the limited amounts that are tinted pale pink, rose, orchid, or blue. Dendritic pieces are sometimes found.

The colored novaculite is available in pieces for carvings, large cabochons, and objets d' art. Local lapidaries have used it for display items and lovely jewelry. Like chalcedony, it is easy to work with and should give the lapidary no trouble. Sand with silicon carbide belts (wet) 120, 220, 320, and 400, finishing stones with tin oxide on felt.

Ohio Flint

A very similar material is Ohio flint, also an official state stone, occurring in Licking and Muskingum counties in an area known as Flint Ridge.

This large deposit was once worked by area Indian tribes. The material, so well suited to weapons and tools, was a prime trade material to other tribes throughout the country. This fine-grained and durable flint was also used for millstones in the early nineteenth century. Because the flint is brightly colored and interestingly patterned, Ohio lapidaries have collected it in quantity from several fee-basis collecting areas and used it for every possible lapidary project. Realistic stone butterflies have been cut from Ohio flint. Eggs, spheres, cabochons, and carvings are other uses of the material. Colors are rose, red, mauve, pink, yellow, gold, blue-gray, ivory, cream brown, rust, black, and white. The rarest colors are green or lilac. Patterns resemble ribbons, waves, clouds, or flames, and are sometimes brecciated or dendritic. Ohio lapidaries are selective about the material they cut, so that many of their cabochons resemble scenic agate, crazy lace agate, or flowering jasper.

Ohio flint dates from the Pennsylvanian period and is found layered with limestone. Geologically it is chert rather than flint; however, it is very fine grained and has a smooth, conchoidal fracture. Easy to cut and polish, Ohio flint is suitable for artistic lapidary work. Finish with tin oxide on leather or felt after fine sanding. Ohio flint is readily available in the Midwest.

Pastelite

This cryptocrystalline quartz variety is an opaque cherty chalcedony often found in hot springs areas. The best-known locality is Burro Creek, Arizona. The colors and patterns are boundless. The material is fine grained and hard, grading into agate and opal. Colors include red, orange, pink, yellow, and lavender as well as several neutrals, usually white, cream, buff, and brown. Patterns are usually swirls, ribbons, clouds, and splashes. A straight banded material also occurs, but the most interesting is a brecciated stone with angular patches of red, orange, and yellow with semitranslucent colorless chalcedony. A small amount of the material is dendritic.

Coatings of most pieces are white and many pieces have holes through them also

Carver Donald Diller made these realistic-looking nuts of light brown flint. Courtesy of Lapidary Journal.

lined with white. Some of the coating on better specimens is common opal.

Another pastelite location is near Ruby in southern Arizona. There are more reds in this location and fewer patterns in the material. Common opal also occurs here.

Jaspery material from Imperial County, California, near Palo Verde, has also been called pastelite. Found as float, the pastelite is vein material in soft pastel colors.

The distinguishing characteristics of the pastelite cryptocrystalline quartz seems to be that it is massive material in pastel colors combining chert, chalcedony, and common opal and associated with hot springs areas. Lapidaries find it easy to work.

JASPER

Jasper is a massive fine-grained or fibrous variety of cryptocrystalline quartz, similar to chalcedony but more impure because it is admixed with greater amounts of other materials such as iron oxides or clays. Jasper can be chalcedonic or microgranular and is opaque or almost opaque. Jasper comes in a wonderful assortment of colors and patterns and is found the world over. It occurs as nodules or veins in ore deposits, altered igneous rock, or in mas-

sive bedded sedimentary or metamorphic deposits. It is common in alluvial gravels.

Although jasper may be banded, the banding is not concentric or precise as in the case of agates. However, some jasper has translucent areas and grades into agate. In lapidary terms it is often hard to distinguish a polished cabochon of high-quality jasper from one of agate. To most lapidaries, if there is any doubt at all, the material is called agate.

Jasper is a gem material known to man for many centuries. It was used for seals, amulets, cylinders, charms, and medicinal purposes. Mentioned in both the Old and New Testaments of the Bible, it was a stone in the high priest's breastplate and the material for the envisioned walls of the New Jerusalem.

Some of the coloring agents of jasper are hematite, limonite, goethite, chlorite, manganese, hornblende, carbon, and clay. Lapidaries commonly call much material jasper which is really chert, flint, silicified ash, silicified rhyolite, or indurated clay. The name is used because it has become the custom to call colorful or richly patterned opaque cryptocrystalline quartz by the term jasper. However, some jasper is earthy and porous. Most of the materials now called jasper by lapidaries are massive, hard, uniform, compact, and well suited to any project the creative lapidary might undertake.

Jasper patterns include spherules, dendrites, bands, eyes, dots, egglike patterns, brecciated areas, and pictures or scenes. Early in this century geologists usually described jasper as red. True red jasper is less often seen than other varieties. Idaho College at Caldwell shows an amazing variety of Northwest jaspers.

Until the next record is set, the biggest cut stone is a 494-pound red jasper sphere cut in Idar-Oberstein from South African rough, now displayed at the Deutches Edelstein Museum. A fine-grained, compact, and uniform jasper can be sanded with 220, 320, and 400 grit silicon carbide and polished with Linde A or cerium oxide on leather.

There are hundreds of occurrences of jasper known by scores of trade names. Many are named for locations, but others are named for pattern or color. A few are misnamed, often for a person with an "ite" at the end. Sometimes a single deposit will have several names and sometimes names change. Of the many jaspers, here is a selection of some that show a variety of desirable characteristics for today's lapidaries.

Algal Jasper

Algal jaspers reveal the structure of the earliest plants. Such jaspers occur in an assortment of colors and in numerous jasper (chert) localities. Sometimes they are unrecognized as being of fossil origin.

A deposit of jasper at the Mary Ellen iron mine in the Mesabi iron range of northern Minnesota has been used for cabochons and ornamental novelties for many years. The jasper is red and blue-gray with some steel-colored streaks of hematite in the graceful swirled banding. Still found as float, or in some of the other old mine dumps, the distinctive jasper is seen in many Minnesota collections. The elaborate patterns caused by the primitive

algae make this an interesting cutting material. Some of the oldest-known algal materials of northern Minnesota are nearly two billion years old. Algal jaspers with different colors—green, pink, maroon, and mahogany—many containing hematite, are found in several mines in the other iron ranges of Minnesota.

Sweetwater County, Wyoming, has a notable occurrence of algal jasper in assorted shades of brown and gray. Stony algae is also found in stromatolites, widely curved, scalloped, and banded masses. The well-silicified stromatolites are found in ancient rock pushed aside by the Rocky Mountain uplift. Most of the occurrences are neutral in color, but the designs are unique and the material is polishable.

The silicified algae of western Oklahoma is outstanding. Exotic cell patterns in dark shades make weird patterns resembling futuristic art, but are in fact nature's ancient art.

Algal jaspers have also been reported in Canada and South Africa. Silicified algae also occurs in some of the more extensive petrified forests. Most algal material is well silicified and uniform in texture so it is worked by normal procedures.

Apache Red Jasp-agate

Small-scale brecciated and mossy patterns of rich, dark red are dense in gray to white agate with a few small fortification patterns widely scattered. This jasp-agate occurs near Ashwood, Oregon. Since the red color is showy and the material takes such a superb polish, it is popular for large cabochons for pendants and bola ties.

Biggs Jasper

Scenic jasper from Oregon, Idaho, and Washington is one of the most popular gem materials with American lapidaries. One of the best is Biggs jasper from Sherman County, north central Oregon. Discovered in 1961, large quantities of jasper were exposed by bulldozers during road construction.

The groundmass colors are warm, rosy beiges, golden or greenish, tans, yellow, pastel blues, and cocoa browns with extravagantly detailed patterns outlined in scallops, swirls, curls, and arcs. Lavish patterns are distinctly drawn in rich dark brown or charcoal. The scenes resemble desert and mountain vistas, plains, valleys, mesas, hills, terraces, volcanoes, distant forests, and stormy skies.

This entire area is volcanic. Successive layers of lava helped form the picture jasper that is really silicified ash. The material is colored by iron, probably goethite.

Lapidaries select mixtures of blues and browns for realistic scenes. Picture jaspers such as Biggs are easy to cut and polish to a high gloss for cabochons, carvings, and ornamental objects. The real challenge to an imaginative lapidary is to get the best possible effect from a carefully chosen piece of rough.

Black Butte Jasper

Rainbow-colored jasper is found near Black Butte Reservoir near Orland, California. Large pieces of jasper occur in and around gullies and washes in the vicinity of Burris Creek and other creeks in Glenn County, northern California.

Colors of the jasper are red, green, purple, yellow, black, orange, and brown. Some pieces are all one color but the most interesting to lapidaries are intermixed greens and reds with marcasite inclusions. The patterns are mottled. The yellow jaspers are particularly bright and fine grained, but very brittle. Blue-white

quartz inclusions are common. Some of the quartz inclusions with the red jasper are clear and colorless. Some of the material is said to resemble Stone Canyon jasper while other pieces are reminiscent of the Lavic Siding jasper. This jasper has been used for jewelry. It tends to undercut, so diamond fine sanding and polishing should solve the problem.

Bruneau Jasper

Bruneau jasper, one of the best known of Northwest jaspers, occurs as nodules in rhyolite in a remote area of eastern Idaho. Lapidaries say that this scenic jasper is somewhat harder than other Northwest picture rocks. It also is noted for its attractive colors, which although monochromatic and neutral, look as if they had been patiently mixed by an exacting artist. Cream, buff, beige, tan, rusty red, and several shades of brown are in perfectly drawn circles, arcs, ovals, ellipsoids, or egg shapes. Darker colors are often near the outer edges of nodules.

Especially interesting for large polished slabs or cabochons, Bruneau jasper has been cut for many years for jewelry, novelty and display items, and specimens. Some of the graceful ovals are light cream in the center and gradually deepen in color until the distinct red-brown outline. Such an oval makes a unique, large cabochon. This is an excellent lapidary material. The big problem is finding the best pattern.

Cave Creek Jasper

There are many jaspers in the washes and dry river beds of Arizona. They are varied in color and pattern and several variations may occur in one area, but a favorite for

Various colors of chert, flint, and jasper are among the most common tumbled stones.

50 years or so has been Cave Creek jasper, a bright red jasper found north of Phoenix near Seven Springs. This jasper has been marketed in many places and used for lapidary projects that called for a good red. Some of the jasper has white streaks and other specimens are orbicular. A mine here once produced red jasper with white quartz and metallic hematite. Jasper is scattered over a large area where the heavier concentrates were commercially mined.

A similar jasper is found on New River Road near Cave Creek. It is fine grained, solid, and available in large pieces. Indian artifacts have been found made of this fine jasper, far from the Cave Creek area.

There is also agate in this region and a cuttable blue copper–stained quartz. Jasper with quartz or hematite inclusions may undercut. It can be fine sanded with 800, 1200, and 2,000 diamond and finished with Linde A on leather.

Chocolate Rock Jasper

This picture jasper comes from Arizona. The chocolate in the name comes from the milk chocolate color of the dendrites that form desert plants, trees, and sometimes thunderclouds. As in some of the other picture jaspers, if there are especially richly colored or dark patterns, there are lighter colors, such as rose, immediately edging the dark colors. There are sprinklings of bright metallic spots, probably native copper, on the darkest colors .

Christmas Jasper

A jasper from Bear Lake County, Idaho, looks as if it were decorated for Christmas. It is bright red filled with bright green grains and needles of malachite. It is fine grained and takes a good polish.

Cripple Creek Jasper

Cripple Creek picture jasper from Homedale, Idaho, has sharply curved hills and horizons in brown and tan tones with gray-blue skies, somewhat more muted than in many jaspers. Some of the borders of various scenes seem to be naturally outlined with crayons. Many of the landscapes resemble receding sand dunes. Some of the material has been used for realistic picture cabochons. The material is uniform of grain, compact, and easy to work with, a favorite of lapidaries.

Deschutes Jasper

Deschutes jasper comes from the same general area as Biggs jasper and is very similar to Biggs, but jasper authority Dale

Bright red Cave Creek jasper predominates in this 1976 flag intarsia by Frank Jeckel.

Huett says it is the best material in the region. It is harder, more even and compact, and richer in color than many jaspers. It is rated as a superior cutting material—so smooth when taken from the saw that it begins to show a prepolish.

A typical slab will show very rich red-browns in scalloped and curvy lines interspersed with dendritic taupe or charcoal outlines, cocoa-colored deserts and hills, and dark blue skies. The exteriors of weathered pieces of vein material show light tan at the top and bottom of the vein, with dark brown outlining the shape of the piece. Then, following the lines of a single pattern area, the color can suddenly change from dark to light without the pattern being disrupted.

Western jewelry artists use cabochons such as this picture jasper cut by Rasmussen for belt buckles, bola ties, and other western-style jewelry. Courtesy of Roland Rasmussen.

curved landscapes outlined in red-brown. The rose patterns are mostly straight bands. There are sometimes small dark dendrites. The scenes are similar to some of the canyon country of the desert states. The warm colors of this jasper are attractive high-fashion colors; this material is for imaginative lapidary uses. Polish with tin or cerium oxide on felt or leather.

Disaster Peak or Picture Rock

From McDermitt, Nevada, actually across the Oregon border, comes this sedimentary jasperlike picture stone, which is a fine-grained polishable sandstone. A lapidary with a good eye can make pictures, cabochons, or slabs with blue skies, brown and tan forested mountains and hills, and detailed foregrounds with winding roads or streams. Developer Frank Sykes finds it in large pieces, polishes it with no trouble, and uses it for a variety of lapidary projects.

Desert Rose Jasper

A picture jasper with the warmest coloring of the Idaho jaspers is aptly named Desert Rose. The Schultz claim near Homedale has a bright rose-colored picture rock characterized by curved arcs and horizons of tan and gray and lacy gray dendrites. The most vivid rose areas are punctuated by red-brown straight streaks. Other colors are a muted rose, mauve, beige, tan, and ivory. Rose cabochons with gray sagebrush patterns look as if they were created by a trendy fashion designer.

A jasper from Malheur County, Oregon, also goes by the Desert Rose name and is probably part of the deposit above, with several shades and tints of muted rose. The second most predominant color is a golden or ivory tint forming gently

Egyptian Jasper

Egyptian jasper is yellow and brown banded jasper according to the Australians, but is a bright orbicular jasper when found in the United States. *Shipley's Dictionary of Gems & Gemology* says it is yellow, red, brown, and black jasper from Egypt and that the term used for the West Coast orbicular jasper is a misnomer. This is but one example of how tricky descriptive names can be, including place names.

Indian Paint Rock Jasper

This very attractive jasper from Nevada is distinguished by light brick-red colors, sometimes called Indian reds. The warm

Channel work is the advanced lapidary/jewelry technique mastered by Betty Crawford for this jasper weasel.

but subtle colors are accented by wonderful treelike dendrites in charcoal black. Pictures resemble forest fires, sunsets, and autumn forests. Quiet reflections are in gray white pools and streams, which look as if they could already have a coat of ice.

Jasper Conglomerate

In many sedimentary formations a material called jasper conglomerate is found. Small rounded pebbles of many colors of jasper, chalcedony, quartz, and chert have been cemented together by impure chalcedony. The material is differentiated from brecciated jasper or agate by the rounded water-worn pebbles instead of jagged angular pieces. It differs from orbicular jasper because the material is not homogeneous—the separate pebbles of various materials can be distinguished. An appropriate common name for jasper conglomerate is puddingstone.

A South Dakota jasper conglomerate consists of red, yellow, orange, brown, and white small rounded pebbles cemented in large masses with red and brown jasper. Called *Buffalo Gap conglomerate* for its location, the material can be slabbed for display, made into cabochons, spheres, or ornamental objects, and polished to a high luster.

A jasper conglomerate from West Texas has smaller pebbles of more uniform size and with less variety in color. Jasper conglomerate occurs as float in many alluvial gravels in Minnesota, Iowa, and Nebraska. Oregon and California also have jasper conglomerate.

Jasper conglomerate may be porous and is prone to undercutting. A filling and coat of Opticon before final polish is used if porous material has good color and interesting configuration, but choice material is solid and can be polished by normal methods.

Keeganite

This name has been given to a compact hard jasper from the Keegan Ranch near Ashwood, Oregon. Several shades of brown combine with a golden color in mossy and mottled patterns. A few translucent areas indicate that the material might grade into jasp-agate, except for the density of the color. The material takes a fine polish.

Kindradite

Lapidary-quality maroon-red chert, patterned with round crystalline spherules in orange, yellow, brown, white, or colorless, has been collected and cut for many years in Marin County, California. High in silica, the colorful chert or jasper, as it is often called, takes a good polish. Kindradite was considered one of the best cutting-quality cryptocrystalline quartzes of northern California and was used for many lapidary projects, but is now quite scarce.

Lahontarite

This is a jasperlike material that occurs in chertlike boulders in Nevada. Hard and fine grained, the basic color is cream or ivory with tints of green, pink, or mauve, and streaks or stringers of darker hues of green or red interspersed with geometric patterns of yellow, orange, tan, or brick. Bands are contrasting and irregularly parallel. A colorful material, it is available in large pieces for almost any lapidary project and is exceptionally easy to cut and polish by almost any favorite lapidary method.

This majestic jasper eagle in the Lora Robins Gallery, carved, by Reiner Stein, is 10 inches high. Photo by Dr. Willie Reams.

Lavic Jasper

A well-known California jasper occurs south of the railroad at Lavic, east of Barstow. This entire part of the Mojave Desert is rich in quartz family gem materials. The Lavic jasper is one of the most colorful and highest quality of regional jaspers. Curvy and mossy red patterns with opaque white chalcedony are choice cabochon material jaspers. Since there is considerable white quartz and chalcedony with the material, it qualifies as jasp-agate. A coating of desert varnish identifies rough material.

The colors are red, rose, maroon, blue, yellow, and orange, all with streamers of white. The plentiful material is useful for the most challenging lapidary projects when carefully selected.

Mohave Jasper

Located in the Black Mountain Range of Mohave County, Arizona, is a deposit of finely banded jasper. The color of the jasper is basically brown, but the variance is from a light yellowish tan to a rich, deep reddish brown. The best of the material has fortification patterns and eyes or fine parallel banding.

The material is fine grained, solid, and uniform and takes a high polish with tin oxide on leather after fine sanding with 600 grit wet. Free-form cabochons, oriented to accent the banding of the jasper, are well suited to pins, pendants, and bola ties.

Morrisonite

Morrisonite has long been a much appreciated cutting material from the rugged Owyhee River Canyon near Ashwood, Oregon. There are still two active mines producing colorful lapidary material. The jasper is in a welded tuff and is characterized by splendid colors of blue, blue-green, green, red, yellow, orange, and brown. Eugene Mueller of Cedarburg, Wisconsin, one of the mine developers, has found some with pink and yellow "egg" patterns on dark blue or blue-green backgrounds; other patterns are scenic. Some of the patterns resemble the graceful egg patterns of Bruneau jasper, but morrisonite is more colorful.

In addition to the Bruneau-type egg patterns, there are scallops, arcs, bands, swirls, eyes, streamers, and brecciated material. A wonderful variety of material is present at the site, but mining is difficult and seasonal.

Morrisonite can be used for beads, jewelry, and art objects. Some of the unusual colors are cut for intarsias, channelwork, or inlay. Silicon carbide or diamond can be used for shaping imaginative cabochons and carvings.

Owyhee Jasper

Eastern Oregon and western Idaho have a superb jasper which is the favorite of many jasper specialists. Called Owyhee jasper for the Owyhee River, the material has its origin in volcanic sediments. Fine grained and compact, the picture jasper has blue and blue-gray skies and lakes, tan, ivory, and brown hills, deserts, and mountain ranges, and graceful desert plants and trees in reds or browns. Outlines of scenic details are sometimes in brown or black and sometimes in dark brick red.

Owyhee jasper found along the Oregon/Idaho border is one of the many fine picture jaspers of the northwestern United States.

Large cabochons with realistic scenes are the specialties of some West Coast lapidaries, who have found that such jaspers as Owyhee are delightful to work with and offer many opportunities for unique lapidary achievements. Dendritic patterns are often extremely lacy in warm red-brown tones with the reddish neutral background curiously lighter than surroundings. Distant hills are sometimes topped with distinct pine forests. Cactus, red ocotillo, and other desert plants are prominent in the foreground of carefully chosen scenes. The blues of the lakes and skies are muted and may have hints of green. Sometimes entire scenes are clearly reflected in the water.

A creative use of scenic jaspers is to find realistic paintings by nature and frame them as one would do with fine oil paintings. Such pictures are more realistic if the polish is not too glassy.

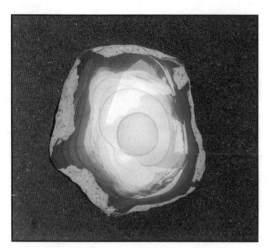

Colorful Owyhee jasper and many others are found in nodules along the Oregon/Idaho border. From the Ed Brandt collection.

Poppy Jasper

In the chert beds of Santa Clara County, California, an exceptionally fine cutting material was discovered in 1935. Called poppy jasper or sometimes flowering jasper, the material boasts designs reminiscent of a poppy field in realistic colors of red, yellow, and green. The best-known occurrence was at Morgan Hill, where the vivid poppies looked as if they had been painted on the brown matrix, sometimes with streaks or small fortifications of white chalcedony.

The structure of the jasper (chert) is called orbicular. This refers to the round inclusions of contrasting color and composition. The name has become generic since several similar materials have been called poppy jasper, including one from Australia. The poppy jasper beads now on the market are not the original poppy jasper.

Now scarce, the California material was used for cabochons, jewelry, and ornamental items. Poppy jasper has a tendency to undercut. It should be carefully wet sanded. A prepolish can be attained by a worn 400 belt followed by rouge on muslin. A final polish is achieved by chrome oxide on chrome tanned leather.

Ribbonstone
(Ribbon Jasper, Banded Jasper)

Fine-grained silicified sedimentary rock with alternating color bands is sometimes called ribbonstone. The layers are varied in thickness from paper thin to about an inch and the colors are usually muted tones of red, brown, yellow, and green. The alternating layers of mudstone and siltstone have different grain sizes, from very fine to medium, which makes the material rather difficult to polish.

Australia and New Zealand have exported colorful ribbonstone for lapidary purposes; however, similar banded jasper is found in many sedimentary deposits in the Americas and on other continents. Cut at right angles to the layering, it makes interesting slabs, cabochons, and ornamental items.

Rocky Butte Jasper

An Oregon jasper that seems to depict Oregon's geologic history is called Rocky Butte jasper. In this material astonishing plumes of red and flows of black show volcanoes of the distant pastel against skies of smoky blue. There are fiery rivers and burning trees, as well as olive green foliage, desert plants, and shrubs. It is interesting that in so many of these scenic jaspers a particularly bright pattern will be surrounded by a lighter and purer color than the rest of the background. For example, a red plume of fire from a rising cone has lighter blue around it than the rest of the smoky blue sky. A realistic picture jasper, Rocky Butte is suitable for many lapidary projects.

Rose-eye

Another Idaho jasper is called rose-eye. The overall pattern is similar to many orbicular jaspers, but the "eyes" are not quite as distinct. The background color is a dark brownish black and the round patterns of dusky rose are more flowerlike than eyelike. The eyes were the results of zeolites and the color is from iron. The irregularly round patterns seem to have been constructed in layers. Very often next to the outer layer there is a concentric arc of the background color reaching about halfway around the circle. This is softer, more porous material. In some of the dark brown arcs the filling material is entirely eroded away. The lenses of this jasper occur in a limited area. The material makes showy cabochons because of its unusual deep rose hue, but it must be carefully selected. Voids are often filled with Opticon.

Spiderweb Jasper

An Idaho jasper with a different type of pattern has a pale greenish gray overall color and is patterned with polygons distinctly outlined in dark brown resembling spiderwebs or honeycombs. The polygons are five- to six-sided and range in size from 3 mm to 10 mm (.118 inch to .393 inch) in diameter. To add to the strange patterns, there are occasional pink or red curves or circles, but these seem to be a softer material, probably common opal. Material which filled some of the circles is completely gone; in other cases the circles are partially filled—few are complete.

Cabochons of select pieces of the material with the best green color could resemble spiderweb variscite. One theory is that the odd patterns are a result of shrinking and later filling of the polygon cracks.

Spring Mountain Jasper

From Craig Gulch, Malheur County, Oregon, comes a banded scenic jasper that combines rose, brown, red-brown, and yellow-gold with a slightly grayed medium or pastel blue. The material is opaque and fine grained with quite fine parallel banding alternating with broader bands of contrasting colors, and more irregular in shape. The lighter colors are often next to the blue bands and the blue bands are not made up of numerous fine lines as are the browns.

Good picture cabochons can be cut from this jasper with blue skies, brown prairies, and distant desert dunes. Parallel bands often resemble plowed fields. The light blue in this material is particularly appealing and can be used when this color is needed for inlay or intarsia. Compact and uniform in grain, the jasper has excellent lapidary qualities.

Stone Canyon Jasper

This California jasper from Monterey County is one of the most beautiful and unique of American jaspers. Some of it is jasp-agate, and some is closer to agate than jasper. It is brecciated jasper with opaque white chalcedony outlining the angular inclusions and lacy inclusions in bright yellow, tan, beige, khaki, and brown.

The material is hard and compact with the broken and recemented pieces being part of a homogeneous mass. It has been

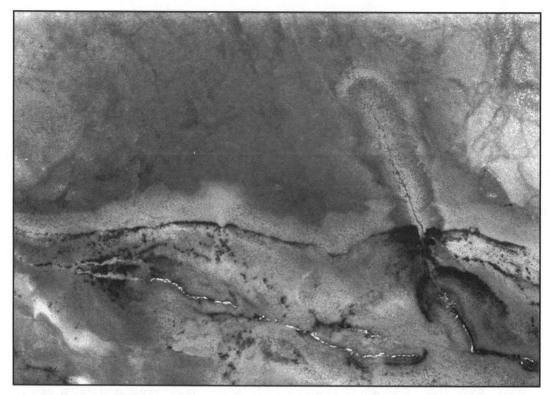

George Frank found this picture of an erupting volcano in Rocky Butte jasper from Oregon.

used for bookends, clock faces, boxes, bowls, slabs, and cabochons. Easy to polish, select material often has high fashion colors and patterns, and has been used for eye-catching jewelry. Extend the wet sanding and polish with cerium oxide.

Stormy Skies Jasper

Another of Oregon's many scenic jaspers has pictures of ivory, tan, and ecru, well defined with seemingly three-dimensional chocolate-brown outlines, and gray skies with just a hint of dark blue. Each scene is in colors that seem dulled by an approaching storm, or perhaps smoke from distant forest fires. Lapidaries can use this material most effectively when lighter blue areas

make the storm look even more threatening. This jasper is well suited to many of the uses for picture jasper.

Succor Creek Jasper

Among the rhyolite outcroppings of the ancient volcanic ash sediments of Malheur County, Oregon, are some of the world's finest jaspers. One of these is Succor Creek picture rock, a fine-grained cherty jasper, brimming with scenes pristine enough to satisfy the most fussy environmentalist. The best of the Succor Creek material has more blues and green-blues than many of the jaspers from these remote and rugged locations. With pictures in the jasper often emulating the local scenery, well-cut jasper shows rough canyons, high mesas, buttes, steep canyons, rocky cliffs, and rough roadways in tones of khaki, brown, ecru, and tan, outlined clearly in red-browns all against endless skies in several shades of blue. In some parts of the deposits dark dendrites suggest hardy desert plants and add to the realism.

The pieces that differ to the greatest extent from other area jaspers are those with multiple closely packed parallel wavy lines in blues, greens, and yellow-greens, filling out a rare color combination for jasper. Well-selected pieces of Succor Creek material are fine grained and uniform, easy to cut and polish, and excellent for jewelry and other lapidary work.

Three-Finger Butte Jasper

This Oregon jasper is a little different. It has numerous dark lacy dendrites and quite a lot of red in scenic areas, looking like watercolor sunsets. The material is not abundant, but is seen in area rock shops and collections. It takes an excellent polish. The only challenge is picking out the most realistic picture.

Turkey Tail

An extraordinarily silicified jaspery rhyolite occurs at Opal Butte, Oregon. It is a rich brown color grading into clear chalcedony and light yellow agate with brecciated patterns. The most interesting patterns are elaborately scalloped fans reminiscent of the spread tail of a handsome turkey gobbler. These graceful fans are white and off-white, contrasting well with the rich brown. The brecciated pieces are angular shapes of several colors of brown and gray with small areas of red.

This material is excellent for polished slabs and large cabochons. A scenic quality piece cut by Dale Huett of West Coast Gemstones looks like a whole yard full of turkeys unknowingly strutting a few days before Thanksgiving. The material makes unusual free-form cabochons.

Wild Horse Jasper

Another Idaho and Oregon picture jasper, wild horse jasper is a uniform, fine-grained material with many earth tones and tints and shades of blue and blue-gray accented at times with ornate black dendrites. Well-cut cabochons can show finely delineated scenes of mountains, foothills, canyons, and streams put into a dimensional-appearing perspective by foregrounds of dendritic trees and shrubs.

A typical scene in this fine-grained jaspery material shows several levels of rugged hills and mountains varying in tint or shade at each level. Such scenes are popular for large cabochons for western-style jewelry such as bola ties, and are also used to make framed "paintings by nature," those polished slabs of gem material (often picture jasper or scenic agate) having natural pictures in them, which are often exhibited at gem shows as features.

RECOMMENDED READING

See lists for Chapters 4 and 5.

CHAPTER VII

Quartz: Strange and Wonderful Pseudomorphs

Animal
    Agatized coral geodes and
        silicified corals
    Agatized dinosaur bone
    Agatized horn coral
    Turritella agate
Mineral

Plants
    Agatized, jasperized, and
        silicified
    Identification of petrified
        wood
    Petrified forests
    Specific and unusual wood

PSEUDOMORPHS OR FALSE FORMS are of major importance to scientists as well as to lapidary artists. In addition to being exotic cutting materials, pseudomorphs are records of the geologic past. A pseudomorph occurs when a mineral replaces another mineral or organic matter. The original form is retained but not the chemical or biological makeup. In this case quartz, which is an excellent lapidary material, is the replacement mineral. The item replaced by quartz may be a mineral, for example, barite, or a part of an animal such as coral or dinosaur bone, or an entire tree trunk such as Araucarioxylon, the dominant tree of the Petrified Forest National Park. For some of these—coral or bone—the quartz could replace calcite or apatite.

Chalcedony replacements after organic or inorganic materials are found worldwide. Mineralogists can learn about the minerals that were in an area in the past. Paleontologists can make studies of extinct species which lived in different climatic conditions millions of years ago. Lapidaries have an amazing choice of colorful materials with unique and desirable patterns which challenge their talent and craftsmanship.

The most common quartz pseudomorph is also the most popular with lapidaries—chalcedony or jasper after wood. In fact, petrified wood is high on the list of all cuttable quartzes and cabochon materials. Since this is a special category which is also important to science, lapidaries should not cut rare specimens, no matter how attractive they are. For example, a dinosaur bone should not be turned into cabochons, unless there are broken scattered pieces of bone in an alluvial nonfossiferous formation, or if a paleontologist says the bone is not essential to research.

Calcite, goethite, pyrite, and hematite are examples of other minerals which replace organic and inorganic materials, but quartz is the replacement mineral of lapidary interest.

ANIMAL

Agatized Coral Geodes and Silicified Corals

The agatized coral geodes of Tampa Bay (actually Hillsborough Bay), Florida, are unique in many ways. Most geodes are spherical, but these pseudomorphs after coral have weird shapes resembling bottles, vases, cylinders, claws, and wings.

The colors are also unusual; some of the best have thick shells of black and royal blue chalcedony, either waxy and botryoidal inside, or sparkling with transparent drusy quartz which seems to borrow its color from the background.

Spread over a wide area of the Tampa islands and peninsulas, the finest geodes were found over 40 years ago during a Florida building boom. They were dug up in the building of Davis Island, in excavations along the bay shores, and in Mac Dill Field and along causeways and road projects.

In the early 1950s collectors would walk out into the bay at low tide and the super low tides which often occurred during "blue northers" to locate geodes in the muck with prodding rods. The standard costume for these expeditions was warm clothing and high rubber boots. The preferred area was just off a city park.

The geodes were usually in a bluish clay and had a ring like fine china when pinged with the prospector's pick. The size range was from an inch (2.54 cm) or so to enormous coral heads over two feet (60.96 cm) in diameter. In addition to the black with blue chalcedony, there were geodes colored like carnelian or sard. Some showed banding, some were multicolored, and some were white with pastel tints. Although the bulk of these strange and aesthetic geodes were cut and polished for award-winning exhibits, some excellent jewelry has been made of choice pieces. Some finger corals about 1–1½ inches (2.54–3.81 cm) in diameter are cut into thin slabs which are natural free-form hoops for earrings. Botryoidal pieces of unusual black and blue colors are preformed and tumbled for striking pendants. Cutters have made calibrated cabochon shapes from colorful coral with drusy quartz coatings, polishing only the edges. Abstract sculptures are also made from agatized coral.

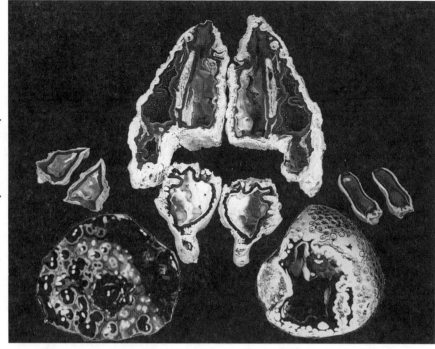

Pseudomorphs of agate after coral from Tampa Bay, Florida, are among the strangest of geodes.

Coral geodes have also been found in other parts of Florida, among them the Suwanee River, Cross Florida Canal, and Withlacoochee River. There are also several places where silicified solid coral is found. The solid coral is nicely patterned but without much color. This type of coral is found in the area of Dunedin, New Port Richey, Tarpon Springs, and other Florida west coast locations. The chalcedony is usually not of as high quality as the Tampa material, but it takes a glassy polish. Agatized coral can be polished with a vibrating lap using 220 to 600 grits and tin oxide. The corals are still sold in Florida and the South.

Agatized shells of numerous species have also been found in Florida, but perhaps the most interesting finds are the translucent chalcedony bottle-shaped enhydros almost full of fresh water.

Silicified coral is found in Georgia, West Virginia, and several other eastern states. Coral heads replaced by chalcedony or chert are also found in the Midwest in the alluvial gravels of the Mississippi River states. Some excellent examples have been found in Iowa and Illinois. In the badlands of South Dakota water-worn pieces of agatized coral occur. Nebraska badlands also have agatized coral. Agatized coral and shells are sometimes found on the beaches of Oregon and California. Other locations are Panama, Cuba, and Australia.

Agatized Dinosaur Bone

Agatized bone of dinosaurs and other extinct animals is a popular cutting material because of its paleontological intrigue as well as the beauty of the detailed cell structure. Some agatized bone is brightly colored, adding to its lapidary desirability.

Colorado, Utah, and Wyoming are all noted for well-silicified bone. Some of the most colorful "dinny bone," as it is locally called, comes from western Colorado near Grand Junction. Found in the Morrison formation, the bone has scarlet cells often outlined in black, an attractive and challenging material for creative lapidaries. Good-quality bone in more muted colors comes from near Canon City in Fremont County.

Wyoming's Big Horn Basin has silicified dinosaur bone and another collectable dinosaur product, the gastrolith. Like birds, dinosaurs swallowed rocks to aid in their digestion. If the dinosaur was selective and the gastroliths or "gizzard stones" are some colorful variety of quartz, novelty conversation-piece jewelry items are the result.

Gorgeous vermillion red dinosaur bone is found near Castle Dale and Green River, Utah. This bone is also found in the Morrison formation. Such bone is often used for jewelry with a story to tell. Because it could undercut, the bone should have extended sanding. Tin or cerium oxide give a bright finish. Good pieces are scarce.

This 6-inch coral pseudomorph is from the badlands of South Dakota.

Agatized Horn Coral

Red, red-orange, and pink agatized horn corals occur in Riley Canyon near Woodland in a mountainous area northeast of Heber City, Utah. The beautifully preserved corals are embedded in limestone. The complete corals may be up to 2 inches (5.08 cm) in diameter and as long as 5 or 6 inches (12.70 or 15.24 cm). Breaking them out of the limestone is difficult but worth the effort because the bright highly agatized corals can be polished for eye-catching specimens for display. Slightly domed heads take a lustrous polish after careful sanding. They have also been slabbed for conversation-piece jewelry, when the dark radial growth pattern is centered like a red wheel with dark spokes.

Another Utah location is for black horn coral. These agatized corals are only an inch or two in length. The black agatized horn corals are occasionally found as float, but most of them are embedded in limestone, similar to the red corals. Sardine Summit, a rugged area where the corals occur, is northwest of Brigham City. These corals are also polished as specimens and make a nice contrast with the red ones in a display. The horn corals are seldom for sale.

Turritella Agate

Perhaps the most famous of Wyoming's many agates is turritella. The agate is composed of graceful spiral pelecypods that once lived in the great lake that covered

This ancient coral replaced by chalcedony is from the South Dakota badlands.

this part of the country. The masses of shells are packed closely together at all angles and have been replaced by translucent chalcedony in contrasting hues of black and white, buff, and gray.

The shells are about 1 inch (2.54 cm) long, or less, and up to nearly ½ inch (1.27 cm) across at the top. The groundmass is usually dense black or charcoal with the shells outlined in white and often changing colors as the spiral winds down to the point. Many shells are complete and others are outlines of partial shells. Complete agatized shells can be found weathered out from some of the poorer matrix which is less solid. These have been tumbled for distinctive earrings, pendants, and bracelet charms.

The location is south and west of Wamsutter and covers many thousands of acres. It matters little to lapidaries that the scientific name of the shells turned out to be Oxtrema instead of turritella. The old name sticks. Well-agatized alga has also been found in this ancient lake bed.

Similar shell agate has been found in other states and has been called turritella, even if the shells are distinctly different. In

some states, shell material for lapidary purposes has been found that is limestone instead of quartz. This has still been called turritella. One such location is in Texas, although Texas also has an agatized variety. Turritella can be polished with cerium oxide after the usual precautions against undercutting. Turritella is usually available.

MINERAL

Pseudomorphs, or false forms, of quartz replacing some other mineral are rarely used by lapidaries, but there are a few exceptions. (The best known is tigereye, which is quartz after crocidolite.) If the pseudomorphs are included in some other cutting material such as agate, jasper, or petrified wood, they make interesting patterns. An example is when agates show chalcedony replacements of halite, argonite, gypsum, or some other mineral.

Needle Peak in Brewster County, Texas, has tabular hexagons of aragonite replaced by brown, yellow, white, and orange agate. The aragonite crystal-shaped agate is polished for display and for ornamental uses like clockfaces. Chalcedony pseudomorphs after aragonite sixlings also come from Mexico.

Oregon agates frequently have sprays of zeolite or gypsum replaced by chalcedony of a contrasting color to the rest of the agate. The pseudomorph section of the agate is surrounded by a halo of pure chalcedony. Cubic quartz pseudomorphs after halite are seen in agatized wood specimens from Oregon. Carnelian replacements of barite roses are unique in Utah. Jasper pseudomorphs after selenite have been found in Utah and southwestern Colorado. In some West Coast agates the original crystal replaced by quartz no longer shows at all, only the dim shapes or

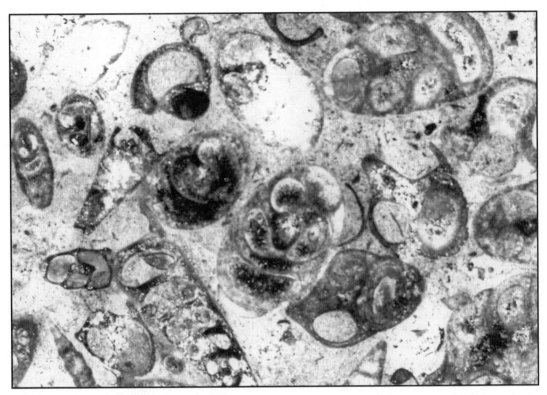

Oxtrema shalle (misnamed Tirritella) from an ancient lake bed in Wyoming have been replaced by agate.

outlines where the replaced crystals once were. Author William Sanborn calls pseudomorphs the "ghosts of minerals past."

A Nebraska occurrence is selenite roses transformed to chalcedony. Calcite and barite crystals replaced by chalcedony occur in the South Dakota badlands. Agate pseudomorphs after barite have been found in Colorado, Nebraska, and Oklahoma. Agate after dolomite is found in Montana.

Pseudomorphs of quartz after calcite are known from France, and pseudomorphs of chalcedony after fluorite come from the Alps. When properly cut and polished to show off their best features, pseudomorphs can make eye-catching cabinet pieces. This is a good specialty for a creative lapidary, who must decide if a specimen should be cut at all, and if so how it should be used to advantage. Usually it is best to keep the specimen as intact as possible, and still bring out its aesthetic potential. Polishable pseudomorphs of chalcedony after another mineral are scarce.

PLANTS: AGATIZED, JASPERIZED, AND SILICIFIED

Wood is just one of the many types of organic materials that can be preserved by silica. The fossil wood may be partially or completely replaced by agate or jasper of

Above, Left: American lapidary artists Harold and Erica Van Pelt create classical and innovative gemstone objects showing exceptional craftsmanship. Vases 4½ inches high are rutilated quartz, quartz, amethyst, and agate. Photo by Harold and Erica Van Pelt. Above, Right: The Van Pelt's 3 x 5-inch faceted egg has walls only 3 millimeters thin. The base is a carved 363-carat aquamarine. Total height is 9 inches. Photo by Harold and Erica Van Pelt. Below: Lapidary pioneer from California, George Ashley, made gem bowls of many fine materials. Shown here are amethyst, variscite, petrified wood, jade, rhodonite, and agate. Photo by Harold and Erica Van Pelt.

*Above, Left: The wonderful colors of opal endear it to lapidaries, collectors, and jewelers.
Opal beads are from Australia. Faceted opal is from Mexico. Courtesy of A.G.T.A.
Photo by Harold and Erica Van Pelt.*
*Above, Right: Idar-Oberstein, Germany, is the center of a great lapidary industry. These
elegant gemstone carvings are by Herbert Klein. Courtesy of Herbert Klein.
Photo by Harold and Erica Van Pelt.*

*Interesting animal jewels
are carved from
facet-quality material
by Herbert Klein.
Courtesy of Herbert Klein.
Photo by Harold and
Erica Van Pelt.*

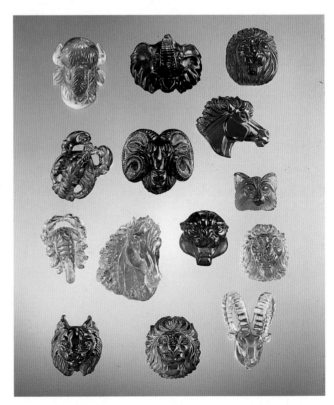

Originator of the trend-setting fantasy cuts, Bernd Munsteiner brought brilliance to this 206-carat citrine and 145-carat aquamarine. Photo by Harold and Erica Van Pelt.

These pansies will not wilt. The amethyst and chalcedony pansies have leaves of jade — the vase is quartz. Courtesy of Herbert Klein, Idar-Oberstein. Photo by Harold and Erica Van Pelt.

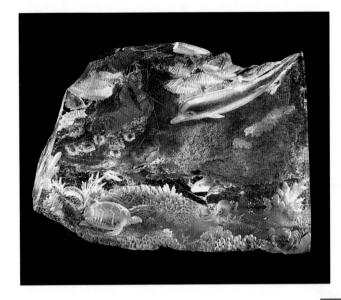

Left: Artist Susan Allen used the technique of internal carving with mastery for this underwater view named "The Reef" done in iron oxide–stained quartz. Photo by Harold and Erica Van Pelt.

Right: Sugilite is one of the colorful new gem materials used for cabochons and carvings. Courtesy Hing Wa Lee. Photo by Tino Hammid.

Left: Hing Wa Lee carvings clockwise from the left are aquamarine beads, jade carving, coral beads, tourmaline snuff bottle, ivory netsuke, and two agate carvings. Photo by Harold and Erica Van Pelt.

any color. In places the only evidence of wood is the branchlike shape which reveals where the wood once was. The mold left by the wood, subsequently filled with chalcedony, is called a *limb cast.*

Sometimes the grain in fossil wood is so well preserved that the species of wood is identifiable. Worm-bored or teredo-bored petrified wood is unique in combining the animal and plant kingdoms with the mineral kingdom.

Certain species of agatized wood are highly desired by lapidaries. One of these is palm wood. Cycad, Tempskya, osmundite, ginkgo, and Lepidodendron are others. Seeds and cones, as well as other parts of ancient trees, are also preserved by silica. Examples are agatized pine cones from Argentina and silicified sequoia cones from North Dakota.

In the west, whole forests are turned to stone. In Yellowstone National Park the remains of 27 petrified forests can be counted. Intense volcanic activity over thousands of years destroyed one forest after another. Trees that were buried by volcanic ash were gradually replaced by silica. The immense forests covering vast periods of time are often standing with some parts exposed by erosion.

Cavities left by some fallen trees have become agate casts after wood. The wood and cavities are sometimes decorated with crystals of clear quartz or amethyst. Similar locations of petrified wood exist in Montana, Colorado, and other states, but none is so impressive as that of Wyoming's Specimen Ridge and Amethyst Mountain.

Other vast deposits of petrified wood are alluvial. Petrified Wood National Park in Arizona is an example. Wood in sedimentary formations was covered by silt from rivers or seas of the distant past and later infiltrated by silica. Broken pieces of petrified wood and huge logs are often found far from where the tree originally grew.

A great deal of agatized or silicified wood has colors unappealing to the lapidary—dark browns, dingy tans, sooty grays. But sometimes the colors are reds, yellows, blues, even greens and violets, making such wood suitable for cabochons and jewelry. However, even if the colors are dark, if the wood has distinct graining and high-quality chalcedony, it is used for display and novelties. Complete rounds are often cut for bookends and desk sets. Large rounds make regal tabletops.

Surface deposits of petrified wood are so vast and widespread that the government has stepped in to try to preserve them by limiting the amount each collector can take from public lands. No collector may take more than 250 pounds a year. This may sound like a lot, but it doesn't take many pieces to weigh 250 pounds.

There are probably many more occurrences of ancient plants in alluvial rock beds than have come to light. The problem is one of recognition. Although field collectors of gem materials scour the surface deposits of quartz family materials constantly, very few are able to recognize the extinct plant species. Lapidaries may collect pieces with fine color or strange patterns without realizing the significance of the unfamiliar patterns, seeing in the material only the possibility of a momentous cabochon.

Some petrified trees such as Lepidodendron and Tempskya represent extinct plants, but the most common species of petrified wood are those which still grow in American forests. Both hardwoods and softwoods are represented. The hardwoods are generally finer grained and more porous than the softwoods. When the woods are replaced by agate, jasper, or sometimes common opal or wood opal, the color does not necessarily represent the color of the wood when it was living. Colors are caused by iron, manganese, and copper minerals and others.

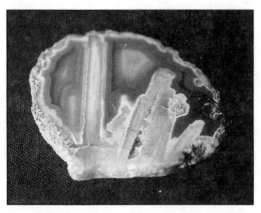

The crystals, which once lined a rhyolite cavity, have been replaced by chalcedony.

The best way to identify petrified wood is to select a piece with distinct cellular and growth ring structure and compare it with a piece of contemporary wood. Thin translucent sections of slabs are an aid in identification. Enlarged close-up pictures also help.

Among the most common types of petrified wood are pine, ash, birch, redwood, elm, hackberry, hickory, holly, larch, locust, maple, oak, cypress, poplar, beech, magnolia, sassafras, cedar, chestnut, sweet gum, spruce, sycamore, willow, and walnut. Not all petrified wood is lapidary material. Wood can also be replaced by barite, marcasite, calcite, coal, and other materials less hard and colorful than chalcedony or jasper.

Even in wood replaced by one of the quartzes, lapidaries must be selective in their choice of material. A particular type of agatized or jasperized wood is called picture wood. This makes gorgeous cabochons. Some wood has fortification or eye patterns that are fascinating to innovative lapidaries.

Wood with wide growth rings and vivid colors also makes excellent lapidary material. The most exotic of woods is that replaced by precious opal such as that from Virgin Valley, Nevada.

Most museums with geological halls have collections of petrified wood. Numerous dealers in the west have specialized in identified petrified wood or petrified wood products, and many lapidaries have specialized in petrified wood collections.

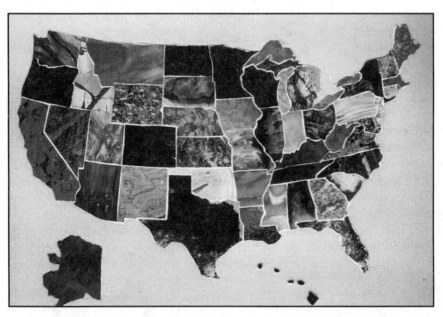

Agatized wood was one of the principal materials used for this intarsia map of the United States by Texas lapidary Wilson Beard.

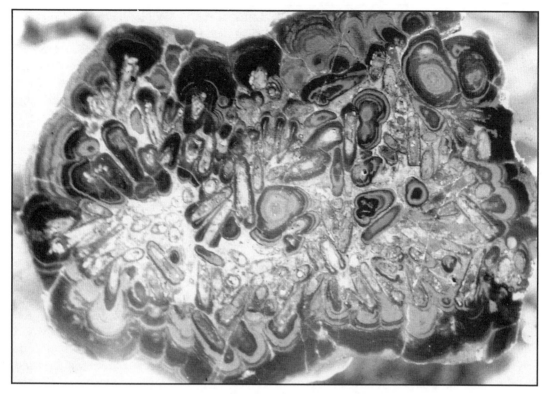

James Slack photographed this weird jasperized algae from western Oklahoma.
Photo courtesy of Lapidary Journal.

Since much petrified wood is located on public lands, lapidaries have the best chance of getting a good supply by finding it themselves or trading for it. Some western dealers are a bit leery about stocking very much.

As a lapidary material, it is easy to cut and polish if it is well silicified. Vibrating laps are often used for petrified wood flats. Polish is achieved with tin oxide on leather or felt, or any preferred polish compound after careful sanding.

A lapidary can do many things with petrified wood.

Tiles, counters, floors. Max Washburn of Houston, Texas, and Wayne Olson of Rapid City, South Dakota, have made tiles out of petrified wood for walls, foyers, counters, and other interior decorations. Dr. Ray Boyce of Rapid City made a bathroom floor of choice polished rounds of colorful agatized wood.

Miniatures and replicas. Melvin Maier of Kalamazoo, Michigan, built a series of scale models of historic stage coaches and pioneer wagons from petrified wood. His "Twenty Mule Team" borax wagon was constructed of 571 polished "boards" of petrified wood. He took the exact measurements from the original in California, at Boron.

Maps. The Puyallup Valley Gem and Mineral Club of Washington made a wall map of their state with each county represented by a different contrasting piece of polished petrified wood. Lapidaries from

Texas and Louisiana make small maps of their states in petrified palm and use them for bola ties, pins, bracelets, and pendants.

Decorative and ornamental items. Award-winning Colorado lapidary Cecil Martin makes intarsia pictures of ducks, quail, and other birds using petrified wood. George Ashley used Arizona wood for some of his beautiful gem bowls.

Jewelry. American Indians use petrified wood in their contemporary channel and inlay work. Colorful agatized and opalized wood has been used for creative jewelry by lapidary silversmiths.

Carvings. Harry Richardson uses colorful rounds of petrified wood as bases for gemstone carvings. Ray Karr carved butterflies from brightly patterned petrified wood. The Malines carved a realistic squirrel from agatized sycamore.

Complete rounds. Some West Coast and Arizona dealers have stunning complete rounds of polished petrified wood and wood casts. Betty Warrington of the Rock-N-Wood shop of Bend, Oregon, says her customers have many favorites, but her own is the petrified sycamore from Post, Oregon, followed closely by the Crooked River limb casts. Identified rounds of petrified wood are both artistic and educational.

Others. Currently, petrified wood has been used for watch faces and watch bands. It has also been used for many casual and sophisticated clocks. Bookends, pen bases, knife handles, paperweights, boxes, bottles, candlesticks, and tabletops are other uses of this versatile and excellent lapidary material.

Identification of Petrified Wood

Lapidaries are aware of the importance of identifying petrified wood, particularly if they have many specimens, large pieces, or unusual pieces. While it does not make a great deal of difference to science if another color or pattern of agate is discovered, it could be very meaningful if a new species of fossil wood came to light. Fossil wood tells science about the climate changes and geological events of the past.

Most species of modern trees arose during the Cretaceous, a period of mild climates, shallow seas, and mountain building. During the late Cretaceous, 90 percent of the trees were antecedents of contemporary flowering trees. Some of these trees are maple, cypress, oak, elm, poplar, magnolia, willow, fig, walnut, hickory, sycamore, sequoia, birch, sweet gum, chestnut, and beech.

Those trees became the source of most of our petrified wood when the volcanoes of the Tertiary in the west covered the forests with ash. Most of the fossil wood found today is related to these Cretaceous families or the even older conifers and palms.

A hand lens is helpful in identifying fossil wood; a microscope is even better. Complete rounds make identification easier. The fibrous outer bark is not always present, but has useful identification characteristics when it is. The bark, phloem, is divided into the outer bark that was dead and the inner bark that was living when the tree perished. The cambial growth was just within the bark. The center, or pith, was surrounded by the xylem or wood, arranged in concentric growth rings. The outer growth rings were the sapwood, and the larger inner section, the heartwood. Modern trees follow this pattern.

Growth rings are more apparent in trees which lived in temperate climates. Other distinctive features of a round of fossil wood are the texture and grain, the specialized cell structure of the storage cells, the water-conducting cells and support fibers. The shapes and sizes and arrangements of the cells are significant. Some trees also have prominent rays.

Cycad, an ancient type of fossil wood, is distinguished by its diamond-shaped pattern.

Cecil Martin of Fort Collins won a trophy with his intarsia bird pictures. Shown here is a Colorado Mountain quail made from petrified wood.

Cell walls may be sculpted or show spiral thickening or pitting. An important feature in the identification of hardwoods is the location and distribution of the pores or vessels in each growth area. These are divided into three groups. In the ring-porous group, the rather large round or oval pores are close to the lighter earlywood part of the growth ring. The latewood pores are much smaller. In the diffuse-porous woods the pores are randomly distributed and are all similar in size. The semiring-porous group is a mixture showing a gradual change in distribution and size of pores. Ash and oak are examples of ring-porous trees, birch and maple are examples of diffuse-porous woods, and walnut and persimmon represent the semiring-porous group. The positions of these pores help determine the distinctive patterns of various woods.

The groupings of cells and pores are separated by rays and growth-ring margins into geometric divisions of squares, rectangles, or curving irregular shapes, usually four sided and similar to squares or rectangles. The pores and storage cells within these structures can form a variety of patterns, for example, in the American elm rather uniform scalloped curves are seen, while the American holly has long chains of regular links, and the sourwood has a polka dot pattern.

When examined with a 10 power lens, the cell structure of the xylem can be round, oval, nearly square, rectangular, or triangular, marquise or tear-drop shaped, diamond or pentagon shaped, or irregular. Both radial sections and tangential sections of the wood should be studied.

It is interesting to note that crystals of quartz, calcite, or various salts are sometimes found in modern wood, so these structures are also seen in petrified wood. But the fossil wood also has crystal growth which occurred long after the tree was dead. Following are some of the things petrified wood experts have seen in their pursuits of identification.

Red maple is diffuse-porous with rings delineated by dark narrow lines and pores small and evenly distributed. Rays varying in width are short but easily seen.

Yellow birch has uniformly distributed pores in units of two, with dim, evenly distributed rays. Under magnification, fine wavy lines are arranged in square fields alternating with rectangles. The pores are bug shaped.

American holly is fine grained with narrow and wide rays and ring edges dividing the surface into squares with radial chains of pores. Margins of growth rings are dense and fibrous.

American chestnut has distinct large pores arranged in quite regular rows close to the growth rings' rims, resulting in an open and lacy look.

Beech is fine and uniform, divided by rings and rays of two widths into square and rectangles full of small pores that are more numerous in the earlywood.

Tupelo has fine, dense rays that make the growth rings appear indistinct. Pores are in short radial groups. Grain is fine and uniform.

Red oak has broad conspicuous rays and abundant pores which are large, round, and concentrated at the beginning of the year's new growth. Broad rays and small pores on either side of these rays finish out the year. Areas of very fine grain alternate with irregular areas of coarser grains. Wide rays provide distinctive patterns.

Red elm has a very regular pattern of alternate tiers with a zigzag appearance and an open lacy appearance formed by large earlywood pores arranged in rows.

Cottonwood has fine texture, even and uniform, with small close pores and tight grain. Some areas when seen under magnification appear to be divided into polka dot–filled squares. Growth rings are rather wide.

Black willow has small numerous pores which are tightly spaced and uniform in is black limb wood with swirling veins of clear or blue chalcedony.

This wood is well suited to jewelry, specimen display, ornamental objects, bowls, tiles, or an assortment of lapidary projects. It is one of the easiest materials to work and takes a brilliant polish with cerium oxide on leather.

Western hemlock shows fine uniform grains a little smaller and denser near the edge of the growth ring. Straight lines of cells are interspersed with equally straight fine rays.

Western white pine is medium to coarse in texture. Specimens may be evenly color zoned with darker, denser latewood. Rays are distinct. Resin canals are present in growth lines as in other conifers. Cells are regular and uniform, arranged in parallel lines.

Ponderosa pine has prominent growth rings with numerous resin canals. There are many wide rays, but they are overpowered by the ring patterns.

Engelman spruce has distinct zoning with darker latewood zones following the earlywood and preceding the growth ring's edge. Rays are inconsequential in the appearance of the wood, which is somewhat like fine hairs transected by light colored strings, slightly frayed.

Western red cedar looks rather like multiple tiered pictures of rainstorms with the latewood denser and coarser in texture and the growth rings gracefully scalloped. Rays are very narrow, but close together.

Redwood or Sequoia semivirens is rather coarse in texture. Growth rings and rays are distinct. Latewood bands are narrow and cells are regular with smooth walls. Storage cells look like strands of oval beads adjacent to the growth ring. Wood cells are like slightly curved parallelograms.

Samples of many kinds of wood are available from several catalogs and from stores specializing in woodworking supplies. Lumber yards have a variety of wood samples and scraps. There are also several books with enlarged pictures of characteristics of many species of wood.

Paleobotanists have sophisticated equipment to use in determining the species of petrified wood. The electronic scanning microscope enlarges the tiniest details that are often significant. They also stain thin sections with analine dyes for a study under a microscope. Three different sections are cut from a specimen: cross section or radial, longitudinal, and tangential. The darker the wood, the thinner the sections must be. If leaf prints or fossil seeds are found in the vicinity of a specimen, they may also aid in identification. Assigning the proper family to petrified wood specimens is fairly easy, but finding the exact species in a family, which may have 50 genera and hundreds of species, is difficult for amateurs. A few dealers in the west have many kinds of identified petrified wood.

Petrified Forests

Arizona Petrified Wood

No doubt the world's most astonishing petrified forest is that of northern Arizona, now a National Park. The sight of the enormous logs of marvelously hued lapidary-quality material covering acres and acres of desert is a view of paradise to the petrified wood collector, except that no wood can be removed from the park. However, to the delight of the lapidary and collector, much of the same brilliantly colored jasperized wood is available from private ranches near the national park.

Arizona was a far different place when these stone logs were living trees. There were many large shallow lakes and sluggish streams as the high country of Arizona was then near sea level. There were junglelike forests of rushes, ferns, and Auracaria pines (like Norfolk pine), and brackish swamps inhabited by ancestral crocodiles. The stone trees did not grow where they now are, but accumulated in these lowlands because of torrential floods. Covered by layers of clay-like silt heavy with volcanic ash, the trees were also buried under a shallow sea that covered the entire region. Silica entered and replaced the wood cells. Then a moun-tain-building period formed the Colorado Plateau, and later the Chinle formation was exposed by erosion, revealing the 200-mil-lion-year-old trees of vivid jasper and chal-cedony.

It is not only modern man who is awed by this remarkable forest. Arrowheads, spear points, and other artifacts have been found meticulously chipped by early tribes from well-selected pieces of petrified wood. Tiffany and Company exhibited mammoth, polished sections of choice Arizona wood at the New York World's Fair of 1900, setting off a rage for any objects made of this wood.

Giant logs from what is now Petrified Wood National Park were once shipped by rail in great quantities to Drake and Com-pany of Sioux Falls, South Dakota, where they were made into clocks for export. Drake also polished huge sections for inte-rior and exterior decorations. Memorial gates, public building fronts, and monu-ments of Arizona wood can still be seen in Sioux Falls.

Much of the Arizona wood was shipped in the rough to Germany where it was made into carvings of animals and other art objects. There is still an industry in Arizona of making bookends and orna-mental slabs of the colorful wood. This wood is obtained from private land.

One of the most beautiful woods from northern Arizona is *Woodworthia*, which is charcoal gray with blue or greenish blue markings. Another is *Schilderia*, which is

black with patterns of a warm golden hue. A beige or fawn-colored wood is *Sigillaria*.

The most striking use of Arizona wood is polished complete rounds for museums and private collections. For home use the Arizona petrified wood bookends and clocks are eye catchers. Large-diameter diamond saws are necessary to make the best use of Arizona petrified wood.

Colorado Petrified Wood

The central plains of Colorado have agatized, jasperized, and opalized wood, mostly subtropical, but including such species as maple, ash, walnut, and pine. Stumps up to 4 feet across and log sec-tions of up to 25 feet have been reported. Elbert County is a particularly productive site. Some of the wood has good color and well-preserved grain patterns. It is cut for display and for cabochons.

El Paso County has yielded many pounds of cutting-quality wood. Numer-ous large pieces of fossil wood have been found in Douglas County, including a trunk 50 feet in length.

Montana Petrified Wood

Tom Miner Basin Forest in the rugged wilderness of northwestern Wyoming and southern Montana is an exceptional petri-fied forest, which to date has revealed over 100 species of trees, including redwoods, pines, oaks, maples, and walnuts. Cellular structure and growth rings may be per-fectly replaced, or the colorful chalcedony may be only a cast of where the wood used to be. The wood in the Tom Miner Basin north of Yellowstone is collectable and under the jurisdiction of the Forest Ser-vice. There is also some private deeded land in the region where wood is collected.

The Tom Miner wood is very colorful in the usual warm wood tones plus hints of blue, violet, and green. A rich gold color and a muted coral are among the out-standing specimens. Some of the golden brown logs are up to 4 feet in diameter. The most elegant specimens have amethyst-lined hollows. Another variation is black limb wood with swirling veins of clear or blue chalcedony.

Nevada Petrified Wood

Excellent-quality petrified wood is widely distributed throughout Nevada. The Hubbard Basin in the Humboldt National Forest has well-agatized wood in a variety of attractive colors, which are stunning for lapidary work, in spite of the fact that the colors are not as saturated as the wood of northern Arizona. The Hubbard Basin wood is pastel blue, pink, violet, and yellow, with contrasting neutrals—gray, beige, tan, and white. In many pieces the cell structure is well preserved with details such as knots and insect or worm holes. Exciting finds have been pieces of colorful logs frosted with sparkling crystals of quartz.

A remote area near Gabbs in Nye County is noted for opalized wood that has bright warm colors and is scattered in alluvial rock beds with agate, jasper, and chalcedony roses. The wood is often completely replaced, showing little evidence that it was once part of a living forest.

New Mexico Petrified Wood

There are several locations for agatized and jasperized wood in New Mexico. The Bisti Badlands of the San Juan basin were once a forested swampland. Well-preserved fossil wood as well as agate and jasper is found in the alluvial deposits. Most of the wood is brown, gray, or black, but some has bright colors. Exceptional specimens are opalized.

Near Las Lunas, fossil wood is found that has a rich chocolate brown color brightened by flaming patterns of saturated red. Brown wood streaked with orange, red-orange, yellow, and gold is found in a volcanic area west of Albuquerque. Wood is also found at Radium Springs south of Hatch.

An extensive fossil forest was discovered near Cerrillos, New Mexico, in the mid nineteenth century. One tree is 6 feet in diameter and over 100 feet in length. Log sections have exceptional detail showing growth rings, knots, splinters, and scars. Assays of the wood have shown traces of gold and silver.

Another New Mexico petrified forest, in Sierra County, has gem-quality petrified wood, including some palm with distinctive dot and eye patterns in earth tones.

Oklahoma's Petrified Forest

Abundant petrified limbs, pieces, and logs of well-preserved petrified wood are found in Cimarron County near Kenton in western Oklahoma's panhandle. Some of the wood is very dark—almost black—but preserves some grain detail toward the center of rounds. Agatized algae is also found here, some resembling the algae of the Eden Valley area of Wyoming. Some of the wood is picture wood; some has inclusions such as quartz crystals or pyrite. The limb sections, 2–3 inches (5.08–7.62 cm) in diameter, are lapidary choices. The logs may be as much as 5 feet (152.40 cm) in diameter.

Most of the wood is locked in sandstone strata, but some continually weathers out. Small pieces of wood are tumbled. Jewelry made of the dark petrified wood resembles black onyx. Some dark petrified wood can be lightened using full-strength household bleach.

Although much of the western Oklahoma wood is unidentified, complete cycads have been found in Cimarron County.

Oregon and Washington Forests

Hampton Butte Wood. Colorful jasperized wood occurs at Hampton Butte in central Oregon. Red, orange, yellow, black, and white are among the colors of the wood, but the sought-for prize is a rare bright green. Knots, twigs, branches, and silica-filled worm holes are other fine specimens. Hampton Butte wood is slabbed for display and made into cabochons for jewelry.

McDermit Petrified Wood. Beautiful, well-preserved petrified wood is found on BLM land in southeast Oregon. Growth rings and cell structures of the highly agatized wood are well preserved, showing many details of the fossil forest. Large trunk sections have been found, many of which have been identified.

Since the preservation is so remarkable, the wood is seldom cut for jewelry, but is used for large slabs, bookends, clock faces, and large lapidary projects. Smaller pieces have been used for cabochons.

Saddle Mountain Wood. Near Mattawa in eastern Washington, some of the most magnificent petrified wood occurs. The prize is called picture wood. In warm earth tones the wood shows panoramic scenes, perhaps similar to the forest in which it once grew. Species are sequoia, sycamore, oak, tupelo, beech, cedar, willow, and cypress.

A typical piece of Saddle Mountain wood is honey colored with rich deep colors toward the edges and streaked with orange, yellow, several shades of brown, and sometimes gray-blue or muted red. Sometimes the structure is sharp and clear and at other times the agate patterns have taken over. While most of the better pieces are about 4–6 inches (10.16–15.24 cm) in diameter, some logs have been found that are 20 inches (50.80 cm) across. This wood has been used for distinctive jewelry and other lapidary purposes, and is often shown as polished complete rounds.

Stinkingwater Petrified Forest. Ugly name—beautiful product! Sulfur-laden hot springs are the source of the name of this Oregon locality in the Columbia Plateau. The well-agatized species of this area are oak, maple, sycamore, and other hardwood trees in natural wood colors of brown, buff, tan, cream, yellow-brown, orange, beige, and taupe. Logs were found here over 2 feet in diameter. Twigs, roots, bark, and knot-hole structure are faithfully preserved as well as the growth rings and cells. One log section even shows plainly where beavers or beaverlike animals gnawed at it before the volcanic destruction.

Some of the wood is brecciated and some is opalized. A rarity in the area is agatized bone from the forest denizens. The wood is high in quality, with few fractures, and is easily cut and polished. The best use for this wood is as polished display slabs, although small fragments make pleasing cabochons.

Sweet Home Petrified Forest. A vast petrified forest is in the area of Sweet Home, Linn County, Oregon. The forest has been known for a long time. Excellent lapidary-quality wood was revealed during the construction of the dam and reservoir on the Middle Santiam River. Some stumps are still vertical.

Authorities say that over 70 species of wood have been found in this area, most of them recognizable as still existing in the forests of today. Some of the wood varieties are fig, cedar, laurel, and oak. In some areas it is necessary to dig for the wood at a depth of 3 to 12 or 14 feet. Douglas fir dominates the living forest. The wood is well agatized and sometimes opalized. The colors are shades of red, red-brown, yellow-brown, yellow, orange, blue, gray, and cream. An oddity is pseudomorphs of chalcedony after halite. The fossil wood is Eocene, from about 50 million years ago, but still remarkable in detail. Lapidaries particularly like the Sweet Home wood that is replaced by bright carnelian—a good jewelry and display material.

Utah Petrified Forests

Escalante. There is a Petrified Forest Park near Escalante, Utah. The wood area extends many miles beyond the park boundaries south and west of Escalante. Large pieces of well-agatized and colorful petrified wood from here are excellent for lapidary projects, including jewelry. The wood grain is well preserved and has contrasting colors of rich browns, reds, yellows, and oranges. It is especially adaptable for large objects like bowls, boxes, and bookends. Many species of plants are represented.

Horse Canyon. Southeast of Boulder, Utah has a significant deposit of silicified wood. Large pieces and sometimes complete rounds of colorful wood are found in the Chinle formation of this rugged area of mountainous desert. The wood has interesting patterns of contrasting colors—blues, browns, whites, reds, and oranges.

Wyoming Petrified Forests

Blue Forest Wood. The Blue Forest Wood north of Green River, Wyoming, is a favorite with Rocky Mountain lapidaries because of its clear blue chalcedony that surrounds much of the wood and fills cracks and crevices, creating handsome patterns against the dense black or warm brown background colors. There is also blue wood with white fortification patterns in the area.

The wood remnants, small or medium-sized logs, limbs, twigs, branches, and casts, are coated with off-white petrified algae. Sometimes the mold left by the algae is filled with blue chalcedony. A layer of blue agate is sandwiched between the algae and the contrasting wood. Annual growth rings and cell structure of some of the wood are preserved in exciting detail in darker and more opaque colors.

Slabbed sections are polished for displays and for large and unique cabochons. Sanding through 600 and polishing with cerium oxide on leather or felt are standard. Most westerners dig their own Wyoming wood.

Wiggins Forks Petrified Forest. Near Dubois, Wyoming, in a rugged mountain area, is a large petrified forest with upright trees of large size. Abundant petrified wood is found north of Dubois toward the 12,000-foot Wiggins Peak and near the Wiggins Fork of the Wind River. The wood is well agatized in natural-appearing wood colors. There are also wood casts here and hollow pieces of agatized wood with quartz crystal lining—occasionally amethyst.

Lamps and other impressive lapidary objects have been made of this wood. Limb casts from this area are very attractive.

Eden Valley Wood. An extensive deposit of unusual agatized wood called Eden Valley wood occurs near Farson, South Pass and Eden, Wyoming. The limb sections, twigs, and branches are glossy black with bluish and clear chalcedony, often with radial markings of pale golden brown, and sometimes a thick rind of cream-colored petrified algae. Small limbs, which still show wood grain, are surrounded by clear chalcedony. In larger limb sections there are often small white mossy or fortification patterns. The dense black chalcedony could pass for jewelers' black onyx.

Eden Valley wood has been used for jewelry and novelties. An example is an old-fashioned lumber wagon miniature replica built of slabs from larger pieces with perfectly round wheels of sections of black wood with natural pale brown radial spokes, the whole wagon loaded high with uniform "logs" of limb sections with deep black polished ends.

The algae found with the wood is light brown with fanciful lacy patterns. Much of it is well silicified, too. The wood occurs in the Green River formation, noted for an abundance of fossil plants and animals.

Specific and Unusual Wood

Bog

Silicified bog occurs in several places in the west, including Oregon, Idaho, and Nevada. Bogs were present in ancient forests, so silicified bog represents a fossil swamp. Residues from many swamp plants, sedges, heaths, mosses, and reeds that once grew in a poorly drained area were covered with silt and infiltrated with silica. Branches and trees also became part of the bog and are called *bogwood*. Scientists find abundant natural history information in the silicified bog. Much of the silicified bog and bogwood is more or less colorless, but the fascinating patterns make up for that lack.

Bogwood is found under a layer of volcanic ash south of Jackpot, Nevada, on the road to Texas Spring. Sometimes the groundmass is a faint pink or a pinkish beige. Bog has been reported near Prineville and Ashland, Oregon, near Alamo Crossing, Arizona, and along the Bill Williams River in Arizona. Chances are that silicified bog occurs in several other areas, but has been thought of as an interesting cutting material instead of a "fossil swamp."

Carnotite in Petrified Wood

Carnotite, a uranium mineral, occasionally occurs in petrified wood or in areas where petrified wood is found. Huge logs with great quantities of carnotite have been found and used only for the uranium contents. However, some western petrified wood has only traces or minimal inclusions of carnotite, which results in yellowish colors in the wood and concentrated intense yellow spots, and causes the wood to fluoresce.

The Morrison formation of southeast Utah is an area rich in uranium and petrified wood. Brightly colored wood from this area is used for cabinet specimens and fluorescent displays. If the wood is highly preserved by silica and has only traces of uranium, it is sometimes cut.

Another area with carnotite in petrified wood is the Anderson Mine in Yavapai County, Arizona. Palm wood with traces of uranium has been found here, sometimes complete trunks. The petrified wood and carnotite are in a sandstone formation that is sometimes fine grained and highly silicified. Spots of canary yellow carnotite in agatized wood make spectacular slabs but are not used for jewelry.

Another state with carnotite in petrified wood is Colorado. The wood is in the Morrison formation near Grand Junction in western Colorado. Some of the wood has been mostly carnotite and sold for premium prices. Small agatized pieces are found with traces of carnotite causing bright colors. They fluoresce neon green and have been cut for display.

Cycad

Now extinct, palmlike plants, cycadeoidales once grew in profusion in mild climates of the Mesozoic. One such area, which at one time was a National Monument, is near Hot Springs in Fall River County, South Dakota. Cycad trunks weighing hundreds of pounds, beautifully preserved in realistic detail by silica, have been found in this mountainous region. Several other counties in western South Dakota are noted for impressive cycads.

Most of these cycads had huge spherical or egg-shaped trunks marked with distinctive diamond-shaped leaf scars and sometimes buds. The colors are usually some shade of brown, varying from rust or brick to chestnut, or lighter hues of reddish brown, buff, or tan and sometimes charcoal black. The regular diamond-shaped patterns appear inside the wood in contrasting lighter or darker shades than the background mass. The patterns are often as perfect as if drawn by

An agatized wood slab shows a natural picture of a pine tree polished and framed by George Frank.

a draftsman and are symmetrically arranged in graceful spirals. Coiled fernlike immature leaves have been found in outer portions of some trunks. Crowns of fernlike leaves grew from the tops of the cycads.

Whole trunks are scientifically important, but broken pieces from alluvial deposits have been used extensively by lapidaries for display and decorative items and sometimes for jewelry. Other locations for cycads are Wyoming, Montana, Colorado, Utah, California, Oklahoma, and Maryland. Cut sections of cycads are dramatic. Quarter sawed pieces give strange patterns that can be used for unique jewelry. Cycad wood is not easy to acquire.

Cythodendron

In south Texas an interesting fossil fern has been found in numerous places. The agatized ferns have been mistakenly called cycad by local lapidaries, although they are very different plants. The agatized fern stems are mainly found in the petrified wood areas near San Antonio. Shaped like elongated cones, the tan and brown fern stems are cut and polished as display pieces, or occasionally made into cabochons. The complex cell patterns are preserved in great detail. Averaging about 3–5 inches (7.62–12.70 cm) in length, the ferns have rough irregular surfaces with a spiraling pattern of eyelike shapes encased in polygons. Patterns are larger at the base end of the cone and smaller at the blunted point. Some Texas petrified wood locations are Livingston, Three Rivers, La Grange, Tilden, Crockett, Zavalla, and Falls City.

Fossil Roots

In the Bowen Basin of Queensland, Australia, there are agatized ancient plants such as osmundite and ancient ferns. Transverse sections of the roots reveal tiny petrified rootlets with starlike patterns in the centers. Although the agatized roots are of special interest, fossil trunks also occur. Calcite and iron are other replacement minerals for these rare specimens. The petrified wood is found in shales interbedded with coal seams. Opalized wood also occurs in Queensland.

Gingko

In the 17-million-year-old forest on the Columbia River near Vantage, Washington, is Gingko State Park, which helps preserve the extinct forest that covers 7,000 acres. There are many stacked layers of well-silicified logs of gingko and other types of wood in the ancient ash. Much of the wood is beautifully opalized.

Gingko trees are gymnosperms that belong to the order of Gingkoales, which originated in the Carboniferous period. Pines are also gymnosperms with long lineage. Gingkos were once widespread. Now they grow in forests in China, but in the United States they are planted in cities as ornamental trees, commonly called Maidenhair trees.

Agatized and jasperized gingkos of Washington have bright colors of red, yellow, green, and blue with brown, tan, cream, and white. Some of the most attractive specimens are blue with black. Most colors are derived from iron and manganese. Cellular patterns are lacy and uniform, rather like a fine mesh. Growth rings are well preserved.

Gingko wood makes impressive polished specimens for display and is high on the priority list of petrified wood collectors. Fossil gingko wood is also found in the John Day River country of north-central Oregon.

Hermanophyton

A mystery plant of the Upper Jurassic found in Utah and other western states had long been an interest of paleobotanist William Tidwell. A few years ago he was aided in his research by amateur collectors, the Leonard Glismanns of Salt Lake City. As a result of Tidwell's study of the Glismann specimens, a new species was identified and named *Hermanophyton glismanni*. For many years specimens of this fossil had been misidentified as Rhexoxylon.

A cross section of this plant resembles a flower, similar to a daisy, encased in a round frame. The plant grew in a moist tropical forest and was unbranched. The arrangement of the wood tissue resembles that of some species of contemporary vines, but this was an erect plant. It was a medium-sized tree with a crown of leaves at the top that fell off as the tree grew. Tidwell studied specimens up to 9 inches (22.86 cm) in diameter.

In addition to the Glismann specimens, Tidwell studied specimens provided by Ken Owens, J. B. Sanchez, and Ruth Kirkby. The specimens showed enough differences that Hermanophyton now includes *Hermanophyton owensi, Hermanophyton taylori,* and *Hermanophyton kirkbyorum*.

This is one of the most interesting-looking types of petrified wood and is often seen in comprehensive wood collections at shows, but is rarely marketed.

Osmundites

Osmundites are a rare form of fossil plant life which belong to the primitive ferns. These plants thrived as early as the Carboniferous. Polished cross sections show contrasting dark round spots which were the basis of the fronds. The exterior of stem pieces are similar to palm trunks with all the fronds broken off.

Osmundites are not found in many places. One location is near Antelope, Oregon. Named *Osmundites oregonensis*, large well-preserved specimens have been found in this vicinity. Another place osmundites have been found is the National Grasslands of western South Dakota and northwestern Nebraska. Here the elaborately patterned pieces are jasperized or agatized and show good coloring of reds, yellows, and browns. Most pieces are rather fan shaped and about hand-sized. The best specimens are translucent when cut and have a pleasing golden color.

Pieces of osmundite have also been found in Wyoming and Idaho. Western Oklahoma has agatized osmundite, tempskya, and cycad in eroded areas of Cimarron County. Osmundites are seldom sold.

Palm

Agatized palm is one of the most sought after of the silicified woods. It comes in many colors, is usually highly agatized, does not have a lot of fractures, and the artistically spaced, dotted patterns make exciting cabochons and slabs. Although agatized palm wood is found in many states, the most and best for the lapidary comes from Texas.

The Texas palm is found in weathered pieces on the surface, in ranch country. Larger sections are found in arroyos and eroded banks, where digging often produces the top prizes, complete agatized palm trunks, sometimes called boles, or in Texas, "palm onions." Caliche pits, gravel pits, ranch fields, and washes have produced superb examples of palm wood. Rocky Byrom, Texas geologist, says the palm is not only on the surface, but is encountered many feet below the surface during oil and mineral explorations. Carefully chipped arrowheads found in the area show that the earliest Americans also appreciated the beauty of the agatized palm.

The colors of agatized palm are like an artist's palette. The round dots in precise patterns that identify the palms are from 1 to 3 mm in diameter. Dots may be light in color on a dark groundmass, or dark on a light ground. The exterior inch or so of a complete round is usually of a contrasting color to the central part. Small pieces showing reverse coloration of the spotted patterns are used for decorator cabochons.

Silicified palm roots have more complex patterns and are also showy for cutting material. Pieces of wood cut longitudinally or tangentially also have exotic patterns. Some of the patterns resemble tangles of strings, yarns, or ribbons.

Some of the Texas counties with palm wood are Fayette, Atacosa, McMullen, Live Oak, Karnes, Hidalgo, Starr, Newton, Sabine, and Shelby. Excellent palm wood is found on both sides of the Toledo Bend Reservoir and the Sabine River, which mark the Texas/Louisiana border.

Other states with petrified palm are California, Arizona, New Mexico, Colorado, and Wyoming. A favorite use in Louisiana and Texas is for bola ties or pins made with cabochons in the shapes of the maps of those states. Texas lapidaries choose colorful pieces with small-scale patterns. Palm wood is seen at most shows and shops in the central south.

Petrified Reed

Two places in California have petrified reeds, which belong to the grasses. One location is near Goffs, which is west of Needles. The silicified reed is often encased in polishable matrix and can be cut into unusual cabochons or slabs. The other location is Brown Butte near Mojave. The petrified reed in matrix has a good color contrast, mostly in neutral tints and shades, and can be imaginatively cut to show eyes, pencils, or tubes, depending on the orientation. The reed occurs in well-silicified bundles, but some of the material will undercut if not carefully selected. This is not commonly found in shops.

Bill Dahlberg, Minnesota lapidary, specialized in scale miniatures. This antique table and chair set is made of jasperized wood.

Sequoia

Fossil remnants of Sequoia trees are widely scattered in petrified wood areas of the central and western states of the United States. The Gallatin petrified forest and the Tom Miner petrified forests of Montana, and the amazing petrified forests of Yellowstone Park in Wyoming, have gigantic Sequoia trunks that must have been 1,000 years old before they were killed and preserved by volcanic ash. Some fossil stumps still standing are 15 feet in diameter. Trees of present forests in the area are dwarfs in comparison to the big trees of the past.

Fossil Sequoia is also found in California, Nevada, Oregon, Washington, Idaho, Colorado, North and South Dakota, Alaska, and British Columbia, Canada. Huge logs are found in place in some areas, while in other areas pieces of Sequoia are found in alluvial gravels. Even weathered and water-rolled pieces often show fine details preserved by chalcedony.

A fossil forest in Sonoma County, north of San Francisco, consists of enormous silicified fossil redwoods, in an area where redwoods still dominate the forest. The original structural detail of the wood is as remarkable as the size of the fossil trees that lie on the surface and up to 100 feet below.

Fossil Sequoia cones have been found in the Cannonball formation in western

North Dakota. About 2 inches (5.08 cm) in length and dark brown in color, these cones have been cut in half lengthwise and polished for display.

Hundreds of the fossil cones have been found by amateurs. Paleobotanists have named the species *Sequoia dakotaensis*. When cut, some of the cones look almost modern, and others have a submetallic luster, probably from hematite. The cones can often be acquired in North Dakota.

Tempskya

Tempskya is a tree fern of the distant past, which grew about 100 million years ago in the forests of the Cretaceous over wide areas where the climates were warm and humid. Agatized trunk pieces are found as float in eroded areas of most of the western states.

The vascular bundles make eyelike patterns when a cross section is cut. The material is opaque with the darker eyes showing off sharply against the paler and smaller cell design of the background.

Colorful pieces of Tempskya including red, yellow, and orange are found in South Dakota, Nebraska, Oklahoma, Wyoming, Montana, Utah, and Texas. An eastern location for large pieces of well-silicified Tempskya is in the gravels of the coastal plains of North Carolina. It has been noted in Maryland also. Huge pieces have been found in Russia. Tempskya is occasionally offered for sale.

Teredo Bored Petrified Wood

Teredo bored petrified wood can be found in locations where fallen trees were once driftwood in shallow seas. The driftwood was bored full of holes by wormlike marine mollusks and later became deeply buried in clayey silt where it was replaced gradually by silica, which preserved every detail of the wood and the passages left by the shipworms.

The overall appearance of a slab of teredo wood is of a polka-dot pattern gone astray. The dots can be filled with clear, gray, white, or faintly yellow quartz, chalcedony, common opal, calcite, or barite, or sections of the borings can be hollow, lined with drusy quartz. The colors of the teredo bored wood are usually drab, but the wood grain is well preserved and the passages of the little mollusks that ate into the trees so many millions of years ago make this an interesting cutting material. So much high-quality teredo bored wood has been found in North Dakota that it is the official state fossil. It is sometimes sold by dealers in the north-central states.

RECOMMENDED READING

See also lists for Chapters 4, 5, and 6.

Arnold, C., *Introduction to Paleobotany*. New York: McGraw Hill, 1947.

Ash, S., and May, D., *Petrified Forest*. Holbrook, AZ: Petrified Forest Museum, 1965.

Core, H., et al., *Wood Structure and Identification*. Syracuse, NY: Syracuse University Press, 1979.

Harlow, W., *Inside Wood, Masterpiece of Nature*. Washington, DC: American Forestry, 1970.

Ransom, J., *Petrified Forest Trails*. Portland, OR: Mineralogist, 1955.

Sanborn, W., *Oddities of the Mineral World*. New York: Van Nostrand Reinhold, 1976.

Tidwell, W., *Common Fossil Plants of Western North America*. Provo, UT: Brigham University Press, 1976.

CHAPTER VIII

Cabochon Favorites of Yesterday and Today

Jade	**Opal**
Jadeite	Common opal
Nephrite	Precious opal
Lapis lazuli	**Sugilite**
	Turquoise

SOMETIMES PEOPLE WHO KNOW little about gems tend to think the really valuable gems are faceted, that gems that are carved or cut into cabochons automatically belong to the former ambiguous classification of semiprecious. The truth is that many translucent to opaque gem materials are used for top-quality expensive jewelry. Fine cabochons include imperial jade and black opal as well as star sapphire and cat's-eye emerald.

Value is not always determined by the transparency of a stone. Beauty is the most important qualification of a gemstone. Several translucent to opaque materials, used primarily for carvings and cabochons, have attained high status and value in the gem and lapidary world. Most of these materials have been used as gems since ancient times. Opal has been cherished since the days of the Roman Empire. One translucent material that achieved rapid acceptance is sugilite, a recent discovery.

One of the old materials, turquoise, is often porous and of inferior hardness, but it has been loved by many cultures for centuries because of its splendid colors. Another of the almost timeless gem materials, lapis lazuli, is a rock not a mineral. Opal is a fragile stone, yet few faceted gems command a higher price than a flashy cabochon of black opal. Jade, honored for centuries in the East and the West, is not one mineral but two, and although there are great quantities of jade, particularly nephrite, in the world, the best colors and qualities are reserved for the finest carvings and exquisite jewelry.

Jade, lapis lazuli, opal, sugilite, and turquoise of high quality are expensive, but other cabochon and carving materials are often in high-price categories too, especially if they have exceptional color and occur in limited quantities.

Jade, lapis lazuli, and turquoise, although beautiful, owe part of their popularity to mystique. Opal's almost hypnotic flashing colors give it an extra quality called phenomenal. Sugilite is a new favorite because its sensational purplish red color fills a slot in the color wheel which is a contemporary favorite with the art and fashion worlds.

Old and new materials were selected for this chapter to illustrate the importance of translucent and opaque materials usually made into carvings and cabochons, but also to show that the old terminology precious and semiprecious have little validity for today's lapidary artists.

Jade (nephrist and jadeite) are among the finest carving materials. Hing Wa Lee carved this traditional Chinese Pi (13 inches).

JADE
Jadeite
Sodium aluminum silicate
H. 7　D. 3.36
Monoclinic

There are two minerals correctly called jade: nephrite and jadeite. Of the two, jadeite is harder than nephrite and the color range is brighter and more varied. *Imperial*

jade, an incredibly rich chrome green translucent material, is one of the most exquisite and expensive cabochon stones.

A tough member of the pyroxene group, good jadeite is as scarce as it is desirable. It has a crystalline structure, a granular texture, and a vitreous luster. Jadeite is found in highly metamorphosed serpentines in masses and veins, and as alluvial boulders. Rocks associated with jadeite deposits are sodium rich.

When pure, jadeite is white; however, the colors include both tints and shades of green, mauve, lavender, red, blue, orange, brown, and yellow. Like nephrite, jadeite has been given many imaginative color names. Some of these are old mine, new mine, pea green, flower green, mutton fat, kingfisher, melonskin, canary, sandlewood, and clouds-in-the-sky. Iron, manganese, and chromium are among the coloring agents. The pyroxene mineral ureyite is found in jadeite deposits and sometimes mixed with the jadeite. Jadeite is sometimes treated in the Orient by a bleaching process that removes undesirable colors, followed by impregnation with polymer.

Jadeite was known in Burma, source of the finest jade, as early as the thirteenth century, but it was not until the eighteenth century that Chinese carvers started working on it. Burma, now Myanmar, became the world's chief supplier of jadeite. Boulders up to 33 metric tons are found in upper Burma, intermingled with serpentine, schists, and dikes of albite, glaucophane, and actinolite. Mining activities are near Tawmaw and in the Kachin Mountains, and alluvial boulders are in the valley of the Uru River.

In 1963, Dr. Edward Gubelin discovered an emerald green jadeite-albite mixture near the Tawmaw mines of Mamshamaw, a material colored by chrome-rich ureyite. The jade-albite-ureyite mixture is a saturated color. At first it was thought to be a variety of epidote, but tests showed the mineral ureyite or kosmochlor, a sodium chrome silicate. This material, subsequently named *maw-sit-sit* sometimes occurs in boulders that are partly jadeite. Since it cuts and polishes in a similar manner to jadeite, it is used for carvings, cabochons, and ornamental objects.

Another source of jadeite is Guatemala. Archeologists have uncovered many elaborately carved jadeite items in Mexico and Central America in the Olmec, Aztec, and Maya sites. Aztecs considered jade a material more precious than gold. Lost for hundreds of years, the Guatemalan deposits have been rediscovered in this century. The jadeite of Guatemala occurs with serpentine in the Motagua River valley near Manzanal in the south-central part of the country. Small boulders are found in the La Palmilla and Huijo rivers.

Not as translucent or color intense as the best Burmese jadeite, the Guatemala jades come in modified green hues, including a lovely blue-green. Some of the greens are mottled with pastel tints of yellow that proved to be pyrite. Guatemalan jade contains 10 percent diopside. Artifacts made from Guatemalan jadeite by ancient cultures show superb artistry.

Jadeite is found in California in Trinity, Sonoma, Mendocino, and San Benito counties. Most of the recoveries have been boulders in alluvial deposits; however, jade has been found in place in the Clear Creek area of San Benito County in contacts of schists and serpentines. Colors of California jadeite are often somber in comparison with the vivid Burma jadeite.

Jadeite is selected for color, grain, and translucency. It is one of the best carving materials and is also used extensively for high-fashion jewelry, especially the more intense greens and mauves. Much of the imperial jade, and other superb colors of translucent jade, is cut in Hong Kong, or marketed through Hong Kong. Elaborate jadeite carvings from China are featured in many museums; however, most of these pieces are antiques, or nearly so. Good jadeite has become so expensive that rough material once used for remarkable carvings, like the Smithsonian's 22-inch (55.88-cm) lavender jade vase, is now being cut into cabochons.

A 24-inch (60.96-cm) incense burner from the Imperial Palace of China is in the collection of Hing Wa Lee, noted carver. A vivid green jadeite reliquary, 18¼ inches high, and a jadeite pagoda splashed with areas of emerald green jade, 21⅜ inches (54.2 cm) tall, are in the jade collection of the Lizzadro Museum. The Carnegie Museum's Hillman Hall has an exquisite carving, "Nut Tree with Birds." A pair of intricate pale green jadeite Mayan plaques are in a private collection in Texas. A graceful white jadeite phoenix is a treasure of the Seattle Art Museum.

Flexible shaft and fixed shaft carving machines, and silicon carbide and diamond tools, are used for carving jade now, but the ancients used only sand, bamboo, and water. Gem lathes are used for such objects as bowls. Jadeite is easily polished on hard leather with Linde A, Rapid Polish, or chrome oxide. Rough jade boulders are scarce at present.

Chloromelanite

Chloromelanite is an impure jadeite close in composition to aegirine. It is distinguished by a very dark but intense green, sometimes almost black. Iron oxide is thought to be the chief coloring agent of this unique jade variety that comes from Burma. It has been found in Burma intergrown with maw-sit-sit.

Chloromelanite, unlike jadeite, never has pastel tints such as lavender or pale green. There are often some streaks of pure white. The material is nearly opaque. Although it is considered scarce, this iron-rich jade is still being found.

The American Museum prizes a chloromelanite Kuan Yin that was carved in China in the nineteenth century. Occasionally magnificent chloromelanite jewelry pieces are seen at major shows. There is some controversy as to whether chloromelanite should be listed as a separate jade, but it is distinctive and recognizable. Well suited to fine jewelry and impressive carvings, it is worked exactly like lighter-colored jadeite.

Nephrite
Calcium magnesium iron silicate
H. 6½   D. 2.95
Monoclinic

Nephrite is more plentiful than jadeite, and has been known far longer. The use of nephrite for tools, implements, and many practical and decorative purposes dates back at least 4,000 years. The toughness, durability, and attractive colors of nephrite led archaic Chinese stone workers to make weapons and ceremonial items from nephrite. Later generations grew to revere nephrite and chose it for magnificent carvings related to their religion, imperial system of government, cultural rites, legends, symbolism, music, customs, and even writing.

Ancient jade items have been excavated in Crete and in the search for Troy. Nephrite tools and carvings have been found in Canada, Alaska, several of the contiguous United States, and in Mexico and South America. Nephrite was used by natives of British Columbia as long ago as 2,000 B.C., and Siberian dark green nephrite objects have been found with organic matter dating to 4,880 B.C. by radiocarbon.

Nephrite comes in a wonderful palette of colors, the best known of which are the greens. Jade authority, Al Youngquist, finds that greens are preferred over all other colors. Most of the greens lean toward the yellow, gray, or brown, although some are almost white or nearly black. Color names applied to jade in various localities include apple green, spinach green, emerald green, leek green, sage green, grass green, and olive green. Other colors are buff, russet, brown, blue, red, gray, mauve, and yellow. Colors are due to iron and magnesium. Most of the colors are a mixture of hues and do not have the intensity or saturation of the colors found in jadeite.

There are also patterned jades with mottling, dendrites, swirling bands, and designs resembling snowflakes or flowers. Such jades are marketed with imaginative names like snowflake jade, moss jade, seaweed jade, polka-dot jade, two-tone jade, twilight jade, tapestry jade, and more.

*Lapidary/jewelry artist Doris Kemp created this
graceful Wyoming nephrite necklace.
Photo by Russell Kemp.*

Nephrite is an amphibole closely related to actinolite and tremolite. Its toughness is due to microscopically fibrous interlocked crystals. The toughness makes up for the hardness, which is lower than jadeite. Associated with serpentines and schists, nephrite is found in situ in highly metamorphosed areas, and also in gigantic boulders and pebbles in alluvial deposits. Small pieces of nephrite are noticeably heavier than surrounding rock such as serpentine. The best nephrite is translucent with uniform consistency and clean, not muddy, color.

Green jade "slicks," polished by wind and sand, are found in the Wyoming jade fields, and, according to Youngquist of Bergsten Jade, they are some of the most beautiful objects in nature. Youngquist also notes that occasionally small boulders of apple-green color are of museum quality. Another interesting Wyoming treasure is pseudomorphic jade, which is patterned with dark geometric shapes that are the pseudomorphs of nephrite after quartz. Even more fascinating are the rare pieces of green nephrite which have inclusions of translucent or transparent, colorless quartz crystals. Pyrite is another jade inclusion. Wyoming also has a bloodstone jade with numerous red spots, clouds, and splotches caused by iron. In the field, Wyoming nephrite often has a rust-colored skin.

California also has several excellent nephrite localities producing fine material for cabochons and carvings. A unique California occurrence of green nephrite has inclusions of lustrous sprays of magnetite crystals, which inventive lapidaries have sometimes treated to the gold plating process. Another distinctive California occurrence is botryoidal jade. Mammoth nephrite boulders have been found in the ocean by skin divers near Jade Cove. There is still plenty of good nephrite in the Indian Creek area of Siskiyou County near Happy Camp in northern California. Sometimes California jade has small inclusions of native gold.

The University of Alaska Museum has a cut nephrite boulder weighing 3,550 pounds from the immense Dahl Creek–Jade Mountain deposit near Kobuk. Even larger boulders exist in this cold and remote region. Alaskan jade was mined for many years by the Ivan Stewarts of Anchorage. After several disappointing tries, government officials are again attempting to help the Alaskan natives to develop the jade field as an income source. Some of the jade is chatoyant and some has excellent color and translucency.

Other U.S. locations for nephrite are Washington, Oregon, and Utah. Geologist Lee Hammons has an active mine for

A stylized red jadeite dragon is the motif for this Hing Wa Lee jewelry carving (3 inches in diameter).

a good-quality black jade in east-central Arizona. Jade of rather mediocre quality has also been found in Wisconsin and North Carolina.

The jade of British Columbia, Canada, is well known. Locations are Lillooet, Fraser River, Ogden Mountain, Shulaps Range, Cadwallader Range, Cassiar, and Deese Lake. Jade mining and processing has become a significant industry in British Columbia. Other Canadian locations are in the Yukon and Northwest Territories. A Canadian nephrite boulder of 175 tons is reported. Fine jewelry and carvings are made from the Canadian jade.

Siberian jade has been mined since the eighteenth century by the open pit method. Huge boulders occur in the Sayan region. Some of the material (closely related actinolite) is chatoyant and will cut cat's-eye cabochons. A newer discovery in Siberia has small veins of high-quality translucent apple-green nephrite along with pastel tints: light blue, off white, and light green. Leonid Prikazchikov, Russian mineral expert, describes it as occurring with calcareous rock on the Vitym River.

The Maoris of New Zealand used nephrite from the Raramakau River and the Whitcombe River for tools, weapons, and decorative objects for centuries. Native lapidaries now make innovative well-crafted jewelry stones and carvings from these deposits. A huge deposit of nephrite of many subtle colors is located near Cowell on the Eyre Peninsula of Australia.

Of all the nations, it is China that has placed the most importance on nephrite, making jade a significant part of the national culture. First used for tools, fetishes, symbols, vessels, and implements, Chinese nephrite was later used for fabulous carvings and ornate items for royalty, religious leaders, and scholars. The Chinese nephrite deposits are in Xinjiang Uygur. The "mutton fat" nephrite of the Kunlum Mountains is considered to be the finest jade of this district. Taiwan also has nephrite. Other nephrite deposits are in Poland, Germany, Zimbabwe, India, and Japan.

Nephrite is used for all types of cabochons, beads, pendants, tumbled baroques, tiles, watchbands, bracelets, rings, and even chains. Contemporary lapidaries also use nephrite for spheres, knives and knife handles, boxes, and bowls.

The most spectacular use of nephrite is for carvings. Amateurs have made translucent carved plates, cups, and saucers of nephrite. A jade pagoda replica carved from British Columbia nephrite from a

Jade and opal are two of the carving material sused by Aubrey Cole for this hummingbird composite carving. Photo by Cook's, Vienna, VA.

10-ton boulder now weighs 1 ton. This detailed reproduction of the historic Buddhist Six Banyon Temple took thousands of hours. A carved seagull of Canadian nephrite has an 18-inch inch (45.72-cm) wingspan. Don Wobber sculpted a 2,400-pound abstract carving from nephrite from Jade Cove, California. J. L. Kraft, cheese magnate, created a nephrite window for a Chicago church. The Lizzadro Museum has a superbly carved five-piece nephrite altar set that was once in the summer palace of Imperial China. An ornately carved apple-green jade bowl that was once a Russian czar's treasure is also in the Lizzadro collection.

Nephrite look-alikes are natural or dyed serpentine, dyed magnesite, or dolomite, green jasper, amazonite, aventurine, prehnite, epidote, chrysoprase, and soapstone. Nephrite itself is sometimes dyed to improve the color. Nephrite selected for jewelry should have the best color available, and be as uniform and translucent as possible.

Some jade is easy to polish by normal methods, whereas other specimens pull and leave a textured surface similar to the skin of oranges or lemons. Considerable pressure may be used in sanding and polishing nephrite. A prepolish should appear with a well-worn 600 silicon carbide sanding belt or disc. Chrome oxide or Rapid Polish or Linde A on leather, worked almost dry, will bring a quick polish. Difficult jades are finished with 50,000 diamond. Nephrite is readily available.

LAPIS LAZULI

A rock, not a mineral, lapis lazuli is an elite carving and cabochon material because of its incredible color. Used and admired for over 6,000 years, lapis lazuli is one of the world's oldest gem materials. It is about 5½ in hardness and around 2.7 in density, and the color is a deep royal blue. The blue comes from lazurite, hauynite, sodalite, and noselite. Other constituents are pyrite, calcite, diopside, feldspar, and mica. A newer theory is that strong absorption of light by molecular sulfur radicals may cause the deep blue appearance. The principal mineral lazurite also forms crystals. Small lazurites are occasionally faceted.

The major source in the past and now is Afghanistan, where the ancient mines are located in the rugged mountains of the Hindu Kush. These mines furnished gem material to the pharaohs of Egypt, the leaders of Babylon, and the rulers and nobility of Greece and Rome. The sapphire of Aaron's breastplate may have been lapis lazuli.

Salah Taj of Afghan Gems says the mine at Sar-e-Sand is still productive and still worked in the old way of heating the rock and quenching it with water. Lapis lazuli was used for amulets, seals, charms, scarabs, cameos, beads, bowls, mosaics, inlay, and many other things. Because blue pigments were rare and much desired, lapis lazuli was ground and powdered and made into the beautiful blue pigment, ultramarine. The use of ultramarine paint became a status symbol for Renaissance artists.

Two occurrences in the Russian commonwealth (CIS) are near the southwest end of Lake Baikal and in the Pamir Mountains. Lapis lazuli was a material favored by the czars and often used by Peter Carl Fabergé.

A lapis lazuli deposit in Chile is not equal in color to the Afghanistan material, but it is often seen in carvings where the numerous gray inclusions can be cleverly hidden or obliterated by skilled craftsmen. This lapis was used for ornaments by South Americans long before the Spanish conquest. The mines in Chile are snow covered 10 months of the year.

Excellent rich blue lapis lazuli comes from Gunnison County, Colorado. A mine on North Italian Mountain at an elevation of about 13,000 feet has been worked periodically. The Blue Wrinkle Mine was worked during the 1980s. The top grade, vivid blue with no calcite and nicely distributed pyrite, is said to equal

From one of the oldest gem mines in the world comes this Afghanistan lapis lazuli carved by Hing Wa Lee. Pendant is 2¾ inches. Zeitner collection.

fine Afghanistan material. Lapis lazuli from this mine has been sent to Idar-Oberstein and Taiwan for carving. Like the deposit in Chile, the lapis lazuli mine of the Colorado Rockies is under a blanket of snow much of the year.

A lapis lazuli deposit was worked for several years in San Bernadino County, California, in the National Forest in Cascade Canyon. In the early 1970s, David Jensen of Rochester, New York, sent a cabochon of lapis lazuli from New York State to the AFMS Smithsonian cabochon collection. The cabochon was of excellent color, well cut and polished, and came from a deposit of dolomitic marble in St. Lawrence County. A deposit on Baffin

Island, Canada, has recently been explored and tested, with results still being analyzed, but looking promising.

Intrusions of magma caused the recrystallization of impure limestones to marble and lapis lazuli resulted from contact metamorphosis. It occurs in pyrite-rich zones of marble and in sheetlike zones.

Lapis lazuli is usually cut into cabochons or made into beads, pendants, or carvings. Sometimes the most intense color is faceted for beads, which are stunning, although opaque. Although not very hard, lapis lazuli is fairly tough and durable. It is often dyed to improve the color. It is also sometimes oiled. Dolomite, howlite, jasper, and quartzite

Carved cabochons of lapis lazuli are among the fine gem materials on this antique stomacher from the Treasures of Chatsworth collection from England. Virginia Museum photograph.

are dyed to resemble lapis lazuli. Lazurite in diopside and sodalite with pyrite can be mistaken for lapis lazuli. Look-alikes are dyed marble, glass, and ceramic. Egyptian faience resembled fine lapis lazuli.

Loreen Haas, gem dealer, designed a lapis lazuli carving, "Christus Dolorosus," executed in fine Afghanistan material. The completed head weighs 827 grams. Hing Wa Lee's intense blue "Chinese Mountain" is 8 inches (20.32 cm) in height and is in a private collection. The American Museum of Natural History has a 6-inch (15.24-cm)-high Chinese junk carved from lapis lazuli. A lapis lazuli carved eagle has a 10½-inch (26.67-cm) wing spread. The Hermitage in St. Petersburg Russia has lapis lazuli urns 6 feet tall.

Selection is a matter of taste as some cutters prefer inclusions of pyrite and mottled material, feeling that the deep, pure blue may appear to be treated or imitation. Lapidaries grind lapis lazuli on fine wheels and work it wet. Lemon peel can be prevented by polishing with diamond; however, some lapidaries get good results with a mixture of chromium oxide and Linde A on hard leather. When there is considerable pyrite in lapis lazuli it may undercut.

OPAL
Hydrated silicon dioxide
H. 5½   D. 1.99

Because of its wonderful prismatic colors, resembling crushed rainbows, opal is one of the most popular gemstones in the world. Black opal and imperial jadeite may be the most coveted of all cabochon stones. Not all opal, however, has the fascinating play of color that excites the imagination, but the many colors of common opal often make elegant cabochons and carvings. Transparent opal can be faceted.

Common Opal

Common opal is widespread with many variations. Common opal is probably an unfortunate term because some of the so-called common opal is translucent and has wonderful color, and is used for excellent cabochons, carvings, beads, and other lapidary purposes. Since common opal is widespread, only a few localities are included here.

An occurrence of gorgeous green opal colored by nickel was found in Poland, and recently in Tanzania. The Tanzanian material has the rich green color of the best-quality chrysoprase and it has been called "prase opal."

Mexican common opal comes in many colors including blue, yellow, and scarce lavender, but the most important are the vivid reds and oranges. Common opal occurs in the same states as precious opal.

Brazil has an interesting green opal with dark dendrites. A vivid blue opal, colored by copper, is now coming from San Patreciao, Peru. Patterned and colored common opal is found in South Africa near Postmasburg and Pella in the Pilansberg Mountains. Common opal in lovely tints comes from Tairua, New Zealand. A green and yellow patterned opal comes from Oamaru, while a dendritic yellow opal deposit is in the Coromandel Peninsula.

An unusual chatoyant Australian gem material called *silicophite* is common opal with asbestos inclusions. Common opal of several pastel colors occurs in a chalcedony field near Wikieup, Arizona. Dendritic opal is also found near Burro Creek.

California has several sites for common opal. Opal Mountain northeast of Mojave has cherry opal and common opal of many vivid colors including green, orange, yellow, honey, and white. Common opal in a host of excellent colors is found in Lemhi County, Idaho. The opal occurs as masses in porphyry, and is green, blue, pink, or

Two areas of translucent opal with vivid color are separated by white matrix in this Mexican opal cabochon.

yellow. The dark blue opal from Owyhee County is prized for its color. It is found in rhyolite nodules. The dumps of cinnabar mines near Riley, Oregon, have yellow and orange common opal. Wood opal of many colors comes from Oregon, Washington, and other western states. Common opal of uncommon colors is usually on the market.

Precious Opal

Precious opal owes its marvelous colors to its orderly layers of silica spheres and the effect of light on the unique structure. The size of the spheres determines the wavelength of the light refraction. Precious opal is that which has play of color. These colors are intense pure hues that shimmer and glow in the light.

The groundmass color of precious opal can be white, clear, or deep brown or black with a myriad of colors in between shades and tints of yellow, orange, red, violet, blue, and green. Some opal is as clear as a drop of water, but alive with points of color. Every new opal strike seems to have its distinctive characteristics. Opal nomenclature differs in some areas, but following is a list of well-known opal varieties and terminology.

Black opal. Opal which has play of color against a black or near black background.

Boulder opal. Ironstone concretion with opal fillings, sometimes with bands of precious opal alternating with common opal.

Broad flashfire. Sheets or flashes of broad fire covering a major portion of the opal's surface.

Cachalong. Porous, porcelainlike opal that absorbs water quickly.

Cat's eye or star opal. The color is concentrated in vertical or hexagonal chatoyant bands.

Cherry opal. Cherry red translucent to transparent opal that sometimes has a play of color.

Contra Luz opal. Opal, often from Mexico or Oregon, which shows its spectral colors against the light.

Crystal opal. Colorless opal with play of color.

Fire opal. Transparent or translucent opal with red or red-orange body color, sometimes with play of color. Mostly from Mexico. Fire opal is not synonymous with precious opal.

Fishscale. Color play resembles fish scales.

Flag. Color play resembles flagstones.

Flame. Precious opal with elongated streaks of flamelike colors.

Flash. Precious opal with broad flashes of prismatic colors.

Girosol opal. Water-clear opal with floating colors.

Harlequin. Precious opal with play of color pattern similar to checkerboard mosaic.

Honey opal. Pale, amber-colored opal usually with play of color.

Hyalite opal. Pure, transparent, colorless opal that forms in crusts.

Hydrophane opal. A variety of cachalong that becomes almost transparent in water, except for the rainbow colors.

Ironstone opal. Opal in dark sandstone.

Jelly opal. Transparent colorless opal with a bluish iridescence.

Lechosos (milk). It has a play of color against a pure white background color.

Mackerel Sky. Opal with bold parallel bands of separate and contrasting color flashes.

Matrix opal. Host rock has small flecks and veins of opal that cannot easily be removed from the matrix.

Moss opal. Usually light-colored opal with dark dendritic growths.

Nobby. A rounded opal found in Lightning Ridge clay.

Peacock. Opal with the vivid colors of a peacock's tail.

Pinfire. Opal with small closely spaced pinpoints of iridescent colors.

Potch. Common opal with no play of color.

Precious opal. Opal with prismatic play of color.

Rainbow opal. Facetable clear opal with pools of reflected colors shimmering on the surface.

Ribbon opal. Has single ribbon of fiery colors.

Rolling Flashfire. Moving sheets of color on the surface.

Seam opal. Narrow rows of opal that have filled cracks and fissures in the rock.

Wood opal. Pseudomorphs of opal after wood.

Yowah Nut. Small concretion from Australia sometimes containing precious opal.

Opal forms near the surface at fairly low temperatures where there has been extensive hydrothermal activity. It is found in many places occurring as seams, nodules, and fillings. The primary source for gem-quality opal for the past hundred years has been Australia. There are opal deposits in Queensland, South Australia, and New South Wales. Well-known fields are Coober Peddy, Andamooka, Mintabie, Opalton, Quilpie, White Cliffs, and Lightening Ridge. Black opal from Lightening Ridge is one of the most spectacular of all gems. The many opal rushes of Australia have been reminiscent of the great gold rushes of the United States. Opal authority Paul Downing has seen Lightning Ridge opals sell for $25,000 per carat.

The largest cut opal at present is a black Australian opal weighing 1,560 carats. A rare opal, "Majestic's Harlequin Sunset," is a glamorous stone of many colors with a rare "mackerel sky" pattern. It weighs 39.8 carats and is set in a necklace owned by Paul Downing. Mackerel sky, a rare pattern, resembles zebralike stripes, or perhaps aurora borealis streamers. Downing also has a rare cat's-eye opal and several unique picture opals.

A possible record-size opal was found 56 feet underground at Coober Peddy in 1989. The smaller of two pieces yielded a 765-carat cut stone and the larger piece is 28,350 carats (11½ pounds). Estimated value of the previous record Olympia Australis at 17,700 carats was $2.5 million. A dense black 574-carat opal in the Los Angeles County Museum is from a new location in New South Wales, Australia.

Another opal-producing country is Mexico. Many opal mines dot the rugged mountains of the state of Queretaro. Some of this opal occurring in rhyolite is fire opal and much of it is extraordinarily translucent or transparent. This material is often faceted. Precious opal-filled amygdaloidal cavities are small, so a high percent of the

Opal cabochons with vivid play of color are suitable for elegant jewelry set in gold and accented with diamonds.
Courtesy of Lapidary Journal.

Mexican opal is used for matrix cabochons and small carvings. A fist-size fire opal found near Queretaro in 1984 is a record for this state. Mexican opal has a reputation for being unstable; nevertheless, a large number of magnificent stones have been cut and set into fine jewelry and seem to be as stable as good opal from other locations. Other locations for Mexican opal are in the states of Guerrero, Chihuahua, Michoacán, and Jalisco. A rare black cat's-eye opal was recently found in Jalisco.

Brazil has excellent opal. American gem engraver Ute Klein Bernhardt says it seems harder and so is easier to work with than other opal. She has made several notable carvings from large colorful pieces of Brazilian opal. The opal occurs in sandstone in the state of Piaui. It has a white ground color and well-distributed rainbow colors. Variations are cat's-eye stones and yellow opal with dendrites.

Clear opal, white opal, and black opal with a promising play of color has been discovered in Java in Indonesia. Another new find of opal is in Ethiopia. Mosaic and flash patterns adorn dark and almost transparent variations.

The United States has several opal-producing areas, the most famous of which is Rainbow Ridge, Nevada, where dazzling dense black opal is found. This opal is often a replacement of wood, and sometimes bone. It is often referred to as unstable, due to excess water; however, many well-cut stones show no crazing after 20 years or more.

The Keith Hodson family, owners of the Rainbow Ridge Mine and until recently the Bonanza Mine, own the breathtaking 11-pound Hodson opal and the fiery 6-pound Bonanza opal. Keith and Agnes Hodson also have a unique collection of fossil pine cones replaced by precious opal. One of their newer finds is a 1-pound opal named "Crowning Glory." Amateurs have been allowed to dig in Virgin Valley and have been well rewarded.

Idaho has precious opal near Spencer. This opal has been mined and set into jewelry for over 30 years by the Idaho Opal and Gem Corporation. One of the claims is operated as a fee-basis collection site, producing hundreds of pounds of cuttable opal.

A lot of the Idaho opal is used for assembled stones, doublets, and triplets. There is a wide assortment of colors and patterns. The harlequin opal from this location is outstanding. Rare cat's-eye and star opal are sometimes cut from Idaho opal by the Idaho Opal Corporation.

Blue opal with play of color is being mined in Santa Cruz County, Arizona. The blue color of this opal is the hue sometimes called Wedgwood blue. The opal occurs in seams up to 12 inches (30.48 cm) across and is intermixed with chalcedony of various colors. A limited amount of pink common opal is also found there.

California has a deposit of precious opal near Randsburg in Red Rock Canyon. Resembling Mexican opal, the gems are found in small gas cavities in volcanic rock. Most of the nodules are small, but some are exceedingly fiery.

A recent producer of magnificent opal is Morrow County, Oregon. Known since 1982, the deposit was not systematically mined until West Coast Gemstones began its successful operations in 1987. The precious opal occurs in thundereggs. It is transparent to translucent and has an extraordinary play of color. Several types of opal occur here: jelly opal, fire opal, hydrophane, and the almost hypnotic contra luz. The scenic opal, or picture opal, with play of color is unusual. An important opal from this mine is a rainbow captured in a 105-carat contra luz stone. Another is the 55-gram (275 carat) scenic opal belonging to Dale Huett, who heads the mining venture. Elegant carvings and jewelry are being created by geologist–lapidary artist–goldsmith Kevin Lane Smith, using high-quality Opal Butte material in innovative ways.

An unexpected opal find was made a few years ago in Louisiana. Opal pinpoints of flashing colors, along with common opal, are present in a quartzite sandstone. The opal-bearing rock is in Vermont Parish. Most of the sandstone that shows opal has been mined out, but the search continues for further deposits.

Precious opal in a resistant matrix is found on the Woodward Ranch in Brewster County, Texas. A large brilliant piece of opal was found near Balmorhea, Texas, in the 1970s by an amateur. A recent find of precious opal in the mountains of British Columbia has led to excitement among opal enthusiasts since it has become a fee-basis collecting area.

SUGILITE
Manganese silicate
H. 6½   D. 2.74
Hexagonal

A dazzling new gem material from the Wessels Mine in the Kalahari Desert of South Africa was introduced in 1979. Because of its red-violet color it became an immediate success. First marketed under trade names of Royal Lavulite and Royal Azel, the material was identified as sugilite, a mineral first reported in nongem quality from Japan.

The material is massive and tough, with a minor amount of the best color being highly translucent, appearing like a glass of concord grape juice held toward the sun. The magical color comes from manganese.

Research by the GIA has shown that two types of material are actually being marketed as sugilite. One is manganoan sugilite and the other is chalcedony mixed with or colored by sugilite. Sugilite has been used for designer jewelry, often accentuated with diamonds. It is a choice stone for cabochons, inlay, fantasy cuts, faceted stones, and carvings. Sugilite beads and pendants are in a class with fine lapis lazuli—in both cases the rich colors recommend them for high-fashion jewelry.

Sugilite is taken from underground mines and from open pits. Since several companies have been marketing it, it is difficult to know how much of the material is still available and how much has been stored.

Jim Kaufman and Nicolai Medvedev have used bright magenta sugilite for innovative intarsia boxes, tables, pendants, candlesticks, spheres, and other art objects combining the sugilite with opal, lapis lazuli, rhodochrosite, malachite, and turquoise. Both have won prestigious awards for their sugilite inlay. Herbert Klein of Idar-Oberstein, Germany, carved a heron over 7 inches (17.78 cm) tall from sugilite. Martin Colbaugh, Arizona turquoise specialist, exhibited an eagle of sugilite in Tucson which was carved for him in Germany. The eagle's wingspread is 10 inches (25.40 cm). Hing Wa Lee has made several museum-quality carvings from sugilite. The Smithsonian has a faceted sugilite of the finest quality and color weighing 23.5 carats.

No other material on the market has the intense magenta color of sugilite; however, attempts have been made to dye materials such as jasper with a sugilite-like color. Most materials which have been compared to sugilite, such as amethyst, lavender jade, and charoite, lack the red highlights of sugilite. Some sugilite is now stabilized and an imitation has appeared.

Since the material is compact and uniform with few inclusions, sugilite is easy to work with silicon carbide or diamond; however, cutters watch for small cracks. When intermixed with chalcedony it is well adapted to the most detailed carvings. Sugilite is polished with Linde A or tin oxide on leather. Lapidaries report that sugilite reacts to cutting and polishing much the same as nephrite or jadeite. Chrome oxide has proven to be the best polish choice. Sugilite is advertised by several dealers.

TURQUOISE
Hydrous copper aluminum phosphate
H. 5–6   D. 2.62
Triclinic

The "sky stone" of the American Indian, turquoise has a long history as a popular gem material on a global scale. A favorite of the ancient Egyptians, it was mined in the Sinai. The hard blue gem turquoise of Persia has been treasured for centuries. So well loved is the green turquoise of Tibet that it is referred to as the national stone.

Good natural turquoise is only 5–6 in hardness and is porous and absorbent, but because of its lovely colors it is cut into cabochons and made into beads, pendants, and carvings. Fine turquoise has a waxy luster and conchoidal fracture. Turquoise with considerable limonite matrix is called spiderweb.

Turquoise was formed by meteoric waters penetrating faulted sandstone. Iron- and copper-bearing sandstone strata with clay and shale often contain superior turquoise. Veins and patches of gem turquoise are distributed through limestone, sandstone, or other rock. While the best quality of turquoise may be used for fine jewelry or intricate carvings, the poorer-quality material or smaller pieces are used for tumbling nuggets or inlay, or for an assortment of enhancing treatments.

Porous or chalky turquoise is routinely improved by adding resins and dyes. It is pressed, powdered, reconstructed, and stabilized. It may even be given fake matrix or webbing. Other treatments are waxing, oiling, and soaking in acid. There are many imitations. They include dyed howlite, magnesite, gibbsite, dolomite, and manufactured imitations such as ceramic and glass. Even the faience of the ancient Egyptians was a pretty fair imitation.

The best color of turquoise is partly a matter of taste, but in the United States, the sky blue tint called robin's-egg blue is preferred by many. Several states in the American Southwest produce excellent turquoise, so the gem has long been associated with the handcrafted jewelry of the American Indians. These jewelry styles, developed from Mexican and Spanish influence, have become a distinctive art style.

Some turquoise fades and some changes color as it ages; however, another occurrence called turquoise of the Old Rock by the Apache Canyon Mining Company of California is guaranteed never to fade. According to Ed Nazelrod,

Turquoise is an oqaque gem admired worldwide for its colors. It is used for beads, cabochons, and carvings.

owner of the mines, each of his mines produces distinctive turquoise, although the color saturation and hardness may vary. For example, one of his mines produces only nuggets and another has only vein material. All of this turquoise is hand mined. Interesting specimens found in the Apache Canyon Mines are turquoise pseudomorphs after beryl.

Nevada has the most turquoise mines in the United States. Others are in Arizona, New Mexico, and Colorado. Many of these have been worked since prehistoric times. Recently a mine was opened near Big Springs, Idaho.

A mine near Kingman, Arizona, owned by the Colbaugh family, once produced exquisite hard turquoise, some with delicate lacy webbing in contrasting black. Material of this type is no longer available in quantity, so the Colbaugh Company is now specializing in processed or stabilized turquoise. Martin Colbaugh says the color is natural, the turquoise is free from resin odors, clean from resin on the outside, and can be cut, ground, and polished by lapidaries exactly like natural stone.

New Mexico has laws regulating nomenclature. They are summarized as follows:

Natural is turquoise that can be cut and polished with no treatment.

Stabilized is turquoise which has been hardened with a clear plastic that has not altered the color.

Treated is turquoise that has been hardened with resin that has been dyed.

Reconstructed turquoise has had its shape altered, such as being ground up and pressed into shape.

Imitation is a manmade or natural product that has been made to imitate natural turquoise.

Turquoise comes from Baja California, Sonora and Zacatecas, Mexico, Bahia, Brazil, and the Quellaceco Mine in Peru. Inca jewelry set with turquoise has been found in Peru.

Other countries that have turquoise are Tibet, Russia, Egypt, Australia, and China. Chinese turquoise is of good quality and apparently plentiful. It is currently being used for beads, pendants, cabochons, carvings, and art objects. It comes from Hubei and Shanyang.

Several intricate Chinese carvings of Persian turquoise are in the Headley-Whitney Museum in Lexington, Kentucky. Many items of the crown jewels of Iran are encrusted with round cabochons of perfectly matched clear blue Persian turquoise. The Geological Museum of Beijing has a huge intricately carved vase of blue spiderweb turquoise.

Three minerals which somewhat resemble turquoise are the closely related *chalcosiderite*, *faustite*, which is a phosphate containing zinc as well as copper, and *prosopite*, a calcite aluminum fluoride considerably less hard than turquoise, which it greatly resembles in color and cutability.

Care should be taken in buying rough from a reliable source. While color variation is a matter of choice, the material should be fine grained, uniform, and solid, slightly lustrous, and with a subconchoidal fracture. Various grades and colors are sold in many states, and at shows and by mail order.

Turquoise should not be cut with an oil-lubricated saw. Some lapidaries soak turquoise in sodium silicate and then cure it before polishing. If kept cool, it can be easily shaped and fine sanded, then polished with tin oxide on leather.

RECOMMENDED READING

Frondel, C., *The System of Mineralogy, The Silica Minerals.* New York: Wiley, 1962.

Sinkankas, J., *Gemstones of North America.* New York: Van Nostrand Reinhold, vol. 1, 1959; vol. 2, 1976.

Sofianides, A., and Harlow, G., *Gems and Crystals.* New York: Van Nostrand Reinhold, 1991.

Webster, R., *Gems*, 5th ed. London: Butterworth-Heinemann, 1994.

SPECIFIC MATERIALS

Desautels, P., *The Jade Kingdom.* New York: Van Nostrand Reinhold, 1986.

Downing, P., *Opal Identification and Value.* Tallahassee: Majestic, 1991.

Eyles, W., *The Book of Opals.* Rutland, VT: Tuttle, 1964.

Hemrich, G., *Handbook of Jade.* Mentone, CA: Gembooks, 1966.

Laufer, B., *Jade.* New York: Dover, 1974.

Leaming, S., *Jade in Canada.* Ottawa: Geological Survey, 1974.

Leechman, F., *The Opal Book.* Sidney: URE/Smith, 1973.

Pogue, J., *The Turquoise.* Glorietta, NM: Rio Grande Press, 1972.

CHAPTER IX

Cabochon and Carving Choices

Amazonite
Azurite
Bustamite
Cancrinite
Ceruleite
Chiastolite
Datolite
Fluorite
Hornblende
Huebernite
Idocrase
Malachite
Microcline
Nepheline
Obsidian

Pectolite
Prehnite
Purpurite
Rhodochrosite
Rhodonite
Shattuckite
Smithsonite
Sodalite
Thomsonite
Thulite
Tugtupite
Variscite
Willemite
Zoisite

THERE ARE FAR MORE MATERIALS for cabochons and carvings than there are faceting materials. Since materials for large cabochons and carvings are usually not rare, they have in the past been dismissed as semiprecious or ornamental. However, these materials often have great beauty. Many are durable, easy to cut and carve, and are excellent materials to challenge the lapidary's creativity and craftsmanship.

Color is more important than anything else in opaque and translucent materials. It is color that makes a common material beautiful. Suitable hardness and/or toughness, size, flaws, grain, and polishability all play a part. Pattern is also important.

Rhodonite is a material loved for its rosy color. Obsidian is often admired for its pattern. Malachite is an example of a material that is desirable for both its saturated color and for its intricate swirly patterns.

As a group, these materials are harder than most of the ornamentals and the organics. It is up to the lapidary to adapt them to the best use. For example, rhodonite, at only 4, is not suitable for a ring, but is stunning for beads and carvings.

Generally, the minerals in this group are available in large sizes, because most are found as massive occurrences. Some of these minerals also occur as transparent crystals and can then be faceted—among them azurite and rhodochrosite—but it is the massive varieties that have become the mainstay of cabochons and carvings. Malachite, rhodonite, and idocrase occur in very large masses, but chlorastrolite and thomsonite are examples of opaque cabochon materials that are limited in size.

A few of these minerals, or their cabochon varieties, are found in many parts of the world. There is often at least one locality known for exceptional quality. But others, such as the Dominican Larimar or the Michigan datolite nodules, are associated with just one locality. Among these materials is obsidian, one of the oldest materials to be worked by man, and also one of the newest gem materials, the gem pectolite, called Larimar. Most of these materials can be used for an incredible number of lapidary projects, and can be cut with either silicon carbide or diamond.

Many of these materials are idiochromic, which means that their coloring agent is an inherent part of their makeup. Lapidaries who realize that idiochromic gemstones are always variations of a single color will find this useful when searching for a specific color for inlay, channel work, or intarsias. Malachite is always some tint or shade of green, rhodonite is always some tint or shade of rose, and azurite is always blue.

The opposite of idiochromatic is allochromatic. These are materials which, if pure, would be white, but occur in a variety of colors because of traces or inclusions of other materials. Both come in a wide array of colors.

An experienced lapidary chooses his cabochon material with great care. It should be carefully examined both wet and dry using magnification and a strong light source. Flaws can be seen easily if a wet slab is held at an angle toward the light as it dries. If some parts of a slab dry more rapidly than the rest, they may be more porous.

Running a fingernail across a slab will reveal tiny cracks, or prove that an apparent crack is in reality healed. Slabs should be held with light shining on them and also through them. Slabs with whitish sugary areas should be avoided.

Some dealers oil slabs, which temporarily enhances the color while hiding defects. A spray of water will disclose oiling. Most of these cabochon/carving materials are not color treated.

When buying large pieces instead of slabs, lapidaries look for color, fractures, and patterns. They determine whether thin edges are translucent. There probably is no such thing as a perfect piece or slab of translucent or opaque material, so the lapidary has to decide which risks to take. For example, if color is more important for a project than size, a large stone with a small amount of excellent color might be a good buy.

After selecting a piece of rough material, windows can be cut in several places before slabbing it. This will help in orienting the slabs to get the desired effect. The lapidary selecting material for cabochons or carvings must learn to avoid the faults or inconsistencies of the material and orient it correctly. An innovative lapidary will find a way to bring out the best in any piece of material.

AMAZONITE (Amazonstone)
Potassium aluminum silicate
H. 6–6½   D. 2.5
Triclinic

A blue, blue-green, or green microcline feldspar, amazonstone is used for cabochons, carvings, beads, and ornamental or decorative items. Amazonite beads on the blue side of the spectrum resemble turquoise at first glance, or a well-cut green cabochon could be mistaken for jade.

Wonderful crystals are found in pegmatite pockets in the Pikes Peak and Crystal Peak areas of Colorado, associated with smoky quartz, goethite, topaz, and fluorite. Broken pieces or small crystals which are not aesthetic or which have only a minor section of good color are used for cabochons, but the finest crystals are seldom cut.

A large quantity of amazonite of superior color and translucent quality was mined in the area of Amelia, Virginia, and is sometimes available to lucky cutters. Virginia dealer Frances Villamagne reports that large crystals and masses are now coming from the Herbb Mine at Powhaton, Virginia. One was estimated at over 30,000 pounds. Other locations are Ontario Canada, Russia, Tanzania, Brazil, Norway, India, and South America.

Amazonstone is colored by iron and the color is stable. Vivid blue-green crystals may be capped with white. Some specimens show an intergrowth of pale buff-colored microcline or white albite feldspar. Frequently buff-colored microcline may cover green areas. The material is not porous, so it is seldom treated.

Vases, bowls, candlesticks, lamps, beads, and carvings have been made of choice amazonstone. With strong cleavage, amazonite should be ground with care. It is not heat sensitive and takes a glassy polish with tin or cerium oxide on leather. Lapidaries can usually order a supply of this attractive and inexpensive material.

AZURITE
Copper carbonate
H. 3½–4   D. 3.8
Monoclinic

The chief appeal of azurite to the gem cutter is the intense blue color. Like malachite, it is found in the upper layer of copper deposits. Azurite eventually changes to malachite, with the two often intermixed, resulting in the gem material called *azurmalachite*. Massive azurite is sometimes banded, but not as elaborately patterned as malachite. Stalactitic sections when sawed yield exotic flowerlike designs in shades and tints of blue, or sometimes blues and greens. Excellent material comes from Australia. Crystals large enough and clear enough to facet come from Namibia.

Azurite seams and veins are deposited in limestone-rich ore bodies. Azurite also occurs as coatings and elegant crystals that slowly become malachite pseudomorphs.

An Arizona occurrence is marble-sized "Blueberry" azurite nodules found south of Globe. Bisbee azurite is among the best for lapidaries. The Morenci mine is noted for azurmalachite stalactites. The Copper World mine of California produced a quantity of compact and colorful azurmalachite which was widely used for jewelry.

Not tough, azurite should be worked slowly and carefully. Masks are advisable for working copper materials. Many cutters prefer chrome oxide as an azurite pol-

American azurmalachite is the material of this Chinese Fo dog carved by Hing Wa Lee.

ish. Azurite is sold at western shops and shows, but is not nearly as plentiful as malachite.

BUSTAMITE
Manganese calcium silicate
H. 5½–6½   D. 3.3
Pleochroic   Triclinic

A recent discovery of this manganese calcium silicate in an attractive color and in a fine cabochon quality was made on the noted Kalahari manganese fields of South Africa. The material is hard, compact, and massive, with a delightful tint of mauve, lilac, or flesh pink. Some of the brighter material resembles sugilite, which also comes from these manganese mines.

The African bustamite was a recent sensation at the Tucson show, selling for as much as $45 a gram. Dealer Bob Smith of South Africa indicates that the material is not that scarce.

Bustamite is often fibrous and somewhat translucent. It occurs in metamorphic and sedimentary deposits and has been reported previously in Arizona; New Jersey; Cornwall, England; Langban, Sweden; and Broken Hill, Australia. Small facet-quality crystals have been found in Japan and Australia.

The recent discovery in the vast Kalahari deposits may make bustamite a more available lapidary material. Select pieces are chatoyant and may yield splendid cat's-eyes, especially if the hue is a violet-tinged red. Pieces without black veins are best.

Lapidaries report that the material is worked in the same manner as rhodonite, a related manganese gem material. Bustamite has easy cleavage and is subject to fraying. Wet sand and polish with Rapid Polish on leather, or fine sand with diamond, finishing with 50,000 (½ micron) diamond.

CANCRINITE
Sodium calcium aluminum silicate
H. 5–6   D. 2.4
Hexagonal

The lustrous warm colors of cancrinite are well suited for cabochon jewelry. Cabochons of bright hues of orange, yellow, pink, and red can be spectacular. Cancrinite can also be used for beads, pendants, small carvings, and areas of inlay or intarsia.

The top producer of cutting-quality cancrinite is the Princess Quarry of Bancroft, Ontario, where large sections of mixed sodalite and cancrinite are often cut for ornamental uses. Another major source of cabochon-quality material is Mont Ste.

Hilaire, Quebec, Canada, where cancrinite is also found associated with sodalite.

Cancrinite masses occur in nepheline syenite rock. The mixture of blue sodalite with orange cancrinite provides a dramatic contrast for unusual lapidary projects.

Other locations are Russia, Romania, Norway, Finland, India, Kenya, and St. John's Island. A Litchfield, Maine, locality of cancrinite is considered worked out. Not often available, cutters should contact Canadian dealers.

Cancrinite can be worked the same as sodalite with cerium oxide on leather after very careful fine sanding, or sanding and polishing with diamond.

CERULEITE
Copper aluminum arsenate
H. 4½–5½   D. 2.7
Triclinic

Cabochons and small carvings, and some rough of a marvelous blue color, surfaced at the Tucson show a few years ago. Resembling turquoise, but of a truer blue, the material was labeled ceruleite and was said to have been mined in Chile. The sky blue material was not treated; however, rough material appeared to be porous, chalky, and lighter in color. The hardness proved to be less than 5.

Ceruleite has been known for most of this century, but was only reported as a gem material in the late 1970s. It occurs in compact claylike concretions, and in small seams with quartz, goethite, and barite. Material similar to that from Chile has come from Bolivia, Mexico, and Corn-wall, England. Originally found in a gold mine, ceruleite is colored by copper. It is an uncommon occurrence in sedimentary formations associated with copper deposits.

The Chilean dealer indicated that more material would become available if a mar-

ket for it was created. Perhaps the worka-bility of the material could be improved by some of the better processes of stabiliza-tion used for porous turquoise. Exquisite small carvings and impressive cabochons are made of this blue material.

Ceruleite should be cut with water, not oil, and used with fine wheels and grits. It is not heat sensitive and will take a good polish. Ceruleite can be used in much the same way as turquoise. It is not often available.

CHIASTOLITE
Aluminum silicate
H. 6½   D. 3.1
Pleochroic   Orthorhombic

One of the strangest-appearing lapidary materials is this opaque variety of andalusite which occurs as long prisms in schists and alluvial deposits. When the prism is cut into horizontal slices, each shows a symmetrical design of a cross, and distinctive variations appear on each slice. The contrasting colors are black with gray, tan, off-white, yellow-ish or khaki brown. The black crosses may be carbonaceous impurities found in con-tact zones of metamorphic rock. Chiastolite is opaque to translucent.

The exterior of the elongated crystals is rough and may be coated with fine flakes of mica. The most attractive examples are yellow with black patterns. Cross sections may be shaped into cabochons or polished and displayed as a fascinating suite of design development.

Nicely contrasting chiastolite prisms are found in Baja California and Sonora, Mexico, in the Transvaal of Africa, and near Bimbowrie, Australia. U.S. locations are Madera and Mariposa counties in Cali-fornia, Cochise County in Arizona, and Lancaster, Massachusetts. Facet-quality andalusite occurs in South Dakota.

Chiastolite jewelry is sometimes popular for religious holiday gifts. Cutters should prolong sanding, as the material undercuts, then prepolish with worn 600, and finish with Linde A on leather. Drilling should not interrupt the pattern. Well-stocked dealers usually have at least a few opaque crystals.

DATOLITE
Calcium borosilicate
H. 5½   D. 2.8
Monoclinic

A unique American gem material is cabochon-quality datolite from the Keweenaw peninsula of upper Michigan. Nodules of fine-grained material in an assortment of wonderful colors are found in the dumps of old copper mines. Although the irregularly shaped nodules are grayish white on the exterior, the surprising interiors are delicate pinks, peaches, yellows, reds, and even greens and violets, due to copper and iron minerals. The colors are further enhanced by inclusions of lacy native copper and occasionally silver.

Although the massive datolite takes a porcelain-like polish, the better nodules are usually cut and polished for displays rather than being cut for jewelry.

A recent find of a light peach-pink nodule, 12 inches (30.48 cm) in diameter and weighing 24 pounds, is in a private collection. Peach is bordered with red and elaborate white edges clearly showing two nodules grown together. Small pieces of datolite are used for rings, pendants, and bracelets. Less colorful pieces have been carved. A nodule the size of a billiard ball, with round concentric rings in contrasting colors, is an unusual new find.

Datolite is not heat sensitive. After meticulous fine sanding, it can be brought to a gleaming polish with cerium oxide on

felt. Yellow, orange, or pastel green crystals of datolite from Norway, Austria, and Massachusetts have been faceted. Michigan dealers often have datolite.

FLUORITE
Calcium fluoride
H. 4   D. 3.1
Cubic

Not often thought of as a lapidary material until the recent mass production of rainbow fluorite beads, the mineral has, in fact, a long history as a decorative material. Blue John fluorite from Castleton, England, has been mined and used as a decorative material since the mid-1700s.

The granular Blue John fluorite is translucent with elaborate concentric bands of purples, blues, and white. Artistic vases, lamp bases, goblets, bowls, and cups were skillfully made by hand from rosin-treated material for England's great mansions. Queen Elizabeth II has a magnificent chalice of purple and white banded Blue John fluorite.

Fluorite comes in many colors. A rare pink fluorite occurs in the Alps of Switzerland and also in Peru. Weardale, England, has green fluorite. Yellow, honey color, raspberry red, lavender, and colorless are among the variations found in the Ohio River deposit in the United States. A chrome green fluorite comes from Columbia. Many crystals are color zoned. Current supplies come from Mexico and China.

The Indians used Illinois and Kentucky fluorite for effigies, and early pioneers made primitive or folk art carvings of the readily available material. A cottage industry in the fluorite district produces colorful, easily cleaved fluorite octahedrons that are used for costume jewelry just as they are. Mike Gray faceted a 1,032-carat yellow fluorite called "Spirit of the Cave." Art Grant faceted a blue-violet and green stone weighing 3,969 carats.

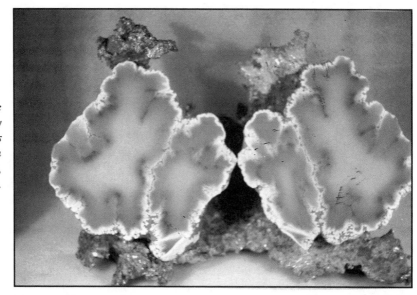

This 12-inch datolite nodule colored by native copper belongs to Herb and Carolyn Jones of Montague, Michigan.

Fluorite occurs in hydrothermal deposits and sedimentary rock. Its perfect cleavage in four directions makes it a difficult material for the lapidary. Nevertheless, it is still used for carvings as well as cabochons and even faceted stones for collectors. Five Minute Epoxy is used to dop fluorite. Grinding and sanding with fine wheels may be followed by chrome oxide on leather, or 800 to 1,200 diamond. Fluorite is easy to acquire.

nephrite, and other minerals. Dark green rock, mostly hornblende, has been mistaken for jade in Wyoming. Hornblende is also present in lapis lazuli.

An amphibole, hornblende is colored by iron. Pargasite, a related amphibole, has been found in Nova Scotia clear enough for small faceted stones. The lapidary, when cutting stones harder than 6, may run into hornblende only as inclusions that undercut.

HORNBLENDE
Sodium calcium magnesium silicate
H. 6   D. 3.0
Monoclinic

Hornblende is a tough rock-forming mineral which is common in igneous and metamorphic rock. Usually dark in color and opaque, it is seldom used as a gem material by itself, but it is often the constituent of cuttable rock such as feldspar or marble. An example is a hornblende-rich dolomitic marble from Baffin Island in northern Canada. Acicular crystals of the variety byssolite are found in quartz,

HUEBERNITE
Manganese iron tungstate
H. 4¼   D. 7.1
Pleochroic   Monoclinic

Metallic-appearing dark crystals of huebernite are sometimes iridescent. The best colors for cutting are yellowish or reddish browns. Many crystals are gray or black.

Occurring in granite pegmatites and high-temperature hydrothermal ore veins, huebernite is found as superb crystals in Park and San Juan counties, Colorado. Metallic-appearing brownish black and red-brown irregular masses and groups of bladed crystals have been found in Lawrence County, South Dakota. Some of the crystals are 4 inches (10.16 cm) in length. These have been locally cut as cabochons. Smaller crystals occur in pegmatites in Pennington County. Other localities are Arizona, Washington, Idaho, New Mexico, Peru, France, Czechoslovakia, and Australia. The best material for faceting comes from dark, transparent crystals from Peru.

Huebernite is brittle and has perfect cleavage. Faceted stones, usually less than 2 carats, are collectors' stones. Cabochons should be finished with 3,000 or 8,000 diamond. Long oval stones are excellent for this material. Huebernite is not common.

IDOCRASE (Vesuvianite)
Calcium aluminum silicate
H. 6½   D. 3.3
Pleochroic   Tetragonal

For lapidaries, the most important variety of idocrase is californite, a massive translucent pastel green or yellow-green occurrence from California. Found in Siskiyou, Butte, and Fresno counties, californite is a mixture of idocrase with grossularite garnet found in the contact zones of metamorphic and igneous rocks. The material has a jadelike toughness. Californite was discovered near Happy Camp a hundred years ago along with nephrite and rhodonite. It still is being collected in the old areas, particularly Pulga, by recreational miners and lapidaries. The best material is apple green in color and very translucent. Chrome green material comes from Asbestos, Canada.

Californite is well suited to cabochons of large sizes and fancy shapes, and to intricate carvings and ornamental objects. Idocrase beads have been made in the Ori-

ent from californite.

A similar material to that from Pulga was found in the Rocky Mountains of Colorado in the mid-1980s and marketed by a Boulder company. Another massive occurrence is in Pakistan. Violet-pink and yellow-green crystals about 4 inches (10.16 cm) long also come from the Jeffrey Quarry, Quebec, Canada, and from Kenya and Pakistan. Faceted stones from the locations are rare. Massive blue idocrase, sometimes called cyprine, comes from Norway.

Because of the admixture with grossular, californite tends to undercut and requires careful, extended wet sanding, finished with diamond. Polish with chrome oxide on leather. It can usually be located through California dealers.

MALACHITE
Copper carbonate
H. 4   D. 3.6
Monoclinic

The massive malachite so popular for jewelry and ornamental objects is opaque to translucent, bright green in color, and exquisitely patterned because of its stalactitic formation. With a hardness of only 4, this material is loved for its color alone, which varies from light muted green to intense grass green, and to an almost black shade. Complex aesthetic banding makes the material interesting for a variety of decorative uses.

Russian czars enjoyed walls, doors, and furniture of malachite from the Ural Mountains. Malachite columns of choice material are a highlight of "The Hermitage" in St. Petersburg.

Excellent material for cabochons, carvings, and ornamental purposes for today's lapidaries comes from Zaire, Namibia, and

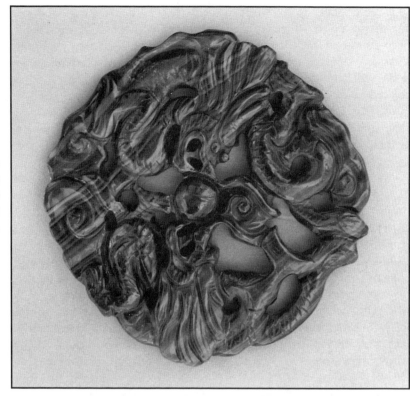

Chinese artists make the pattern fit the stone. Malachite carving by Hing Wa Lee.

Australia. The Monster Mine at Burra produced 10,000 tons of malachite, but only a small quantity got into lapidary hands. Recently, superb malachite with gem chrysocolla has been coming from Peru. Inlaid malachite boxes, beads, pendants, spheres, eggs, carved animals, bowls, and candlesticks are some of the many uses of malachite for the current market.

Malachite is hydrous, occurring as a secondary deposit in the upper layers of copper deposits. Crystals are drusy or very small. Smooth botryoidal coatings on copper-bearing rocks are often found. Bisbee, Arizona, has been the source of excellent malachite in the United States.

Saw malachite parallel to the botryoidal pattern. Toxic to work with, malachite is porous, not tough, subject to undercutting, and difficult to polish. It should be worked wet and slowly and meticulously

sanded before polishing with Linde A on leather. Malachite is readily available.

MICROCLINE
Tektosilicate
H. 6   D. 2.5
Triclinic

This feldspar species is usually opaque to translucent, occurring in large crystals in pegmatites in an assortment of pleasing colors. It is abundant in granite pegmatites in many areas. Lapidaries often use the best colors for large cabochons, spheres, eggs, and other items. Preferred colors are red, red-orange, coral, flesh pink, rose pink, and pink. (The greens have been given a special name, amazonstone.)

Large crystals, up to 6 feet in diameter, and masses up to 10 feet in diameter, have been found in the Black Hills of South Dakota. Manufacturer Wayne Olson made floor, wall, and counter tiles from peach-colored microcline with black and white inclusions. Other brightly colored microcline comes from California, New Mexico, Colorado, Canada, Mexico, Russia, Kenya, India, Japan, and many more.

Microcline has perfect cleavage in three directions, but the cleavage is seldom a problem. The structural lamellae present a cross-hatched grating, which may be the reason the material is somewhat difficult to polish. Tin oxide on leather is a good choice. Sometimes there is a pearly glow on the surface of a well-polished stone. Microcline is tumbled, used for beads, inlay, intarsia, and many other lapidary purposes. It can be purchased in states where it is found.

NEPHELINE
Sodium aluminum silicate
H. 5½–6   D. 2.5
Hexagonal

Nepheline or nephelite occurs in compact masses, or as crystals in pegmatites associated with nepheline syenites. Translucent and opaque material in suitable colors is used for cabochons and carvings. Colors are green, gray, yellow, white, and red.

Gray nepheline with red-brown and black inclusions from Lawrence County, South Dakota, has been used for cabochons. Blue-gray nepheline from near Raton, New Mexico, has also been used by local lapidaries. Nepheline-syenite rock from Greenland—mottled red-brown with black, white, and yellowish areas—has been used by natives for ornamental objects, cabochons, and carvings. Gray and pink nephelite with white streaks from the

nepheline-syenite pegmatites of Bancroft, Ontario, is used for interesting cabochons.

A chatoyant variety of nepheline in colors of green and brownish red, called *elaeolite*, has been used as an ornamental stone by creative lapidaries. Other nepheline localities are Norway, Finland, and Russia.

Nepheline may undercut, so extra sanding is required. Linde A gives a good polish.

OBSIDIAN

Nature's own glass provides a wonderful variety of lapidary materials with assorted colors, patterns, and phenomenal effects. About 5–6 in hardness and 2.4 in density, and very brittle, obsidian is found in many volcanic areas, sometimes as small nodules (Apache tears), and sometimes as immense deposits, such as Glass Buttes, Oregon. It is amorphous and has no cleavage planes.

Some of the most elegant obsidian is the iridescent *peacock* obsidian of northern California. Layered prismatic colors create a rainbow in the dark, translucent rock. Other iridescent obsidians are called *rainbow* and *iris*.

The area in northern California known as Davis Creek or Lassen Creek also produces iridescent rose-colored and violet-colored obsidians, locally known as Pink Lady and Royal Purple, as well as gold sheen, silver sheen, mahogany, and, rarely, blue and green. *Fire* obsidian has a mixture of colors in each layer. Fiery iridescent banded obsidian is found in nodules north of Guadalajara, Mexico.

Glass Buttes, Oregon, has produced an enormous amount of cuttable obsidian for many years. All varieties are found there, with a brecciated material being of unusual interest. Lapidaries like translucent smoky-colored obsidian with wisps of swirling black called Midnight Lace. Green obsidian is found north of Burns. Utah is noted for its snowflake or flowering obsid-

Mexican artist Eduardo Oblés interprets that country's culture with its most common cutting material, obsidian. "Caballero Iztli" is texturized obsidian 12 × 9 × 5 nches. Photo by Adrian Bodek.

ian. The material is abundant near Delta and Milford. Nevada's unique contribution is a double-flow material with odd twists and bands of transparent gray.

Arizona has Apache tears galore. Some of these are glassy nodules in perlite, and others released from their mother rock resemble lumps of charcoal on the desert floor. The weathered surface hides high-quality silver sheen, gold sheen, and other aesthetic obsidians. Nodules suitable for large showy cabochons are found near Wickenburg and Burro Creek. Red obsidian with black inclusions, known as Mountain Mahogany, comes from Idaho. A huge deposit in Yellowstone National Park is off limits for lapidaries.

There are numerous obsidian deposits in Mexico and Central America. An attractive pink snowflake obsidian from Mexico

is new on the market. Other locations are Iceland, Siberia, New Zealand, Australia, and Japan.

American aborigines used obsidian for tools, weapons, ceremonial items, mirrors, and delicate surgery, which according to archeological evidence, was highly successful.

Peter Carl Fabergé used obsidian from the Caucasus for many of his delightful composite Russian figures and animal carvings. Mexican carver Eduardo Oblés specializes in obsidian carvings with an Aztec accent from choice material from Hidalgo, Queretero, and Jalisco. His graceful bamboo- and cactus-inspired vases are superb.

Robert Miller of South Bend, Indiana, won the AFMS carving award with a perfect score for his iridescent obsidian relief carving of a unicorn. Like other carvers, Miller makes some of his own tools. He likes to work with a flexible-shaft handpiece such as Foredom or Dremel.

Light yellow or green obsidian from Peru has been faceted. Some of the pale to nearly colorless gray obsidian of the California, Oregon, or Utah deposits has also been faceted.

Varieties such as snowflake or iridescent obsidian should be carefully oriented before cutting. Obsidian is amorphous and has no cleavage, but is extremely brittle. It cannot stand thermal shock. Grinding should be on fine, smooth, flat wheels. Wet sanding must be meticulous. Cerium oxide on felt will bring a high polish. Obsidian is one of the most available materials.

PECTOLITE (Larimar)
Hydrous sodium calcium silicate
H. 5   D. 2.8
Triclinic

An enchanting gemstone appeared on the market in the 1970s. Called Larimar, the material was soon identified as a unique form of the mineral pectolite, allied to the zeolites. To date, the new gem material has only been found in the Dominican Republic.

An exquisitely patterned stone in tints of blue and greenish blue, Larimar has a suitable toughness for jewelry and ornamental uses. Sometimes dendritic, and often chatoyant, Larimar cabochons are distinctive. A small portion of the material is a replacement of wood; some of this is brecciated. The blue colors come from copper.

The mine in the Dominican Republic is in a remote and rugged area at an elevation of 5200 feet. Worked by a cooperative, the hazardous mining is done by hand. There are few lapidaries in the Dominican Republic who can make acceptable cabochons of Larimar, but more are being trained. Larimar is also cut in the United States. Exceptional stones, and some rough, are often seen at the Tucson show.

Cuttable pectolite is found in Alaska and California, but those occurrences do not resemble Larimar and are seldom seen. Facetable pectolite has come from Quebec, Canada.

Dr. Robert Woodruff, who has cut considerable Larimar and lectured and written about the material, says its exact nature is still under study. Final identification is somewhat clouded, since analysis of some samples is closer to natrolite than to pectolite.

The material should be selected for color and pattern. Carefully sanded pieces take a glistening polish with tin oxide on leather.

PREHNITE
Calcium aluminum silicate
H. 6½   D. 2.8
Orthorhombic

Lovely green prehnite associated with zeolites occurs in vugs, crusts, and stalactitic masses in basaltic rock, such as the trap rock of New Jersey. The color range includes white, apple green, yellow-green, pale yellow, blue-green, and pastel green. The transparent to translucent material is fibrous and sometimes chatoyant.

Cuttable material has come from quarries in New Jersey and Virginia. The material from Virginia is known for its fine color. In place, prehnite resembles a pile of green marbles with individual globes sometimes measuring 1½ inches (3.81 cm) in diameter. Some of the Virginia material has inclusions of dark green byssolite. Unusual pink prehnite, formerly thought to be thomsonite, occurs as amygdule fillings in the copper-bearing rock of Michigan's Keweenaw Peninsula and Isle Royale in Lake Superior. Native copper is an inclusion in this prehnite.

Prehnite makes large, good-looking cabochons and carved pendants. Delicately colored jadelike prehnite beads are now on the market. It is also used for bookends, clock faces, desk sets, inlay, and intarsia.

Attractive prehnite suitable for jewelry comes from South Africa; Scotland, where it has long been a jewelry stone; and Australia, where yellow material has been faceted. A 15-carat lime-green stone from Australia is in the Australian Museum of Earth Science.

When cut, prehnite resembles jade, green quartz, or green beryl. Said to fade upon exposure to strong sunlight, it is best to carefully shape it as high-domed cabochons, and polish with Linde A on leather. It is often found for sale or trade in the eastern states.

PURPURITE
Manganese iron phosphate
H. 4–4½   D. 3.6
Pleochroic   Orthorhombic

An alteration product of decaying granite pegmatites, purpurite is another of the cutting materials admired for its color alone. The red-purple color is due to manganese. The rose-purple is so desirable that cutters tend to forget the inferior hardness. It is opaque to translucent and can be made into large cabochons for jewelry which is not subject to abrasion, such as bola ties or pendants. Art objects are carved from purpurite.

Most cutting material on the market has been from Namibia, but some magnificently colored purpurite from Larimer County, Colorado, appeared at the Tucson show in 1991. Mined by Terry Hicks and David Ratoike of Boulder, the material polishes well and can be used for carvings, intarsia, and decorative objects.

Other locations are Custer County, South Dakota; San Diego, California; Yavapai County, Arizona; Gaston County, North Carolina; and Western Australia and Afghanistan.

Besides being soft, the material is brittle, but should create no major problems if worked slowly and wet. It can be polished with Linde A or tin oxide on leather. Supplies are intermittent.

RHODOCHROSITE
Manganese carbonate
H. 4   D. 3.5
Trigonal

Although there are facet-quality rhodochrosite crystals, most of the rhodochrosite seen in beads and other jewelry is the massive stalactitic material from San Luis, Argentina. Low on the hardness scale, rhodochrosite is a gem loved for its color. The tints of pink and rose vary from baby pink to hot pink and deep rose. Several colors plus white may enhance an individual piece with swirls, bands, flowers, and eyes, not unlike the patterns in another carbonate, malachite.

Rhodochrosite may be transparent, translucent, or opaque. A preferred quality for beads is a translucent unpatterned deep rose, but flowerlike patterns of rich pink are preferred for cabochons. Once called Inca Rose, because the mine was said to have been worked by Incas centuries ago, the material is highly decorative for objects such as lamps, clocks, bowls, bookends, and carvings. It is used in intarsias, inlay, and dioramas, wherever an intense pink is needed. The Smithsonian has a 10-inch (25.40-cm) stalactite slab.

Rhodochrosite is formed in low-temperature hydrothermal veins in ore deposits of silver, lead, zinc, and copper and also in sedimentary manganese deposits. Oxidation may alter the surface to black. Other locations are Colorado, Peru, and Brazil. Beautiful stones have been faceted from crystals from Colorado, Peru, and South Africa's Kalahari Desert.

Not easily mistaken for another material, massive rhodochrosite used for jewelry and ornaments is not treated. Besides its low hardness, it has distinct cleavage and is somewhat heat sensitive. The finest translucent rose material, sometimes called Ortiz, is scarce. The banded material can be polished with white rouge. Zam on leather works for the translucent material, after wet sanding with 600 sanding cloth by hand. Rhodochrosite must be kept cool. Soft, and with differential hardness, it can be shaped with a 220 sander instead of a grinder. Some cabochon rough is available, and sometimes facetable crystals. Faceting is difficult because of easy cleavage.

RHODONITE
Manganese calcium silicate
H. 6   D. 3.5
Triclinic

This lovely rose-colored manganese mineral is a popular massive material for cabochons,

*Stalactitic rhodochrosite is skillfully used for this
jewelry set by Doris Kemp.
Photo by Russell Kemp.*

Coola, British Columbia. The Sea Rose
rhodonite is currently mined and used for
jewelry made in Sea Island. The pink, rose,
and black rhodonite is interbedded with
chert in a large exposure. Inclusions are
quartz, garnet, and calcite. Some of the
material is exceedingly fine grained and
translucent, but the larger veins are coarser.
Over 200 tons of prime rhodonite have
been mined in recent years. Several of the
best specimens are in the British Museum.

Rhodonite from Fulford Harbor, British
Columbia, has yellow and green streaks to
contrast with rose and black. Other locations are Oregon, Mexico, Sweden, Tanzania, and South Africa. A vivid rose-red
material comes from Australia. A richly colored deposit from Russia has been used lavishly and skillfully by artists for the czars.

Rhodonite with black veining or other
impurities may undercut, or pitting may
occur. An extended period of fine sanding
with a worn 400 silicon carbide belt can be
followed by Rapid Polish on leather for a
bright polish. Working cabochons or carvings with diamond is an alternative. Transparent material from Australia and Japan has
been faceted. Rhodonite is readily available.

beads, carvings, and decorative items. At
present, the solid-color light rose-pink
material is most used, but there are also
pleasing variations which include red and
brown mottling and lacy black veins.

Rhodonite is found in masses in metamorphic deposits. Although found in many
localities, Massachusetts alone chose
rhodonite as its state gemstone. The Massachusetts rhodonite is uniform and pure pink
in color. Its toughness and translucency add
to its value as a gem material. It was made
into vases, boxes, and other large decorative
objects in the nineteenth century. Pretty
Cherry Blossom rhodonite comes from the
Spider Mine near Redding, California.

Mine developer Anthony Karup tells
about an excellent deposit near Bella

SHATTUCKITE
Hydrated copper silicate
H. 5   D. 3.8
Pleochroic   Orthorhombic

Lapidaries searching for another blue
stone for cabochons might be able to
locate some of the now scarce shattuckite
which was readily available at Ajo, Arizona, in the 1950s. A rich blue in color,
shattuckite resembles azurite more than
lapis lazuli, but is often a little closer to a
greenish blue than pure azurite. The
material from Ajo is sometimes mixed

with a little malachite and inclusions of red quartz. Because of its fibrous nature, it has a good toughness which makes it suitable for jewelry.

First discovered at the Shattuck Mine in Bisbee, it was subsequently found near Clifton, Wickenburg, Jerome, and San Manuel, Arizona. Most of the lapidary material has come from Ajo. The mineral has also been observed in Zaire and Namibia.

Shattuckite is an oxidation product of secondary copper minerals and is present in the upper levels of only a few copper mines. It is seldom found as crystals, but forms fibrous masses, often radiating and silky. It sometimes replaces malachite. Shattuckite makes splendid cabochons which take a glassy polish with tin oxide on leather, but rough is scarce.

SMITHSONITE
Zinc carbonate
H. 4–5½   D. 4.3
Hexagonal

Smithsonite, named for James Smithson, benefactor of the Smithsonian Institution, is found in the oxidized zones of many deposits where zinc is present. The beautiful blue-green material would be an expensive gemstone if it had a better hardness. Other colors of smithsonite are pink, green, blue, yellow, and lavender. The cabochon material is translucent and has a subchatoyant glow. Occasionally, clear facet-quality pieces are found, but most will yield stones of less than 10 carats.

An interesting occurrence in the Magdalena District of New Mexico is the complete replacement of a limestone formation including perfect pseudomorphs of smithsonite after crinoids and mollusk shells. Exquisite specimens are still occa-

sionally found in Kelly Gulch. The New Mexico School of Mines Museum at Socorro displays superb examples.

Canary yellow, botryoidal, translucent smithsonite, known as "turkey fat" ore, was found in the Morning Star Mine, a zinc mine near Rush, Arkansas. Other smithsonite localities are Colorado, Utah, and Montana. Excellent pink comes from Mexico, banded yellow massive smithsonite from Italy, and transparent yellow, pink, and green facetable crystals from Tsumeb, Namibia.

Large and showy cabochons and small carvings are made from translucent smithsonite. The greens can be mistaken for jade. Cabochons are suitable for pins and pendants which take a minimum of wear damage. Lapidaries find the material rather brittle, but not overly heat sensitive; however, cold dopping is advisable. Cutters achieve good results with tin oxide on leather, or fine sanding and polishing with diamond. Cutting-quality material is not common.

SODALITE
Sodium aluminum silicate
H. 5½–6   D. 2.2
Isometric

Since it is blue and opaque to translucent, this stone is often mistaken for lapis lazuli, and is sometimes substituted for the more expensive material. When it is almost transparent, it resembles blue corundum. Although sodalite has a similar hardness to lapis lazuli, the colors never quite reach the intense blue of the top-quality lapis lazuli.

Sodalite occurs in metamorphic calcareous rock and nepheline syenites. Closely related to hauyne, nosean, and lazurite, it has been found in meteorites. Sodalite is actually a component of the rock lapis lazuli. Ontario, Canada, has been the most prolific source. Massive royal blue material from the Princess Quarry has been used for lapidary projects around the world. Pink feldspar and white calcite are common inclusions. Nepheline-rich gneisses and pegmatite-like patches have been replaced by sodalite, the result of hydrothermal action.

Canadian geologist Anna Sabina writes that the vast deposit was discovered over a hundred years ago and is worked now as an open-pit mine. An official wedding gift to Princess Diana from Canada was a gold brooch set with sodalite.

Sodalite is also found in the provinces of British Columbia and Quebec. The Quebec Ministry of Mines notes that sodalite from the Poudrette Quarry at Mont Ste. Hilaire, Quebec, has been cut into world-class faceted stones for this species. Sodalite is also mined in Brazil, Norway, Namibia, India, and Bolivia. The Bolivian mine has been producing evenly colored translucent material, but not in great quantity, since the mine is at an elevation of 14,000 feet. It is recovered by hand and packed by llamas to the nearest road.

Locations in the United States include Colorado, South Dakota, and Maine. The variety *hackmanite* is found at Magnet Cove, Arkansas, and also at Mont Ste. Hilaire, where a light yellow faceted stone of 15.33 carats originated.

Cabochons are polished with tin oxide on felt after fine sanding. Sodalite is currently available in large pieces and is often advertised.

THOMSONITE
Hydrous sodium calcium aluminum silicate
H. 5½   D. 2.4
Orthorhombic

Thomsonite is a zeolite, a member of a complex family of minerals that form in

Minnesota silversmith Tania Feigal specializes in free-form thomsonite cabochons for her jewelry.

basalt and other igneous rock. The most cuttable thomsonite occurs as small, fibrous, rounded nodules in basalt matrix on the north shore of Lake Superior in Minnesota.

The nodules have radial structure of needle-fine crystals with patterns resembling eyes and targets. The colors are often complementary harmonies of red or pink with tints and shades of green and blue-green, and accents of black against a snowy groundmass. Several contrasting colors may appear in one stone.

Waxy green nodules, facetiously called Minnesota jade, are a variety of thomsonite with no radiating crystals or "eyes." They are named lintonite for chemist Laura Linton.

Thomsonite has been used for beads, and cabochons for pendants, bracelets, earrings, and even large and showy bola ties. Some of the best cabochons are free-form, because the choice patterns and colors are near the surface. Thomsonite jewelry and polished nodules up to several inches across are displayed at the Thomsonite and Zeolite Museum at the Thomsonite Beach Motel near Lutsen, Minnesota. Colorful carvings of thomsonite in basalt are also shown.

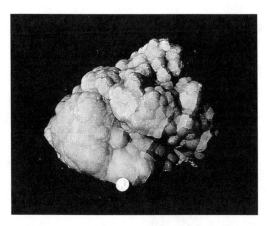

Blue-green smithsonite from Kelly, New Mexico, is a splendid cabochon material. Courtesy of New Mexico Bureau of Mines.

Other thomsonite locations are Michigan, Switzerland, and Denmark. Small crystal groups occur in many zeolite areas. Thomsonites can be tumbled successfully in small batches. Instead of sawing, cabochons can be shaped with fine grinders. This rather fragile gem must be worked slowly with care using fine silicon carbide wet sanders. But results can be so attractive that the work is well worth the extra effort. Rough and polished thomsonite is usually available in Minnesota.

THULITE
Calcium aluminum silicate
H. 6½   D. 3.4
Pleochroic   Orthorhombic

Thulite is a pink or rose variety of zoisite, a member of the epidote group. Found in the alluvial boulders of the nephrite jade fields of Wyoming, thulite was called pink jade in the early days of exploration. Thulite was often found intergrown with nephrite and associated rocks, in which case it was named flowering jade. Massive

thulite is fibrous with the needles often penetrating other rock; however, the rose-pink color is so predominant that such rocks are often merely called thulite. Pink thulite cabochons resemble pale rhodonite.

Thulite was discovered in Norway and named for Norway's ancient name. The pink lapidary-quality deposit was in Telemark. A similar occurrence is in Greenland. Western Australia also produces thulite.

In the United States, rich rose-colored thulite occurs near Pilar, New Mexico. A long, narrow vein of thulite with quartz runs through, and sometimes replaces, the mica schist. Author Stuart Northrop writes that some of the needles are piemontite, a related mineral. Thulite suitable for cutting also occurs west of Taunk Mountain in north-central Washington. Pink and lavender thulite is sometimes mixed with greenish zoisite here.

Tough enough to accept fine detail in carvings, thulite is also used for beads, eggs, and cabochons. Small, clear pieces have been faceted. Due to the varying hardness and texture of mineral inclusions, the material may undercut unless given extended periods of careful wet sanding. Cutters can usually acquire a piece or two.

TUGTUPITE
Sodium aluminum silicate
H. 4–5½   D. 2.3
Pleochroic   Tetragonal

Distinctive rose-red cabochons from a Tugtup, Greenland, occurrence are flashy stones. The compact massive material occurs in nepheline-syenite pegmatites. Other colors are pink, light blue, white, and light green. The material is also known to occur in the Kola peninsula of

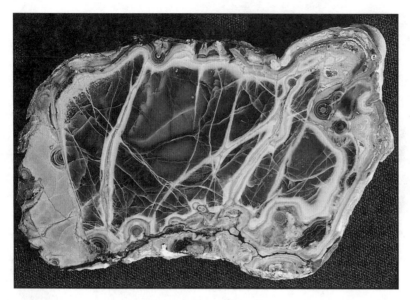

*One of the most elegant
American cutting mate-
rials is Fairfield
variscite from Utah.
Photo courtesy of
Lizzadro Museum,
Elmhurst, Illinois.*

Russia. A few small transparent stones have been faceted.

Some of the material is mottled with white and cerise patches. The material has been a popular tourist item in Greenland since the discovery of gem-quality masses in the early 1960s.

Translucent tugtupite has been used for spheres, eggs, and carvings as well as jewelry. Because of the rich color, it can also be used for intarsia, channel work, and other lapidary projects. The lighter colors seem harder. Polish is easy with tin oxide or Linde A on leather or rock-hard felt.

VARISCITE
Aluminum phosphate
H. 4½   D. 2.2
Orthorhombic

One of the most elegant of American cabochon gemstones is variscite. Sometimes mistaken for turquoise, this gem mineral is found in tints and shades of green and blue-green. When mixed with other phosphates, such as the superb material from

Fairfield, Utah, it has marvelous patterns in yellow, taupe, and muted earth colors such as sand and rust. The gem material is massive, fine grained, compact, and has a toughness which somewhat alleviates its lack of hardness.

Great deposits were discovered in Utah about 100 years ago. Marketed under such names as *utahlite* and *lucinite*, variscite was mined extensively and was used for decorative purposes and jewelry.

The most beautiful variscite came from Fairfield, where it was found in large nodules. The other phosphates which furnish its intriguing patterns are light yellow crandallite, dark green wardite, brown hydroxylapatite, and smoky gordonite. Large spectacular slabs were available at shows until the early 1950s, and are now seen in private collections and museums.

Claude Atkin, who mined the Amatrice Hill deposit for many years, says there are still plenty of nodules in the ground. The Amatrice Hill material is aqua or medium blue-green with muted neutral inclusions forming eyes, clouds, veins, lace, and breccia.

Variscite forms near the surface from the action of phosphoritic waters on aluminum-bearing rock. Other locations for variscite are Nevada, Australia, Brazil, Germany, and Spain.

In the 1970s a gem material turned up at shows that resembled variscite except that it had black spiderweb patterns. Called *variquoise*, for its resemblance to turquoise, the Utah occurrence was followed by a similar discovery in Lander County, Nevada. Called Verde Web and then New Lander, the material was identified by Dr. Parsons of Arizona State University as chalcosiderite, a member of the turquoise group.

The American Museum of Natural History has a striking sphere about 3 inches (7.62 cm) in diameter of choice Fairfield material. Variscite is often porous and rather heat sensitive, so it should be worked wet with little pressure, then polished with tin oxide on leather. Cabochons of patterned material may undercut. Variscite carvings and bowls are exquisite. Recently variscite has been used in American Indian–style jewelry. Variscite can be purchased in Utah and neighboring states.

from Quebec and Arizona. A red-brown variation, also from Franklin/Ogdensburg, colored by manganese, is known as *troostite*. Other locations are Mexico, Belgium, Algeria, Zaire, and Namibia.

The primary use by lapidaries has been the creation of ornamental objects, mosaics, pictures, and fancy cabochons of the combined materials for sensational fluorescent displays. Willemite will fluoresce a vivid green under short- and long-wave light; zincite will fluoresce orange under long-wave light; and hydrozincite will fluoresce rich blue under short-wave light. The calcite matrix provides the maximum contrast with flame red.

Since the cabochon material is usually a mixture of minerals of different hardness, it is likely to undercut. Ornamental objects can be shaped using silicon carbide tools with a flexible shaft machine. Sanding should be extended before polishing with tin oxide on leather. Cabochon material can be bought in the eastern states at times.

WILLEMITE
Zinc silicate
H. 5½   **D. 4.1**
Pleochroic   **Hexagonal**

Cabochons, spheres, carvings, and small faceted stones have been made from willemite from Franklin, New Jersey, both from the green or orange crystals and from massive calcite containing franklinite, willemite, and zincite. Large cabochons can be cut from massive material, but faceted stones are small and rare. Small chatoyant stones have been cut from massive willemite.

Willemite usually occurs as a secondary mineral in oxide zones of ore bodies. Other colors of willemite come from the various locations in which this mineral occurs. Dark blue comes from Greenland and a light blue

ZOISITE
Calcium aluminum silicate
H. 6–7   **D. 3.1**
Pleochroic   **Orthorhombic**

Although it was tanzanite that really put zoisite on the gem map, opaque to translucent varieties are also exciting lapidary materials. One is the chrome-green massive zoisite-rich rock from Tanzania which is embedded with dark red, almost opaque ruby crystals, sometimes of large sizes up to 8 inches (20.32 cm) in diameter. The zoisite occurs in alteration areas of basic igneous rock. Many pieces are coated with dark schist.

The zoisite is grainy and has black chromite and hornblende inclusions. It varies in color from an intense green to

Vibrant green zoisite from Tanzania, with or without its ruby inclusions, is a versatile material for cabochons, carvings, and beads.

almost black-green, with a few lighter areas still rich in color. Blocks of green zoisite, up to a ton, are reported from the Longido Mine. The material has been used for cabochons, beads, and carvings. Some artists have made vivid carved pendants and small elegant carvings of the green zoisite with the ruby inclusions, a job made difficult because of the huge difference in hardness. Lapidaries also like the contrasting red and green slabs for displays. Some of this zoisite is marketed in Africa under the name *anyolite*.

A gray-green zoisite found in the jade fields of Wyoming has sometimes been tumbled and cut into cabochons. Zoisite is also found in South Dakota, Massachusetts, Canada, Mexico, Finland, Russia, and Japan.

Massive green zoisite with ruby inclusions has been popular on the lapidary market for vivid display slabs, colorful carvings, spheres, cabochons, beads, and pendants. Since undercutting is a problem, it is advisable to use diamond all the way. Chrome oxide on hard leather gives an improved polish. Zoisite can be purchased by mail or at shops or shows.

RECOMMENDED READING

Arem, J., *Color Encyclopedia of Gemstones.* New York: Van Nostrand Reinhold, 1987.

Arem, J., *Rocks and Minerals.* Phoenix: Geoscience Press, 1992.

Bancroft, P., *Gem and Crystal Treasures.* Fallbrook, CA: Western Enterprises, 1984.

Palache, C., et al., *Dana's System of Mineralogy,* 7th ed. New York: Wiley, 1963.

Parsons, C., *Practical Gem Knowledge for the Amateur.* San Diego: Lapidary Journal, 1969.

Roberts, W., et al., *Encyclopedia of Minerals.* New York: Van Nostrand Reinhold, 1990.

Smith, H., *Gemstones.* New York: Pitman, 1962.

Webster, R., *Gems,* 5th ed. London: Butterworth-Heinemann, 1994.

SPECIFIC MINERALS

Odiorne, H., *Colorado Amazonstone.* Denver: Forum, 1978.

CHAPTER X

Ornamental and Decorative Gem Materials

Alabaster
Anhydrite
Argillite
   Zebra stone
Barite
Bauxite
Bowesite
Calcite
   Calcite onyx
   Coquina
   Marble
   Petoskey stone
   Tufa
Catlinite
Charoite
Chicken-blood stone
Copper rocks
   Campbellite
   Eilat stone
   Imperialite Dancer
   Mojave stone
   Natural mosaic
   Patricianite & Michigan copper
   Tanundaite

Georgia Midnight
Granite
   Colored granites
   Graphic granite
   Larvikite
   Orbicular granite
   Unakite
Howlite
Lapis Nevada
Lepidolite
Mariposite
Meerschaum
Ocean Picture Rock
Oil shale
Orthoamphibole
Rhyolite
Serpentine
Spurrite
Staurolite
Stichtite
Talc
Thaumasite
Verdite

Through the years the public became indoctrinated with the idea that some gemstones are precious and some are semiprecious. Even lapidaries came to consider ornamental materials as somehow inferior and less desirable. The truth is that many ornamental materials are more colorful and have more interesting patterns than some gem materials that are considered more sophisticated.

The greatest sin of the ornamental materials is that they are plentiful and usually available in large pieces. They are usually softer than other materials, or have varying hardness, because many of them are rocks rather than minerals. Although the original material may be inexpensive, elaborate and valuable items in the world of art have been made of the so-called ornamentals. Examples are the Egyptian alabasters, the carvings of Michelangelo or Leonardo da Vinci, the mosaics of Pompeii, old Chinese soapstone carvings, elaborately carved meerschaum pipes from Turkey, and magnificent buildings like the Taj Mahal. It is the lapidary's own skill, not the cost of the material, that is of highest importance.

Many of these materials, for example, calcite, are found around the world; others like *mariposite* are of regional significance. Alabaster is a timeless ornamental material, carved for the Pharaohs of Egypt and perhaps before. Ocean picture rock is a relatively new find in Canada. Almost every country has some rock or mineral that has been used with success as a folk art material.

Ornamental materials are a real challenge to the lapidary. First they must be carefully selected and well suited to the projects for which they are intended; then they must be worked with expert craftsmanship aided by originality. It is the talent of the artist that adds value to readily available materials. An expertly done serpentine carving should be worth more than a poorly made nephrite carving.

The creativity and craftsmanship of the lapidary can clearly be seen in the multitude of uses of ornamental materials. In some cases they lack the rarity that would qualify them as gems. An example is marble, by no means rare, but it can be used for truly artistic achievements. In other cases the material lacks the hardness that would qualify it for some jewelry. Alabaster is a case in point; however, talented lapidaries regularly turn alabaster into lovely decorator items. Calcite onyx, which has only a hardness of 3, is widely used for such jewelry as beads.

A patient, persistent, and gifted lapidary can take many materials, such as common granite or basalt, and turn out interesting stones and carvings. Some rocks are excellent for jewelry, having good hardness, toughness, and grain. The important distinction here is color. If a rock such as granite—a mixture of minerals—has good color, such as the greens and pinks of unakite, it is well adapted to jewelry. A number of rocks colored by copper are desirable for lapidary uses. It is the rich hues of blue and green that make the difference.

Some rocks have been neglected in the past because differential hardness made them hard to work with. Undercutting was a common problem. New technologies, plus new freedoms for the cutters, make many materials accessible.

Many of the ornamental and decorative rocks and minerals have been given trade names and sometimes one material may have several local or trade names. Not all of the lapidary rocks are common—some are rare occurrences from certain levels of early mines and are no longer available, except from old collections.

Some of the abundant ornamental stones, flint, and chert, are well silicified and included in the cryptocrystalline quartz chapter. This chapter includes rocks that form a significant part of Earth's crust, rocks that are a combination of several minerals, and minerals that are usually considered too soft for most jewelry uses. But all of the varied materials included here are suitable for at least some lapidary uses, and some, for example, marble, are the materials of great art.

Lapidary rocks and soft minerals are suitable for carvings, clocks, bowls, vases, boxes, intarsia, inlay, and interior and exterior decoration. More and more they are being used for jewelry in innovative ways, particularly for beads and earrings which do not have hard wear. A good point in favor of most of these materials is that they are available in pieces of suitable sizes for large projects. There are enough variations in color, grain, and patterns that the lapidary can usually find exactly the right material for the project he has in mind. Lapidaries should study these widely varied materials and learn to be highly selective, then try these materials to demonstrate their originality and craftsmanship.

ALABASTER
Hydrous calcium sulfate
H. 2   D. 2.3
Monoclinic

This compact fibrous gypsum is a widely used lapidary material in spite of its very low hardness. The best qualities are translucency, delicate colors, and availability in big enough pieces for lamps, bowls, and large carvings. Easily carved with steel tools, good alabaster has uniform grain and few fractures.

Alabaster has been treasured as a decorative rock since the days of King Tutankhamen of Egypt, and even earlier. It is a sedimentary rock, with massive deposits occurring in many areas where mineral waters have evaporated. When freshly quarried the hardness is only 2, but the material hardens after being exposed to the air for a while.

Pure alabaster is white, but traces of iron and manganese minerals and other impurities produce bands and veining of browns and blacks, against subtle tones of peach, yellow, pink, pale orange, lavender, and green. Patterns are like webs of fragile lace, or sometimes like faded dendrites.

Excellent peach-colored alabaster is found near Loveland, Colorado. White alabaster is plentiful in and around Rapid City, South Dakota. A large quarry in Grand Rapids, Michigan, now used for natural cold storage, yields pink and red material. Alabaster is found in England, Italy, Australia, New Zealand, and many other places.

Dyed alabaster ornamental objects such as bowls of artificial fruit are common in Italy. One of the best uses of the material is for objects like the innovative bowls and lamps made with precision craftsmanship by sculptor Susan Zalkind of California. Much of Zalkind's work is done with steel tools and hand tools, but she uses a Foredom electric tool for detail carving.

Alabaster for lapidary work should be stored where it is dry. Rasps, files, steel knives, sandpaper, and steel wool (to 0000) will shape and refine small carvings and pendants. If worked by machines, the material should be kept cool and worked slowly. Wax is often used for final polish or tin oxide on muslin. Inexpensive and abundant, alabaster is ideal for the beginning carver.

ANHYDRITE
Calcium sulfate
H. 3– 3½   D. 2.9
Orthorhombic

Anhydrite is found in gypsum or halite beds and in traprock. Although very soft,

Susan Zalkind and Paul Hawkins specialize in carving American alabasters. This free-form candle lamp glorifies a common material.
Photo by G. Frost.

its lovely colors recommend it for ornamental uses and for cabochons which will not be exposed to wear. The colors are pink, violet, blue, and gray. Massive anhydrite is granular or fibrous and sometimes has marblelike veining. It alters to gypsum. That which is suitable for cutting is siliceous and often has a pearly luster. Small collectors' stones have been faceted from Swiss and Canadian material. Anhydrite was promoted as a lapidary material, especially for carvings at Tucson. The material, which went by the trade name Angelite, was pale blue. The source of Angelite was probably Mexico.

A fancy purple-colored material is found at Bancroft, Canada. Blue masses are found in Chihuahua, Mexico, and a marblelike white variation from Italy has been used for many ornamental purposes. In the United States it comes from South Dakota (lavender and pink), New Mexico (blue banded), and Texas (gray blue).

Pendants, cabochons, and small carvings can be made with steel tools, sanding cloth, and tripoli. Hard wax applied to a slightly warm stone and buffed with strips of flannel gives a protective finish. Hand buffing is an appropriate treatment for soft material.

ARGILLITE (SLATE)

Slate—a lowly rock? Sometimes, but as with other rocks and minerals, there are standout examples which have attracted attention for centuries.

For several thousand years the natives of western Canada mined the black material called Haida slate. Tribal artists patiently transformed the slate into tools, ceremonial objects, and exquisitely designed plates, plaques, and carvings. They also added a decorative touch—black dye.

The slate, composed of serpentine, pyrophyllite, graphite, and kaolin, was hardened by volcanic activity of the Tertiary. It is found with sandstone and shale on Queen Charlotte Island, British Columbia, near a channel separating several small islands.

Black slate was also used by stone workers of West Coast tribes in the United States. In the Midwest, a banded slate was a choice material for prehistoric craftsmen. Effigies, gorgets, birdstones, bannerstones, and pendants of highly polished slate show delicate handwork. The bands on the slates are mostly monochromatic, and some have a metallic luster.

Wewee slate from northern Michigan is used by lapidaries there for clocks, bookends, boxes, and carvings. The fine-grained slate is lighter in color than most slates, with tones of tan, brown, cream, and peach taking the best polish.

Slate is soft, only 2 to 3 in hardness, so it is easily worked with common steel tools. It should be worked wet. The Indians finish it by rubbing to a matte or semi-shiny finish. Natural fauna carvings, plates, and trays are still made. Lapidaries frequently coat a soft material like this with an epoxy or resin and rebuff the item after the coating has cured. Slate can often be purchased at stone yards for architectural materials.

Zebra Stone and Green Slate

An unusual ornamental stone from Australia, Zebra stone is used for bookends, pen bases, clock faces, carvings, and other large-scale projects to make use of its interesting red-brown and white stripes. The rock classified as argillite is composed of clay, silica, and iron and is of sedimentary origin, although it is slightly metamorphosed.

Found near Lake Argyle in the Kununurra district of western Australia, Zebra stone's unique patterns are not entirely understood by geologists. One theory is that the patterns are ripple markings. When skillfully cut, the stripes can become dots, rods, or waves. I. A. Mumme reports that Australian lapidaries like to work with the material in spite of the fact that it is difficult to polish. They are looking for new sources since the original source is now under the waters of a new dam on the Ord River.

Creative carver Leonard Stoller of California turned a piece of Zebra stone purchased in Tucson into fascinating ceramiclike vases or containers. June McKenzie of Newton, Australia, who reports a recent find in western Australia, says flats are easier to polish than domed cabochons. She gets her polish with cerium oxide on the smooth side of a leather buff. The rock comes from a very ancient formation, about 500—600 million years.

A slatelike rock from southern Australia is massive and heavily impregnated with bright green malachite and isolated veins of red cuprite. Australian writer Patrick Murphy says it also appears to contain vanadium. It takes an excellent polish and is a popular lapidary material.

BARITE
Barium sulfate
H. 3–3½   D. 4.5
Orthorhombic

Barite is a common vein mineral in many ore deposits and because of its softness it is seldom used as gem material. However, some crystals have such desirable colors that they have been made into cabochons or faceted stones. Pure barite is colorless, but barite can also be white, yellow, blue, green, brown, black, or golden in color. A stalactitic type of barite from England has been used as an ornamental material.

One of the most attractive barites for lapidaries is the so-called golden barite from Elk Creek near Wasta, South Dakota. Shining, well-shaped transparent crystals of a desirable light golden brown occur here in large concretions in the Pierre Shale formation. The concretions are difficult to open to reveal the fragile barites. Most crystals are ½–1½ inches (1.27–3.81 cm) in length, but crystals up to 12 inches

(30.48 cm) are known. Lustrous small crystals have been used as found for pendants and earrings.

Another prime locality for facetable barite is Stoneham, Colorado, where tabular blue crystals are found in clay banks of rugged gullies. Milky crystals are sometimes used for small cabochons.

Canada, England, and France have facetable barite. Barite is too soft for jewelry, except perhaps a pendant. Cut stones should have protective mountings. Lapidaries must be cautious because of the perfect cleavage. Very heat sensitive, barite should be preformed with fine wheels. After cold dopping, use a fine lap and polish on a wax lap with tin oxide. Barite for cutting is not common.

BAUXITE

Bauxite is an aluminum-bearing rock consisting of concretionary masses of white clay, red iron oxides, and various impurities. Produced by decaying granite and other igneous rock, surface deposits are widespread and immense. The material is often brightly colored with red, green, and yellow pisolitic patterns against a white, buff, or gray groundmass. Selected pieces can be cut into large cabochons. Much of the best cutting material has come from Bauxite, Arkansas, from immense deposits discovered in 1887. The cutting material has been called heliotrope bauxite. Other deposits are in New Mexico, Virginia, Tennessee, Alabama, Brazil, France, Germany, and India.

With variable hardness, the material is difficult to polish for cabochons or ornamental objects. Some lapidaries coat a cut stone with resin and repolish it after the resin has cured.

BOWESITE

A polishable rock used by Australian lapidaries, bowesite is a mixture of diopside, feldspar, actinolite, garnet, sphene, epidote, and calcite. It comes from Queensland and has been widely used for animal carvings, figurines, and objets d'art.

All examples of this rock are some tint or shade of green, pale green, yellow-green, medium green streaked with white, or deep green that is almost black. Carefully chosen pieces are used for assorted decorative purposes.

CALCITE
Calcium carbonate
H. 3   **D. 2.7**
Hexagonal

Although calcite is a common and very soft material, lapidaries have found numerous uses for it. It can be opaque, translucent, or transparent, and it comes in a kaleidoscope of colors from pastel tints to deep rich shades. Fibrous calcite is chatoyant.

Calcite occurs in all rock types in massive veins and as an amazing array of collectable crystals. It is abundant in mines and caves. Lapidaries use pink, peach, orange, and green calcite for cabochons and other projects. Considering its many difficulties (low hardness, easy cleavage, and heat sensitivity), the most unusual use of calcite is for faceted collectors' stones. Clear stones of over 1,000 carats have been faceted. The New York State Museum has a calcite of 1,800 carats from Ontario, Canada, material faceted by Arthur Grant. Grant also cut a sensational stone of 1,156 carats which reflects the colors of the rainbow. A 70-carat calcite

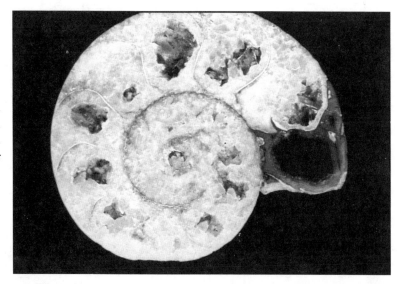

Calcite fossils like this 4½-inch ammonite from South Dakota are often cut and polished as specimens by lapidaries.

with spectral colors cut by Elvis Gray is in the Los Angeles County Museum.

Cabochons and faceted stones are cut from red, yellow, and green calcites from Mexico. Orange banded calcite from Mexico is now marketed as eggs, spheres, pyramids, and carvings. Yellow and orange calcite from South Dakota has been cut. Pink cobaltian calcite from Zaire is now a temptation for lapidaries as well as cerise-colored cobaltocalcite from Spain. Peach-pink crystals from northern Michigan and black calcite from New Mexico are other choices.

Although calcite is found in many lovely colors, it is often dyed to imitate jade, lapis lazuli, turquoise, and rhodochrosite. Dyed calcite is most often used for beads. The difficulties for cutters are perfect cleavage planes in three directions and heat sensitivity. Also, the cabochons are resistant to polishes, so cutters add a few crystals of oxalic acid to the final tin oxide slurry. Various forms of calcite for lapidaries are abundant.

Calcite Onyx

This variety of calcium carbonate, deposited by water, is composed of translucent fibrous crystals. It comes in a wonderful variety of colors and often immense massive deposits, so it is widely used as a decorative and ornamental material.

In spite of a hardness of 3, it is usually compact and uniform with intricately banded patterns. Onyx can be cut into large objects such as counters, tiles, tabletops, bookends, clocks, candlesticks, vases, bowls, and lamps. It is also used for beads, pendants, small carved animals, and other souvenir-type items.

Important onyx deposits are in Mexico. Huge quarries at Oaxaca, Puebla, and other places have been producing onyx for many years, and the term Mexican onyx is heard so often that the word Mexican is sometimes an adjective for any calcite onyx. Puebla had large manufacturing companies specializing in onyx, as well as an extensive cottage industry. This may be playing out, but other onyx quarries are still at work. Mexican onyx comes in colors of honey, white, tan, golden, brown, and light green, but some of the material is now dyed for brighter colors. The patterns are concentric bands of varying widths and configurations. Mexican products are customarily acid polished.

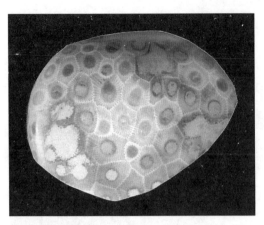

Hexagonaria coral, replaced by calcite, is the popular Petoskey stone of Michigan.

There are many notable onyx deposits in the United States. An onyx with exotic multicolored patterns comes from Kokoweef, near Baker, California. A quarry near Trona produces green, red, gold, brown, and white onyx. Another quarry near Trona produces Aquarius Lace, a delicately patterned gray and white onyx. The popular Silver Onyx comes from Mule Canyon near Calico.

A gypsy-colored onyx—red, yellow, orange, and peach—comes from Mayer, Arizona. The best material is fine grained and makes colorful ornamental lapidary products. Other Arizona occurrences are

Art Grant faceted this 1,170-carat calcite for Harvard University's Museum.

white onyx at Kingman and amber onyx at Canyon Diablo. In Utah, excellent red and white banded calcite onyx comes from Mt. Nebo near Nephi. Onyx is also found near Escalante. In New Mexico, green onyx occurs in Dona Ana County near Organ. Pale neutral onyx comes from near Pringle in Custer County, South Dakota. Cutting-quality onyx has been quarried in Kentucky, North Carolina, Tennessee, and several other states.

A modern find of useful onyx is the intricately patterned, highly colored onyx of Pakistan. Other onyx locations are Argentina, Austria, Czechoslovakia, Gibraltar, and several counties in Africa.

Calcite onyx can be carved with steel tools or worked with standard lapidary machinery. Coarse wheels should not be used. Polish on onyx is improved by the addition of a small amount of muriatic or oxalic acid to the tin oxide slurry. Manufacturers of onyx ornamental products polish by acid dipping, a dangerous method for amateur lapidaries or small shops.

Coquina

Shell fragments are obvious in this loosely aggregated limestone. In some places the formations are old and the fossiliferous limestone is used for decorative purposes. A large and geologically recent deposit is off the coast of St. Augustine, Florida. The Spanish cut this material into blocks and built the walls and fortifications of this old city from the coquina limestone. Most of the shells are the small mollusks that are still prevalent on the coast.

That the stone is durable is proven by the fact that the old walls are still standing. Souvenirs are made from the coquina rock today. It is especially used for garden ornaments, gates, and exterior decoration. Some compact shell limestone from other states has been loosely called coquina.

Marble

Marble is a crystalline calcareous rock formed by the metamorphism of limestone. The composition may be mainly calcite or dolomite, but impurities and inclusions give this rock, which is white if pure, an artist's palette of colors and a decorator's book of patterns.

Marble has a hardness of 3. The grains are varied from extremely fine and uniform to coarsely crystalline. Massive deposits of marble occur worldwide, and some have been used for history's finest examples of art and architecture. Examples are the carvings of Michelangelo and the Taj Mahal.

While limestone is sedimentary and marble is metamorphic, the term marble has been used to cover decorative materials of either group—materials which occur in large deposits and have the beauty of color and pattern required for ornamental and decorative lapidary work. Several new marble quarries are producing and promoting material for the lapidary. From Beaver County, Utah, comes Picasso marble, a fine-grained material with colors of orange, yellow, gray, and tan crisscrossed in every direction with lines of dark brown. Mined by Lita Smith-Gharet, it is used for beads, pendants, earrings, and cabochons.

Smith-Gharet also mines Zebra marble from Utah. It is a dolomitic marble with contrasting black and white irregularly shaped markings. Her third marble, from Washington state, is a pastel green dolomitic marble laced with white. The unnamed marble looks like lime sherbet. It is translucent, fine grained, and takes a good polish. The light green hue with a slight hint of yellow fills a color gap in lapidary marbles.

A white marble with pale tints of pink or green in some areas is found near Etna, near Yreka, California.

From Nevada's old silver district in Lincoln County comes Heritage marble, a brecciated material consisting of yellowish-white calcite and dark green serpentine. In some places there are areas of light green calcite and pink rhodochrosite. The marble occurs in an area of intensely altered rocks. According to mine operators it is really a low-grade silver ore.

A fossiliferous marble is from the Lambert Ranch in San Saba County, Texas. Fragments of crinoids and other marine animals are white or pastel against a charcoal gray or black background. Fascinating patterns make conversation-piece spheres, art objects, and cabochons. Beautifully preserved gastropods on multicolored material are highly prized here.

From upper Michigan comes an attractive material called Kona dolomite. This dolomite is a rock, not a mineral. The Lindberg quarry near Marquette has mined many tons of this elegant decorators' stone. Michigan cutters use this dolomite for fireplaces, doorways, counters, altars, and jewelry. The material also occurs as float over a large area. Kona dolomite has geometric and brecciated patterns and gracefully undulating bands with light muted ground colors dominated by a splendid coral pink, and accented with rust, brown, tan, and beige.

A high-grade dolomitic marble is also quarried in Le Seur County, Minnesota. Called Kasota stone, the material has interesting mixtures of pink, yellow, white, gray, and tan. It is popular with architects, decorators, and local lapidaries.

Tennessee has a marble industry centered in Blount County. One of the varieties of this rather coarse-grained marble which is favored by lapidaries is called French Pink. Colors are from pale pink to deep rose and the material is translucent. Other Tennessee marbles are white, red, blue, honey, gold, and yellow.

In this slab of Picasso marble, George Frank captured a moonlight scene of a wintry forest. Zeitner collection.

Some excellent marble quarries are located in Georgia. A delicate pink marble with patterns of fluffy white clouds comes from Pickens County. Marble with inclusions of pyrite crystals is also found here. There is a black marble quarry in Gordon County.

Quarries in Alabama's Talladega County have produced showy white marble as well as black crystalline marble. An ornamental marble from Morelos, Mexico, has pink grossular garnet crystals in fine-grained white marble. Green marble has been quarried near Madoc, Ontario, Canada.

There are many more notable marbles in the United States, but some of the European marbles deserve mention also. The marbles of Greece are historic. These are true metamorphosed crystalline marbles, many of them pure white, translucent, and with a texture suitable for fine arts. Great museums have famous classic statues sculpted from Greek marble. Some of the quarries are on the islands of Paros and Thassos and some come from the Athens region. There are also occurrences of black, red, green, and cream-colored marbles in Greece.

A most exciting marble is the Ruin marble, or landscape marble, of Tuscany, Italy. The colors are warm, chiefly tints of reddish brown, with subtle banding and bold pictures in rich dark shades of brown. The scenes bear astonishing likenesses to ruins of ancient cities or collapsing skylines of modern cities, perhaps after an earthquake.

A recent creative use of marble by lapidary Edwin Gueck is a sphere made from seven colors of marble cut into parallelograms, cemented together and then ground into a sphere with a checkerboard pattern. Sculptor Thomas Miller of Minnesota created a likeness of Indian hero Sitting Bull from a 10-ton block of Kasota stone.

Fine-grained massive marble is easily polished with hand tools or mechanical wheels. Cold dop cabochons to be used on machines. Polish with tin oxide on felt with several drops of muriatic acid added to the slurry. Marble is readily available for almost any size project.

Petoskey Stone

Michigan's state rock is Petoskey stone, a calcium carbonate fossilization of a coral called Hexagonaria. Petoskey stone is found in lower Michigan in the Traverse Bay region of Lake Michigan. The pieces of coral have a distinct honeycomblike pattern with each cell having intricate radial markings. Colors are beige, tan, cream, and several shades of brown. Sizes vary from small pebbles to pieces several inches in diameter. Other marine species from the Devonian are found here, but Hexagonaria is preferred because of its contrasting and complex pattern.

Michigan lapidaries use Petoskey stone for jewelry and carvings. Particularly realistic are the carved turtles and serpents. A few crystals of oxalic acid vastly improve the polish that is often achieved by tin oxide on felt. Some local lapidaries use a velvet lap. The decorative stones are marketed throughout the Midwest.

Tufa

One of the strangest materials to be cut and used for decorative purposes is tufa, a calcareous deposit from hot springs. The calcite from the hot water sometimes covers and kills such vegetation as moss, watercress, ferns, and cattails. The vegetation is killed but the calcite coating remains. Sometimes the delicate moss and leaf shapes in buff-colored calcium carbonate are aesthetic, showing in detail what the plant life looked like.

If a material is interesting and available, someone is bound to try to cut it. An unusual fireplace in Fall River County, South Dakota, is made of well-chosen blocks of tufa from local hot springs. Shelves and niches have been cut in the blocks for objects such as Sioux pottery or polished agates.

Tufa from Cascade Creek near Hot Springs was also used by Indians hundreds of years ago. Garould Fairhead, Nebraska rancher, found a strange-looking artifact of tufa when he was digging a pit on his ranch. Several feet underground he found a dirt-filled tufa carving, a huge masklike head, similar to the Kiva heads of the Mimbres culture. Tufa also occurs in California, Arizona, Wyoming, Italy, and Australia.

CATLINITE

The sacred pipestone of the Midwestern Indians is an indurated clay colored several shades of red by iron. Easy to shape, the material is fine, uniform, and compact. The principal locality is Pipestone, Minnesota, where a large quarry has been worked for hundreds of years. Even warring tribes came to this quarry in peace. Now a National Monument, the quarry is still worked by Indians who use it for peace pipes, ceremonial objects, and souvenirs for tourists.

Catlinite is a mixture of pyrophyllite, kaolinite, sericite, diaspore, and limonite. The grain is fine and even, and the hardness is only about 2½ to 3 when mined, but quickly increases in the atmosphere.

Catlinite, similar to that from Minnesota, is found near the Big Sioux River north of Sioux Falls, South Dakota, and also east of the town of Rice Lake, Wisconsin. There are also several catlinite claims north of Prescott, Arizona.

A similar material, but black in color, is found on Blackpipe Creek near Martin, Bennett County, South Dakota. Many of the northern plains Indians considered this black pipestone ideal for their ornate religious and ceremonial objects. The black pipestone was often inlaid with colorful materials. Pipestone is easily carved with household tools, and readily polished, sometimes with steel wool and wax. Catlinite is sometimes advertised.

CHAROITE
Calcium potassium silicate
H. 5–6   D. 2.6
Monoclinic

A massive and strikingly beautiful ornamental rock from Yakutsk, Russia, was introduced in the United States in the 1970s and was immediately ranked as a major opaque lapidary material. The attractive colors range from lavender to lilac to purple with contrasting patterns in

Charoite is a striking lavender lapidary material from Russia that has been used for vases, wine decanters, bowls, boxes, and jewelry. McNamar collection. Courtesy of Lapidary Journal.

orange, green, and black. The needles of black aegerine-augite give dramatic scenic effects, especially when combined with orange tinkasite and green microcline. Some of the tints and shades of violet occur as silky swirls of fibrous chatoyant bundles.

Found near the Chary (Charo) River in the Lake Baikal region, the material is present in syenite/limestone contact zones. It was first misidentified as the mineral canasite, which occurs with it. The cutting material is a rock rather than the mineral charoite alone. It has been available in large blocks. Leonid Prikazchikov writes that charoite occurs in thick lenses and scattered boulders in a remote area. It is now mined by open cut. In Russia the material is known as Sirenevy Kamen, lilac stone.

Charoite is distinctive and easy to recognize. Russian artists have used the material for large vases, candlesticks, decanters, goblets, and other useful and decorative items. It has been used in the United States for jewelry, carvings, and intarsia. Lapidaries should look for red-purple and black sprays of radiating needles or chatoyant stone.

A foremost cutter of charoite is Charles Laloma, an American Indian artist who uses charoite for his innovative inlay and channel work. Choice items and pieces have been marketed for several years at shows and by mail.

Because it is fibrous and has inclusions of unequal hardness, charoite should be cold dopped and worked with diamond using water as a coolant. Diamond paste (½ micron) produces a good finish. Charoite cabochons and carvings are suitable for jewelry and combine well with sugilite, lapis lazuli, turquoise, amethyst, and black onyx. Rough charoite and slabs are now on the market.

CHICKEN-BLOOD STONE

Certainly with the exception of Stinking-water wood from Oregon, Chicken-blood stone has to be the most inappropriate name for a comely lapidary material. A traditional carving material from China, it is a clay mineral with pyrophyllite, dickite, and kaolinite in its composition. It is compact, translucent, and waxy appearing with exotic red colors due to cinnabar inclusions in the matrix. The Chinese have used it for elegant carvings for over 1,000 years.

The cinnabar is distributed in the translucent material in the form of large spots, swirled streaks, and filmy clouds. The best material is evenly colored by fine dissemination of cinnabar through the pastel or neutral matrix, which can be yellow, gray, greenish, white, or black. Fragments of quartz or pyrite which are sometimes present devalue the material. Occasionally some material has a pearly luster.

There are two major locations in China, but the material is becoming scarce. Similar material has come from Mongolia. Clay minerals have been used for soft carvings in other areas. They can be worked with hand tools or flexible shaft tools and are usually finished with hard wax. Chickenblood stone is only 2 or 3 in hardness and 2.6 in density.

The material has become so popular in the Orient for carvings and seals that the Chinese have come up with an imitation consisting of a talclike core with a cinnabar-treated resin coating. When carved, the imitation is very realistic.

COPPER ROCKS

Campbellite

Campbellite is a copper mixture from Bisbee, Arizona—a show hit for discriminating lapidaries at Tucson a few years ago. It consists of pure copper, white quartz, malachite, and several copper minerals. With tones of red, green, blue, white, and copper, the rock is a riot of color. The section of the mine where the material was found is now flooded, but West Coast dealers may have a few hundred pounds in stock.

Michael Taterka, a Texas jeweler and designer, has cut many cabochons of the material for pendants, rings, and other jewelry uses. He says it is difficult to work with because the copper seams tend to rip out diamonds. He uses tin oxide and Zam for a finish. This is an uncommon material.

Eilat Stone

From the city of Eilat on the Red Sea comes a colorful lapidary material composed of silicified chrysocolla with malachite, azurite, and turquoise. The predominant color is a vivid blue-green. Large impressive cabs have been cut of the intricately patterned material and exported to many countries. Some rough was also exported. Supplies are now very limited.

Imperialite Dancer

This harmonious mixture of blues and greens is primarily malachite, azurite, chrysocolla, chalcocite, and copper. It is mined in Imperial County, California, from a vein that was discovered in 1965. Wesley Koerner of King Solomon's Mine U.S.A. stated that the mine was first worked for copper, but now only for gem material. The largest gem-quality piece to be mined is about 900 pounds.

The chrysocolla in the rock is not entirely the gem chalcedony variety, but there is some of the translucent chrysocolla-colored chalcedony in the mix. The malachite is not banded in the manner of the African material. Electric blues are the dominant colors in graceful patterns with just enough black to set off the brighter colors.

Imperialite Dancer is used for cabochons and jewelry. It should be worked wet and takes a good polish, although undercutting may be a problem.

Mojave Stone

This mixture of copper minerals was discovered in the Mojave Desert of California by Laurence Stalling in the late 1970s. Stalling named it for the desert and mined and cut it for several years, selling it as finished oval and freeform cabochons through distributors. Some cabochons are nearly 3 inches (7.62 cm) in length.

A bright and vibrant material for jewelry, Mojave Stone consists of copper, brochantite, antlerite, covellite, linarite, bisbeeite, tenorite, malachite, and several other colorful minerals plus chalcedony. Examination of the stunning patterns reveals interesting hexagonal crystal pseudomorphs. Some of the most sensational stones are metallic black with patterns of intense blue-green.

The material is 5 to 6 in hardness and is fairly tough. It takes an excellent polish with chrome oxide or 50,000 diamond. Little has been available to cutters, but it may soon be on the market again.

Natural Mosaic

In the late 1970s a geologist at Ajo, Arizona, found a deposit of brecciated copper-bearing rock near Ajo. The angular patterns and the wonderful blues and greens led discoverer Ronald Boatman to test its lapidary qualities. It passed the test, turning out to be well cemented by quartz and near 7 in hardness. He named it Natural Mosaic.

Resembling a fine Florentine mosaic, the stones have "tiles" of green, blue, orange, pink, white, and brown; creating the inlaid effect are epidote, malachite, feldspar, chrysocolla, and chalcocite. The individual polygons seldom exceed 5 millimeters. The material was initially shown at Quartzsite and Tucson. Lapidaries should wear masks when working with coppers. Linde A or ½ micron diamond on leather are polish choices.

Patricianite and Michigan Copper Rocks

Patricianite is the local name for a Keweenaw Peninsula cutting material which is an intergrowth of chlorite, prehnite, epidote, quartz, and native copper. The copper flecks and lacy veins against the variegated green groundmass provide an arresting contrast. Found in the copper mine dumps or as beach pebbles, the rock is used for cabochons by Michigan lapidaries who place the hardness at around 6.

The Michigan copper mines have several other rocks which can be used for gemstones and jewelry. A cuttable epidote is often streaked with copper, and sometimes even includes native silver. Selected pieces of copper-laced basalt are also polishable. A black shale with webs of bright copper can sometimes be used for stunning cabochons.

Lapidaries must watch for undercutting in any of the copper materials which consist of several minerals. Richard Whiteman of Red Metal Minerals writes that the Michigan copper rocks that are not suitable for jewelry are often used for spheres, clock faces, pen sets, bookends, and carvings. Several cuttable coppers are available in Michigan.

Tanundaite

This is a local name for an Australian lapidary material from the Barossa Valley. It is a metamorphic rock with actinolite and several other minerals with complex swirling patterns in several shades of green, probably due to copper.

Patrick Murphy of Australia, editor of *Informs*, writes there is a substantial deposit of this ornamental material and local lapidaries use it in many ways. Wet sanding should be followed with Linde A on hard leather.

GEORGIA MIDNIGHT

A dense black ornamental rock from Georgia has been given the trade name Georgia Midnight. The material is opaque, fine grained, and hard. Minute sparkles are reminiscent of a cloudy sky with an occasional star peeking through.

Patented by the C. R. Smith family of Kennesaw, Georgia, the material has been analyzed and found to contain many ele-

ments—among them gold, silver, iron, chromium, aluminum, calcium, zinc, lead, and silicon. No two specimens are alike except in the density of the velvet black.

Some specimens have metallic flashes and some have pearly flecks which look similar to aventurine or sunstone. The material takes a glassy polish and can be used for rings, pendants, pins, and earrings. The cabochons are striking when mounted in yellow gold, especially with gold castings which appear to give depth to the stone. Rough is not presently available.

GRANITE

Granite, a common igneous rock, is by no means at the bottom of the list for lapidaries. Colorful granite, and granites with fascinating patterns, exist in many places. Granite is a durable material consisting mainly of quartz and feldspar, but with other constituents—epidote, mica, hornblende, tourmaline, and magnetite—often added to the mix. The grain size varies

Red granite from Wisconsin is used for many colorful lapidary projects.

from fine to coarse as in the case of pegmatite dikes. Granite takes a good polish and has been used for centuries for decorative purposes, buildings, memorials, and monuments. A few types of granite have outstanding possibilities. Lapidaries can always locate some kind of granite.

Colored Granites

Fine-grained granites with uniform textures and good color are the most commonly used for lapidary work. The primary color and the accessory colors, their sizes and shapes, all go into the lapidaries' choice of material. Lapidaries who wish to use granite have an incredible choice.

One granite used for monuments and decorative objects such as clocks and bookends is a deep red granite called Mahogany granite, from a quarry at Milbank, South Dakota. A pink granite is from St. Cloud, Minnesota. From Morton, Minnesota, comes a red granite with swirling tone-on-tone patterns. A dark green granite was once quarried at Buyck, Minnesota.

A red granite of uniform grain is quarried near Redgranite, Wisconsin. Called Rapakivi granite, a Wisconsin granite from Wuapaca County has complementary colors of green and red. The name comes from a noted Finnish deposit with similar colors. The green is due to chlorite.

Of the granites of the eastern states, that from Barre, Vermont, is best known. The Rock of Ages quarry has produced granite for major public buildings and monuments in many places. Granites from New Hampshire and New York have been widely used. A large granite quarry is located at Mt. Airy, North Carolina. The largest exposure of muscovite granite in the United States is Stone Mountain, Georgia. A relief carving here illustrates heroes of the Civil War.

In South Dakota, the uniform, beige-gray granite of the Harney Range was carved by dynamite for the National Memorial, Mount Rushmore, a deep relief carving of Washington, Jefferson, Theodore Roosevelt, and Lincoln. A monument to the American Indian hero Crazy Horse is being carved from a nearby granite peak.

Vibralaps are excellent for sanding and polishing large blocks of granite, starting with 100-grit silicon carbide followed by 220, 320, and 400. After cleaning the granite and the machine, a felt pad is inserted and charged with cerium oxide.

Graphic Granite

Quartz and feldspar crystals intertwine in graphic granite to produce patterns not unlike an exotic alphabet. Glassy dark "letters" against a cream or white groundmass make a pleasing contrast. Graphic granite is often a sign of nearby pegmatites, where the crystals of feldspar and quartz cooled even more slowly, and are separated, or in clusters, such as the amazonstone (microcline) and smoky quartz of the Pikes Peak, Colorado, area.

Locations for graphic granite are California, Montana, Colorado, South Dakota, Connecticut, New York, and Maine. A graphic granite with polishable qualities comes from Hybla, Ontario. A blue-green and dark gray graphic granite occurs in the Illmen Range of the Ural Mountains.

Like many granites, graphic granite will undercut or chip if not worked slowly and carefully. A vibralap does a good job on flats. Extended fine wet sanding is followed by Linde A on leather.

Larvikite

A decorative rock found near Larvik, Norway, has been popular for many years and is still being quarried for interior and exterior uses and for innovative lapidary projects. Called larvikite, the rock is a feldspar, mica, and augite mixture with coarse grains and colors of gray, white, and black, accented by chatoyant rhombs of pale feldspar with flashes of silvery blue. Lapidaries have used it for large handsome spheres, eggs, bookends, desk sets, and many ornamental items. The material undercuts unless sanded with special care. Alumina or tin oxide will polish when used on hard leather.

Orbicular Granite

In some places the mineral grains of the granite are arranged in round or eye-shaped clusters of varying and contrasting colors. The round structures at first glance look like a pebble conglomerate, but upon examination orderly configurations of crystallized minerals can be observed. Orbicular granite occurs in Rhode Island, Vermont, Canada, Sweden, and Finland. A significant deposit is at Rapakivi, Finland.

Since granite is made up of several minerals of varying characteristics, lapidaries might consider making doublets or triplets of pieces that have good color and pattern. The highly polished transparent rock crystal caps are used in lieu of polishing the granite.

Porphyry

Porphyritic granite is granite that has large crystals or phenocrysts of orthoclase feldspar in a matrix of finer grains. Porphyry as a granite is composed of grains of quartz, feldspar, biotite, and sometimes hornblende. The phenocrysts of quartz or feldspar often form flowerlike patterns, in which case it is called chrysanthemum rock. There is also labradorite porphyry in which the phenocrysts consist of labradorite and a porphyritic basalt, with green or yellow phenocrysts against a dark, finely crystalline groundmass.

Some pieces of porphyry resemble snowflakes, stars, or daisies, rather than chrysanthemums. The phenocrysts are arranged in radial patterns, sometimes randomly and sparsely scattered, and sometimes closely packed. Often found as beach stones, these igneous rocks sometimes weigh many pounds. Not all porphyry has these desirable patterns, but even if the porphyry is not the flowerstone type, it is an interesting material because of its boldly contrasting crystal patterns.

In many cases the groundmass of porphyry is dark, and the feldspar crystals that form the patterns are white, or nearly white. In some instances the groundmass may contain epidote, so there is a hint of green, and in other instances the feldspar may be a light pink or orange.

Porphyries can be found in many large areas of igneous rock. Porphyritic granite is found west of Twenty-Nine Palms, California. Locally called *bakerite*, it is used for bookends, clocks, and spheres. A handsome syenitic porphyry is found near Negaunee in the Upper Peninsula of Michigan. A black porphyritic granite is found near Mellen, Wisconsin.

Porphyry with flesh-colored phenocrysts occurs in the Black Hills of South Dakota. Other variations are found throughout the Rocky Mountain states. A pink and smoky porphyritic granite occurs in the hill country of Texas.

Aesthetic porphyries come from Ontario and British Columbia, Canada. Fine, water-worn specimens come from the beaches of Vancouver Island. The flowerstone porphyries of British Columbia are often gray-green with white phenocryst flowers. Another type has charcoal gray ground color with green flowers. White flowers etched on a dark velvety black background are handsome. Flowers of salmon-colored microcline feldspar are rare and choice. A strangely patterned brecciated green and white igneous material called *dallasite* is found on Vancouver Island. The pattern resembles crystals that have been crushed to bits and carelessly put back together again.

Chrysanthemum stone from Japan is used for a type of decoration called Suiseki. A green porphyry is found in Greece and a red porphyry comes from Egypt.

Lapidaries have used porphyries for carving and decorative objects historically as well as recently. Handsome clocks, pen bases, paper weights, bookends, and large cabochons for bola ties are made of porphyry. The chief drawback of working porphyry is the tendency of crystals to chip or pull if not kept cool and worked slowly. After extended wet sanding, polish on hard leather with Linde A.

Unakite

Unakite, a favorite American cabochon, jewelry, and carving material from the Appalachian Mountains, is an epidotized granite. Numerous areas of Virginia, Tennessee, and North Carolina have produced quantities of colorful high-quality cutting material.

The unakite is found in place and as stream-worn pebbles and boulders. Although there is much variation in the hues of greens and reds of the material, the most appealing is a light leaf green with rose-colored flowerlike patterns, set off by swirls of black and dark green. The green is epidote; the pinks, roses, and reds are feldspar; and the neutrals are quartz, and occasionally tourmaline or mica.

A well-known location is the Unaka Mountains in Unicoi County, Tennessee,

both names derived from an Indian tribe. The Max Patch granite has several outcrops of unakite, extending into Mitchell and Madison counties in North Carolina.

Pebbles of unakite are found in alluvial deposits in other states, including South Dakota, Wyoming, Colorado, and New Mexico, but the materials of these gravels are used only locally and are not available in any quantity. Epidotized granite also comes from South Africa and Zimbabwe; however, the colors and patterns are not equal to the Appalachian materials.

Unakite beads of many shapes, plus unakite cabochons, pendants, spheres, and carvings, are seen at most shows. Lapidaries have to work carefully to avoid chipping, especially if the crystal grains are large. Wet sanding is slow and a polish should result by using Linde A on hard buffs. Tumbling also works well. Unakite is plentiful.

HOWLITE
Hydrous calcium borate
H. 3½   D. 2.5
Monoclinic

This California mineral, a product of the borax mines, occurs in compact nodules lightly laced with black veining. For many years the soft material was used for small carvings, as backgrounds for paintings, and for novelties. Recently howlite has made the jewelry scene, primarily as beads. Pure white howlite beads are exquisite, but unfortunately most of the howlite beads have been dyed, because the porous material takes dye easily. Some artists have painted pictures on howlite slabs.

Howlite has been used to imitate lapis lazuli, coral, red jasper, and other opaque materials, but it is as turquoise that

Leonard Sires used California howlite for his daisy wall plaque.

howlite masquerades most often. Most of the turquoise dye jobs have been too intense and uniform to look real, although if the material is carefully chosen with black veining and given a pale variegated aqua-blue dye, it can be a close optical imitation of turquoise.

Howlite does not take a mirror polish, nor does it hold its polish. The best lapidary use for the whitest howlite is for carvings. It is soft enough to be carved with steel tools and tough enough to accept good detail. Tin oxide on a felt buff will give a fair polish. California dealers may stock howlite.

LAPIS NEVADA

This rather recent discovery in western Nevada is a rock of many colors. It is composed of thulite, zoisite, clinozoisite, scapolite, sericite, diopside, epidote, and piemontite with minor amounts of feldspar, quartz, actinolite, and apatite. The material is found in five deposits, two predominantly green and pink, two with mostly tints of pink and rose, and one that includes lavender with the pink and green. These delightful colors combine to produce a myriad of fascinating patterns for jewelry. A typical cabochon may have five or more minerals, each a different color.

The choice patterns resemble fields of primroses in the spring, with a few bluebonnets and Indian paintbrush thrown in. As a jewelry material, Lapis Nevada has suitable hardness and toughness.

The mine owners, David and Barbara Smith, grade the material according to colors, polishability, freedom of fractures, and translucency. The material is available for lapidaries in the rough and also is sold as beads, cabochons, spheres, and ornamental items. It has been used for delicate Oriental carvings and lovely jewelry. Carved pendants and heart-shaped cabochons are handsome.

Found in a metamorphic area of an igneous batholith, the material occurs as a thulite diopside endoskarn. The trade name, meaning Nevada rock, is rather unusual since the word lapis has come to be substituted commonly for lapis lazuli. Lapis refers to a rock or stone, but people think blue when they hear the word.

This is an interesting material which offers choices and challenges to the lapidary. Cutters should watch for undercutting. Fracture healer may be needed for large projects, but cabochons can be flawless. Working with diamond may bring the best results. A similar material—thulite, epidote, zoisite, and piedmontite—occurs in Norway and is a popular cutting material there.

Carved in the Orient, this new cutting material, Lapis Nevada, is a mixture of thulite with zoisite, scapolite, diopside, and epidote.

South Dakota, and Maine. Other sources are Brazil, Sweden, Czechoslovakia, Madagascar, Zimbabwe, and Japan. Material from Brazil has been faceted according to Maine lapidary Richard Oates. Maine lepidolite has been used for vases, bowls, boxes, and bookends.

Fine-grained lepidolite, especially if other fine-grained pegmatite materials are present, can be carved or cut into impressive cabochons. Flat ornamental objects are often finished on a vibrating lap. A high sheen can be developed also by using 50,000 diamond.

Soft and with perfect cleavage and variable hardness, lepidolite is difficult to work with. The first hurdle is careful selection of material. Besides good color, it should have uniform fine grains and a compact texture with few fractures. Cuttable lepidolite is not often available.

MARIPOSITE

This California lapidary material, named for the county in which it is found, is a mottled green dolomite colored by chrome-bearing green fuchsite mica. The groundmass color is white or pale green and the material is enhanced by veining of vivid green. Since it is found in California's Mother Lode gold country, mariposite sometimes contains native gold. California lapidary Vernon Korstad has a green sphere with many shining flecks of gold.

Mariposite is used for spheres, bookends, clock faces, and other ornamental items. Cabochons for jewelry which will not be subjected to hard wear are also cut. Building supply companies in California have sold the material for interior and exterior decoration. A quarry near Coulterville is sometimes open to collectors.

LEPIDOLITE
Lithium aluminum silicate
H. 3–4   D. 2.8
Monoclinic

Although lepidolite has not previously been used much as a lapidary material, lepidolite beads, pendants, and carvings have been seen on the market recently. The lilac color is the chief attraction of this fine-grained sparkling material that seems to be intermixed with quartz and feldspar. The carved Oriental beads have a splendid color but a poor polish. Pinkish purple cabochons have been cut from lepidolite from near Pala, California.

This lithium mica is often found in gem pegmatites. Some U.S. locations are California, New Mexico, Colorado, Wyoming,

Mariposite is soft and has differential hardness, so it is considered difficult to polish. Chrome oxide on leather is often used, but the best polish is with diamond.

MEERSCHAUM (SEPIOLITE)
Hydrous magnesium silicate
H. 2   D. 2.0
Orthorhombic

This soft, lightweight, porous material is a decomposition of serpentine. As a lapidary material it is easily carved with hand tools. Historically it has been carved in Turkey, the principal locality, for pipes, decorative objects, and even jewelry. A classic pipe is an intricate lady's hand holding a realistic skull. Such carvings are now collectors' items.

Meerschaum is polished with wax. The white material turns golden yellow as the pipe is smoked. The material also seems to harden with age.

An American location for carvable meerschaum is the Gila Wilderness of New Mexico, where pieces were originally found floating down Salt Creek. Other states having meerschaum are California, Arizona, Utah, and Pennsylvania. Foreign localities in addition to Turkey are Greece, Morocco, Spain, and Czechoslovakia. Meerschaum is fibrous and dusty to work with, so lapidaries should wear masks when working the material by hand.

OCEAN PICTURE ROCK

One of the most attractive of the ornamental and decorative rocks is called Ocean Picture Rock. Altered and silicified serpentine, the material is dramatic for large-scale lapidary work, such as clocks, desk sets, carvings, boxes, bowls, and framed rock pictures. Clock faces are a sensational use.

The colors of this picture rock are so unique that well-chosen pieces make exceptionally realistic scenes with blue and white Pacific surf, rocky peninsulas of red and browns, green foliage, and sandy beaches. The scenes are reminiscent of British Columbia where the rock is found.

Artistic scenes are the results of the brecciated composition of the rock. Large angular pieces of colorful material seem to have been captured in the sea of blue and white fine-grained rock. Some of the dark rock pieces seem to have been brecciated themselves before becoming part of the picture rock. There are also areas of small-scale patterns suitable for delicate cabochons, and small sections of opaque light blue which are used in intarsias and inlay.

Mined by Joe Carlton of Rock Creek, British Columbia, Ocean Picture Rock is quarried about 10 miles from that community. Regional rock is highly metamorphosed. Carlton says that because the rock contains considerable silica, much of the material approaches 6 in hardness. A good supply is available.

The material is usually homogeneous and will not undercut. The lapidary's main concern is selecting the appropriate stone for a project. It is for sale in British Columbia and sometimes in the Northwest.

OIL SHALE

Stone souvenirs of the west slope of the Colorado Rockies often elicit questions from visiting lapidaries. The material is fine grained, banded, and colorful and appears in gift shops as jewelry, bookends, clocks, paperweights, desk sets, and carvings. The answer is that it is oil shale, a plentiful material which, according to the government, was supposed to have become the answer to our energy problems. Millions of dollars were invested in trying to find a way to remove the oil in an economically feasible manner. Now an immense area is good only for this unusual lapidary material.

The fine bands, usually on a cream or buff groundmass, are blue, gray, yellow, and light red-orange. The shale is not difficult to polish but should be kept cool, worked wet, and cut slowly.

ORTHOAMPHIBOLE

An unusual iridescent rock from near Douglas, Wyoming, was recently reported (*Gems and Gemology,* Fall 1988) and was compared to the popular iridescent orthoamphibole from Greenland, reported in 1987. The Greenland trade name is Nuummite. The Wyoming material was described as being ferro-anthophyllite with goethite, opaline silica, quartz, and calcite occurring in metamorphic rock. This discovery seems to be the same material which was described in the December 1966 *Lapidary Journal.* At that time the material was identified by the Smithsonian and the University of Wyoming as grunerite, an iron magnesium silicate.

Chet Humphrey of Douglas is credited with finding the material originally in veins on his jade claims. Float material was later found over a wide area by Bob Berry, a Wheatland dealer, who first had it analyzed. Locally it is called *fire jade.*

The amphibole has a fibrous structure and silky luster. Iridescent patches on the surface are shaped like jigsaw or intarsia

pieces. It has the glow of bronze with patches of metallic yellow, rose-red, and red-orange against a predominantly brown body color. Wyoming lapidaries have cut cabochons from the material for many years. A cuttable cummingtonite-grunerite occurrence in North Carolina and another in Lawrence County, South Dakota, may be similar.

Greenland Nuummite is now on the market. With gold, yellow, orange, green, and violet patches, it is an attractive jewelry material. Nuummite has recently been discovered near Risor in southern Norway. European cutters call it a sensational cutting material.

With its striking golden glint, this iridescent amphibole is being used for men's jewelry. Cabochons are often free-form. Lapidaries place the hardness at over 6 and also comment on the toughness. Most of the material has large grains, and much of it is badly fractured. Few cabochons are as large as 30 x 40 mm. Linde A on muslin was an early polish choice, but now all diamond produces better results.

RHYOLITE

Rhyolite is an igneous rock, usually fine grained, and often very colorful and boldly patterned. There are many fascinating occurrences for lapidaries. Most useful for cabochons, beads, pendants, and other jewelry items is *wonderstone*, a banded siliceous material in bright colors of yellow, red, cream, brick, brown, and orange. Wonderstone is found in many of the western states.

Orbicular rhyolite, often called bird's eye, is found in the Ord Mountains, California, northwest of Lucerne Valley. The round eyes, measuring up to an inch (4.54 cm) in diameter, have a wide spectrum of

From Donald Diller's bowl of gem fruit comes this lustrous bunch of obsidian grapes.

colors. A banded pink and green rhyolite wonderstone, a superb decorative material, is found in the Rawhide Mountains, north of Wenden, Arizona.

Near Fallon, Nevada, a fine-grained, highly colored, and generously patterned wonderstone suitable for jewelry is found. Disaster Peak wonderstone, from the Oregon/Nevada border, is a scenic rock with mountain scenes of red-browns, yellows, grays, and tans against a gray-blue sky. The bands are highly convoluted.

South of Texas Springs, Nevada, is a deposit of wonderstone banded in purple, yellow, red, white, and brown. The larger pieces are used for clocks and bookends. An elaborately banded wonderstone in shades and tints of red, orange, green, and brown comes from north and east of Pine Creek, Oregon.

An especially popular occurrence from New Mexico is locally called Candy Rock, a reference to its bright candy-colored stripes. Found just outside of Truth or Consequences, the material is used for cabochons, carvings, spheres, clocks, bowls, and many other purposes. Another

New Mexico occurrence with swirling bands and eyes in decorator colors, including violets, reds, and golds, is at Eagle Peak in Sierra County.

Northwest of Eureka, Utah, is a variety of wonderstone with elaborate patterns of reds, oranges, yellows, creams, and browns. It is used for cabochons and larger lapidary works.

Bird's-eye rhyolite from Thistle Station, Utah, is a top material for interesting cabochons, carvings, clocks, and an assortment of lapidary projects. A similar material with startling round bull's eyes occurs at Yuba Lake, Utah. This is also called bird's-eye rhyolite. The brightly banded *Hickoryite* from near Rodeo, Mexico, is a fine-grained wonderstone, suitable for almost any lapidary work.

A spheroidal rhyolite from Australia, with the trade name Rainforest Jasper, has a green groundmass in variegated colors with little lakes and rivers of translucent chalcedony, sometimes with a tint of blue. Some of the material is brecciated with the broken green spheres recemented by red-brown silica.

Lapidaries must be careful to select fine-grained wonderstone. The porous material will not polish well, but the fine-grained material can be worked the same as jasper. Many colors and patterns of rhyolite are marketed.

RODINGITE

A quarry in Montgomery County, Maryland, was the source of an attractive lapidary rock about 30 years ago. This rock was a mixture of green diopside with garnet, prehnite, calcite, and other minerals, but the overall effect was green. The texture resembled a medium-grain granite. Area lapidaries eagerly gathered the material for an assortment of lapidary uses including bookends, paperweights, and cabochons.

The quarry at Rockville was used for road material. Local clubs were allowed to take field trips there in the 1960s and reported that the material found was excellent for cutting. Collectors at first called the material diopside, but later it became known as Rodingite.

The material had to be carefully selected as some was badly flawed or fractured. In cutting there was a tendency to undercut. Rodingite is still seen occasionally at eastern shows.

SELWYNITE

This soft rock, with a hardness of about 2, is a claylike mixture from Mount Ida, Victoria, Australia, which has been used as a carving material. It is massive and translucent with a waxy luster and is similar to steatite. Carvers like selwynite for its excel-

lent shades of green including an emerald-like color. Often mottled in several shades and tints of green, the material is more colorful than most soapstone and just as easy to carve. Numerous ornamental objects have been carved either by hand or machine.

SERPENTINE

This metamorphic rock is widespread, but some occurrences have wonderful color and translucency and are suitable for jewelry, carvings, and many lapidary uses. Two serpentines, bowenite and williamsite, are referred to as "noble," meaning they have superior qualities which make them the aristocrats of this rock.

Bowenite, the state gem of Rhode Island, is a stone that is often sold as jade, mistakenly or otherwise. The translucent waxy green material is a massive hydrous magnesium silicate of about 5 in hardness. The colors vary from light to apple green to yellow-green, greenish yellow, yellow, and pale pure green. The material is tough and well adapted to the many elaborate Oriental carvings made from it. It is also used for beads and other jewelry. Bowenite is also found in Afghanistan , South Africa, China, New Zealand, and Pennsylvania. The bowenite from New Zealand is often a bluer green than that of Rhode Island, and is sometimes chatoyant.

Williamsite from Pennsylvania and Maryland is more translucent than bowenite and the color is a superb emerald green or apple green, often marked by black chromite inclusions. Found in seams in chrome deposits that were first worked about 200 years ago, the Maryland material is becoming scarce. Most williamsite cabochons are less than 25 x 18 mm in size. Although of inferior hardness,

Translucent yellow-green serpentine was carved into a tropical fish by Hing Wa Lee (fish is 4 inches long).

williamsite has a suitable toughness for lapidary purposes. It takes a high polish and can be used for pins, earrings, and pendants. Working it with diamond will prevent undercutting. Williamsite is difficult to acquire.

A decorative banded serpentine is found in Ash Creek Canyon, New Mexico. Called *ricolite*, the unique serpentine is used for spheres, bowls, bookends, carvings, and jewelry. Most of the bands are some tint or shade of green, but some are yellow, red, blue, and brown. The colors and patterns are so varied that lapidaries can be very discriminating when selecting their material. Soft but tough, ricolite can be worked with steel tools. Lapidaries

report they get the best polish by using a vibrating lap.

Verde antique is a name of a decorative opaque serpentine with many uses, ranging from carvings to interior decorations and building materials. It has been mined in large quantities in Vermont, and has been found and used locally in Michigan's Upper Peninsula, and in the Sidewinder Mountains of California. Other locations are Greece, Italy, and South Africa. Usually dark green in color, the material is often enhanced by sinuous veins of white calcite.

Satelite is a California serpentine similar to bowenite, which is pale green, gray-green, or blue-green in color and fibrous

Otis McDermitt made this organ pipe cactus from serpentine.

in structure. It can be used for superb cat's-eye cabochons. An unusual California serpentine is patterned material from near Livermore, which has contrasting irregularly outlined polygon shapes in complex arrangements. The colors are predominantly light and dark green.

Yalakomite is an altered serpentine from near Lillooet, British Columbia, Canada. Colors are pink, white, and green, with the green areas colored by platelets of fuchsite mica. This material seems to be silicified and takes an excellent polish for cabochons or ornaments.

Serpentines are often soft enough to be carved with hand tools. Better-quality material such as bowenite or williamsite can be beautifully finished with chrome oxide following diamond shaping and sanding. Serpentines often pose as jade, particularly on Oriental markets.

SPURRITE
Calcium silicate
H. 5   **D. 3.0**
Monoclinic

Spurrite is occasionally seen as an ornamental material, or for cabochons, and jewelry such as bola ties or pendants. Usually gray or with a lavender tint, spurrite with a desirable purple color was shown at Tucson in 1986. The rough material came from Mexico where it occurs in metamorphic contact zones of limestone and silicates in Durango, Hidalgo, Michoacán, and Queretaro. Nicely polished slabs accompanied the rough. Spurrite has also been found in New Mexico, California, Ireland, Turkey, and Japan. Facet-quality spurrite is rare.

A recent discovery of a massive amount of spurrite in the American West was greeted with excitement, but so far has shown little promise as a facetable gem. The color is grayish purple and efforts to brighten it have failed. It might turn out to be a good material for cabochons and large lapidary projects. However, studies are continuing.

The material is massive and granular. It is not heat sensitive and cleavage is not a problem; however, it is a little difficult to polish. Linde A on leather works best. Spurrite is not often available.

STAUROLITE
Iron magnesium zinc
aluminum silicate
H. 7–7½   **D. 3.7**
Monoclinic

Although staurolite can occasionally be cut into cabochons and, rarely, tiny faceted stones, the chief use is for novelty uncut jewelry and curios. When the dark, reddish brown crystals form perfect crosses, Roman or Maltese, they are attractive novelties, often used for pendants, charms, and earrings after brief treatment. They are rarely perfect as found, so they may be filed and oiled before being drilled for jewelry. In fact, they are such good tourist items in areas where they are found that inventive lapidaries carve twinned Fairy crosses out of soapstone or other soft material. The crosses have always excited awe and superstitions. They are used as amulets, talismans, pendants, earrings, and charms. The treatment may include filing, grinding, sanding, and oiling or waxing

Staurolite crystals occur, sometimes with garnets, in metamorphic rock, schists, and gneisses. In the United States, large well-formed crystals twinned at right angles are found in New Mexico. South Dakota and Minnesota are two Midwest locations. Some of the most attractive staurolite crystals for folk jewelry come from the eastern states of Virginia, North Carolina, and Georgia. Other locations are Canada, Brazil, Switzerland, and Zambia.

Staurolite is usually almost opaque; however, small stones have been faceted from rough material from Switzerland and Brazil. Faceted stones are dark and are not used for jewelry.

STICHTITE
Hydrous magnesium
chromium carbonate
H. 2½   D. 2.16
Trigonal

The delectable lilac, orchid, blue-violet, and rose-pink colors of stichtite recommend it to lapidaries for such projects as intarsia, inlay, carvings, and ornamental objects. Occurring with serpentine, partic-

ularly when associated with chromite, stichtite is an alteration product. It is usually fibrous and lamellar, but sometimes granular with platy micaceous crystals. The decorator colors are attributed to chromium.

Stichtite was discovered in Tasmania and subsequently a spectacular occurrence was found in an asbestos mine in the Eastern Transvaal of South Africa. There, the material is streaked with black and white, accenting the blues, mauves, and hot pinks. Later a large quantity was obtained from a road cut near Barberton, East Transvaal. Mineral collector Horst Windisch of Groenkloof, South Africa, states that the stichtite mine at Kaapsche Hoop is no longer active but that as late as 1989 some material was still coming from Barberton.

An occurrence of stichtite in Quebec, Canada, has veins and segments of light

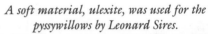

A soft material, ulexite, was used for the pyssywillows by Leonard Sires.

green complementing the bright pink. A similar but more granular material has been found in Russia. It has also been reported from Algeria.

Stichtite is best used for small carvings which can be made with hand tools. It has been used for dramatic cabochons for competitive display. It should be worked slowly and kept wet. Finish with 8000 diamond after fine sanding.

TALC (STEATITE)
Hydrous magnesium silicate
H. 1   D. 2.2
Monoclinic

Easily carved, talc has been used by primitive tribes and contemporary lapidaries for a variety of useful and decorative items. Talc is formed by the metamorphism of siliceous dolomites. The massive, fine-grained, compact material comes in many tints and shades of green, plus neutrals such as white, beige, and tan. Its hardness of 1 is at the bottom of the Mohs' scale.

Often associated with serpentines, steatite is found worldwide. Steatite was used for bowls and ceremonial objects by many Indian tribes in the United States. The natives of Alaska still carve sensitive scenes and animals of the far north from steatite. Soapstone is sometimes dyed, but the subtle natural colors are usually preferable. It can be hardened by heat.

Some U.S. locations for soapstone are California, Arizona, South Dakota, Vermont, Virginia, North Carolina, and Georgia. Other locations are Canada, Brazil, England, Sweden, Italy, Russia, Egypt, India, and China. Antique soapstone carvings from China are now collectors' items. Natives in the region of Agra, India, make a variety of tourist items of soapstone, based on the timeless designs of the Taj Mahal.

Lapidaries can carve soapstone with steel tools and finish it with files, sandpaper, and tin oxide followed by wax. This is an inexpensive common material.

THAUMASITE
Calcium silicate
H. 3.5   D. 1.9
Hexagonal

Thaumasite occurs with spurrite and zeolites in metamorphic rock as minute crystals or in crystalline or fibrous masses. It is one of the minerals that is soft when first dug from the ground, but rapidly hardens when exposed to the air. It is colorless or white and translucent to opaque.

Silky massive material from several states has been used for chatoyant cabochons up to 3 inches (7.62 cm) in size. Some of the locations are Crestmore, California; Beaver County, Utah; Cochise County, Arizona; Patterson, New Jersey; Centerville, Virginia; and Langban, Sweden.

In Virginia, thaumasite is associated with prehnite in cavities in igneous rock. In California, it is associated with spurrite and ettringite. Material from the Great Notch Quarry in New Jersey is found in trap rock with zeolites.

Thaumasite is soft enough to be shaped with steel tools, especially when newly excavated. Cleavage is no problem, but the material is brittle. Cat's-eyes are not particularly showy, but cabochons have a silky shimmer. It is not hard enough for jewelry.

VERDITE

This attractive green rock is colored by fuchsite, the chrome mica. Verdite has interesting variations of color, including reds, blues, oranges, and browns. Only about 3 in hardness, the massive material from Zimbabwe is available in large pieces for carvings. Natives have used it for charms and medicines for thousands of years, and now there is a cottage industry producing verdite sculptures of native animals and tribal heads for Western markets. Many of these carvings are exceedingly well done and have become collectors' items.

The rock is much like serpentine, and lapidaries report that cutting and polishing it is like working with serpentine. There are also examples of marble and syenite being colored by fuchsite. There is some disagreement as to whether the rock called verdite in Africa is unique. Originally the material was reported to come from South Africa, but importers are now getting the carvings from Zimbabwe.

E. K. Macintosh in his book *Rocks, Minerals and Gemstones of South Africa* defines verdite as a serpentine with constituents of quartz, talc, chlorite, albite, corundum, and fuchsite. It is easily shaped with steel or corundum and polished with tin oxide on leather. Little is sold in the United States.

RECOMMENDED READING

Desautels, P., *The Mineral Kingdom*. New York: Grosset & Dunlap, 1968.

Dietrich, R., *Minerals, Rocks and Fossils*. New York: Wiley, 1983.

Dietrich, R., and Skinner, B., *Gems, Granites, and Gravels*. New York: Cambridge University Press, 1990.

Caillois, R., *The Writing of Stones*. Charlottesville: University Press of Virginia, 1985.

Fenton, C., and M. Fenton, *The Rock Book*. New York: Doubleday, 1946.

McFall, R., *Collecting Rocks, Minerals, Gems , and Fossils*. New York: Hawthorn, 1963.

McFall, R., *Rock Hunter's Guide*. New York: Crowell, 1980.

Pearl, R., *How to Know Minerals and Rocks*. New York: McGraw Hill, 1955.

Pough, F., *Field Guide to Rocks and Minerals*. Boston: Houghton Mifflin, 1976.

Sinkankas, J., *Gemstones of North America*. New York: Van Nostrand Reinhold, vol. 1, 1959; vol. 2, 1976.

CHAPTER XI

Phenomenal Gems: Stars and Stripes

Actinolite	Fibrolite
Chlorastrolite	Gypsum
Diopside	Mordenite
Enstatite	Scapolite
Feldspar	Tremolite
Labradorite	Ulexite
Moonstone	Wollastonite
Perthite	
Sunstone	

THE MOST CHALLENGING of cabochon materials are the phenomenal stones, those with properties which yield cabochons with gleaming eyes, glittering stars, or shimmering prismatic colors. The ultimate beauty of such stones depends on the skill of the lapidary. Some of these stones are at the bottom of the price scale—gypsum, for example—while others are among the most expensive, for instance, chrysoberyl. All help capture some of nature's fleeting moments of rapture—tropical butterflies, hummingbirds, rainbows, and sunbeams.

A phenomenal gem is one which exhibits a special optical effect in visible light. About four dozen species and varieties are known to exhibit such effects, which are usually limited to only a minor proportion of the stones of each species.

Inclusions of other minerals such as acicular rutile, or the structure of the mineral itself, such as fibrous, spherical, or tubular structure, are the primary causes of optical phenomena. There are several categories of phenomena in these gems.

Adularescence. A glowing effect as seen in moonstones.

Asterism. Stars of four, six, or more rays displayed by stones with oriented inclusions.

Aventurescence. A sparkling look because of metallic or glassy reflections from spangles of mica or another mineral.

Chatoyancy. A gleaming effect including all-over shimmer or distinct cat's-eyes.

Iridescence. Play of color, or rainbow colors, sometimes metallic in appearance.

Labradorescence. A broad multicolor flashing surface.

Schiller. A directional sheen or shimmer.

Opalescence. A milky appearance similar to a moving cloud.

Not all phenomenal stones are included in this chapter. Star rubies, sapphires, beryl, spinel, and others are included in the historical favorites chapter. Cat's-eye tourmaline is included in the chapter on newer faceting materials, and star quartz is described in the crystalline quartz chapter. Opal is included in cabochon and carving materials. This chapter includes species and varieties which are particularly known for their phenomenal effects or are dominated by the phenomenal effects, or which possess unusually aesthetic phenomena. Many of these materials are sometimes transparent and are then used for faceting. Here is a list of gems which are known to yield cat's-eyes or stars:

Actinolite
Alexandrite
Andalusite
Apatite
Beryl: aquamarine, emerald, goshenite, heliodor, morganite
Bustamite
Chrysoberyl
Corundum: ruby, sapphire
Diopside
Ekanite
Enstatite
Feldspar: albite, clevelandite, labradorite, orthoclase
Garnet: almandine, demantoid, rhodolite
Gypsum
Hexagonite
Iolite
Kornerupine
Mesolite
Nepheline
Opal
Peridot
Petalite
Prehnite
Quartz: blue, rock crystal, rose, white
Rutile
Scapolite
Sillimanite
Spinel
Tanzanite
Topaz
Tourmaline: elbaite, indicolite, rubellite
Tremolite
Ulexite
Wollastonite
Zircon

In some locations none or very few specific gems will have phenomenal effect, while in other places, such as the Emerald Creek garnet location of Idaho, a significant number of stones will have a phenomenal display. Precious opal has a play of color while common opal does not. One might expect that all labradorite would have the quality of labradorescence, but such is not the case.

Some lapidaries specialize in cat's-eye or star stones or in other phenomenal stones.

Phenomenal gems show cat's-eyes or stars. These superbly cut cat's-eye cabochons are multicolored tourmalines. Courtesy of Gerhard Becker.

The process of finding the best way to cut these gems is called orientation. Each stone has an inherent cut that will bring out all of its potential beauty. The lapidary must learn to inspect each rough stone carefully to find its best color and its strongest optical phenomena, and then visualize the best shape, size, and proportions.

Closely packed needles oriented in one direction give chatoyancy to a material, which will produce a cat's-eye if properly cut. Two sets of needles, arranged according to the crystal system of the mineral, cause the inclusions to form a four-rayed star. Three sets of oriented needles enable the lapidary to cut a six-rayed star. In some cases there are tubes instead of needle inclusions.

In cat's-eye gems the fibers must lie flat for the bottom of a cabochon and horizontal to the length of the stone. For star stones the bases of cabochons should be at right angles to the length of the crystal. Star stones are often cut round with high domes. To find stars, material should be dipped in star oil or water and inspected under a single clear incandescent light bulb. The spot is marked where two lines cross.

Cat's-eye and star stones, along with other phenomenal stones, are popular for jewelry if the materials have adequate hardness. Since many of the best cat's-eye and star stones are rather small, they are used more for rings than other types of jewelry. Soft phenomenal stones such as satin spar gypsum are used for carvings.

ACTINOLITE
Magnesium silicate
H. 5½–6　　　**D. 3.05**
Pleochroic
Monoclinic

The fibrous nature of actinolite and its chemical makeup are close to tremolite and the two are similar to nephrite, one of the two jades. Actinolite occurs in metamorphosed limestones and dolomites in the contact zones. The elongated aggregate crystals are usually some tint or shade of green—light green, medium green, bright green, yellow-green, gray-green, or greenish black.

Compact fibrous masses of actinolite can be used for excellent cat's-eye stones, sometimes sold as cat's-eye jade. When the color is a light to medium green and the eye is silvery, the stones are exquisite, durable, and suitable for jewelry. The emerald green stones are the most desirable, and also the rarest. Chatoyant actinolite comes from Alaska, Siberia, and Taiwan. Facet-quality actinolite comes from New York, Vermont, Tanzania, Madagascar, and Uganda. Other locations are California, Arizona, Idaho, Oregon, Colorado, Wyoming, South Dakota, New York, Tennessee, North Carolina, Canada, England, Sweden, New Zealand, and Japan. Actinolite is moderately tough and not heat sensitive, but it has easily developed perfect cleavage. The best lapidary use is for chatoyant cabochons.

Many materials such as Mojave Blue are
chatoyant because of fine rutile needles.
These stones will often cut cat's-eyes or star stones.
Photo courtesy of Bill Nicks.

CHLORASTROLITE
(PUMPELLYITE)
Hydrous calcium magnesium silicate
H. 6   D. 3.10
Pleochroic   Monoclinic

An alluring chatoyant gem is Michigan's state gem, chlorastrolite. Found in the Keweenaw Peninsula of upper Michigan, the small green stones occur in basalt matrix and as float. The nodules are fibrous and silky, sometimes hollow and sometimes filled with another material. The solid nodules are the ones which are cut for fascinating turtle-back patterned cabochons with shimmering silvery chatoyancy. Related to the zeolites, the nodules are coated with chlorite. The polygon-shaped radial patches gave rise to the name "green star."

Of the various tints and shades of green, a rich emerald color is preferred. One of the more unusual occurrences of chlorastrolite is a mixture of this green material with salmon pink laumantite. Michigan cutter Bruce Deter reports pink laumantite patterned with green veins and eyes of chlorastrolite. Native silver or copper is sometimes found in chlorastrolite.

A few stones have yielded cabochons up to 2 inches (5.08 cm), but the average nodules yield finished stones of less than an inch. Bruce Deter has a rectangular piece of chlorastrolite that measures 2½ x 4 inches (6.35 x 10.16 cm), which would probably make a 3-inch (7.62-cm) cabochon. Chlorastrolite jewelry known by the name Isle Royale Greenstone was popular on the East Coast for jewelry shortly after its discovery in the late nineteenth century. Deter says that mainland stones are darker and more chatoyant than those from Isle Royale. Fine stones are sometimes brought up by scuba divers from Lake Superior's cold waters.

The best patterns are directly under the skin, so cabochons often follow the contour of the nodule. Michigan lapidaries sometimes bleach their stones by placing them in intense sunlight for a week or so.

The needlelike crystals of the polygons that form the turtle-back patterns have opposing directions, so the shades and tints of green seem to twinkle and reverse color as the stone is moved. High-domed cabochons have the best chatoyancy.

Michigan lapidaries sometimes grind the surface of a nodule slowly with electric hand tools to find the best pattern and color. Grinding and sanding should be slow and careful. Tin oxide is used for the polish. Chlorastrolite is sold in Michigan.

DIOPSIDE
Calcium magnesiuin silicate
H. 6   **D. 3.29**
Pleochroic   Monoclinic

Cat's-eye diopside has distinct eyes of various shades of green, brown, and gray. The darker green and brown colors are caused by iron. The green cat's-eye stones from Burma, colored by chromium, are especially elegant. White cat's-eye stones come from Australia. A dark green, almost black, diopside from India will cut cat's-eyes and four-ray stars. Some star stones are in the 100-carat range. Other diopsides with

Cat's-eye actinolite has a silvery eye highlighting a lustrous deep green.

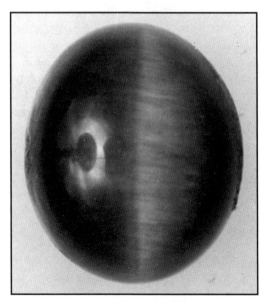

ilmenite needle inclusions may cut six-rayed stars. Tremolite pseudomorphs after diopside are of interest to collectors. Diopside is used for carving. Small diopside carvings made for jewelry resemble jade. A faceting material is found as transparent prismatic crystals. Rough from New York has yielded stones over 20 carats.

An unusual color for diopside is violet, sometimes called *violane*. This variety, originating in Italy, is used for inlay and other projects where small areas of violet are needed. Green diopside also occurs in Italy. Other cuttable diopsides are from the Black·Hills of South Dakota; Fowler, New York; Ontario and Quebec, Canada; Sweden; Madagascar; Kenya; China; and Sri Lanka.

Usually diopside, a pyroxene, occurs in calcium-rich metamorphic rocks, but it has also been found in diamond-bearing kimberlites in South Africa and occasionally in meteorites.

Cat's-eye or star diopside cabochons are worked wet at slow speed on fine wheels and polished on leather with Linde A or tin oxide. Fairly expensive, diopside is usually advertised by major suppliers.

ENSTATITE
Magnesium iron silicate
H. 5–6   **D. 3.30**
Pleochroic   Orthorhombic

Enstatite is a part of a series that includes bronzite and hypersthene. The colors are mainly greens, browns, and yellows and may deepen to almost black. Black enstatite from India often has distinct four-ray stars, bright contrasts to the dark ground color. The California Academy of Sciences has a 196.45-carat star enstatite from India.

Bronzite may have six-rayed stars against a bronzy, almost metallic, body color.

*Ed Clay of Houston cut this gleaming free-form
from albite moonstone.*

Bronzite is also found in India. Other localities are Arizona, North Carolina, Greenland, Australia, Brazil, Sri Lanka, Burma, Kenya, and Tanzania. Both enstatite and bronzite are found as water-worn pebbles in some of these locations. Pale brown enstatite from Sri Lanka is faceted, but with weak dispersion, stones are not very attractive. Sri Lankan stones in greenish hues yield cat's-eyes.

Hypersthene is translucent with a sub-metallic sheen due to inclusions of minute bright scales, probably of an iron mineral. The contrasting schiller is especially effective in dark stones. Occurrences are in Labrador, Quebec, Greenland, Mexico, and Norway. Violet hypersthene from Finland is used for cat's-eye stones.

Enstatite and its varieties can be found in igneous and metamorphic rocks, sometimes with serpentines. The toughness of enstatites is only fair and cleavage is easy. The hardness of a stone is variable accord-

ing to direction and cleavage, so it must be worked with care. Enstatite is not difficult to obtain.

FELDSPAR

Labradorite
Sodium calcium aluminum silicate
H. 6–6½   D. 2.72
Triclinic

Orthoclase
Potassium aluminum silicate
H. 6   D. 2.55
Monoclinic

Labradorite

With prismatic iridescent colors and metallic glint, labradorite from Labrador, Canada, has been known for centuries and is still being mined. Native Inuits are helping develop the productive quarry on Tabor Island. The vibrant colors, pools of spectral hues, float on the surface of this dark feldspar gem in a unique manner called labradorescence. Massive labradorite is translucent to opaque with dark neutral body colors that show off the violets, blues, greens, and golds of the schiller.

The distinctive iridescence of labradorite is caused by the gridlike lamellar structure, the result of repeated twinning. The colors change as the stone is moved. Additional inclusions of needles and platelets of magnetite or some other mineral give reflected light and add to the phenomenal effect.

A fantastic occurrence of high-quality labradorite is the Finnish material called *spectrolite*, named for its spectrum of pure rainbow hues. It is continually quarried at Ylamaa. Highly translucent, the body color is gray or slightly blue-gray. Bright, almost metallic, colors dance across the surface of rough or cut stones. A well-cut cabochon may resemble black opal. The play of color is dominated by a rich royal blue which grades into violet and green. Faceted spectrolite makes an elegant stone.

The recently popular Rainbow moonstones from India are labradorite. Cabochons of 15 carats have been advertised. With pastel ground colors and splendid iridescence these stones were immediate best-sellers.

Labradorite from some localities is transparent and facetable. One such locality is the Woodward Ranch in Texas where light yellow pieces are found in fields of disintegrating igneous rock. Nevada and Utah also have facetable material. Other labradorite localities are California, Oregon, Nevada, Arizona, New Mexico, Utah, New York, North Carolina, Mexico, Greenland, Norway, Sweden, Madagascar, and Australia.

A critical step in cutting a cabochon stone is correct orientation. The cut should be parallel to the best color plane, which can be found with a wet stone and a single source of light. Cutters should remember the pronounced cleavages in the feldspar group. The rough is also brittle and often fractured. Cabochons, usually long ovals, should be nicely domed. Labradorite is an acceptable jewelry stone. It is plentiful at present.

Moonstone

Moonstone can be one of several kinds of feldspar—albite, adularia, perthite, peristerite, or sanidine. A lovely gem with the limpid glow of a winter moon, moonstone is known for the quality of adularescence.

Star stones are among the most beautiful of cabochon gems. From Idaho comes this star garnet, the official state gem.

Feldspars are among the most important rock-forming minerals and are widely distributed throughout the world. Attractive blocky crystals are found in pegmatites and water-worn pebbles are present in alluvial gravels. Moonstones of delicate pastel tints with flashes of silver or blue adularescence are among the most desirable of feldspar gems. Some moonstone combines two or more feldspars.

Burma and Sri Lanka have been the source of pastel moonstone with blue sheen. Hastings County, Ontario, is noted for fine peristerite with a sky blue flash on soft ground colors of pink, yellow, and white. A fascinating peristerite from Haliburton County, Ontario, is blue intermixed with red feldspar and smoky quartz. Grains of fluorite and scapolite are also seen in the cutting material there. Translucent blue sheen moonstones have been found in gravels of Hanover County, Virginia, and sanidine moonstones with blue and silver adularescence come from the Black Range of New Mexico.

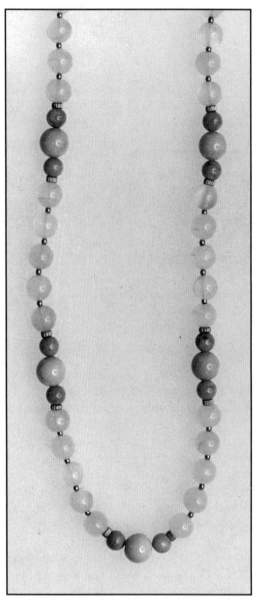

Groups of Persian turquoise and Afghanistan lapis lazuli beads are accented by pale chatoyant moonstone.

In the nineteenth century white moonstones were popular for engagement rings. A shimmering pure white moonstone resembles bridal satin. Well-cut moonstones may show sharp eyes and occasionally four-rayed stars. Both the structure and the inclusions of moonstones have roles in the phenomenal effects. Chatoyant chalcedony is often incorrectly called moonstone.

Properly oriented moonstone should have the base parallel to the horizontal structural planes. Round or oval cabochons are traditional for moonstones, but elegant free-form and fantasy cut stones are growing in popularity. Beads and small carvings are other uses of moonstone. Moonstone is suitable for jewelry and is usually available.

Perthite

This material is an intergrowth of several feldspars. It was discovered as a lapidary material by a Canadian gem enthusiast, Dr. James Wilson, and named for the locality near Perth. The light orange-red material is aventurescent, highlighted by shimmering golden and coppery platelets against ground colors that range from flesh pink to brownish red-orange. The rough material is cross hatched and ribbed. Bright colors are intertwined with white in the lamellar structure. The white sections often have pronounced schiller.

Large masses of the material have been found and used for many ornamental purposes such as exterior and interior decoration, urns, bookends, clock faces, counters, and tiles. Jewelry cabochons are also made from choice pieces. Perthite is rarely seen in the United States.

Sunstone

Sunstone is an aventurescent labradorite, microcline, or oligoclase feldspar, distinguished by minute hematite or goethite

Kenya and Madagascar are recent sources of attractive yellow moonstone. Madagascar also has a moonstone with blue labradorescence. A light green moonstone is among the pastels from India. Orthoclase moonstone beads on the market are blue, pink, peach, and white.

inclusions which reflect the light. Sunstone cabochons may be in the 25-carat range.

A top locality for labradorite sunstone is Lake County, Oregon. Oriented platelets of hematite give schiller to the transparent or translucent material that presents an array of warm colors—straw-yellow, yellow, orange, red-orange, and red. The vibrant transparent-quality material with little or no schiller from this location has been dubbed heliolite.

A microcline sunstone called Rainbow Lattice is a surprising new material from Australia's Harts Range. It shows both aventurescence and adularescence. The precise geometric lattice structure of the feldspar is heavily accented by bronzy colors of greens, yellows and blues, caused by inclusions of ilmenite and hematite. The appearance is similar to an iridescent plaid silk with metallic threads in the weave. Large striking cabochons were recently shown in Tucson. Sunstone also comes from California, Arizona, New Mexico, South Dakota, Maine, Virginia, Canada, Mexico, Norway, Russia, and India.

Lapidaries must watch the cleavages in the feldspars. Interesting effects are achieved by altering the orientation of the base of select pieces of cabochon material. Much of the rough is fractured, but large cabochons are possible and wearable as jewelry.

Moonstone rough shows the glow of promising chatoyant cat's-eyes.

FIBROLITE
Aluminum silicate

H. 6–7	**D. 3.23**
Pleochroic	**Orthorhombic**

Sillimanite or fibrolite, so called because of its finely fibrous structure, can be used for showy cat's-eyes. The usual colors are tints of green, yellow, bluish gray, and shades of green and brown. Fibrolite occurs in metamorphic rocks and granites. Chatoyant material has come from Idaho, South Dakota, South Carolina, Sri Lanka, Burma, and Kenya. Brown-black fibrolite from Sri Lanka is used for sharp cat's-eyes. The best-known locality in the United States is Idaho, where chatoyant waterworn pebbles of pastel grayed blues and yellows are found in the gravel bars of the Clearwater and Salmon rivers. Almost black sillimanite from South Carolina has been used for chatoyant cabochons up to 10 carats.

Andalusite and kyanite are polymorphs of sillimanite. Closely packed fibers are responsible for the chatoyancy, which seems more pronounced in stones of darker colors. The most chatoyant stones have come from Sri Lanka. Some are gray and gray-green. Blue, green, and violet fibrolite from Sri Lanka and Burma is faceted. Kenya also has facet-quality material, found as colorless crystals.

The best colors of sillimanite are quite rare. Cabochons and faceted stones are difficult to cut. Sillimanite has perfect cleavage, brittleness, and a tendency to fray, pull, or split. Lapidaries should not saw the stones but shape them on a lap using fine grits and finishing with Linde A. Cat's-eye sillimanite is suitable for jewelry. Sillimanite is not commonly seen in shops.

GYPSUM (SATIN SPAR)
Hydrous calcium sulfate
H. 2   D. 2.32
Monoclinic

Although it is too soft to be durable, satin spar gypsum has such pronounced chatoyancy that it has been used for small carvings and other ornamental objects. The pastel tints of pink and yellow, as well as the snowy white, shine like slipper satin. Parallel fibrous material has been used for beads and pendants. A few years ago numerous native animals of Russia were cut from satin spar and were exported to gift shops in the United States. The carvings were white, pale silvery gray, and honey colored.

Chatoyant gypsum is translucent and owes its chatoyancy to fine parallel fibers. It is heat sensitive and has perfect cleavage. Gypsum is common in sedimentary rocks around the world. Pink satin spar is found in Colorado, lily white material is found in South Dakota, and yellow fibrous gypsum is found in California.

Gypsum is soft enough to be worked with knives, files, and other steel tools; however, it is fragile to work with. Kept

cool, with plenty of water, it must be sanded slowly with worn sanding cloth. Carvings and spheres have a pleasing glow. Gypsum is easy to obtain.

MORDENITE
Aluminum silicate
H. 4–5   D. 2.12
Orthorhombic

Mordenite is one of several zeolites that can be cut into chatoyant cabochons. It is found in veins and cavities in basic igneous rock as crystals and as fibrous masses. The silky material is mostly white but sometimes is stained yellow or pink by other minerals. Cabochons are usually small, not much over an inch.

In the United States mordenite is found in California, Idaho, Utah, Colorado, and Wyoming. Cuttable cream-colored material is found in Nova Scotia, Canada. It has been used for beads and cabochons. Other localities are Mexico, Scotland, Ireland, Italy, Russia, Japan, and New Zealand.

Brittle, and with perfect cleavage, mordenite cabochons are shaped on fine wheels. They are cold dopped and wet sanded. Cabochons are sometimes suitable for jewelry, such as pendants, if in protective mountings. Rough is not easily available.

SCAPOLITE
Aluminum calcium silicate
H. 6½   D. 2.60
Pleochroic   Tetragonal

Cat's-eye scapolite cabochons are strikingly beautiful, obtainable in a desirable suite of colors including white, green,

Scapolite is elegant as a faceted stone as well as for cabochons and carvings. Michael Dyber's original cut is a 39.3-carat example.

pink, blue, yellow, lilac, and gray. With these luscious colors come sharp eyes, making these stones among the most attractive of the lesser-known phenomenals. Scapolite can also be faceted. Mark Smith, Thailand gemologist, cut a pink Burmese scapolite of 50.45 carats. A 288-carat colorless scapolite from Burma was recently reported by the GIA.

Scapolite occurs in metamorphosed rock and is found in Massachusetts, Canada, Brazil, Australia, Burma, Kenya, Zimbabwe, and Tanzania. Pink-purple and red-brown scapolite comes from Kenya. Excellent violet scapolite came from East Africa in the late 1970s. Brazilian and Tanzanian scapolite is yellow. Mineralogically, scapolite is part of a series that includes melonite, wernerite, mizzonite, and marialite. Star scapolites are known from Sri Lanka. Cat's-eye stones of up to 50 carats have been shown at Tucson. One was a yellow-green round stone of over 52 carats. Scapolite from Brazil, Madagascar, Zimbabwe, and Burma has been faceted for stones 100 carats or more.

An altered pearly scapolite from Canada is noted for its elegant lilac color. Geologist Anna Sabina notes that Canadian gem

collector, Dr. James Wilson, discovered it in Ontario in the mid-1880s and it was called wilsonite because it was thought to be a new species. Subsequently it was also found in Quebec.

Cutters should have no trouble cutting scapolite cabochons if the long fibers lie in one direction and the length of the oval is at right angles with the fibers. Scapolite is used for jewelry. Cutters can usually buy rough.

TREMOLITE
Magnesium silicate
H. 5–6   D. 2.90
Monoclinic

Fibrous tremolite makes exquisite silky cat's-eyes. White and pastel green cabochons are entrancing. Other colors include pink, gray, and brown. Hexagonite is a variety of tremolite from St. Lawrence County, New York, with transparent crystals of pinkish violet or lilac color. Small stones have been faceted. Brown, green, blue, and gray tremolite from Ontario is cut into cabochons. Chrome green tremolite occurs in Sierra Leone. Material from Burma yields green cat's-eyes. Small stones have been faceted from tremolite from New York, Ontario, Quebec, and Tanzania. Michigan cutter Bruce Deter reports facet-quality hexagonite has been found near L'Anse, upper Michigan.

Tremolite is an amphibole in a series that includes actinolite and nephrite. It is found in metamorphosed dolomites and limestones. More locations are Brazil, Switzerland, Austria, and Italy. Compact varieties are tough, which makes them suitable for durable gemstones. Translucent to transparent, long-bladed tremolite crystals are brittle with easy cleavage and parting planes.

The best lapidary use is for cat's-eyes. Faceted stones are worked at slow speed on an extra-fine lap. Cat's-eye cabochons are polished with Rapid Polish or tin oxide on leather. Shimmering pure white or green cabochons are especially aesthetic and suitable for jewelry. Tremolite is not often advertised.

ULEXITE
Sodium calcium borate
H. 2–2½　　　D. 1.95
Triclinic

Not a jewelry material, although highly decorative, ulexite will cut the most distinct cat's-eyes imaginable. The stone is fibrous and colorless or snowy white. When fibers are fine, straight, and parallel, large shimmering cabochons can be cut as collectors' stones or conversation pieces. Ulexite spheres are splendid.

The source of most cabochon material has been the California desert. It has also been found in Argentina, Peru, Chile, and Turkey. Another phenomenal effect of ulexite is that clear pieces, when cut and polished perpendicular to the fibers, will transfer a picture placed under the slab to the top of the slab. This has been called TV rock.

Because of heat sensitivity and brittleness, ulexite should be cold dopped and worked with great care with fine grits. It may also need frequent repolishing. Ulexite can be acquired in California.

WOLLASTONITE
Calcium silicate
H. 4 ¼–5½　　　D. 2.87
Monoclinic

This pastel silky material yields chatoyant and cat's-eye stones. Often white or light green, or more rarely pink, red, or yellow, the massive material that furnishes the chatoyant stones occurs in metamorphic limestones and sometimes in igneous rock. Some of the localities are California, Michigan, New York, Canada, Mexico, Finland, and Australia. Compact gray-green wollastonite is used for carvings.

Brittle and fibrous, wollastonite also has perfect cleavage in one direction, so it is somewhat difficult to shape for perfect cabochons. It should be carefully ground on fine wheels only and should not be subjected to stress. It has recently been advertised.

RECOMMENDED READING

Barth, T., *Feldspars*. New York: Wiley, 1969.

Gubelin, E., *Internal World of Gemstones*. Zurich: ABC, 1974.

Hoffman, D., *Star Gems*. Spokane: Aurora, 1967.

Hurlbut, C., *Manual of Mineralogy*. New York: Wiley, 1972.

Kunz, F., *Curious Lore of Precious Stones*. New York: Dover, 1968.

Parsons, C., *Practical Gem Knowledge for the Amateur*. San Diego: Lapidary Journal, 1969.

Schumann, W., *Gemstones of the World*. New York: Sterling, 1977.

Sinkankas, J., *Gem Cutting, A Lapidary's Manual*, 3d ed. New York: Van Nostrand Reinhold, 1984.

Webster, R., *Gems*, 5th ed. London: Butterworth-Heinemann, 1994.

CHAPTER XII

Metallic Lapidary Materials

Algodonite
Bayldonite
Bornite
Breithauptite
Chalcopyrite
Chromite
Cobaltite
Columbite-Tantalite
Copper Rhyolites and Basalt
Covellite

Cuprite
Goethite
Hematite
Meteorite
Niccolite
Proustite
Psilomelane
Pyrite
Pyrrhotite
Rutile

A FEW LAPIDARY MATERIALS are distinguished primarily by their metallic luster, which resembles polished gold, silver, copper, steel, or bronze. The mirrorlike gleam is due to selective absorption of light on the surface as well as strong reflective power.

Some materials with metallic characteristics are discussed in other chapters. Examples are gold in quartz, which is included in the crystalline quartz chapter, and pyritized Nipomo agate, which is listed with other agates.

Most of the metallic gem materials are dark, or will turn dark with tarnish. Many acquire vivid iridescent surface colors. The metallic materials are generally softer and much heavier than quartz. Though easily polished, they may need occasional repolishing.

Although the greatest number of these materials are cut as collectors' gems, some of this group, such as hematite and pyrite—"marcasite"—are popular favorites in jewelry. At times, small pieces of these metallics can be faceted, but for the most part they are used for cabochons, spheres, pyramids, and decorative items.

Many of these minerals are common—bornite and chalcopyrite—but only the best quality of each species is cuttable, so although the distribution may be worldwide, only certain localities have produced material for lapidaries.

Lapidaries should take great care when working with metallic materials because some are highly toxic. Precautions include working in a well-ventilated area, keeping the stone wet and cool, and wearing a protective mask.

ALGODONITE, DOMEYKITE, AND MOHAWKITE
Copper arsenides
H. 4   D. 8.3
Orthorhombic/Cubic
Streak, black

This family of arsenides is rare with a major occurrence in the Keweenaw Peninsula of Michigan. Michigan lapidaries recover the silvery white or gun-metal-colored massive algodonite from the old copper mine dumps and cut large impressive cabochons. The best material for cutting is when the arsenide mineral is intermixed with white quartz.

In addition to lack of hardness, the material tarnishes rapidly, so some lapidaries spray their cabochons with clear lacquer after polishing. Small carvings are also made from the material.

Mohawkite is a rock containing algodonite, domeykite, and other copper minerals. It is opaque and the mixture of minerals produces attractive patterns. Like algodonite, it eventually tarnishes, sometimes becoming iridescent.

Other deposits of copper arsenides are in Canada, Mexico, Chile, Sweden, Czechoslovakia, Namibia, and Iran. The striking big cabochons, finished with tin oxide on leather, are used for display or for such items as bola ties, which lapidaries repolish when necessary. The material is usually available in Michigan.

BAYLDONITE
Lead copper arsenate
H. 4½   D. 5.5
Monoclinic

Green bayldonite, a secondary oxide zone mineral from Tsumeb, Namibia, has been used for cabochons for collectors, and for jewelry such as pendants or bola ties which do not receive hard wear. Massive bayldonite is fibrous or granular and has a submetallic luster. Greens are mostly yellowish, but sometimes approach a bright apple green. Crystals may be greenish black and under ½ inch (1.27 cm) in size.

Brilliant crystals occur with cuproadamite in the arsenate zone with adamite and olivinite. Only the fibrous material from Tsumeb has been used for cabochons. Bayldonite has also been found in England, France, and Durango, Mexico. In the United States, it occurs in the Santa Rita Mountains of Arizona.

The center cabochon (30 × 40 mm) from Colorado has inclusions of marcasite in chalcedony. The long oval is native gold in quartz from Colorado. The third one is copper in calcite from Michigan.

The material must be worked wet and a protective mask should be worn. A metallic polish results from an alumina slurry on leather. It is not often available.

BORNITE
Copper sulfate
H. 3   D. 5
Cubic
Streak, gray-black

Bornite, sometimes called peacock ore, is occasionally cut for novelty cabochons. It occurs in copper mines as a metallic-appearing bronzy mineral. The surface, when oxidized, has strongly iridescent colors starring rich purples, blues, and greens. Cabochons are dramatic, but with low hardness they do not hold a polish.

Bornite is compact and opaque, occurring with pyrite, chalcopyrite, and chalcocite in hydrothermal veins. The mineral is brittle and the cleavage indistinct. In spite of low hardness, bornite is cut for display-type cabochons or small carvings by lapidaries from Arizona and Montana. Other locations for massive bornite include Utah,

Hematite and pyrite beads are enlivened with blue agate and azurite.

Copper-bearing rock from Upper Michigan is locally used for cabochons and lapidary projects.

cabochons have lacy networks of native silver, making them even more distinctive. The material used for cabochons is compact, opaque, and massive, with no cleavage planes.

Breithauptite occurs in calcite with sphalerite, galena, and silver. In addition to the Canadian location, which has supplied most of the rough, the material is found in Germany, Norway, Spain, India, and Australia.

Keep the material cool and be careful not to grind deeply into the silver. Linde A on leather produces a brilliant polish. Although the material is more durable than the previous metallics, it is seldom seen in collections or in jewelry.

Colorado, Alaska, Canada, Chile, Peru, Germany, Namibia, and South Africa.

Cabochons are polished with some difficulty because pitting is common. Alumina or Linde A on Pellon after meticulous fine sanding brings a mirror luster. Some lapidaries spray the finished stones with lacquer, but it is best to repolish them when necessary. Cutters should have no trouble getting bornite.

BREITHAUPTITE
Nickel antimonide
H. 5½   D. 8.2
Hexagonal
Streak, red-brown

With a metallic luster and a lovely pale red-violet color, a cabochon of breithauptite is very showy. Large cabochons have been cut from the material found in the silver mines of Cobalt, Ontario. Exotic

CHALCOPYRITE
Copper iron sulfide
H. 3½–4   D. 4.3
Tetragonal
Streak, greenish black

A brass yellow mineral which occurs in high-temperature ore deposits, chalcopyrite is a major copper mineral. Cabochons and small carvings have often been made, but the glowing yellow brasslike finish soon tarnishes to a splendid suite of iridescent colors.

Chalcopyrite is common in the copper deposits of Arizona, New Mexico, and Montana. Most of the cabochons are from Arizona materials. Other occurrences are in Mexico, Chile, Peru, Spain, Norway, Czechoslovakia, Tasmania, and Australia.

Highly brittle and with low hardness, chalcopyrite is not often seen in jewelry except for novelty items. A high polish results from Linde A on leather. Cutters can usually get what they need.

CHROMITE
Magnesium iron chromium oxide
H. 5½   D. 6.0
Isometric
Streak, brown

With a black metallic luster, massive chromite is sometimes enhanced by a reddish cast that recommends it for cabochons for exhibitors and collectors. Chromite occurs in igneous and metamorphic rocks, often with serpentines. It is brittle and has no distinct cleavage. The massive material is sometimes almost translucent in thin pieces, but as far as is known, no areas suitable for faceting have been found. Maryland and Pennsylvania provide chromite. Other localities are Canada, Norway, Zimbabwe, India, and the Philippines.

Chromite cabochons have as good a hardness as some more commonly used lapidary materials, but lacking color and individuality, they are cut for collectors or display only.

COBALTITE
Cobalt arsenic sulfide
H. 5½   D. 6.3
Isometric
Streak, gray-black

This silvery white to steel gray mineral sometimes has red or violet highlights. It is found in metamorphic rocks in high-temperature deposits in masses suitable for cutting large cabochons. Cobaltite from the silver mines of Cobalt, Ontario, Canada, may be laced with fine threads of native silver, giving an unusual spiderweb appearance. With a red or red-violet metallic gleam, the cabochons are elegant, but seldom seen, collectors' stones. Although Canada is the major locality, other masses are found in Mexico, Brazil, Sweden, England, India, and Australia.

Cabochons with a brilliant metallic red-black finish are used mostly for show. After fine sanding with diamond, the stones are polished with Linde A on leather. Rough is not often for sale.

COLUMBITE-TANTALITE
Iron manganese columbate tantalates
H. 6   D. 5–8
Orthorhombic
Streak, black

Large black crystals of columbite-tantalite have a submetallic luster which becomes iridescent with time. Tantalite has a greater density than columbite. Both are opaque and compact with one distinct cleavage plane and considerable brittleness. Crystals up to 200 pounds have been found in the Black Hills of South Dakota, so cabochons of large size can be cut for collectors. Other locations are Colorado, California, Canada, Brazil, Finland, Zimbabwe, and western Australia.

COPPER CONGLOMERATE, COPPER IN RHYOLITE, AND COPPER IN BASALT

Native copper cementing other rocks together or as a major inclusion in igneous rock, such as basalt or rhyolite, furnishes many interesting materials for the creative lapidary. In the famous copper peninsula of upper Michigan, jaspery pebbles are cemented together by the red metal copper. The rounded pebbles vary in size from small to medium. The material is locally used for cabochons and decorative purposes. Like the copper itself, the pebbles take a good polish, but as is the case with most combinations of different hardness, undercutting is a problem.

The Michigan copper conglomerate is even more attractive when bright blue bits of chrysocolla are included in the mix, such as the material from the Allouez Mine, locally called Allouez Conglomerate. The material from the Centennial and Tamarack mines, called Calumet and Hecla Conglomerate, is made more colorful by pebbles of olive green epidote. These materials make stunning cabochons, sometimes of large size, and some of them suitable for limited jewelry use.

A red-brown basalt with webs and splashes of bright native copper also occurs in the Keweenaw Peninsula. The more copper this basalt contains, the more interesting it becomes to the lapidary. Since all copper tends to tarnish, local lapidaries use clear acrylic spray to seal their cabochons.

The classic locality for *copper rhyolite* is in Adams County, Pennsylvania. The copper rhyolite from the Bingham mine is a tough material with wonderful colors. At first glance it may resemble unakite, because the best colors are moss green and a bright apricot hue. There are a few areas of richer green and some small dark areas of biotite and smoky quartz. The material is patterned with ovals and ellipses, a structure called amygdaloidal. It was widely used for striking cabochons and small art objects in the 1960s, but is seldom seen now except in private collections.

Another metallic-appearing copper combination used for lapidary purposes is *copper altering to malachite*. Native copper

with its green carbonate, malachite, is found in the mine dumps and as float in the Keweenaw Peninsula of Michigan. Some of the copper/malachite nuggets contain native silver as well. The malachite is not banded and swirled as in stalactitic deposits, but is a solid color and grainy, rather than fibrous.

Both the copper and the malachite are soft, but spectacular cabochons can result from careful cutting, sanding, and polishing. Such cabochons or art objects are showy for displays, but the material is seldom used for jewelry. Exceptions are nuggets that have been gold plated. All copper must be worked wet in a well-ventilated room, and the lapidary should wear a mask and be aware of possible health hazards. Care must be taken to avoid undercutting by prolonged wet sanding or using 325 to 14,000 diamond. Copper material can usually be purchased in the states of origin.

COVELLITE
Copper sulfide
H. 2   D. 4.6
Hexagonal
Streak, black

Lustrous and iridescent, this indigo blue material can be used for splendid cabochons. The blue iridescence is from tarnish. The vivid stones are only 'for exhibitors or collectors, although some lapidaries have successfully made useful doublets with covellite cabochons.

Covellite is an uncommon mineral in copper mines. Covellite from Butte, Montana, has been cut by amateur lapidaries in the west for many years. South Dakota, Alaska, and Colorado also have cuttable covellite. Other locations are Argentina,

Chile, Yugoslavia, Greece, Namibia, and New Zealand. A secondary mineral in copper sulfide deposits, it is found with other cuttable metallics such as pyrite, chalcopyrite, and bornite.

A few years ago a suite of pyrite-spangled covellite cabochons caused a minor sensation at the Tucson show. The largest of the cabochons was 25 carats. Because of its low hardness and its inclusions of varying hardness, covellite should be finished with diamond compounds. It is not often available.

CUPRITE
Copper oxide
H. 3½   D. 6.1
Isometric
Streak, red-brown

Cuprite is not often used as a gem material, but in recent years there have been numerous crystals from Onganja, Namibia, cut as collectors' stones. Some of the magnificent red metallic crystals in a recently mined group have weighed over 150 carats; however, earlier material from this location was used to cut a cabochon of 300 carats. The California Academy of Science has a faceted cuprite from Namibia weighing 103.73 carats. A 647-carat cuprite faceted by Mike Gray may be the record.

Cuprite is a secondary mineral in copper deposits and is rare as a gem material. Before the discovery in Namibia, only very small gems had been cut. Bingham, Utah, copper mines produced large crystals. Other locations are New Mexico, Arizona, Mexico, Bolivia, France, the Ural Mountains, and Zaire.

Considered difficult to cut, cuprite is brittle and soft. It should be worked with

great care in every step, using only fine grits followed by Linde A. It is not suitable for jewelry. To bring out the best color, stones should be shallow. Cuprite tarnishes readily, quickly developing a submetallic "bloom" on polished surfaces. Cuprite for cutting is uncommon.

GOETHITE
Iron oxide
H. 5–5½   D. 4.2
Orthorhombic
Streak, yellow-brown

Goethite is usually included in lapidary material information only as inclusions, such as the spangles of aventurescence. However, blackish-brown metallic-appearing nodules found in the iron ranges of Minnesota have been polished for years by amateur collectors and lapidaries. First thought to be hematite, the nodules proved to be goethite when analyzed in the mine laboratory. These nodules were abundant in the immense Hull-Rust-Mahoney Mine near Hibbing.

In the 1960s the nodules were successfully tumble polished for souvenir-type jewelry, and later some were made into cabochons which were polished with tin oxide on rock-hard felt.

Goethite is an alteration product of iron minerals and is found in many places. A similar occurrence to the Minnesota goethite occurs in the upper peninsula of Michigan near Negaunee. Another is in the Gogebic Range of Wisconsin. Worldwide localities include Mexico, Brazil, England, France, South Africa, and Australia. As ironstone, goethite is the matrix of some of Australia's colorful opal.

HEMATITE
Iron oxide
H. 5½   **D. 5.0**
Trigonal
Streak, red

Best known of the metallic cutting materials is shiny, near black hematite, which has often masqueraded under the glamorous but misleading names of Black diamond or Alaska diamond. Hematite has a long history of use by man. It was the war paint of the American Indian. In the old world, it was used for seals, talismans, amulets, and medicine. It was engraved for classic cameos and intaglios. It is now a common metal polish, "rouge," which is also sometimes used to polish stones.

Crystals of hematite can be large and lustrous, sometimes arranged in exotic "iron roses." Other crystals, fine and platy, occur as inclusions in other minerals such as feldspar or quartz, creating the optical effect known as aventurescence. Hematite is a species of the hematite group, which includes the gemstone corundum. Botryoidal and stalactitic shapes are sculpturally elegant, particularly the type called *kidney ore*.

Now a common lapidary material for beads, pendants, and other jewelry, hematite is even used to simulate black pearls. Although hematite is opaque, it is sometimes faceted, mostly in round and oval shapes with flat backs and a minimum of facets.

Hematite occurs in thick sedimentary beds and is an abundant iron ore. Important localities in the United States are Minnesota, Wisconsin, and Michigan. Other deposits are in Canada, Mexico, Brazil, England, Switzerland, Italy, South Africa, and Australia.

The variety of hematite called *specularite* shimmers with tiny splendent scales. Mixed with a jaspery material, it is cut for large objects such as clocks, bookends, and desk sets. A large deposit called *jaspilite* is in the iron country of northern Michigan. Similar material comes from Minnesota and Vermont. Jaspilite is abundant in several mines in western Australia. Metallic bands of dark hematite contrast with red, yellow, and green jaspery material in the vicinity of Pilbara.

Mixtures of hematite with other materials will undercut, but patterns and contrasts are interesting and most lapidaries find the material challenging, although messy to work with. Linde A on wood after extended fine sanding brings a glassy luster. This mineral is not difficult to acquire.

METEORITE
Nickel-iron
H. 4–5   **D. 8.0**
Streak, black

Artifacts of early man have been made of meteoric iron and evidence is that early man was aware of the source of this metal. Oxidation may mask the lustrous interior of nickel iron meteorites.

Meteorites are of great scientific value and should not be cut for ornaments. Small meteorites have been used for pendants without being cut. Gem materials, for example, diamond and peridot, are found in some meteorites.

Meteorites are worked by scientists and lapidaries who surface polish them or slab and polish them and often etch the polished surface with dilute nitric acid. This is a determinative test for metallic meteorites when the acid reveals geometric patterns called Widmannstatten structure. These figures resemble ancient intricate basket weaves, with fine reeds splayed and broken. Polished and etched meteorites are seen in museums and are used for educational purposes and research.

Black nephrite with magnetite inclusions from California is sometimes gold plated to add a gleaming contrast to the cabochon.

Meteorites are found worldwide. Best known in the United States is the crater at Canyon Diablo, Arizona. The crater, 4,100 feet across, has yielded thousands of small fragments of meteoric material. In contrast, a meteorite found in the Hoba crater of Namibia weighs 66 tons. Meteorites can often be purchased, but should seldom be cut.

NICCOLITE
Nickel arsenide
H. 5–5½   D. 7.7
Trigonal
Streak, brownish black

Niccolite, when it is a pastel orange-red or peach color, makes brilliant and stunning cabochons. It is found in veins in silver, cobalt, and nickel mines. Large cabochons are possible, but, unfortunately, tarnish with time. The most important locality for this attractive material is Ontario, Canada. Others are California, New Jersey, Mexico, France, and Japan.

Niccolite occurs as veins in igneous rock as a massive, opaque material. It is brittle and without cleavage. Cabochons are usually coated with lacquer to prevent tarnish. Niccolite can be finished with diamond. Cabochons have a fair hardness and have been used for jewelry which does not get hard wear. Niccolite is seldom marketed.

PROUSTITE
Silver arsenic sulfide
H. 2–2½   D. 5.5
Hexagonal
Streak, red

Too soft for anything except a rare collectable, proustite cuts sensational semimetallic-appearing stones. With its deep red glow and its high refraction (greater than diamond), it is one of the most splendid soft lapidary materials. A great fault with the material is that it will tarnish to black if not kept out of the light.

The world's finest proustite for faceting comes from Chanarcillo, Chile, but most of these crystals are too superb and rare to be cut. Crystals from Freiberg, Germany, have been faceted. Proustite occurs in low-temperature hydrothermal veins with silver, pyrite, galena, calcite, and quartz. Locations are Cobalt, Ontario, Canada; Chihuahua, Mexico; France; Czechoslovakia; and Romania.

Larger stones tend to be too dark, so the best faceted stones are around 5 carats. Subject to tarnish, proustite is also exceedingly brittle and heat sensitive, so it must be worked with extra care. Stones

Shining crystals of rutile form the fixed star in this quartz and are the source of many stars and cat's-eyes in gemstones. Gerhard Becker photo.

are cold dopped and faceted with diamond. Polish is fast with Linde A on a wax lap. Cuttable proustite is rarely sold.

PSILOMELANE (Romanechite)
Manganese oxide
H. 5–5½   D. 3.5
Monoclinic
Streak, brownish black

Psilomelane is now a group name and romanechite is the species name for the jet black material with the lustrous swirling patterns. (This change was made by the International Commission on New Minerals and Mineral Names.) Reminiscent of watered silk when cut by lapidaries, the stalactitic and botryoidal material occurs in manganese mines, often associated with pyrolusite and limonite. The hardest and most compact material has been used for cabochons, carvings, and jewelry. Small contemporary carvings of lustrous

psilomelane have been made by creative lapidary Bart Curren.

The elegant psilomelane popular in the 1960s was mostly chalcedony. The source was Mexico and the material was called Crown of Silver. Polishable banded psilomelane now comes from near Blythe, California. Other locations are Michigan, Virginia, Mexico, Brazil, and France.

Psilomelane is a dirty mineral for lapidaries to work with, but takes a good polish with Linde A on wood or leather. It is sometimes available.

PYRITE
Iron sulfide
H. 6–6½   D. 5.0
Isometric
Streak, greenish black

Pyrite is the dimorph of unstable marcasite. Marcasite is sometimes seen in lapidary materials, such as inclusions in agate, but the marcasite of the jewelry industry is pyrite. Pyrite has been used as a jewelry stone by the ancient Greeks and by the Incas of the New World. Popular in Victorian times, marcasite (pyrite) jewelry is now experiencing a fashion revival. The distinguishing characteristic is a brilliant metallic luster with a mirror like finish that may be bronzy or silvery. Stones are cut with flat backs and a minimum of facets, most often round in shape. Small stones are commonly set in silver, and are often combined with cabochons of bright material, such as malachite.

Cabochons are also cut from pyrite, and recently there have been pyrite beads on the market, although they are too dark and heavy to have much success. Bright natural pyrite cubes in dark matrix and naturally etched pyrite are used for contemporary jewelry.

Pyrite occurs in igneous and metamorphic rocks and in sedimentary deposits. Excellent crystals come from Peru. Other localities are Colorado, Utah, Canada, Mexico, Chile, Bolivia, Italy, Spain, and Tasmania.

Fossils are often replaced by pyrite. Pyritized fossils, such as brachiopods, have sometimes been cleaned and brightened and coated with clear lacquer to be used for bola ties, key chains, or pendants. Aesthetic pyritized fossils are found in New York, Ohio, Illinois, and Germany.

Flattened radial disks of brilliant pyrite, golden yellow in color, are found in the coal beds of southern Illinois. Known as pyrite "suns," and occasionally as pyrite "dollars," the gleaming disks are used for bola ties and pins after being treated.

Lapidaries find pyrite brittle and heat sensitive. It also undercuts and pits easily. It should be cold dopped and worked wet, sanded thoroughly, then prepolished and finished with diamond. Pyrite is commonly stocked by dealers.

PYRRHOTITE
Iron sulfide
H. 3½–4½   D. 4.6
Hexagonal
Streak, gray-black

With a metallic bronzy yellow to red color, pyrrhotite is usually massive and opaque. It is found in igneous and metamorphic deposits with pyrite and other sulfides in numerous worldwide locations. Massive material is used for large cabochons and for carvings and ornamental items. Locations in the United States include South Dakota, where it is abundant in the Homestake Gold Mine at Lead, Lawrence County, and also in Pennington and Custer counties. Other locations include Tennessee and Pennsylvania. Major occurrences are in Mexico, Bolivia, Brazil, and Norway.

The material is brittle, but cleavage is not a problem. Although the cabochons are resplendent at first, they tarnish rapidly to an iridescence typical of many metallic materials. A coat of lacquer prevents rapid tarnish.

RUTILE
Titanium oxide
H. 6–6½   D. 4.2
Tetragonal
Streak, light brown

Rutile crystals are a metallic black or dark brown, often with red highlights. Select crystals can be cut as cabochons and rarely faceted. Rutile is found in igneous and metamorphic rocks. It is brittle material, sometimes massive and granular with distinct cleavage in one direction. Rutile is better known to lapidaries as the lustrous needles and straws that form spectacular inclusions in transparent quartz. Needles of rutile are also responsible for star stones.

Cabochons are cut from large crystals from North Carolina and Georgia. Other locations are South Dakota, Arkansas, Canada, Norway, Austria, Russia, and Madagascar. Clear areas of large crystals have been faceted for collectors' stones. Rutile is brittle and has distinct cleavage in one direction; however, rutile cabochons can be ground and sanded with silicon carbide and polished with tin oxide on leather. Crystals are sometimes sold at shows in eastern states.

RECOMMENDED READING

Arem, J., Color *Encyclopedia of Gemstones,* 2d ed. New York: Van Nostrand Reinhold, 1987.

Fenton, C., and Fenton, M., *The Rock Book.* Garden City, NY: Doubleday, 1976.

Hurlburt, C., *Minerals and Man.* New York: Random House, 1970.

Palache, C., et al., *Dana's System of Mineralogy,* 7th edition. New York: Wiley, 1951.

Parsons, C., *Practical Gem Knowledge for the Amateur.* San Diego: Lapidary Journal, 1969.

Pough, F., *A Field Guide to Rocks and Minerals.* Boston: Houghton Mifflin, 1976.

Roberts, W., et al., *Encyclopedia of Minerals.* New York: Van Nostrand Reinhold, 1989.

Schumann, W., *Gemstones of the World.* New York: Sterling, 1977.

Sinkankas, J., *Gemstones of North America.* New York: Van Nostrand Reinhold, vol. 1, 1959; vol. 2, 1976.

Smith, G., *Gemstones.* New York: Pitman, 1958.

Webster, R., *Gems,* 5th ed. London: Butterworth-Heinemann, 1994.

SPECIFIC MATERIALS
Nininger, H., *Catch a Falling Star.* New York: Erickson, 1973.

CHAPTER XIII

Organic Gem Materials: Gems from Life

Abalone	**Ivory**
Amber	**Mellite**
Ammolite	**Odontolite**
Bone	**Ostrich Egg Shell**
Coal	**Pearls**
Anthracite & Cannel Coal	**Tortoise Shell**
Jet	**Vegetable Ivory**
Conch Pearls	**Wood**
Coral	

ALTHOUGH MOST GEM MATERIALS are minerals or rocks, a few beautiful and important gems such as pearls or amber are of organic origin. Organic gems can come from the plant or animal kingdoms and can be recent or incredibly ancient in origin.

Most of these materials combine mineral matter with organic components. Some, like tortoise shell, are totally organic. These organic materials are usually far less hard than most gem materials that are minerals, but they do have toughness and durability, as seen by the historic organic gem treasures in great museums. They are found around the world from the fossil ivory of Siberia to the black pearls of Tahiti, from the ox-blood coral of Italy to the Kauri gum of New Zealand.

Organic materials have been used by primitive man from the earliest days of prehistory, in some places becoming a rich part of the native culture. First used for charms, amulets, and fetishes, organic materials have been used for religious and royal items, objects of trade, dowries, games, magnificent carvings, and stunning jewels.

At present, pearls are among the most popular gem materials. Amber beads are among the most desired gem products of Europe. Some of the organic materials, however, are from endangered species and have been the subjects of legislation, so substitutes are being found.

Organic gem materials often have important regional use. In the American West, antlers and horns are used for ranch, rodeo, and square dance styles of jewelry, and also for Native American jewelry. In Poland, amber was once considered so valuable that the bride's bulky necklace of carefully polished amber nuggets was her dowry.

Organic materials are soft enough to be worked with ordinary steel tools, so they still appear in folk art, such as Inuit carvings from Alaska. Lapidary artists use amber, jet, and ivory for small carvings, and jewelry designers often use aesthetic pieces or cabochons of bright coral or baroque pearls in custom-made pendants, enhancers, earrings, or rings. Carvings can be made with flexible shaft tools. Material should be worked slowly and kept cool.

Most large museums have superb examples of organic gem materials in their collections, some of historic significance. These items may combine organic material, such as in composite carvings, or they may combine organic materials with diamonds or colored stones. The organic materials are wonderful foils or accents for metal and colored stones.

This chapter also includes materials which are not lapidary materials, but which are used for jewelry by some cultures, or by contemporary artists who use fashions of the past for inspiration.

ABALONE AND SHELL

Lustrous iridescent abalone and other shells with colorful mother-of-pearl lining have been used for ornaments since Neolithic times. Shell ornaments have been used by African tribes, natives of the South Pacific Islands, and the American Indians, as evidenced by many archeological digs.

A particularly vivid abalone, or ear shell, is the Paua shell from off the coast of New Zealand. Its intense blues, greens, and violets have made it a desirable material for inexpensive silver jewelry and for souvenir items, although gifted designers have sometimes been inspired to use it in intricate designs because of its high iridescence. New Zealand also has an iridescent mollusk, aurora shell, the green-lipped mussel, which is reportedly dyed for jewelry.

Mexico and California use abalone shell in jewelry. (Abalone meat is a delicacy in some Pacific areas.) Abalones also occasionally produce dark, lustrous, baroque-shaped pearls. A 365-carat elegant abalone pearl was shown at Tucson. The pearls are usually elongated and extremely iridescent.

Mother-of-pearl from both saltwater and freshwater species has been used for carvings in the Mideast since the eighteenth century. The glowing material also provided a great industry along the Mississippi about 100 years ago in such states as Iowa, where the town of Muscatine had many factories manufacturing buttons, buckles, brooches, frames, stick pins, trays, boxes, and other items of shell. Lustrous pieces of shells were used for inlay on musical instruments.

A 3-inch carved ivory chicken by Hing Wa Lee has a personality of its own.

A time-honored use of shell is for cameos. The helmet shell is often used for these delicate carvings because of its vari-colored multiple layers. The Italians of the nineteenth century made shell cameo carving a fine art, often covering an entire shell with intricate and realistic pictures. California lapidary artist Raymond Addison created shell cameos of famous living people in the late 1950s and early 1960s. He used homemade power tools and lots of patience.

Other shells used for jewelry and a variety of ornaments are turbo, trochus, strombus, and various other mollusks. Mother-of-pearl, or MOP, is dyed in a wide spectrum of colors.

The operculum or shell door has also been used for jewelry. Some univalves protect themselves by thick-domed covers which are sometimes lustrous and colorful. The shining round white and green opercula with eyelike patterns from the South Seas were popular souvenirs of World War II and were made into attractive pieces of keepsake jewelry.

Shells have been cut into round discs for beads which the American Indians call Hishi. Small lustrous shells are used in their natural form in ethnic, antique, and contemporary jewelry.

Shell is mainly calcite, only 3 in hardness, so it can be worked with common tools from the shop or kitchen or with regular machinery; however, the shell should be kept wet. Shells are also successfully tumbled. Lapidaries should protect themselves from inhaling the dust of shells. Tin oxide on leather or hard felt will polish shell.

AMBER

Amber is one of the oldest of lapidary materials, since it accompanied salt on the earliest trade routes. The fossilized sap of prehistoric pines, *Pinus succinifera*, amber is known for its glowing colors, its warmth, and its lightness in weight. Its density is 1.04. It was used for a fumigant, incense, amulets and charms, bridal dowries, and carvings and jewelry.

The classic locality for this condensed sunshine of primeval forests is the Baltic. Transparent hues of pale yellow, clear golden, and a tint of burnt orange are among the popular colors. There are also cloudy and opaque variations, and fascinating pieces that contain some of paleontology's most complete fossil insects. Baltic amber is still being brought to the market from Germany, Poland, Lithuania, and eastern European locations.

At present a major producer of amber and amber items is the Dominican Republic. This amber was gathered for centuries, but because Germany bought almost the entire output until 1979, little was known about its characteristics and inclusions. Some of the Dominican amber fluoresces bright blue. Most of the amber is a transparent gold, though much of it is heavily included.

Other locations for amber are Romania, Burma, Canada, Mexico, and Sicily. In the United States amber has been found in numerous places including Alaska, California, Texas, Arkansas, and New Jersey. It has recently been found at three locations in South Dakota. A significant discovery is now under water.

There are several resins similar in appearance to amber that have often been used as substitutes. They have not undergone metamorphic change as true amber has. Copal is the best known of these. The New Zealand variety is called Kauri Gum.

Amber darkens with age, so "antique" amber is sometimes the result of heat treatment. Amber is also clarified, spangled, oiled, and reconstructed. About 70 percent of amber now on the market has been baked to improve clarity and color. Amber has been used in countless ways throughout history, including for pipe stems, parasol and cane handles, religious items, game boards and chess sets, cups, vases, bowls, candlesticks, snuff bottles, boxes, and jewelry.

Many excellent ancient and modern amber objects exist. Among the best is the carving "The Judgment of Paris" in the Victoria and Albert Museum in London. The Hugh Leiper collection included two large dark amber Foo dogs carved in China.

Amber can be worked with steel tools, sandpaper, and tin oxide. When worked with power machines, it should be kept cool and wet and not subjected to coarse grinders. It is brittle and heat sensitive. It should not be worked with diamond. Clear amber is sometimes faceted. Powdered pumice is often used for the polish.

AMMOLITE

A beautiful iridescent gem material from Alberta, Canada, is Ammolite, the mineralized shell from Cretaceous marine creatures known as ammonites. The choice material is intricately brecciated in geometric patterns and has spectacular colors including reds, violets, oranges, blues, and greens, some almost metallic in their brilliance.

The material, once promoted as calcentine, is marketed principally by the Korite Company, although there are other claims in the Bear Paw formation in which the fossils occur. Most of the cuttable material comes from the ammonite *Placenticeras meeki*, from crushed and altered shells that may be 12 inches (30.48 cm) or more in diameter. Similar fossils are found in Montana, Wyoming, and South Dakota, and although the colors are just as bright, the shells have not been metamorphosed as in the Bear Paw formation.

Worked by the open pit method in Alberta, the shells may be deeply buried, so the mining is slow and expensive. Rene Vandervelde, president of the Korite Company, says that the International Colored Gemstones Commission recognized Ammolite as a gemstone in 1981. Vandervelde, who shows Ammolite at Tucson and a few other shows, has a museum at Banff, Canada, with some of the most extraordinary fossil specimens as well as the illustrated story of ammolite. Ammolite is sold as calibrated or uncalibrated cabochons or as graceful free-forms, and as finished jewelry.

The harder, thicker seams are cut to be mounted in custom-made gold jewelry. Mountings are designed to protect the rather soft but tough material, which is basically hardened aragonite or calcium carbonate. The thinner layers of material are made into doublets with quartz or synthetic spinel caps. The popularity of the material is based on its remarkable opal-like colors, which are all natural, enhanced only by skillful cutting and polishing.

BONE AND HORN

The uses of bone and horn for ornamentation lie deep in the roots of prehistoric times. Tribes from all the continents have used bone and horn for tools, implements, utensils, weapons, fetishes, amulets, and body ornaments. Many of these items have been made with extreme care and artistry. Bone was particularly important to tribes in the far north where wood was not readily available. American Indians used bone for breastplates, bibs, hair ornaments, and beads. They used bison horns

for spoons, ladles, bowls, and for headdresses in dance costumes. In Europe stag horn was used for inlay. The Art Nouveau artists Lalique and Gaillard used horn for fine jewelry.

Bone and horn are still used for jewelry. Camel bones or beef bones are used for beads and carvings, often as a substitute for ivory. Pieces of antler are now widely used in the western states for western jewelry such as belt buckles, buttons, and bola ties. Bone and horn are also used by scrimshanders. Handsome knife handles are often made of horn.

Lapidaries boil the leg bones of beef to free them from the marrow. Some add washing soda to this process. A hacksaw can be used to make the rough shape. Details are carved with dental burrs or steel tools. The bone can be hand sanded and polished with any white polishing agent on leather or chamois. Lapidaries should be careful not to inhale dust while working with bone or horn.

COAL

Anthracite and Cannel Coal

The hard and durable anthracite of Carbon and Luzerne counties in Pennsylvania has been used for carvings and novelties for several generations. In the past, many folk objects have been carved by the miners and their families and offered for sale in area stores and shops. Coal carvings were once popular in Newcastle, England, where some miners specialized in carving miniature Bibles of hard, black coal. Anthracite is produced by contact metamorphism and is almost pure carbon. It has a glassy luster and a hardness of about 2. Anthracite is dense, compact, opaque,

Garry Van Ausdle uses the natural shape of tusks for his intense portraits.

ebony black, layered, and brittle. Frequently pieces are iridescent.

Archeologists have found coal artifacts in several countries. There are large deposits of anthracite in Wales, Indochina, China, the Russian Commonwealth, and South Africa.

Cannel Coal is a variety of bituminous coal, a dense, deep black coal found in lens-shaped patches in Kentucky, Alaska,

France, and Scotland. It has been used as a substitute for jet.

Coal is soft enough to be worked by hand with steel tools. With some patience it will take a glistening polish. Indiana award-winning carver Robert Miller created a 6-inch carving, "Moses at the Burning Bush," from coal using a flexible shaft handpiece, diamond points, and tools made of dowels.

Jet

Jet is a fossil driftwood allied to lignite coal. Archeological evidence shows that it was used for ornaments as early as the Bronze Age. It reached its height of popularity for jewelry and decorative objects in England during the reign of Queen Victoria, when it was favored for memorial and mourning jewelry by the royal court.

Whitby, England, was the center of an enormous jet industry. Jet was engraved, carved, faceted, and inlaid, and made into beads, buttons, boxes, and dozens of novelties. Over 100 shops were engaged in manufacturing items of jet.

Jet from western states in America was used by the Hopi and other tribes for fetishes, beads, and inlaid jewelry. A carved jet frog from the Anasazi period was among the artifacts found at Chaco Canyon, New Mexico. Contemporary Indian artists still use jet.

Jet is only 2½ in hardness but possesses a toughness that compensates to a certain degree. It is capable of accepting fine detail and a mirrorlike polish. Other qualities that have made jet an acceptable gem material are its warmth to the touch and its dense black color.

When found, jet is dull, dark brown, and has an obvious woody structure. In the United States jet occurs in Utah, New Mexico, Colorado, North Dakota, South

Dakota, and Texas. Other sources are Germany, Poland, Spain, Russia, and Japan. The Whitby Museum in England has fabulous examples of intricately carved jet. A jet Pieta is in the Swabish Gmund Museum in Germany.

Jet can be worked with steel tools and sandpaper. Jewelry designer Doris Kemp uses a 220 grinding wheel to shape cabochons, followed by worn 220 sanding cloth on a drum sander. Worn 600 sanding cloth brings a glossy prepolish. For the polish a hard felt wheel is rotated slowly. Doris warns that jet gives off a strong and unpleasant odor similar to hot automobile grease, so it must be worked with proper ventilation.

has more than one pearl. Other shells produce calcareous concretions, but none as fine as the Queen conch. Only 10 percent of these are jewelry quality.

The delicate pink colors are not stable, so the gems should be kept out of direct sunlight, and the jewelry should be worn only for special occasions. The hardness of the pink pearls is about 5 and the density is 2.8. The concretions also have a certain toughness that recommends them for jewelry.

Some Caribbean fisheries cultivate conchs. (The meat is used for chowder or grilled.) At least one attempt to produce cultured conch pearls is recorded, but as far as is known, no one is pursuing this at

CONCH PEARLS

Calcareous concretions from the mollusk known as the Queen conch, *Strombus gigas*, are desirable because of the wonderful array of tints of pink—baby pink, flesh pink, coral pink, rose pink, and hot pink. Not true pearls, the nodules are usually under 10 carats. They have a silky or porcelainlike sheen, and a flamelike structure, attributed to thin layers of aragonite crystals with intersecting angles. Very few conch pearls are truly round, but many are shaped like miniature eggs, jelly beans, or footballs. Others are baroque.

The lovely pink colors match the pink linings of the conch shells that are often found by shrimpers in the Gulf of Mexico or the Caribbean. The shells have been used for cameos for many years, and the pearly pink concretions were used for jewelry by famous designers in the nineteenth century.

Paleontologist Susan Hendrickson, who has a collection of 150 of these rare organic gems, says that a single shell never

Oriental ivory carvings are combined with black onyx for this necklace by Eleanor Anderson.

present. A univalve off the coast of Australia called the Baler shell also produces pink nonnacreous concretions similar to conch pearls.

CORAL

Corals as living marine organisms are found in many tints and shades of color, but historically it is the reds that have inspired jewelry designers. The reds range from a delicate tint of pink, sometimes called angelskin to a deep rich red called oxblood. But the pastel red with a hint of orange or yellow is the color responsible for the word coral becoming a well-known color name. There are also corals that have soft tints of blue, violet, gold, and yellow, plus black and white. Gold color is quite rare, so black coral has been bleached to imitate this almost metallic color.

Coral is calcium carbonate, only about 3½ in hardness, but tough and durable. Mediterranean coral has been used for fine cabochon jewelry and gem engravings such as cameos for centuries. Drilled bright branchy pieces called frangia were made into necklaces popular in the early 1900s. The Chinese have been successful in making incredibly artistic carvings of coral. Coral was a fashion favorite during the Baroque period in Europe. The Italians did much of the delicate carving.

Some coral is bleached and some is dyed, so the coral beads on today's market may not be a natural color. Black coral is from the deep waters off the Hawaiian Islands. It is not related to the precious coral of the Mediterranean. Black coral is also found off the coast of Mexico near Cozumel, where a cottage industry has sprung up to make jewelry from this coral, which is really conchiolin rather than calcium carbonate. Coral is also found in the

waters off the coast of Africa, in the South China Sea, the Red Sea, and near Taiwan, Japan, Malaysia, the Philippines, and Australia.

An elaborate 9-inch (22.86-cm) tall carved vase made from precious coral by Hing Wa Lee is in the Lora Robins Gallery at the University of Richmond in Virginia. The Jack and Elaine Greenspan collection has an Oriental carving of a large treelike piece of red coral 12 inches (30.48 cm) across with elaborately carved details.

Coral can be cut and polished with care. It must be kept cool and wet, and the lapidary should protect himself from breathing fumes. Coral can be worked with a Foredom handpiece and silicon carbide tools of various shapes. Cerium oxide is a good choice for polish.

IVORY

Ivory as a material for art dates back to the dawn of history. Smooth, fine grained, soft but durable, its mellow glow and easy workability have inspired ancient and modern craftsmen. Cultures as diverse as the Egyptians of King Tutankhamen's time, the Ming period of China, the Victorian romantics, and the whaling villages of New England have prized ivory as an important lapidary material.

It has been used for amulets, charms, picture writing, implements, tools, weapons, netsuke, scrimshaw, carvings, and jewelry. In fact, it has been so popular that it may become the first gem material to become extinct by law. Nations have united to protect the elephant, the chief source of ivory.

Ivory is dentine, calcium phosphate, related to apatite. It also contains organic matter. The structure is striated and elastic.

An Alaskan native carved this effective primitive mask of whalebone. Photo by Russell Kemp.

Only a little over 2 in hardness, ivory is lightweight and warm to the touch. It yellows with age.

Other animals from which ivory is obtained are hippopotamus, walrus, narwhal, and boar. An excellent and still legal source of ivory is the tusks of extinct mastodons and mammoths. Much of the fossil ivory is dark in color rather than white. Fossil ivory is found in Alaska and many other states. Probably the most beautiful fossil ivory is from the Snake River near Valentine, Nebraska. Found in tusk sections up to 30 to 40 pounds, this superb ivory is white with blue-black dendrites, and areas of dusty rose and gray-blue due to mineral inclusions. Fossil ivory is also found in Canada. Huge tusks of mammoths and mastodons sometimes on the frozen animals are found in Siberia.

The Chinese are noted for their complex multidimensional ivory carvings, some of which are tinted in pastel colors. Carved whole tusks are seen in museums. Eskimos still make poignant carvings of Arctic life with fossil ivory or walrus ivory. American artists still carry on the scrimshaw tradition of New England whalers. The Nantucket Historical Associ-

ation's Whaling Museum has a large scrimshaw room. A soaring American eagle was carved from a 90-pound mammoth tusk. The eagle has a 32-inch (81.28-cm) wingspan. Contemporary ivory carvers use flexible shaft tools for the delicate details of ivory carvings.

Ivory is easily worked with steel tools or power tools. A Pro-slicer blade will cut it easily. Sanding with 120, 220, 320, and 400 grit sandpaper brings a prepolish. It is extremely heat sensitive, so much so that it should be kept cool even after working—out of the sun and bright, hot lights. (In lighted cases, the Orientals place small open vials of water at strategic locations to keep the ivory from drying out and crazing.) Tin oxide or a calcium carbonate polish known as *whiting* are among the finishes for ivory.

MELLITE

This is an unusual mineral that occurs in cracks and cavities in lignite and brown coal. It is honey yellow or golden in color,

A model of a whaling ship in ivory shows the skill of the Alaskan natives in portraying their history and their world. Photo by Russell Kemp.

or brownish or reddish, and rarely color-less. It occurs as masses, coatings, or nod-ules. Only 2 to 2½ in hardness, it has a slight toughness to compensate. It belongs to the tetragonal crystal system.

When clear, mellite can be faceted for very small collectors' stones. It is mostly resinous and translucent. Seine, France, and Saxony, Germany, are notable loca-tions. Others are Italy, Czechoslovakia, and the Russian Commonwealth. The first successful faceted stone cut by Art Grant from German material is 1.06 carats.

It is an organic mineral formed by an inorganic process. Described by Arem and others as unique, it is weakly pleochroic. Cleavage will not bother lapidaries, but the material is extremely heat sensitive. Tiny cabochons resemble amber. Mellite is rare.

ODONTOLITE

Resembling turquoise, odontolite is fos-silized bone colored blue by the iron phosphate vivianite. The replacement min-eral is apatite, giving the material a greater hardness and density than natural bone. The hardness is near 5 and the density is 3.

Odontolite can be the teeth and tusks as well as bones of such prehistoric ani-mals as mammoths, mastodons, and dinosaurs, or ancestors of such animals as whales. When found, odontolite still retains the natural organic shape, although the color may be blue-gray instead of the bright blue that can be attained by heat treating.

Odontolite has been found in France, Australia, Siberia, Alaska, South Dakota, and Florida, in paleontological digs or phosphate deposits, but usually in amounts too small for processing as a gem material. It is used for cabochons and small carvings. It has varying hard-ness as some of the replacement mineral may be calcite and a small amount may still be natural organic material. A pre-ferred technique is to wet sand thor-oughly and prepolish with white rouge on muslin, then finish with chrome oxide on leather.

*Jet from Whitby, England,
sometimes has fossil impressions.
Jet is metamorphosed wood.
Photo courtesy of Doris Kemp.*

PEARLS

Pearls are not really a lapidary material in the usual sense. The people who prepare pearls for market are professionals who work only with pearls and do not use traditional lapidary equipment, except perhaps in drilling. However, throughout history no gems have been more admired and desired by women than pearls.

There is a natural pearl industry centered mainly in the Persian Gulf, the Gulf of Mannar, Australia, and the South Seas. Natural freshwater pearls are also used for jewelry. A few are found in unpolluted waters of the United States, Nova Scotia, Canada, Scotland, China, and a few other countries, but usually not in industrial quantities.

*Pearls are the most popular of organic materials.
Courtesy of Lora Robins Gallery, Richmond,
VA. Photograph by Dr. Willie Reams.*

OSTRICH EGG SHELL

Relief carvings and engravings have been made from the large thick shells of ostrich eggs. With extreme care, the shell can be shaped and polished by hand, using steel tools, sandpaper, steel wool, and wax. A craft known as "eggery" cuts the shells in two, installs hinges, decorates the shells lavishly, often with jewels, and then adds a surprise à la Fabergé. Scrimshaw-type items and cameo cabochons have also been made from ostrich shell. Jewelled cups are another use. Shops that stock supplies for eggery artists carry shells.

Most pearls now on the market are cultured pearls, produced by a method developed in Japan in the early 1900s. Cultured pearls are now grown in Japan, China, Tahiti, Australia, the Philippines, New Guinea, Korea, and the United States.

Cultured pearls are grown both in saltwater and freshwater and have as many shapes and colors as natural pearls. A universally popular color is a creamy white with a slight hint of pink in the pearlescence. Exotic and expensive are the gorgeous so-called black pearls of Tahiti, which have iridescent colors of rich green, blue, violet, and sometimes rose and yellow.

Pearls are found in several species of oysters and mussels. The generic name of the Pacific pearl oyster is Pinctada. The freshwater mussel Unio is a pearl producer. Pearls are calcium carbonate, aragonite, plus an organic secretion, conchiolin, plus water. They are 3½ in hardness and 2.8 in density. Overlapping platelets in concentric layers create the iridescent surface of nacre. This lustrous sheen is referred to as "orient."

Pearls have a rich history as treasured gem materials, from the one Cleopatra supposedly dissolved in wine, to the two rows worn by Pocahontas on her beaver hat to denote her high status when she was presented at court. The Russian czars wore caps of fine pearls.

So far the most expensive pearl in the world is the Pelegrina, once in the collection of Russian nobility, which sold recently at Christie's for $467,123. The Canning jewel is a spectacular pearl pendant in the Victoria and Albert Museum in England.

Some of the pearls on today's market are bleached or dyed. There are many imitation pearls, some of which are quite believable. The traditional use of pearls in modern times is for necklaces, which may by graduated or all one size, and strung with a knot between each bead. Contem-

Many species of shells have been used for ornamentation since prehistory. Cameos are often made from helmet shells.

porary designers use pearls with colored gems, such as amethyst, lapis lazuli, onyx, or jade, often accented with gold and diamonds. Baroque pearl *enhancers* are elegant new jewels. Pearl rings, bracelets, pins, clips, and earrings are steady fashions.

TORTOISE SHELL

Tortoise shell is another material that will probably disappear from the lapidary scene because it is obtained from the endangered Hawksbill sea turtle of the tropics. The translucent mottled shell has warm coloring of ivory, yellow, and orangy brown. The shell is a tough, horny material high in carbon, about 2½ in hardness and 1.3 in density. The bright patterns are reminiscent of abstract modern art. In the past, large turtles were collected for their 8-pound shells.

The Romans used tortoise as a decorative inlay and as a veneer. In the nineteenth century, tortoise shell was made into boxes, vanity sets, lorgnettes, decorative combs, and jewelry. An unusual jewelry technique in England and Europe was called piqué. The tortoise shell was inlaid with dainty designs of gold, silver, and mother-of-pearl, mainly in the forms of small dots. Piqué jewelry pieces are now collectors' items. This technique was perfected because tortoise shell is so thermoplastic that it can be softened in boiling water.

The shell sometimes has been artificially colored, and chips and crumbs have been melted and fused together. The shell is easily shaped and sometimes laminated. It can be smoothed with whiting. In more recent times a major use of tortoise shell has been for designer eyeglass frames, knife handles, buttons, and buckles.

VEGETABLE IVORY

An ivory substitute comes from the vegetable kingdom. Called Corozo or Tauga nuts, the hard ivory-like nuts or seeds from certain palms are used for scrimshaw and carvings. The best of these come from the Ivory palm of Peru or Columbia. About the size of hen's eggs, the nuts are ivory-white and about 2½ in hardness. Similar nuts come from the Doum palm of central Africa. Unlike the Ivory palm, which yields clusters of six to nine nuts, the Doum (or Doom) palm has a single nut in the center of an edible fruit. The nut is hard, white, and translucent.

These nuts are easy to carve with steel tools and finish with sandpaper, steel wool, and buffs. American scrimshanders have turned to these nuts since the shortage of ivory. The scrimshaw designs can be finished with India ink, as in ivory scrimshaw patterns, or the material may be dyed or tinted.

WOOD

With the new freedom in jewelry, such natural materials as wood and rubber are frequently seen, even in award-winning high-fashion designs. Easily shaped with

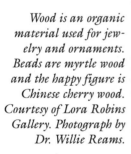

Wood is an organic material used for jewelry and ornaments. Beads are myrtle wood and the happy figure is Chinese cherry wood. Courtesy of Lora Robins Gallery. Photograph by Dr. Willie Reams.

ordinary shop or kitchen tools, wood is used for mountings, inlay, bases of carvings, display of jewelry items, and beads, buttons, buckles, and other decorative items.

Manzanita and desert ironwood have been used in the West for jewelry displays. Ironwood has also been cut and used for inlay. Popular for mountings are knots, burls, black walnut, rosewood, laurel, sycamore, teak, tulip, and ebony. Ebony, a very hard, dark wood, has been used for ornamental items for many years.

The Orientals have successfully used fine wood for elaborate decorative items. Examples are wood with cinnabar and lacquer. The Japanese have used cypress, persimmon, and mulberry for intricately carved netsuke. Sometimes gracefully shaped and highly polished wood has been used to mount items such as small fossils or gemstone arrowheads for bola ties.

Carvings and souvenir items of wood have become cottage industries in some areas. For example, walnut is used in many ways in the Ozarks, and myrtle wood products are made in Oregon. Ironwood was often used in Arizona until it became so scarce that it needed protection. Dark wood was used with silver for the original jewelry of William Spratling, who founded the silver industry of Taxco, Mexico.

Wood can be carved with steel knives. Various grades of sandpaper, successively finer, followed by 0000 steel wool, will make wood satiny smooth. It can be stained, oiled, waxed, shellacked, or varnished according to desired use.

RECOMMENDED READING

Bauer, M., *Precious Stones.* Rutland, VT: Tuttle, 1969.

Desautels, P., *The Gem Kingdom.* New York: Random House, 1970.

O'Donoghue, M., *Gemstones.* London: Chapman & Hall, 1988.

Sofianides, A., and Harlow, G., *Gems and Crystals.* New York: Simon and Schuster, 1990.

Webster, R., *Gems,* 5th ed. London: Butterworth-Heinemann, 1994.

SPECIFIC MATERIALS

Dance, S., Collectors *Encyclopedia of Shells.* New York: McGraw Hill, 1974.

Dickinson, J., *The Book of Pearls.* Philadelphia: Chilton, 1968.

Farn, A., *Pearls.* London: Butterworths, 1986.

Fraquet, H., *Amber.* London: Butterworths, 1987.

Hunger, R., *The Magic of Amber.* Philadelphia: Chilton, 1977.

Kendall, H., *The Story of Whitby Jet.* Whitby, England: Whitby Museum, 1977.

Ritchie, C., *Organic Jewelry You Can Make.* New York: Sterling, 1973.

Shell, H., *Is It Ivory?* Tulsa, OK: Ahio, 1983.

CHAPTER XIV

Rare, Little-Known and Unusual Gem Materials

Adamite
Anatase
Anglesite
Apophyllite
Aragonite
Augelite
Beryllonite
Boleite
Boracite
Carletonite
Cassiterite
Catapleite
Celestite
Cerussite
Childrenite
Chondrodite
Clinohumite
Colemanite
Dioptase
Ekanite
Eudialyte
Friedelite
Grandidierite

Hambergite
Haüynite
Hemimorphite
Herderite
Hureaulite
Inderite
Jeremjevite
Kammererite
Kornerupine
Kyanite
Lazulite
Legrandite
Leucite
Linarite
Ludlumite
Manganotantalite
Microlite
Mimetite
Painite
Parisite
Petalite
Phenakite
Phosgenite

Phosphophyllite
Pyroxmangite
Realgar
Sapphirine
Scorodite
Serandite
Strontionite
Sturmanite
Taaffeite
Triphylite
Vivianite
Wardite

Wavellite
Whewellite
Witherite
Wulfenite
Zectzerite
Zeolites
   Analcime
   Mesolite
   Natrolite
   Pollucite
Zincite

Most books call these *collectors' stones.* They are often hard, beautiful, and suitable for jewelry, but they may be too rare or the gem crystals too small for the lapidary/jewelry market. On the other hand, many collectors' stones are too soft or fragile for jewelry—or completely uninteresting. These rare and unusual materials are a challenge to creative lapidaries who want to master as many materials as possible, and an equal challenge to gem collectors who eagerly look for at least a small stone of every transparent mineral conceivably cuttable.

The definition of *rare* could include well-known stones such as emerald, which is rare in fine large stones, but here it refers to materials rarely used as gems. *Unusual* refers to materials that may be too soft for jewelry, or considered exceptionally difficult to work with, but are nevertheless cut as collectors' stones.

Some of these soft or fragile stones are exceedingly difficult to cut. Some are found in only one place in the world. Some are radioactive. There are other reasons for stones being put in this category—among them, the fact that many rare stones are rather plain and mediocre in appearance, and there is little reason to cut them or to buy them except for the challenge. The rough may be very small, heavily included, and almost impossible for a cutter to obtain.

Some collectors' stones are cabochon stones, but the most sought-after are facet-quality stones. In several cases less than a handful of cut stones of a species exist. New discoveries may remove some of these materials from the rarity and collectors' category.

There is always a certain amount of rivalry between cutters to see who can cut the biggest or best collectors' stone and among the collectors to see who can have the largest and most complete collection. Museums like to show a rare stone, such as hiddenite, along with the common mineral, in this case, spodumene, in order to make the common material appear more interesting. Altogether, this adds up to a brisk market for collectors' stones. In some ways it is an intriguing gamble to buy a new or strange material for its possible collectable potential.

There is also always the chance that an enormous amount of previously rare material will be discovered somewhere and flood the market, so that what was rare and expensive will become popular and moderately priced. However, collectors have learned that the time to buy a new material is as soon as they see an affordable piece they like. Often a fine gem discovery is a dramatic splash on the market and in a year or so there is none to be had at any price.

The public knows little about this group, and indeed, many lapidaries and jewelers are not familiar with rare stones not commonly used for jewelry or ornamental purposes. Collectors of rare stones may be gemologists, advanced or professional lapidaries, scientists, prospectors, or connoisseurs of the unusual. Every field collector dreams of finding a new gem or a gem-quality occurrence of a previously undistinguished or uncut mineral. Every lapidary hopes to cut a material never cut before, or the largest or the best of a rare species.

In the last half of the twentieth century, new minerals have been discovered faster than ever before. The ballpark figure for minerals used to be around 2,000 and is now over 3,000. Two dozen new minerals have been discovered in the state of South Dakota alone. The fact that there are new minerals is naturally a great challenge to gem cutters to see how many of these minerals can be cut into faceted stones or cabochons. Some of these new minerals which have been found to be cuttable have yielded only a few small stones which were cut with difficulty. Others have produced exciting stones in the 10-carat range, which if found in adequate amounts, may be the new gems of the future.

Another factor which influences rare gems is that new locations are constantly being found for some of the well-known materials of the past that have never before been found in cuttable quality or size. So cutters eagerly follow each new

location for a mineral in hopes of acquiring a piece that will cut a bigger or more sensational stone than has ever been cut from a rare species. As an example, Art Grant, master faceter from Hannibal, New York, has cut many rare stones not listed in major gem books; some of these are the first to be cut of the species, and others were the world's largest when cut, and perhaps even now. Table 14-1 lists some of these stones.

To date such stones qualify as rare collectors' stones only. When enough pieces with the proper qualities are found and cut, some may, in the future, be used as gemstones. There are probably numerous other examples of minerals that have provided enough transparent material for one or two small stones.

Gemologists and recreational lapidaries owe a lot to the dedicated and skilled cutters who keep trying to find the best way to cut and polish new materials, thereby improving the science and art of faceting. Most of these materials are worked by master cutters who find the best cut and the best technique for each stone.

ADAMITE
Zinc arsenate

H. 3½	**D. 4.32**
Pleochroic	**Orthorhombic**

Transparent small crystals of adamite have sometimes been cut into attractive stones with high dispersion. Transparent yellowish green and violet crystals from Tsumeb, Namibia, and Mapimi, Mexico, have furnished the cutting material to date. The violet color from Namibia is from cobalt. Cabochons have also been cut from massive material from Mexico.

Adamite is in a group that includes olivinite. It occurs as a secondary mineral

Cutters vie for new faceting materials, while collectors search for the rarest of rare.

in the oxidized zone of ore deposits in California, Utah, Chile, Greece, Turkey, and Algeria, as well as Namibia and Mexico. Other colors are rose, blue, and yellow. Soft, heat sensitive, and brittle, adamite is cold dopped and faceted on fine laps only. Cut stones are small and rare but have good color and fire. Art Grant cut a Mexican stone of 4.38 carats.

ANATASE
Titanium dioxide
H. 5½–6   D. 3.82
Pleochroic   Tetragonal

Some interesting small cabochons have been cut from anatase grains mixed with metamorphic rock. Pyramidal and tabular

crystals have adamantine luster, but are seldom transparent enough or large enough for faceted stones. Dispersion and birefringence are strong.

Colors of anatase are red, red-brown, black, blue, green, violet, and rarely colorless. It is found in gneisses, schists, and diorites. In the United States it is found in Mono County, California, Utah, Arizona, New Mexico, Colorado, South Dakota, Pennsylvania, Maine, and Massachusetts. The source of the limited number of faceted stones is Brazil. Other anatase occurrences are England, Norway, France, Switzerland, Austria, Czechoslovakia, and Tanzania.

As a lapidary material, it is brittle and has perfect cleavage. Arem reports faceted stones in the 6-carat range. Vargas says slow speeds are best and polishing is easy.

ANGLESITE
Lead sulfate
H. 2½–3   D. 6.30
Orthorhombic

Fiery faceted anglesites from Namibia, Morocco, Tunisia, and Mexico are excellent stones for display, in spite of the low hardness. Art Grant cut a 171.20-carat stone from Moroccan rough, but most anglesites are small. The tabular crystals are colorless or some tint of yellow, gold, blue, or brown. Massive and stalactitic material also occurs.

Anglesite is a secondary mineral in lead deposits, often as an alteration of galena. Belonging to the barite group, it has extremely lustrous crystals, high refraction, and diamondlike dispersion.

In the United States fine crystals have been found in California, Arizona, Idaho, Colorado, New Mexico, Utah, and Pennsylvania. Other locations are Brazil, Argentina, England, Scotland, Germany,

Table 14-1
RARE STONES CUT BY ART GRANT

Mineral	Locality	Hardness	Carats	Chemistry
Burbankite	Mont Ste. Hilaire	3½	6.62	Sodium calcium carbonate
Gaudefroyite	Germany	6	1.86	Calcium manganese borate
Görgeyite	Russia	5	.89	Potassium calcium sulfate
Kainite	Germany	2½	10.40	Potassium magnesium sulfate
Kröenkite	Chile	2½	2.29	Sodium copper sulfate
Leucophanite	Mont Ste. Hilaire	4	1.43	Sodium calcium beryllium silicate
Leucosphenite	Russia	61.2	40	Barium sodium silicate
Mosandrite	Russia	5	3.97	Calcium sodium cerium silicate
Narsarsukite	Mont Ste. Hilaire	6–7	.14	Sodium titanium iron silicate
Preobrazhenskite	Russia	4½	10.62	Magnesium boron hydroxide
Stillwellite	Russia	NA	53	Cerium lanthanum calcium silicate
Tunellite	California	2½	1.56	Strontium borate hydroxide
Väyrynenite	Germany	5	6.41	Manganese beryllium phosphate
Virgilite	Peru	6	1.06	Lithium aluminum silicate
Xenotime	NA	4–5	.86	Yttrium phosphorous oxide
Yugawaralite	India	4½	.16	Hydrous calcium aluminum silicate

Zaire, Australia, and New Zealand. Sometimes stalactitic, anglesite often has galena as an inclusion.

The material is highly heat sensitive, brittle, and has perfect cleavage. After cold dopping, it should be worked slowly on a fine lap. Suggested polishes are Linde A, alumina, chrome oxide, or diamond. Not a jewelry stone, anglesite livens up a display or collection.

APOPHYLLITE
Potassium calcium silicate
H. 4½–5   D. 2.37
Tetragonal

Green, pink, and colorless faceted stones of apophyllite from India and Brazil are collectors' items. The best color is a lovely

Pastel anglesite is seldom used as a lapidary material. These crystals are from New Mexico. Photograph by New Mexico Bureau of Mines.

apple green that is sometimes found in the crystals from Poona, India. Occurring in many places in cavities in basalt and related igneous rocks, apophyllite rarely occurs in cuttable quality or size. Colorless apophyllite yields exceptionally white stones.

The green variety from India is known as fluorapophyllite. Minor occurrences are in California, Oregon, Colorado, Michigan, Pennsylvania, Canada, Brazil, Finland, and Czechoslovakia.

Apophyllite is difficult to cut because it is brittle, heat sensitive, and has strong cleavage. Cold dopped material should be worked carefully at slow speed. Stones are usually small and not particularly attractive, but Grant cut a lovely stone weighing 24.92 carats from a crystal from India.

ARAGONITE
Calcium carbonate
H. 3–3½   D. 2.94
Orthorhombic

Faceted aragonites are rare collectors' stones, regardless of the fact that aragonite, as a mineral, is widely distributed. The faceted stones are usually small and colorless, but a yellow stone from Czechoslovakia weighs 110 carats. Light golden-brown aragonite is also faceted. Other colors of aragonite are pink, green, lavender, blue, and brown. Massive, fibrous, and stalactitic material exists in addition to crystals. Chatoyant cabochons are sometimes cut. Some cabochon-quality aqua-colored material from Peru has recently been marketed.

Aragonite is found in sedimentary and metamorphic rock, being deposited by low-temperature solutions in caves, hot springs areas, and oxidized zones near the surface of ore deposits. Blue aragonite occurs in Greece and Chile, yellow aragonite comes from Mexico and Germany, pure white silky aragonite and gray banded material occurs in South Dakota, brown banded aragonite is from Germany, and a greenish-white variation comes from Sicily. Other locations are Peru, England, Spain, and Namibia, and in the United States, California, Colorado, and Wyoming.

Brittle and heat sensitive, aragonite has distinct cleavage in one direction. It is easier to cut than its dimorph, calcite. Polish with tin oxide or alumina at a slow speed.

AUGELITE
Aluminum phosphate
H. 4½–5   D. 2.70
Monoclinic

Massive augelite in pastel colors of rose, yellow, blue, and white can be used occasionally for cabochons, but faceted stones are rare and small. Colorless crystals from Mono County, California, have furnished most of the rough for the faceted stones. Tabular crystals occur in pegmatites and ore bodies. White augelite in small pearly masses occurs in Lawrence County, South Dakota, and small cloudy crystals occur near Keystone, Pennington County. Other locations in the United States are New Hampshire and Maine. Fine crystals also occur in the Yukon Territory, Canada, and in Bolivia, Brazil, Sweden, and Uganda. Some crystals from Bolivia and Sweden have been faceted. The material is brittle and has an easily developed cleavage. Polish with Linde A on a plastic lap.

BERYLLONITE
Sodium beryllium phosphate
H. 5½–6   D. 2.84
Monoclinic

A rare gem material found near Stoneham, Maine, beryllonite is yellow or colorless. Found as massive material or crystals in pegmatites, it occurs in several townships in Maine—Stoneham, Greenwood, Newry, Albany , and Warren. Only small areas of crystals are clear enough to be faceted as most of the material is opaque. Cat's-eye beryllonites are known.

Since the discovery in Maine, which was unique for years, beryllonite has been found in Minas Gerais, Brazil, and at Devon, England. Beryllonite alters to herderite.

Cleavages are perfect and easily developed, but properly oriented pieces are easily faceted after cold dopping. Cerium oxide on a tin lap works well. Art Grant recently faceted a beryllonite of nearly 25 carats.

BOLEITE
Lead copper silver chloride
H. 3–3½   D. 5.05
Cubic

A super rare mineral, little used by lapidaries except for comprehensive collections, boleite from the Boleo district, Baja California, Mexico, is usually opaque to translucent.

Numerous showy groups of azure boleite cubes on beige-colored claylike montmorillonite matrix were shown at Tucson in 1976 by Edward Swoboda. The sensational mineral specimens were purchased by crystal collectors and lapidaries who were entranced by the royal blue color of the ½-inch (1.27-cm) dicelike crystals.

Boleite, a secondary lead mineral, is also found in Arizona, Chile, Germany, Iran, and Broken Hill, Australia. Crystals from these areas are not large enough to cut. It has perfect cleavage in two directions and is brittle and heat sensitive with strong parting planes. Fine grits only are advised followed by polish with Linde A or alumina.

BORACITE
Magnesium chloroborate
H. 7   D. 2.95
Cubic

The most attractive boracite is green, blue-green, or a pale tint of green. It can also be yellow or colorless. Fine-grained or massive material and modified cubic crystals, translucent or transparent, furnish cutting material. In the prime location, Stassfurt, Germany, it is found in bedded sedimentary deposits with anhydrite and gypsum in salt mines. Some material is fibrous. Other locations are California,

Louisiana, Canada, England, France, and Poland.

The best crystals for cutting are the cloudy, muted green crystals from Germany, but since these are usually less than ¼ inch (0.63 cm) in diameter, most cut stones are very small. The Louisiana crystals and the Polish crystals were found in salt domes.

Boracite has good color, medium dispersion, adequate hardness, and no major problems for the lapidary. It also has toughness and a lack of heat sensitivity. The major drawback is rarity. If more were found it could be used for jewelry.

CARLETONITE
Potassium sodium calcium silicate
H. 4½   D. 2.45
Tetragonal

One of the rarities from Mont Ste. Hilaire, Quebec, is the transparent blue mineral, carletonite, which occurs in marble xenoliths in contact with igneous and dark green hornfels. The blue crystals are tetragonal prisms up to 2½ inches (6.35 cm) in length and usually color zoned. Less common crystals are pink or lilac, a few with silky luster. Crystals may have blue centers surrounded by water-clear zones with silky luster. Color zoning is common, varying from pale tints to intense hues.

With strong cleavage and layered structure, the mineral is fragile; nevertheless, several small collectors' gems have been successfully cut, mostly in the 2-carat or less range. Masses of translucent material with pearly luster have rarely been used for cabochons.

CASSITERITE
Tin oxide
H. 6–7   D. 6.99
Pleochroic   Tetragonal

Faceted cassiterite stones with no inclusions of around 1 carat are rare and exciting, with a high refractive index and a fiery dispersion of light almost twice that of diamond. The gem-quality material is red, yellow, gray, or colorless. Opaque material with concentric bands reminiscent of fossil wood is called wood tin. Opaque material has an adamantine luster. Spectacular pieces have come from Mexico.

Found in granite pegmatites and alluvial deposits, cassiterite has a good hardness, no cleavage problems, and a suitable toughness for durable gems. Facet-quality material comes from Bolivia, Spain, England, Namibia, and Australia. Wood tin suitable for interesting cabochons is found in Durango, Mexico, and in Catron County, New Mexico. Cabochon-quality small masses of lustrous dark cassiterite occur in the Black Hills of South Dakota. Gem dealer Frances Villemagne found a 2.16-pound crystal in the Herbb mine of Virginia.

Only outer portions of crystal faces are transparent, so sections for faceting must be sawed off parallel to the surface of the face. The material is difficult to saw, so the thinnest of blades should be used. Wood tin has areas of varying hardness and will undercut unless sanded with unusual care.

CATAPLEITE
Sodium zirconium silicate
H. 5–6   D 2.80
Trigonal

Catapleite is a handsome mineral found with alkali rocks in the pegmatites of

Mont Ste. Hilaire, Quebec, Canada. Translucent, transparent, and opaque vitreous crystals are usually tan or a neutral color, but also occur in yellow, pink, blue, and orange. Catapleite has also been found in Greenland, Norway, Madagascar, and Hot Springs County, Arkansas. The twinned crystals have perfect cleavage in one direction. When found, some of the crystals are iridescent. Several collectors' faceted gems have been cut for stones of about 1 carat. Cabochons from red or yellow Norwegian material are larger. The material is brittle and has perfect cleavage in one direction.

CELESTITE
Strontium sulfate
H. 3   **D. 3.97**
Pleochroic   **Orthorhombic**

Rare as a faceted stone, celestite has been cut into some ice blue cat's-eye cabochons from material found at Chittenango Falls, New York. A vein of fibrous celestite occurs below the falls. Geologist James Young found that the chatoyance was due to the fiberlike crystals of the celestite itself rather than to any inclusions. The showy cabochons are collectors' stones only because of low hardness. Celestite belongs to the barite group.

Faceted stones have been cut from blue celestite crystals from Ohio and Texas. Fibrous greenish-blue material from Texas will cut chatoyant cabochons. Stones have been faceted from orange crystals from Ontario, Canada. Most cut stones are from Tsumeb, Namibia, rough.

Celestite is widespread in sedimentary rocks. Spectacular facet-quality blue crystals in geodes come from Madagascar. Grant faceted a 32.7-carat stone from Madagascar. Other localities are Mexico,

Switzerland, Sicily, England, Egypt, and Tunisia. Besides blue and orange, celestite crystals are pink or colorless. With perfect cleavage in two directions, celestite is soft, heat sensitive, and brittle—a difficult material for lapidaries.

Cold dopping and working with diamond is preferred. James Young polished his cat's-eyes with rouge on a cotton goldsmith's buff. Cabochons should be worked wet at slow speed on fine wheels and sanders.

CERUSSITE
Lead carbonate
H. 3½   **D. 6.55**
Orthorhombic

Colorless yellow, gray, and brown cerussite from Tsumeb, Namibia, has been faceted for spectacularly brilliant stones with higher dispersion than diamonds. Some of the stones seem to have a submetallic luster. The largest cut stone known may be the 408-carat stone reported by Arem.

Cerussite belongs to the aragonite group. It is a secondary mineral found near the surface in oxidized ore zones, and although it is common and widespread, faceted cerussite stones are among the super-rare cut stones. Some locations are Arizona, New Mexico, Montana, South Dakota, Massachusetts, Pennsylvania, Scotland, Morocco, Australia, and New Zealand. Material from Arizona has been used for small cat's-eye stones.

Cerussite lacks most of the qualities of a good lapidary material except for its refraction and dispersion. It has a distinct cleavage plane, is very brittle, and is exceedingly heat sensitive and soft. Only skilled faceters are able to cut a presentable stone.

CHILDRENITE
Iron aluminum phosphate
H. 4½   **D. 3.20**
Pleochroic   **Monoclinic**

In a series with eosphorite, childrenite is the darker of the two in color. Pyramidal or prismatic crystals are reddish brown or yellowish brown and transparent to translucent. The mineral occurs as crystals in hydrothermal veins and in granite pegmatites.

Locations are South Dakota, New Hampshire, Connecticut, Maine, and North Carolina. It is found in several localities in England and Germany. Fine crystals come from Brazil. There are also several locations in Australia. Facetable material comes only from Brazil and stones are small, so they hide the strong dispersion.

Childrenite is brittle, but cleavage is no problem, nor is heat sensitivity. Clean rough is difficult to get. A slow speed with a fine lap is recommend.

CHONDRODITE
Magnesium fluosilicate
H. 6½   **D. 3.16**
Pleochroic   **Monoclinic**

Chondrodite has a vibrant garnet red color and an adequate hardness for cut stones, but the source of the facet-quality material, the Tilly Foster Mine of New York, has been closed for some time.

Chondrodite, a member of the humite group, which includes clinohumite, humite, and norbergite, occurs in contact zones of limestones and dolomites in massive veins and as crystals. Yellow, orange, and brown chondrodite is found in California, Arizona, Ontario, Finland, Sweden, and South Africa. A new find of crystals

from South Africa has furnished a few faceted stones.

The material is transparent to translucent, heat sensitive, and brittle. There is no distinct cleavage. After cold dopping, only small stones can be faceted and polished with cerium oxide on tin at slow speed. Stones should be shallow if the color is dark. Small cabochons have been cut from dark material.

CLINOHUMITE
Magnesium fluosilicate
H. 6–6½   **D. 3.17**
Pleochroic   **Monoclinic**

Clinohumite is a new gem from the Pamir Mountains of Russia. One discovery in 1983 yielded a limited supply of material for the world market, and no more has been discovered at this location. Vivid orange in color, faceted clinohumites seldom exceed 2 carats in weight, although Dr. Aris Mallas has seen three stones of over 2 carats. Small quantities of rough were brought into the United States in the late 1980s by Bennett-Walls of Rotan, Texas. These were well cut and taken to Tucson where they were immediately sold to discerning collectors. Nicely cut stones were released from Russia a few at a time as the demand rose. Dr. Aris Mallas of Bennett-Walls estimates that all of the gem material was from a single find and that the total number of carats of facetable material may have been less than 2,000. Most of the faceted stones were ovals. The largest was nearly 3 carats. Only a small parcel was left in early 1992.

Clinohumite occurs as modified crystals in contact zones of dolomite and in veins in serpentines and schists. While the gem material is a vivid orange, ordinary clinohumite may be yellow, white, and brown. Nongem locations are California, Canada,

Utah, Greenland, Italy, Spain, and Finland. The Russian find may never be repeated. Clinohumite is a perfect example of the interest and intrigue brought about by rare gem materials.

Cleavage and heat sensitivity are not a problem in cutting, but the very brittle quality demands extra care. A bright polish comes easily on tin with Linde A or cerium oxide. With great clarity and exceptional color, this rare gem material has made a big impact on the market. Faceters and collectors are hoping for a new find.

COLEMANITE
Calcium borate
H. 4½ **D. 2.42**
Monoclinic

Yellowish or greenish or colorless crystals of colemanite from Boron, California, have been faceted for collectors. Colemanite occurs in saline deposits and in dry lake beds of the Death Valley area. Large-size stones have been cut, but they are too soft for jewelry and are also plain-looking stones with little going for them, since there is no good color and very weak dispersion. Large crystals from Turkey have also been faceted. Colemanite occurs in Nevada, Argentina, and Kazakhstan.

Colemanite is brittle, heat sensitive, and has perfect cleavage, so it is difficult to work with and the polish is also a problem; however, the material is a challenge to American lapidaries. Collectors' stones are finished with cerium oxide.

DIOPTASE
Copper silicate
H. 5–6 **D. 3.28**
Hexagonal

With brilliant faces and vivid emerald green color, dioptase crystals and clusters have been set into jewelry uncut. Small

Vivid green dioptase is sometimes faceted, but more often used as natural crystals for jewelry purposes.

stones have been faceted from the excellent crystals from Tsumeb, Namibia. Crystal clusters are found in cavities with calcite in the oxidation zones. Single crystals can be as large as 2 inches (5.08 cm) from this extraordinary locality.

Dioptase is also found in Arizona, Chile, Iran, and Zaire. Its sufficient hardness is blunted by brittleness and perfect cleavage in distinct planes in most crystals. All of the cut stones are very small. Cold dopping and lapping on ultrafine laps is the advice of experts.

An ostrich-size dioptase egg was cut from Tsumeb material in Idar-Oberstein, Germany, showing a brilliant pocket of dioptase crystals, enhanced by sparkling quartz in a polished shell. Chrome oxide is the polish choice.

EKANITE
Calcium thorium silicate
H. 6–6½   D. 3.28
Tetragonal

This rare gemstone was discovered in the mid-twentieth century in Sri Lanka. Subsequent discoveries were made in Mont Ste. Hilaire, Quebec, Canada, and in the Yukon Territory. Since its structure has undergone great change because of its uranium and thorium content, the cutting material has been classed as metamict. It is often translucent and chatoyant, more suitable for cabochons than faceted stones. Some ekanite is suitable for cat's-eyes.

The colors are various browns and greens, including a vivid emerald color. The best Sri Lanka stones are yellow-green, found as small water-worn pebbles in gem gravels. A 320-carat uncut stone is owned by a Sri Lanka gemologist.

GIA reports a square-cut stone of 41.7 carats. Most large Sri Lanka pebbles of ekanite are dull and dark in color, some almost black. The Canadian ekanite is brown, found as small stubby crystals. Ekanite is not suitable for jewelry.

EUDIALYTE
Sodium zirconium silicate
H. 5–5½   D. 2.74
Pleochroic   Trigonal

Another of the rare facetable materials from Mont Ste. Hilaire, Quebec, Canada, eudialyte is a pink, red, or brown mineral found in nepheline syenites with microcline, nepheline, and aegirine. The crystals, tabular or prismatic, are mostly translucent. In addition to Quebec, crystals and massive eudialyte are found at Magnet Cove, Arkansas, in Greenland, Norway, Russia, and Madagascar. The tints and shades of red are thought to be from manganese.

For cutting, the most attractive material is the transparent rose-red eudialyte from Kipiwa, Quebec. Small stones in the 1- to 2-carat range have been cut from rough from this locality. (Art Grant's is 1.20 carats.) Cabochons have been cut from the Magnet Cove material. The material is brittle, but cleavage is not a problem.

FRIEDELITE
Manganese chlorosilicate
H. 4½–5   D. 3.04
Monoclinic

Transparent or translucent, colored in warm tones of pink, rose, or red, friedelite occurs in fibrous aggregates, or as cryptocrystalline masses resembling fibrous chalcedony, or as tabular crystals. It cuts brightly colored cabochons which are appealing stones for collections and displays. The chief locality for cuttable material has been Franklin, New Jersey, although some fine material is now coming from the Kalahari manganese field of South Africa. The color of the African material is rose-red with a hint of violet in contrast to the orange-red of New Jersey. Rhodochrosite and calcite are inclusions. Cabochons cut from the Kalahari material may resemble sugilite. Small carvings have been made of the brittle material.

GRANDIDIERITE
Magnesium iron
  aluminum borosilicate
H. 7½   D. 2.85
Pleochroic   Orthorhombic

This is an opaque to translucent mineral with blue-green color and suitable hardness for durable gemstones, but it is not a common material and is seen in only a few collections. It is not plentiful enough for jewelry use.

It is strongly pleochroic, translucent, and jadelike in appearance when polished as cabochons, which are usually less than 1 inch (2.54 cm) in length. Often found in prismatic masses, it occurs in pegmatites in Madagascar, and also in Norway, Scotland, Italy, Algeria, New Zealand, and India.

A few small stones of about 1 carat have been cut from the Madagascar material. It is brittle with perfect cleavage in one direction.

HAMBERGITE
Beryllium borate
H. 7½   D. 2.35
Orthorhombic

Colorless, yellowish, white, or gray crystals of hambergite have been faceted in the 10-carat or less range, rarely larger. White, prismatic crystals up to 2 inches (5.08 cm) are sometimes double terminated. In the United States, it is found in San Diego and Riverside counties in California. Other locations are Madagascar, Brazil, Norway, Czechoslovakia, Pakistan, Afghanistan, and India. It occurs in syenite pegmatites and gem gravels.

With perfect cleavage in two directions and quite brittle, the material is difficult to facet. It is also heavily included, but is not heat sensitive. Hard enough for jewelry, cut stones are rare and not distinguished.

HAÜYNITE (HAÜYNE)
Sodium aluminum silicate
H. 5½–6   D. 2.40
Cubic

This rare mineral, a constituent of lapis lazuli, has furnished a few elegant blue faceted stones of small size. In 1969, a few hundred pounds of dolomitic marble with haüyne were collected in St. Lawrence County, New York. Haüyne had previously been found only in igneous rock. (Coincidentally, it is also found in Lawrence County, South Dakota.) The rich blue New York material, flecked with pyrite, was used for stunning cabochons. A large cabochon from this locality was given to the Smithsonian. New York lapidaries wrote that the major problem was undercutting and only thorough sanding would solve that problem. They polished it with Linde A on leather.

Haüynite is a member of the sodalite group. Transparent to translucent, it occurs in white, green, yellow, and red besides the preferred blue. Small faceted gems have been cut from the bright blue material from Germany, but they are rare and extremely collectable. Other locations for haüynite are Colorado, Montana,

Quebec, Canada, France, Italy, and Morocco.

Faceted stones are worked on a diamond lap and polished at slow speed, while cabochons are polished with cerium oxide on leather.

HEMIMORPHITE
Zinc silicate
H. 4½–5   D. 3.43
Orthorhombic

Blue hemimorphite from Mexico has been used for cabochons resembling smithsonite. The sky blue botryoidal masses from Durango, Mexico, were shown at Tucson several years ago and were eagerly purchased by mineral collectors and lapidaries alike. The material was translucent, slightly silky, and suitable for cabochons up to 30 x 40 mm and small carvings. Colorless, clear material from Chihuahua, Mexico, has been faceted, with most cut stones being under 10 carats. Facet-quality material is rare.

Hemimorphite occurs in oxide zones of zinc/lead ore deposits, in stratified calcareous rock, or in granitic pegmatites. Colors, in addition to blue, are yellow, red, gray, brown, and white.

White radial fibrous masses from Lawrence County, South Dakota, have been cut into small cabochons. Other U.S. localities are California, Washington, Nevada, Arizona, New Mexico, Missouri, Pennsylvania, and Virginia. It also occurs in Brazil, France, Spain, Greece, Iran, Zambia, and Australia.

With perfect cleavage and high heat sensitivity, hemimorphite should be worked wet on fine wheels only, using a light pressure. Chrome oxide or Rapid Polish are the best polish choices.

HERDERITE
Beryllium calcium fluophosphate
H. 5–5½   D. 3.02
Monoclinic

Green and violet facet-quality crystals, which will cut up to 20-carat faceted stones, are found in Minas Gerais, Brazil. Herderite is found in granite pegmatites as a late-stage hydrothermal mineral, altering from beryllonite. Gemmy green crystals up to 2 inches (5.08 cm) are a recent find in Pakistan. Stones reported from Stoneham, Maine, are colorless and less than 5 carats. Herderite also occurs in New Hampshire and in Germany, Austria, and Russia. Other colors are yellow and pink.

Too soft for anything but moderate wear, the stones are, nevertheless, attractive and collectable. Crystals are cold dopped and polished with Linde A on tin.

HUREAULITE
Manganese phosphate hydrate
H. 3½–4   D. 3.19
Pleochroic   Monoclinic

Massive hureaulite from Black Hills pegmatites in Custer and Pennington counties in South Dakota have been cut into small cabochons. The material is translucent. The best material for cutting is compact, massive, and delicately colored in pink, white, or coral. Pink crystals occurring in masses of white phosphates can also be cut. Some pink crystals from Brazil are translucent, though small.

Other locations are Connecticut, California, Poland, France, and Namibia. Cabochons are not common but very attractive.

INDERITE
Magnesium borate
H. 2½   **D. 1.78**
Monoclinic

The borax mines in the California desert have been the source of cuttable inderite, a colorless mineral. Found as nodules and prismatic crystals, the material is extremely difficult to cut, but transparent crystals are large enough for faceted stones of 30 carats or more. Russia and Turkey also have inderite in borax deposits.

The massive material can be pale pink and suitable for soft cabochons that are difficult to polish and do not hold the polish well. The mineral is water soluble, so it should be lapped with clear cutting oil, or mineral oil, instead of water, and polished with glycerine. Inderite is also extremely heat sensitive and has perfect cleavage; it is a fragile and delicate stone to work with, and some say hardly worth the effort.

JEREMJEVITE
Aluminum borate
H. 6½–7½   **D. 3.29**
Pleochroic   Hexagonal

Long blue-green crystals of facetable quality were discovered in Swakopmund, in Namibia, and found to be the first gem-quality examples of the mineral jeremjevite, previously known only as microscopic grains. Mostly yellow, brownish, or colorless, it was first found in Siberia in the nineteenth century and named for a Russian mineralogist. The jeremjevite from Namibia, so far, is from a limited area, so it is known only as a collectors' stone, although it has good hardness and color. It

This cabochon (16 × 26 mm) is light blue hemimorphite from Mexico.

has been found in an igneous region of Germany.

Faceted stones to 5 carats have been cut. The gem is said to be easy to work as there is no cleavage and it is not heat sensitive.

KAMMERERITE
(CHROMIAN CLINOCHLORE)
Magnesium aluminosilicate
H. 2–2½   **D. 2.64**
Pleochroic   Monoclinic

A member of the chlorite group, kammererite is the chromium variety of clinochlore. This soft material is admired only for its vivid violet-red color. The principal gem occurrence has been in Turkey where small hexagonal raspberry red and cerise-colored crystals occur. The micaceous mineral is found in chromium deposits, in serpentines, and schists. First found in Russia, it was named for a St. Petersburg mining director. A few small cut stones exist and several cabochons have been cut from opaque material shown in the 1970s. Kammererite or clinochlore has perfect easily developed cleavage and is brittle and difficult to facet. Other colors of clinochlore are yellow and green. Clinochlore occurs in California, Montana, South Dakota, Pennsylvania, and Vermont, and in Switzerland, Japan, and New Zealand.

KORNERUPINE
Magnesium aluminum iron borosilicate
H. 6½–7   D. 3.28
Pleochroic   Orthorhombic

Originally discovered in Greenland, and later found as pebbles in the Elahera gem field of Sri Lanka, kornerupine can be colorless, white, pink, brown, yellow, greenish brown, blue-green, or yellowish green. The pleochroic colors are yellow, green, and reddish brown. Kornerupine has been found in upper Burma also, in desirable hues of green. Superior shades of green also come from Kenya and Tanzania. Star and cat's-eye stones have been reported. Other locations are Quebec, Canada, Germany, Madagascar, and Natal. A yellow stone from Sri Lanka is an oval of 17.01 carats. Most museums and private collections have examples of this collectable gem, but it is seldom seen in jewelry.

Lapidaries must watch for the brittleness of the stone and the perfect cleavage in two directions. However, it is not heat sensitive. Cabochons are sometimes cut from the less transparent material from Green-

Among the rare cabochons in the bicentennial tiara by Honey O'Sullivan are a hauynite from New York and a wavellite from Arkansas. An Arkansas diamond and a California benitoite are among the faceted stones. All gems are from the United States.

land and elsewhere. It polishes easily with alumina or tin oxide.

KYANITE
Aluminum silicate
H. 4–7½   D. 3.53
Pleochroic   Triclinic

Blue gems are among the most popular, but unfortunately kyanite, although possessed of a wonderful true blue color, is seldom cut. Crystals are thin, splintery, and brittle, and cleavage is pronounced. In the United States gem-quality crystals have been found in North Carolina that yielded a few stones over 5 carats. Specimen-type crystals are also found in Virginia and Georgia. Cuttable crystals have come from Brazil, Kenya, and Zaire. A chrome green kyanite comes from Tanzania. Pink, gray, yellow, and brown crystals are also known. Not many cut stones are over 10 carats. The largest cut stones are from Brazil.

The formula for kyanite is the same as that for sillimanite and andalusite. Kyanite occurs in schists and pegmatites, especially in strongly metamorphic areas. It is transparent to translucent and often color zoned. A major fault as a lapidary material is that the faces of the crystal have extreme variations in hardness.

Some of the other best-known kyanite occurrences are California, Washington, Utah, Colorado, South Dakota, Canada, Sweden, Switzerland, France, Austria, Italy, India, Burma, and Australia.

Occasionally kyanite is chatoyant, so small cat's-eye cabochons can be cut, but cutting the cat's-eye is as difficult as faceting, so cut kyanite stones are not at all common. Avoiding the cleavage planes is critical in cutting.

LAZULITE
Iron magnesium aluminum phosphate
H. 5½–6   D. 3.10
Pleochroic   Monoclinic

Lazulite has a wonderful blue color, but is rare as a gem material. Facet-quality rough comes from Brazil and India and stones are small and seldom clean.

Azure blue crystals occur in granite pegmatites and highly metamorphosed rocks such as quartzite. Lazulite also occurs as granular masses, mostly opaque or translucent. Crystals as long as 6 inches (15.24 cm) are found in Sweden. Other locations are Graves Mountain, Georgia; Mono Mountain, California; Custer County, South Dakota; Bolivia; and Madagascar. Small cabochons have been cut from massive material and from opaque crystals. Crystals, some of gem quality, from the Yukon Territory, Canada, are over ¾ inch (1.90 cm) in diameter.

Cabochons are used for jewelry that does not undergo heavy wear, such as earrings, pendants, and bola ties. Cabochons have been cut from material from California, Georgia, and Canada. The sky blue color is exotic, and the stones are fine for displays and collections.

There is no cleavage and little heat sensitivity. Cabochons can be worked by normal methods and polished to a high luster with Linde A or chrome oxide on leather.

LEGRANDITE
Zinc arsenate hydroxide
H. 5   D. 3.98
Pleochroic   Monoclinic

Some 30 years ago the most astonishing crystals at the Tucson show were legrandite crystals from Mapimi, Durango, Mexico. Golden yellow, canary yellow, and yellow-orange in color, the sheaflike crystals with their shining surfaces were grabbed up as aesthetic and rare mineral specimens, but a few dedicated faceters obtained broken pieces large enough to cut. The fanlike sprays of better specimens are as long as 2½ inches (6.35 cm). Many are quite transparent. The crystals occur in cavities in a compact, neutral-colored limestone. Other localities are Nueva Leon, Mexico, and Japan.

A few long, narrow cabochons have been cut from Mapimi rough, as well as some faceted, step cut stones. Cleavage is no problem, but legrandite is very brittle. Faceting is easy, but polishing (with alumina at slow speed) is more difficult.

LEUCITE
Potassium aluminum silicate
H. 5½–6   D. 2.47
Tetragonal

The best source of cuttable transparent leucite is the Alban Hills of Italy. Crystals are translucent to transparent, and colorless. Massive granular leucite and almost opaque crystals, white, gray, or yellow, occur in potassium-rich igneous rocks. Other notable locations are Wyoming, Arkansas, New Jersey, Canada, France, Zaire, Uganda, and Australia. Although leucite is found in many lavas, facet-quality material is a rarity. Sleepy-appearing cut stones are usually less than 3 carats.

Not heat sensitive, and only moderately brittle, the material is comparatively easy to cut and polish. Cerium oxide on a plastic lap is recommended.

LINARITE
Lead copper sulfate
H. 2½   D. 5.30
Pleochroic   Monoclinic

Linarite is a collectors' stone known for its lovely blue color. Found in copper mines, the shining blue crystals make showy specimens but are seldom large enough to facet. The tabular crystals, up to 4 inches (10.16 cm) in length, are often quite transparent in spite of the deep blue color.

Linarite is a secondary mineral of the oxide zone of copper deposits. Fine specimens occur in Namibia, Australia, Chile, Peru, England, and Canada. In the United States, linarite display-type crystals come from California, New Mexico, Montana, Idaho, and Nevada. At a Tucson show at the Desert Inn in the 1970s, dealers featured excellent linarite crystals from Arizona. Quite a few of these were large enough to facet stones in the 3–4-carat range, but were exciting cabinet and competition specimens. Grant cut a stone of 1.49 carats.

Lapidaries consider the material difficult to work with because it is extremely heat sensitive, brittle, and has easily developed cleavage planes. Transparent areas are small and included. Chrome oxide at slow speed gives a good polish.

LUDLUMITE
Iron magnesium phosphate
H. 3½   D. 3.19
Monoclinic

Facet-quality apple-green ludlumite has been found in the Blackbird Mine of Lemhi County, Idaho, and translucent crystals from South Dakota's Black Hills are large enough to cut attractive cabochons. Ludlumite is found in oxide zones of ore deposits as tabular crystals, colorless, white, pale green, apple green, and occasionally vivid green. Some Idaho crystals are transparent and emerald green in color. Massive material is also found. Locations are South Dakota, New Hampshire, Connecticut, Mexico, Brazil, England, France, and Germany. Mexican material is facetable.

There is perfect cleavage in one direction that is easily developed and the material is highly sensitive to heat, but careful cutters can sometimes facet a small collectors' stone of ludlumite probably in the 1-carat range. Lapidaries have also been successful in polishing unusual cabochons.

MANGANOTANTALITE
Manganese tantalate
H. 6½   D. 8.0
Pleochroic   Orthorhombic

A brownish-red gem with vitreous submetallic luster, manganotantalite is found as short prismatic crystals with scarlet-red highlights in the translucent material. Massive material is found as well. It occurs in granite pegmatites and occasionally in placer deposits. The material is rarely transparent.

Facet-quality crystals come from Mozambique, Zambesia, and Brazil. Well-cut gems of paler material are fiery because of high dispersion. Cut gems are seldom over 5 carats. Other locations are San Diego County, California; Taos County, New Mexico; Park County, Colorado; Newry Township, Maine; Amelia, Virginia; and England, Sweden, Japan, and Australia.

Faceters claim that manganotantalite is difficult to work with because of the easily developed cleavage, brittle composition, and somewhat heat-sensitive nature. They polish it with alumina, or Linde A, or chrome oxide.

MICROLITE
Calcium sodium tantalate
H. 5½–6   D. 5.50
Cubic

Microlite is a rare gem material, formerly known from only one locality. Facetable olive green crystals of microlite were found in the pegmatites of the Rutherford Mine near Amelia, Virginia, with quartz, topaz, amazonstone, and garnets. The Virginia crystals are sometimes over 2 inches (5.08 cm) in diameter, while a previous discovery in Massachusetts yielded crystals too small to cut. A more recent find of gem-quality green crystals was in Brazil. Other microlite colors are red, yellow, and brown.

Occurring as crystals or irregular masses, microlite is found in pegmatites, often with lepidolite and spodumene. Indistinct crystals of 1 inch (2.54 cm) in diameter and brown masses 3–4 inches (7.62–10.16 cm) thick have been found at the Tin Mountain Mine in the Black Hills of South Dakota. Other locations are Colorado, New Mexico, Brazil, Norway, Sweden, Finland, Afghanistan, and Australia. Microlite is used for cabochons if the material is translucent or opaque. Faceted microlite, from green crystals from Brazil, is a rare collectors' stone. Most stones are less than 5 carats. The material is not heat sensitive but is moderately brittle, yet it gives no significant problems in cutting and polishing.

MIMETITE
Lead chloroarsenate
H. 3½   **D. 7.24**
Pleochroic   **Monoclinic**

Mimetite cabochons from Mexican material have been occasionally exhibited for a number of years, but recently facet-quality mimetite appeared from Tsumeb, Namibia. The colors of mimetite are bright yellow, orange, yellow-orange, red-orange, white, and colorless. The Mexican material from Durango and Chihuahua is globular or botryoidal and sometimes silky. The crystals from Namibia are yellow, transparent, and rare. Only small faceted stones have been cut.

Mimetite occurs as a secondary mineral in lead deposits. Other locations are California, Nevada, Utah, Colorado, South Dakota, Pennsylvania, England, Scotland, Sweden, France, Algeria, and Australia.

Because of their low hardness, neither the cabochons nor the faceted stones are suitable for jewelry, but their high refractive index and intense colors make them especially collectable. Brittle and heat sensitive, mimetite is shaped on fine wheels and kept very cool. Polish is achieved with chrome oxide on leather.

PAINITE
Calcium aluminum borosilicate
H. 8   **D. 4.03**
Pleochroic   **Hexagonal**

This gem is so rare that only several pieces are known. A single lustrous garnet-red crystal was found in 1951 by Mr. A. C. Pain in the gem gravels of upper Burma. It proved to be a new species. The crystal had a pseudo-orthorhombic appearance and well-developed faces. It is possible other painites exist that have never been analyzed. Excellent gem possibilities cannot be proven unless more rough is found.

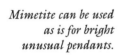

Mimetite can be used as is for bright unusual pendants.

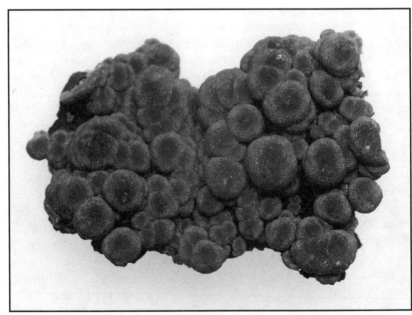

PARISITE
Calcium cerium lanthanum fluocar-
bonate
H. 4½   D. 4.36
Pleochroic   Hexagonal

Crystals of parisite are usually small, and the colors, browns and grays, with yellowish tints at times, are somber and unappealing. However, small stones have been cut in the 3-carat range. (Grant has a 3.21-carat faceted stone he cut from Colombian rough.) The only locations for cutting material to date are Muzo, Columbia, and Ravalli County, Montana. The material occurs in shales and pegmatites. Other locations are Massachusetts, Canada, Brazil, Greenland, Norway, Switzerland, and Madagascar.

The material is brittle and splintery. Cleavage could be a problem. This is a collectors' stone only.

PETALITE
Lithium aluminum silicate
H. 6–6½   D. 2.32
Monoclinic

Petalite occurs as masses and, rarely, crystals in granite pegmatites with lithium minerals such as spodumene and lepidolite. The colors are white, gray, yellow, pale pink, and green. Cabochons have been cut from material found in Oxford County, Maine, and pink material from Namibia. Facet-quality transparent petalite from Brazil and western Australia is sometimes available. Colorless or light yellow pieces from Brazil will cut stones up to 50 carats. Some of the material is chatoyant.

Other locations for petalite are California, Wyoming, Canada, Sweden, Italy, and Zimbabwe. The Zimbabwe petalite is mixed with analcime and can be used for cat's-eyes, pinkish brown in color. A translucent 20.3-carat cat's-eye cabochon of light pink color from South Africa was recently examined by the GIA. Webster, in *Gems,* reports a 206-carat faceted stone from Brazil. Grant has a faceted petalite of 100.80 carats from Brazilian rough.

Cabochons of petalite are not difficult to cut in spite of the perfect cleavage in one direction. Not heat sensitive, the material is easily polished with cerium or tin oxide on felt or leather. Faceted stones are finished with diamond.

PHENAKITE
Beryllium silicate
H. 7½–8   D. 2.93
Pleochroic   Trigonal

Minas Gerais, Brazil, furnishes the best colorless phenakite for faceting, but few stones are over 10 carats. The largest stone reported is over 500 carats, a Sri Lanka gem. Phenakite resembles colorless quartz, and is hard enough for jewelry wear, but is not an especially interesting stone since it has low dispersion.

Usually colorless, crystals are often tinted yellow, pink, or brown by impurities. Phenakite occurs in granite pegmatites, mica schists, and hydrothermal veins. Some U.S. locations are Pala, California; Mount Antero, Colorado; Oxford County, Maine; and Amelia County, Virginia. Norway, Switzerland, Poland, Austria, the Ural Mountains of Russia, Namibia, and Tanzania all have phenakite. Austria's is pale yellow, and Russia's is light red. The colors are beautiful and the hardness is good, but many crystals are small and large crystals are heavily included, so most cut stones are less than 5 carats.

Phenakite is tough in addition to being hard. It is not heat sensitive and the cleavages, though distinct, are not easily developed. It is somewhat difficult to polish, but Linde A, tin oxide, or cerium oxide on tin should bring a bright finish.

PHOSGENITE
Lead chlorocarbonate
H. 2–3   D. 6.13
Pleochroic   Tetragonal

A secondary mineral in lead deposits, and in granite pegmatites, phosgenite has strong dispersion and will yield brilliant small gems. Its colors are pastel green, pink, yellow, or brown or gray shades, or colorless.

It occurs as excellent crystals up to 5 inches (12.70 cm) in Sardinia and also at Tarnowitz, Silesia, Poland; Matlock, England; Larium, Greece; Tsumeb, Namibia; and Tasmania and Australia. In the United States, it is found in the Mammoth Mine, Arizona; at Oak Creek, Colorado; and at Eureka Hill, Utah. Besides prismatic and tabular crystals, it occurs in massive form.

While the massive material is used for delicate cabochons, the transparent material is faceted, although the stones are usually small. The largest known is a 119.66-carat stone cut by Art Grant.

For cutters, the distinct cleavage can be a problem. It is better to cold dop the stone, then preform it on a fine wheel.

PHOSPHOPHYLLITE
Hydrous zinc phosphate
H. 3–3½   D. 3.13
Monoclinic

Spectacular crystals of blue-green phosphophyllite were discovered in the sulfide deposits of Potosi, Bolivia, in 1960. Small sections of these crystals have been faceted for rare collectors' gems. The Smithsonian had Victor Pribil of Long Island, New York, cut its first faceted phosphophyllite shortly after the discovery. The phosphate is a late hydrothermal deposition. Crystals from Bolivia occur in vugs in sulfides. Other localities for phosphophyllite are Bavaria, Germany; Pennington County, South Dakota; and South Australia. Some occurrences are in pegmatites with an assortment of other phosphates.

Brittle, soft, and with strong cleavage, the material is extremely difficult to work with. Sinkankas writes that the hardness of the lapidary material is considerably greater than 3½ and that the grinding should be done with diamond and the polishing with Linde A on tin or wax.

PYROXMANGITE
Manganese silicate
H. 5½–6   D. 3.61
Pleochroic   Triclinic

Found in metamorphic rocks, schists, and quartzites, especially in manganese deposits, these tabular transparent crystals are admired because of the rich and delicate pinks, rose-reds, orchids, and lilacs. Crystals are often found in association with rhodochrosite, rhodonite, and other manganese materials. Scotland, Finland, Sweden, Japan, and Australia are some localities, while in the United States crystals and massive material are found in California, Idaho, Colorado, and South Carolina. The massive material can be used for cabochons and decorative objects.

Facet-quality material, in small clear grains, comes only from Japan. Most cut stones are under 3 carats. Pyroxmangite is brittle and has to be oriented carefully because of perfect cleavage in two directions. However, it is not difficult to polish.

REALGAR
Arsenic sulfide
H. 2   D. 3.56
Monoclinic

Soft and fragile, realgar is noted for its sensational red and red-orange colors. It occurs in low-temperature hydrothermal veins or as a hot springs deposit. It is sometimes faceted for small collectors' stones, but must not be exposed to the light. It may alter to orpiment and decompose.

In the United States the best crystals come from Humboldt County, Nevada. Masses are found in Nye County, Nevada. Other good crystals come from Tooele County, Utah. It is also found in California, Washington, and South Dakota. Washington and Nevada have provided the small amounts of facetable material. Other locations are Peru, Switzerland, Romania, and China. Grant cut a 1.76-carat stone from Chinese rough.

Extremely brittle and heat sensitive, the material should be cold dopped and handled with great care. Stones should be shallow and cuts simple.

SAPPHIRINE
Magnesium aluminum oxide
H. 7½   D. 3.43
Pleochroic   Monoclinic

This rare gem is often an intense blue, but GIA has examined some that are a purplish pink, and a strange brown-green stone. It occurs as a high-temperature metamorphic mineral in low-silica magnesium-rich rock. Although it occurs in several localities, the facetable material to date has come from Madagascar and Sri Lanka. A recent discovery is on Somerset Island in the Canadian Arctic. The type locality is in western Greenland.

Several cut stones in blue, brownish green and purplish pink have been examined in the GIA laboratory in recent years. Very few stones are over 2 carats. Mark Smith faceted a blue-black sapphirine of 2.72 carats. The rough was from Sri Lanka. Recently *Gems & Gemology* reported a Madagascar specimen of corundum covered with a layer of green spinel and the whole encased in blue sapphirine.

Sapphirine can be faceted on a tin lap with alumina. The few who have cut it report that it handles much like garnet.

SCORODITE
Hydrated iron arsenate
H. 3½–4   D. 3.27
Pleochroic   Orthorhombic

Related to variscite, scorodite occurs in facetable crystals in Tsumeb, Namibia, and Zacatecas and Durango, Mexico. The Manuel Ontiveros collection of Mexican minerals had several fine large crystals of rich blue facet-quality material that might yield faceted stones of up to 5 carats. The Tsumeb crystals are violet-blue and blue-green. Other colors are green, brown, and yellow. Gem crystals of small size have recently come from Brazil.

Scorodite occurs in arsenic-bearing metamorphic rock, in cavities in basalts, and in schists in many places. Other locations are Canada, Brazil, Algeria, and Australia. The material is sometimes silky and can be used for cabochons.

Scorodite has an indistinct cleavage, but it is brittle and heat sensitive. If the color is dark, shallow cuts are preferred. Professional cutters advise cold dopping the material and working it at slow speed.

Rough for this 3-carat blue scorodite came from Durango, Mexico.

SERANDITE
Sodium manganese silicate
H. 4½–5   D. 3.41
Triclinic

An analogue of pectolite, peach-orange serandite of cutting quality, is one of the unique handsome minerals of Mont Ste. Hilaire near Montreal, Quebec, Canada, an extensive area of nepheline syenite rocks. Other occurrences are in Japan and Australia. In the United States, it has been found in New Mexico.

Its marvelous colors are pale and bright pink, peach-pink, salmon, rose-red, bright orange, and orangy tans and browns. It occurs in large splendid crystals and in silky aggregates that are usually of duller colors. Translucent orange crystals from pegmatites have been cut into vivid cabochons and a few small stones have been faceted. Faceted stones over 3 carats are rare and usually flawed or included. A step cut stone of 3 carats is in the Royal Ontario Museum. Grant's largest Mont Ste. Hilaire serandite may be a record at 5.4 carats. A cross-hatched structure shows in many cut stones but is less apparent in high-domed cabochons.

Rather soft, brittle, and with perfect cleavage, the material is difficult to work at all stages, but worth the effort for stunning collectors' stones. Cabochons are oriented so that the strongest structural lines cross at acute angles down the center of the stone. They are polished with cerium oxide on leather. High heat sensitivity makes it necessary to keep the material cool in every step. Faceted stones are small and rare.

STRONTIANITE
Strontium carbonate
H. 3½   D. 3.63
Orthorhombic

This rather colorless mineral sometimes occurs in small clear areas which can be faceted for collectors of rarities. Occurring in veins and sometimes geodes, it is a low-temperature mineral, found as crystals or massive material. The best of the bland colors for cutting are greenish and yellowish tints. It is transparent to translucent, a member of the aragonite group.

South Dakota is one of the many places this mineral is found. White and green radial masses, sometimes chatoyant, were collected in Lawrence County in the Homestake gold mine. Several cabochons were cut from this material.

The few faceted crystals, mostly colorless or pale, have been cut from material from Canada, Germany, and Austria. Other locations in the United States are California, Washington, New Mexico, Texas, Pennsylvania, and New York. Strontianite is also found in Mexico, Scotland, Switzerland, and India.

It is brittle and has near perfect cleavage and uneven fracture. It should be worked wet on fine wheels and polished with a slurry containing a small amount of oxalic acid.

STURMANITE
Iron sulfate
H. 2½–3   D. 1.84
Trigonal

Yellow, yellow-orange, and yellow-green crystals of sturmanite, associated with barite and hematite, were found in the Black Rock Mine of South Africa in 1982. The attractive transparent to translucent, vitreous, prismatic crystals were determined to be the iron member of the complex ettringite group. They occur in metamorphic rock. Cal Graeber, a California collector, acquired a magnificent crystal 4¾ inches (12.06 cm) in length and another over 5 inches (12.70 cm) long.

Found with barite and hematite, sturmanite's long formula includes calcium, iron, aluminum, manganese, sulfur, and boron. The sturmanite crystals have ettringite cores. The outstanding color is golden yellow, but there are other tints of yellow plus white and colorless.

A few small collectors' stones have been cut. Graeber says the material is not sensitive to light and that there is a perfect cleavage parallel to the long axis. The vivid color makes sturmanite a desirable collectors' stone.

TAAFFEITE
Beryllium magnesium aluminate
H. 8   D. 3.60
Hexagonal

Until about a decade ago there were only six examples known in the world of this rare facetable gem, first found in a parcel from Sri Lanka. Count Taaffe, a Dublin gemologist, was studying a stone that was thought to be a spinel, but it was doubly refractive and had a refractive index of 1.72. After further testing, it proved to be a new species. Since its discovery, taaffeite has been found in Burma, Siberia, China, and Antarctica. A recent report mentions taaffeite in schist in Australia. Most taaffeites are found as water-rolled pebbles. The gem has graduated in the past 20 years from super rare to merely rare.

Taaffeite occurs in metamorphic limestones and alluvial gravels. The coloring agents may be iron, manganese, or chromium. The colors of these elegant and hard gemstones are delicate mauve, lilac, pink, blue, violet, and, very rarely, red (originally called *taprobanite*). Mark Smith, of Thailand, recently faceted an intense red taaffeite. A 46.17-carat crystal was a big attraction in Tucson.

Two minerals thought to be taaffeite and very closely related have been under investigation. They are taprobanite and musgravite. These studies have had the effect of changing the formula of taaffeite. It is known that the occurrence in Antarctica is quite different from that of Sri Lanka.

Director Thahis of Zam Gems, Sri Lanka, calls their finest taaffeite a colorless, flawless brilliant of 9.63 carats. A mauve oval faceted stone in Columbo is 13.22

Not many lapidaries have had a chance to cut taaffeite, but Jerry Call, faceting instructor, who cut a lilac-colored stone as a show demonstration, says that taaffeite handles much like spinel. It presents no major problems and takes an excellent polish.

TRIPHYLITE
Lithium iron phosphate
H. 4–5   D. 3.42
Orthorhombic

Massive triphylite occurs in granite pegmatites and in metamorphic rock. Prismatic crystals are rare, and very few have clear areas. There are several attractive colors: honey yellow, pale blue, blue-gray, green, coral, and brown. Colors come from iron and manganese.

Irregular masses up to 8 feet in length and some large crystals are found in Custer and Pennington counties in the Black Hills of South Dakota. Olive-green material, greatly resembling turquoise, has been cut into cabochons. As far as is known, none of the South Dakota material has been faceted. Siderite pseudomorphs

after triphylite have been found near Keystone. Triphylite is rather unstable.

Other locations are California, New Hampshire, Maine, Canada, Brazil, France, Sweden, Germany, and Finland. A few dark faceted stones have been faceted from Brazilian rough. What may be the largest cut stone is gray-brown and weighs 65 carats. Triphylite has perfect cleavage in one direction, but is not brittle. Porous material like this should be cold dopped and should not be cut with oil as a coolant. Polish with tin oxide on leather.

VIVIANITE
Iron phosphate hydrate
H. 2   D. 2.68
Pleochroic   Monoclinic

Vivianite is colorless when found but quickly turns dark blue, blue-black, greenish blue, or violet. A fragile mineral, it occurs in long thin crystals as an alteration of primary phosphates. Vivianite also occurs in coal seams. It is sometimes the

Bright yellow or orange wulfenite is popular with collectors, but faceters seldom find suitable material.

coloring agent in organic material in sedimentary deposits, such as the blue dendrites in mammoth ivory, or the turquoise color of odontolite (fossil bone). Fossil ivory, colored by vivianite, is found in Nebraska. Vivianite is part of a group that includes annabergite and erythrite.

Excellent crystals come from Lemhi County, Idaho, and Salt Lake County, Utah. Vivianite has also been found in California, Colorado, South Dakota, New Jersey, Maine, North Carolina, and Florida. Large crystals come from Bolivia, Brazil, Camaroon, and Japan.

A very sensitive stone for the cutter, vivianite can only occasionally be faceted for rare collectors' stones. It has easily developed perfect cleavage and is very heat sensitive and splintery. Vargas recommends cold dopping and making no attempt to cut or polish a girdle. Work is done with the cleavage, not against it.

WARDITE
Hydrous aluminum phosphate
H. 5   D. 2.81
Tetragonal

Wardite occurs in pyramidal crystals, but more often as masses in sedimentary rock with other phosphates and occasionally in pegmatites. Colors are bluish green, white, and several tints of green. Small faceted stones have been cut from pale green crystals from Brazil. However, wardite is mainly used for cabochons, usually with other phosphates. The best example is the superb blue-green variscite from Fairfield, Utah, which occurs in nodules including white or green wardite with yellow crandallite, white englishite, beige gordonite, deep green or yellow montgomeryite, light green overite, and others. Magnificent cabochons can be cut show-

ing mostly wardite and variscite, or wardite mixed with several of these cuttable phosphates. Spheres, eggs, and slabs of mixed phosphates including wardite are showy display items.

Clear wardite crystals have been found in California, New Hampshire, and Maine. Well-formed crystals almost ¾ inch (1.90 cm) in length are found in the Yukon Territory, Canada. Other locations are Brazil, France, and Australia.

The few faceted stones of wardite that exist are cut from greenish-white crystals from Paraiba, Brazil. Undercutting is a definite problem with the cabochon material. Sanding should be with fine wet sanding cloth. Tin oxide on leather brings a good polish. When intermixed with other phosphates, wardite makes handsome cabochons that can be used for certain jewelry styles for light occasional wear.

WAVELLITE
Aluminum phosphate
H. 3½   D. 2.36
Orthorhombic

Wavellite suitable for small cabochons is occasionally found in the Hot Springs area of Arkansas. Occurring as radial green aggregates of acicular crystals resembling piles of marbles, wavellite is varied in color from medium green to light green to white, and sometimes yellowish green or yellow. It occurs in hydrothermal veins with other phosphates and as fracture fillings in sandstone. It is prized for aesthetic cabinet specimens.

There are several locations in Hot Springs, Garland, and Montgomery counties, with many collectors choosing one near the town of Buckville as their favorite. Wavellite has also been found in California, Colorado, Pennsylvania, Alabama, and in

Bolivia, England, France, Germany, Romania, and Australia.

Prismatic crystals are rare and faceting-quality wavellite is unknown. Cabochons of 2 or more inches (5.08 cm) have been cut from Arkansas material. Difficult to cut, the radial crystals splinter. Wavellite is heat sensitive and has perfect cleavage, but well-shaped high-dome cabochons are interesting to collectors.

WHEWELLITE
Calcium oxalate
H. 2½   D. 2.21
Monoclinic

An unusual white, yellow, brown, or orange mineral, transparent to translucent, whewellite occurs in concretions and coal seams. Cabochons and small faceted stones have been cut, mostly from material from Germany and South Dakota. The South Dakota occurrence is of yellow prismatic crystals in the 2½-inch (6.35-cm) range in large concretions that are found along the Cheyenne River in Meade County. The whewellite occurs with yellow calcite and sometimes golden barite in concretions which may measure 2 feet (61 cm)—or more in diameter. Coarsely crystalline masses are up to 3 inches (7.62 cm).

Crystals several inches in length are found in a coal seam near Dresden, Germany, and in concretions near Hohenneggelsen. Most of the faceted stones have been cut from German material. Other locations are Czechoslovakia, France, and Hungary, and in the United States, San Juan County, Utah; Erie County, Ohio; and Havre, Hill County, Montana.

Faceted stones are small and colorless, but brilliant because of high dispersion. The material should be worked wet at slow speed and with fine wheels or laps. It is heat sensitive and brittle.

WITHERITE
Barium carbonate
H. 3–3½   D. 4.29
Orthorhombic

Yellow and greenish colorless, translucent witherite has been cut into cabochons and a few faceted stones. The fluorite district of southern Illinois and neighboring Kentucky has produced large crystals of witherite in the past. Massive material occurs as well as prismatic and tabular crystals. Witherite is a low-temperature mineral occurring in hydrothermal vein deposits. Some coarsely fibrous material cuts interesting cabochons, especially if the material has a green or yellow tint.

Witherite is also found in California, Arizona, Montana, and New York. Other localities for witherite are Canada, England, Germany, Czechoslovakia, and Japan. The yellow crystals from near Rosiclare, Illinois, have been faceted into small translucent stones up to about 5 carats and sometimes near the size of Grant's 12.90-carat stone.

Witherite is brittle and has distinct cleavage in one direction. Illinois cutters say cabochons present no difficulty when worked wet on fine wheels. Long narrow stones look the best. Faceted stones are difficult to polish and require slow speed.

WULFENITE
Lead molybdate
H. 2½–3   D. 6.50
Pleochroic   Tetragonal

Wulfenite is such a bright and lively mineral that it would be a leading gem if only it were harder and available in larger crystals. The intense yellows, oranges, and reds and the excellent refraction and dispersion are not offset by the thin crystals, the heat sensitivity, and the brittleness. Nevertheless, some beautiful stones, up to 50 carats, have been faceted for the determined collector, from material from Tsumeb, Namibia, and Mexico. Stones from Namibia are light yellow. Smaller stones have been faceted from the incredibly vivid red-orange crystals from the Red Cloud Mine of Arizona. Most collectors' stones are only a carat or two. The Arizona Sonora Desert Museum in Tucson has three faceted Arizona wulfenites in the 2-carat range. Cuttable crystals also come from the Old Yuma and Seventy-nine mines.

Wulfenite occurs as a secondary mineral in oxidation zones of ore deposits with such minerals as cerussite, vanadinite, mimetite, and pyromorphite. In addition to the Mexican and Arizona localities, wulfenite crystals of cutting quality come from Czechoslovakia, Algeria, Morocco, Iran, and Australia.

Wulfenite is a challenge to lapidaries and a goal of collectors. Cutters cold dop wulfenite and shape it on ultrafine laps, using chrome oxide as a polish.

ZECTZERITE
Lithium sodium silicate
H. 6   D. 2.79
Orthorhombic

Tabular crystals of colorless zectzerite have been found in granite in Okanogan County, Washington. A few crystals are light pink. Crystals are small with pearly luster. Most are translucent. To date, cavities in the granite of the Golden Horn batholith are the only source of this mineral that was discovered only a few years ago.

The cleavage is perfect in two directions and the mineral is fluorescent. Cut stones

are great rarities for collectors. Art Grant reports cutting a 1.25-carat gem. Grant cold dops sensitive stones with Five Minute epoxy.

ZEOLITES

Analcime
Sodium aluminum silicate
H. 5–5½   D. 2.22
Cubic

Analcime is a common zeolite found in cavities in basic igneous rock. Small facetable specimens are rare, so few cut stones exceed 1 or 2 carats. The pastel colors are pink, blue-green, violet, white, and colorless. The luster is vitreous and crystals are doubly refractive.

There are several locations in the United States for fine crystals. Among them are California, Oregon, Washington, and upper Michigan. An excellent locality is Mont Ste. Hilaire, Quebec, Canada, where large crystals have furnished both faceted stones and cabochons, mostly for collectors. Analcime is also found in Iceland, Norway, Italy, Germany, Czechoslovakia, and Australia. The massive material from Australia is used for cabochons.

Analcime is brittle, but does not have a cleavage problem. The most interesting cabochons are from analcime crystals intergrown with orange serandite from Mont Ste. Hilaire.

Mesolite
Sodium calcium aluminum silicate
H. 5   D. 2.26
Monoclinic

Mesolite is a zeolite found in cavities in igneous rock as slender white or colorless crystals in radiating clusters. Compact fibrous material also occurs.

In the United States, the best-known localities are in the zeolite-rich areas of California, Washington, and Oregon. Small cat's-eye cabochons have been cut from some of the other localities that include Colorado and Pennsylvania. Other countries with mesolite are Canada, Iceland, Greenland, Scotland, Italy, Sicily, India, and Australia.

Mesolite is brittle and the closely packed fibers make uneven ends. Faceted stones are narrow because crystals are long and slender. Cabochons are shaped and sanded on fine wheels and kept cool because of high heat sensitivity.

Natrolite
Sodium aluminum silicate
H. 5　　　　D. 2.22
Orthorhombic

Facetable colorless prismatic crystals of natrolite have been found in basalt in New Jersey. Collectors' stones have been faceted up to the 20-carat range. Facetable crystals also are found in California and Montana. British Columbia has facetable crystals. Other locations are Norway, Greenland, Scotland, Germany, France, South Africa, and India. Natrolite is one of the constituents of maw-sit-sit, a jade-like rock from Burma.

Extremely heat sensitive, natrolite is worked wet. It is brittle and has perfect cleavage that is easily developed. For faceting, it should be cold dopped.

Pollucite
Cesium aluminosilicate
H. 6½–7　　　D. 2.93
Isometric

With a better hardness than many zeolites, pollucite is white, gray, yellow, blue, violet, pink, or colorless. Found in small crys-

tals or massive form in granite pegmatites, material suitable for cabochons is compact and fine grained, while transparent facet quality is rare. Faceted stones are less than 10 carats, but cabochons can be as large as 20 x 30 mm. Small masses and facetable crystals are collected at the Emmons quarry in Maine. White and cream-colored masses suitable for cabochons are found at Tin Mountain, Custer County, South Dakota. Facetable colorless material has come from Connecticut. Massive lilac-colored material has come from Sweden and Finland.

Cleavage and heat sensitivity pose no problems for cutters. Cerium oxide on leather or felt will bring a satisfactory polish.

ZINCITE
Zinc oxide
H. 4–4½　　　D. 5.68
Hexagonal

Transparent red crystals of zincite colored by manganese from the noted zinc ores of Franklin, New Jersey, have been used for small faceted stones and also a few cabochons. At the 1991 Tucson show, however, some brilliant dark greenish-yellow and orange zincite crystals from Poland were shown. Art Grant cut an orange zincite weighing 83.04 carats and a yellow-green one of 87.03 carats. With high refraction, the stones are sensational. A 20.05-carat stone, cut from Franklin material by John Sinkankas, is in the Smithsonian. Other zincite localities are Colorado, Namibia, Spain, Italy, and Tasmania.

Zincite has perfect cleavage but it is not easily developed. It is used only as a collectors' stone because of scarcity and low hardness. Linde A on tin yields a good polish.

Fluorescent cabochons have been cut from Franklin calcite with inclusions of blackish-red franklinite, green willemite, and brownish-red granules of zincite. Franklin's mixed fluorescents are also used for carvings and novelties, such as eggs, spheres, and fluorescent pictures.

ADDITIONAL MINERALS THAT HAVE BEEN CUT

There are probably numerous other minerals that lapidaries have experimented with, perhaps resulting in a successful stone or two. Such stones will continue to come to the attention of collectors, jewelers, and the gem media as long as new minerals (and rocks) come to light.

Recently Sy and Ann Frazier bought some polished gemstone eggs cut in Germany from Algerian *mansfieldite*, a member of the variscite group. Gray-green in color, the eggs have a dark spiderweb pattern. This is the first known use of this arsenate as a lapidary material.

A periwinkle blue opaque mineral related to *crandallite* has been imported from China. Bluer than turquoise, it too has a spiderweb pattern. Only a small quantity is stable enough for cabochons, but the rest may be stabilized.

Light brown *zunyite* crystals from Arizona have been faceted. *Pinite*, a chromium green mica, has been examined in the form of a bead sold as jade. Another cuttable mica is purplish-red *paragonite* from Brazil.

Rare materials continue to come from Mont Ste Hilaire, Canada. A 5-carat *villiaumite* was recently reported as well as a 1.22-carat *leifite*. *Gadolinite*, a matamict material from Norway, has yielded large green cabochons.

Here are some more rare stones, some of record size for the material, cut by Art Grant.

Bastnasite 3.65
Cobaltocalcite 18.28
Cryolite 1.75
Ettringite 1.0
Ezcurrite 2.45
Hodgkinsonite .98
Hornblende 3.03
Inderborite 2.53
Mooreite 0.14
Nahcolite .32
Nambulite .58
Powellite 6.41
Probertite 2.00
Pyrargyrite 13.20
Pyrrhotite 32.71
Remondite 3.18
Samarskite 10.57
Sellaite 5.30
Senarmontite 4.67
Serandite 5.41
Shortite 2.37
Struvite 0.90
Vlasovite 1.41
Wollastonite 4.05

RECOMMENDED READING

Arem, J., Color *Encyclopedia of Gemstones*, 2d ed. New York: Van Nostrand Reinhold, 1987.

Bancroft, P., *Gem and Crystal Treasures*. Fallbrook, CA: Western Enterprises, 1984.

O'Donaghue, M., *Gemstones*. London: Chapman & Hall, 1988.

Palache, C., et al., *The Systems of Mineralogy*. New York: Wiley, 1963.

Panczner, W., *Minerals of Mexico*. New York: Van Nostrand Reinhold, 1987.

Schumann, W., *Gemstones of the World*. New York: Sterling, 1977.

Sinkankas, J., *Gem Cutting: A Lapidary's Manual*. New York: Van Nostrand Reinhold, 1984.

Tschernich, R., *Zeolites of the World*. Phoenix: Geoscience Press, 1992.

Vargas, G., and Vargas, M., *Faceting for Amateurs*. Thermal, CA: Private, 1990.

Webster, R., *Gems*, 5th ed. London: Butterworth-Heinemann, 1994.

CHAPTER XV

Gem Materials from the Laboratory and Factory

Synthetic Faceting Materials	Garnet
Beryl	Rutile
Corundum	Strontium Titanate
Chrysoberyl	Silicon Carbide
Diamond	**Simulants and Imitations**
Quartz	Amber
Spinel	Coral
Synthetic Cabochon Materials	Emerald
Coral	Glass and Steel Simulants
Jadeite	Jade
Lapis Lazuli	Jet
Malachite	Lapis Lazuli
Opal	Opal
Turquoise	Quartz
Synthetic Laboratory Originals	Turquoise
Cubic Zirconia	Victoria Stone

THERE IS AN ONGOING CONTROVERSY about synthetic and laboratory grown gem materials. The trouble on the part of the public is misinformation and misunderstanding. Many people think that synthetic, such as ruby boule, is the same as imitation, such as a piece of red glass. They fear that the word synthetic denotes something of little or no value. While some dealers sell attractive birthstone rings set with man-made stones without ever mentioning the word synthetic, others refuse to even stock man-made stones.

One person may brag, "My emerald is better than hers because it came from a mine," but the hidden meaning of such a statement may be, "I can afford a mined emerald and she can't." So "mined" or "natural" to the fashion world may be little more than a status symbol.

If people could be properly educated about man-made stones, they would know that the gemologist's definition means that the stone has been developed in a laboratory by humans, to duplicate the chemical and physical properties of the natural mined gem. Synthetic does not mean a stone is inferior, or fake, or cheap. In fact, a synthetic emerald is likely to have far less inclusions and better color than the average natural emerald, and a luxury synthetic ruby is far more valuable than a poor-quality mined ruby.

The chief quality of a gemstone is beauty, and the chief attribute of beauty in most cases is color. In these respects, synthetics may rival even high-quality natural stones. The purpose of jewelry is to decorate, enhance, or accessorize, so to the fashion world it should make little difference as to the source of the stone as long as it is beautiful and durable.

There is a difference between synthetic and man-made stones in some cases. While a synthetic has the chemical and physical qualities of the natural material, some man-made stones have no parallel in nature. However, they are still not the same as an imitation, which may be glass, ceramic, or plastic. Many laboratory stones are carefully made to bring out the qualities the inventor dreams about: superior color change, higher dispersion, less heat sensitivity, larger pieces, greater clarity. So these man-made stones, too, are excellent products.

What bothers many people is the fear of fraud or of paying too high a price for a manufactured material. Dealers, of course, know how the public feels, and want to find some way to break the news gently that a much admired stone did not come from the ground. An example of a man-made stone that has made good is *cubic zirconia*. This diamond substitute, or simulant, is seen in all kinds of jewelry in department stores, gift shops, gem shows, and even in jewelry stores. It is openly called CZ, cubic zirconia, or by some trade name, but the public knows it is not mined and accepts it.

It will probably be some time, however, before the public understands synthetic and laboratory gems, because gemologists do not even agree among themselves exactly what the nomenclature should be. Some feel that the term *homocreate* (man-made) should be used for a synthetic replicating nature. This would make laboratory gems, such as YAG and CZ, for which there is no natural counterpart, the true synthetics. To the public, it adds to the confusion, since people are only beginning to understand that synthetic is not synonymous with ersatz, fake, or imitation. The word *created* has also been used for fine laboratory gems.

Synthetic stones are not something that just happened over night, although we hear more about them all the time. Man has been trying to imitate or duplicate nature's gems for over 5,000 years. An early substitution was the faience of the pharaohs of Egypt and later the bright enamels of seventh-century Europe. Among some of the successful look-alikes have been paste, goldstone, vulcanite, Wedgewood's jasper, bakelite, and a strange nineteenth-century material called Gutta Percha.

The first true synthetic gem did not appear until the early twentieth century when Auguste Verneuil of France produced rubies in his laboratory. The technique he developed was called *flame fusion*. Preliminary work on this process occurred when Verneuil worked under Dr. Edmund Fremy in the late nineteenth century.

There are four principal methods of synthesizing gem materials with some variations of each, and constant improvements to equipment and technique.

1. *Flame fusion.* The powdered chemical elements present in the original gem material are sprinkled onto a flame, melting the constituents at high temperature to settle on a seed crystal to recrystallize. This was the method used for early synthetic corundum. It is also called the *Verneuil* method or technique.
2. *Hydrothermal.* A melt occurs in water containing a seed plate. Crystals form slowly as the superheated water cools. Quartz and emerald commonly use this technique, which is said to be close to natural growth.
3. *Flux grown.* The chemical elements of the original gem material are dissolved in a platinum crucible with compounds added as solvents. Emerald, alexandrite, and ruby have been grown this way. The flux synthetic ruby development was spurred by the need for optical-quality corundum for lasers.
4. *Czochralski pulled.* A small seed crystal on a rotating rod is lowered into a crucible containing a chemical melt and slowly pulled away from the melt after the initial touch. The melt crystallizes on the seed as it is removed. This technique is capable of producing very large crystals. It has been used for YAG, GGG, and a variation, known as *skull melting*, is used for CZ.

The flame fusion and Czochralski techniques are faster and less expensive in the production of laboratory gems, while the slower and more expensive methods are sometimes called "luxury" synthetics.

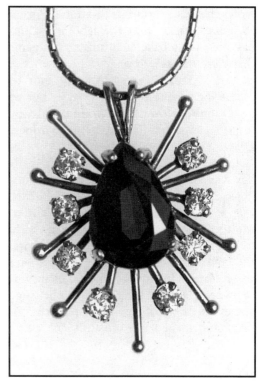

High-quality laboratory gems are faceted for fine jewelry. Shown is a Kashan ruby (9 × 13 mm) set in yellow gold.

Research on synthetics must continue. Synthetic minerals and gemstones have many purposes. They are useful in industry, beautiful and affordable for lapidaries and artists, and can be used for acceptable duplicates of irreplaceable jewels. Synthetic research is teaching us a great deal about the processes of nature.

Laboratory gems are also very important to the economy of some countries. For example, Dr. Aris Mallas says that the production of synthetic gems is Russia's top export business, surpassing even gold and oil. The Russians have produced excellent emeralds, sapphires, amethyst, and other gems and may market as many as 10 million carats a year of high-quality synthetics.

Dr. Mallas, a principal importer and distributor of natural and synthetic gems, writes that the present generation has tried to replicate nature in the laboratory and has met the challenge, producing gems that rival nature's own. "It is up to the next generation," warns Mallas, "not to repeat the technology of the past, but to try to improve on nature, for example, by growing large bright blue gems, hardness 10, with no cleavage problems."

In the future man-made gem technology will continue to grow, and as the public learns more about laboratory gems, they will gain prestige. San Diego cutter, Martin Cademy, thinks synthetics are ideal for amateurs. The cost is low to moderate, the color choices are almost endless, and there are few fractures or heavy inclusions to worry about. The entire challenge comes in developing new patterns or becoming adept at the most difficult cuts.

SYNTHETIC FACETING MATERIALS
Beryl

Emerald

Biron

The Biron emerald was originally called the Pool emerald for a mine of the same name in western Australia. It is a hydrothermally grown emerald, and at least some of the beryl is said to come from the Pool Mine. The stones are clean and have high clarity and a bright bluish-green color. Inclusions of gold have been noted as well as "fingerprints," "comet tails," liquids, gas, and phenakite. The name has recently been changed to Kimberley-Created Emerald, and the stones are faceted for jewelry.

Chatham

Carroll Chatham of San Francisco, California, startled the gem world in the mid-1940s by producing high-quality facetable emerald crystals in his laboratory. He had worked on the project since high school and was still in college when he entered the gem market.

In color, the Chatham crystals are similar to those of Muzo, Colombia, but they do not contain as many inclusions as the natural stones. Chatham Created Gems, Inc., has crystals and crystal clusters.

Before the Chatham emerald, experiments at IG Farben in Germany had resulted in a laboratory emerald after 31 years of work. Called Igmerald, little was ever revealed about these stones until 1960.

Gilson

Pierre Gilson's Created Emeralds made an impact on the market in the 1960s. The Gilson flux process uses nongem-quality natural beryl crystals, which are melted at high temperature and recrystallized on seeds. Less fragile than natural emeralds of similar color and quality, the Gilson emerald costs only one tenth of the price. Crystal clusters are marketed, but larger single crystals are all cut on automated machines before distribution. The Japanese Nakazumi Company now produces Gilson synthetics.

Inamori

Kyocera's emeralds are medium green and flux grown. Inclusions are described as resembling icicles and globules. On occasion, the natural seed crystal can be seen.

Lechleitner

The Lechleitner emerald is color zoned hydrothermal beryl. A thin layer of medium green emerald, slightly muted in intensity, is deposited on nongem-quality beryl. The material makes impressive cabochons after being lightly polished on the top surfaces. Step cut coated faceted stones have been said to crack easily.

Lennix

This rich green, flux synthetic emerald is grown in Cannes, France. It closely resembles the emerald of Africa with gemological properties like natural emerald except for a lower refractive index and lower density. It is now being marketed by a Canadian company. The tabular crystals are transparent to translucent, showing wispy veil inclusions, tubelike inclusions, and acicular crystals, sometimes resulting in a jardin reminiscent of natural stones.

Linde (Regency)

This hydrothermally grown emerald became a product of Vacuum Ventures of New Jersey and California after they bought the Linde emerald equipment and process in 1978 and acquired the Linde license.

Pleochroic, with a rich blue-green color, the Linde stones were colored by chromium and were marketed for about 10 years without much success. Renamed Regency Created Emerald by Vacuum Ventures, crystals and preforms soon caught on with creative faceters. The Regency process has recently been sold to Levix of New York City.

Magnification of these emeralds shows straight, uniform parallel growth, some metal inclusions, and a wavy zoning. The clarity is good and the color is a saturated green. Crystals weighing many grams have been grown.

Overgrowth Emeraldolite

This laboratory material, similar to flux-grown emeralds, is a synthetic emerald layer coating natural white beryl. Unlike

Crystals of synthetic gems are used in one-of-a-kind contemporary jewelry. This is a super-rare Kashan ruby rosette.

the Chatham or Gilson emerald, the Emeraldolite is not transparent, so it is used for cabochons. The emerald layer is only about 1 millimeter, so this material is grown more rapidly than the transparent flux-grown emeralds. The overgrowth technique can be used on preformed beryl cabochons, but the layer will show a stair step appearance even after polishing. Small crystals coated with emerald are sometimes used "as is" for jewelry.

Russian Synthetic Emerald

Russia is certainly one of the foremost producers of high-quality synthetic gemstones. In the 1980s, they introduced a flux-grown emerald that was distributed for several years. Then in the latter 1980s, they produced a sensational hydrothermally grown emerald of the most remarkable color and clarity, very similar to the highest-quality natural emeralds. The process may be a new variation of the hydrothermal technique.

Other Beryls

Russia also markets blue beryl, aquamarine, and morganite or peach-colored beryl. Their aquamarine is an excellent blue, colored by iron, as is natural aquamarine. They also have a blue beryl colored by copper and a yellowish-green beryl colored by nickel. Of course, any laboratory that can grow excellent emerald can also grow the less expensive beryls, and since emeralds are so much more profitable than other beryls, the research for other beryls is not as concentrated.

Synthetic pink beryl is also made by Regency. A company called ANICS has produced a fascinating red and green watermelon beryl, and also a red beryl similar to that from Utah.

Corundum

Ruby

Chatham

The Chatham Created Ruby is a medium dark red or red with a hint of violet. Its physical and optical qualities are much the same as natural ruby. Transparent crystals are flux grown. Color zoning is irregularly swirled and resembles some of the natural rubies from Burma. Rough has been available to professional cutters who have produced large and elegant stones. Chatham began marketing ruby crystals in 1959, the first successful flux-grown synthetic rubies. Superb crystals have been used uncut for innovative modern jewelry.

Douros

A newcomer among synthetic rubies is being produced by a Greek laboratory. The owners, John and Angelos Douros, are growing deep red crystals by the flux method. The crystals are described as color zoned with darker cores and nearly colorless edges.

Kashan

So excellent are the Kashan laboratory rubies that professional gemologist and cutter, James Semmes, Jr., said that he would recommend them to be purchased in lieu of most commercial-grade corundum. He states that he examined a suite of Kashan stones and found them to rival the finest Asian rubies.

Kashan rubies are flux-grown from seed in a platinum crucible. The process takes several months, using aluminum oxide and sophisticated equipment and technique. Flawless stones have been cut. The color spread is remarkable with dozens and dozens of tints and shades of red including rich pink, rose, rose-red, crimson, purplish red, fuschia, orangy red, coral-red, cerise, magenta, and more. Only the Kashan has duplicated the color of the rare Macedonian ruby. When these rubies, perfected by Dr. Truehart Brown, first appeared on the market, well-trained jewelers mistook them for natural. Dr. Bob Mallas notes that jewelers were soon provided with determinative information. A small amount of material was made available to cutters and at least one dealer sells some rough from time to time. Kashans are no longer being made, but cut stones are sometimes available from Bennett-Walls, gemstone specialists.

Knischka

Professor P. O. Knischka, of Steyr, Austria, produces exotic ruby crystals that have yielded faceted stones of 67 carats. The crystals are noted for their multiple faces. The material is marketed as faceted stones, preforms, and as rough crystals and clusters.

The colors are close to the Burma or Thai stones and the materials are graded for quality. Cutters can hope to facet stones over 10 carats. These rubies are flux-grown and were brought to the gem market in the 1980s, introduced by Dr. Edwin Gubelin.

Kyocera

Japan has been active in producing man-made gems. Inamori, a division of the Kyocera company of Japan, has produced highly convincing star corundum with slightly imperfect stars and a natural-appearing purplish-red color, very close to nature's own. GIA reports that they are not flame fusion, but are probably crystallized from a high-temperature melt. Marketed as rough or oval cabochons, the stones are remarkably translucent.

Lechleitner

A recent addition to ruby synthetics is the product of the Lechleitner laboratory of Austria. Purplish-red rubies with wispy veils led gemologists to conclude that the rubies are flux-grown.

Lechleitner also uses its overgrowth process to deposit a layer of gem-quality corundum over common natural corundum, or over the flame fusion corundum, which is less expensive to grow than flux synthetics.

The rubies are pleochroic with a good purple-red color and are transparent with some cloudy areas. The Lechleitner process, that which combines the flux-grown and Verneuil techniques, has a combination of distinctive inclusions—veils, bubbles, and grains of flux.

Ramaura

It is seldom a woman is credited with either mining or developing a gemstone. Judith Osmer of California is the exception.

Osmer has been successful with her flux-grown ruby crystals of red, orangy red, and purplish red. The crystals are transparent, clear, and aesthetic. Faceted stones looked so much like the real thing that GIA asked Osmer to dope the Ramaura Created Ruby, as she called her product, so it would be easier for jewelers to identify. She complied by making her stones fluoresce yellow under ultraviolet light. Customer reaction to this tagging was poor when it was disclosed. Gemologists have said their first clue that a stone is a Ramaura rather than an Oriental ruby is that the cut is superior to a native cut stone.

Sapphire

Chatham

The Chatham sapphires are flux-grown transparent crystals, color zoned from nearly colorless to dark rich blue. The physical and optical qualities are the same as fine natural sapphires. Under magnification, meshlike patterns and platinum can be observed.

The Chatham Created blue sapphire is popular because the excellent blue color is better than many of the Oriental blue stones now on the market. Chatham also makes orange-colored synthetic *padparadscha*, a rare color for mined sapphires. The Chatham crystals appeared in the late 1980s.

Lechleitner

Johann Lechleitner of Innsbruck, Austria, produces blue and orange sapphires in his flux-grown process, or in the flux–flame fusion combination. The blue is strongly pleochroic. Inclusions are fingerprints and veils. There are also curved growth lines in the Verneuil type. Lechleitner also produces a pink sapphire overgrowth over colorless corundum.

Linde

Linde "stars" were grown in the United States from 1947 to 1973, using the Verneuil flame fusion technique. They manufactured both boules and rods in many colors of synthetic corundum. Later, the Linde Air Products Company, then a division of Union Carbide, switched its corundum-growing process to the newer Czochralski pulling.

A wide range of colors in the star stones was available, including pink, lavender, red, yellow, green, blue, and brown. Dramatic stones with splendid stars were cut by orienting the optic axis perpendicular to the base of the cabochon.

Linde promoted its star corundum at gem shows with items such as a sapphire-encrusted dress and a sapphire castle. Titanium oxide in the feed powder provided the silk in the boules, which would have been transparent if the titanium needles were not present.

Calibrated star cabochons were produced by automated machines. Over 2 million carats of star stones were cut until production ceased in 1973. Since then, the Heller Hope stars and others have filled the gap in man-made star stones.

Chrysoberyl

Alexandrite and Catseye

There are at least four countries and seven companies worldwide using variations of the four methods of producing synthetics to grow two types of chrysoberyl. They are attempting to reproduce the beauty and magice of the color-change alexandrite used for faceted stones and the splendid catseye chrysoberyl used for cabochons.

The Russian product, grown by the Czochralski method, is particularly fine, which is appropriate since the first alexandrites with the distinctive red/green color change were mined there. Russia has also used the flux-grown method successfully. Czechoslovakia has perfected the hydrothermal techniques for its synthetic crystals. Their color-change alexandrite is excellent.

Several companies in Japan are marketing synthetic chrysoberyl. Kyocera produces large alexandrite crystals using the Czochralski melt. They market faceted stones and also catseye chrysoberyl under the Inamori name. The chatoyancy of synthetic catseyes is brought about by heat treatment after the crystals are grown. Seiko uses the Verneuil technique for its chrysoberyl. Sumitomo Electric Industries also produces catseye stones.

Growing crystals by the flux technique, Creative Crystals of San Ramon, California, is marketing a color-change alexandrite. Another U.S. company, Litton Airtron, is using the Czochralski method. There is also an imitation cat's-eye chrysoberyl made of fiber optics by Galileo. Called "Catseyte," the stone has strong phenomenal properties.

The first so-called synthetic alexandrites were not alexandrite at all, but synthetic spinel or corundum made with a color change which bore little resemblance to the genuine stione. Nevertheless, tens of thousands of these stones were sold in jewelry to unsuspecting tourists.

Diamond

Just as alchemists dreamed of creating gold in the laboratory, people have dreamed of producing gem-quality diamonds. There were several false claims before true synthetic diamonds were achieved, with intense work being conducted in several countries over many years. The credit for the first laboratory diamond goes to General Electric Company Research Laboratories of the United States, with their memorable announcement of a breakthrough in 1955.

The General Electric diamonds are crystallized carbon, high in quality, with a hardness of 10. However, they were produced for industry, not for jewelry. Since then, synthetic diamond has revolutionized most industrial processes. General Electric's first products are in the Smithsonian. Recently, gem-quality "carbon-13" diamonds have been produced by General Electric.

Several other countries and corporations now make synthetic diamond; even the DeBeers diamond cartel has entered the synthetic diamond business and recently announced the growth of a 14.2-carat yellow diamond that took 500 hours to produce.

Sumitomo Electric Industries produces gem-quality yellow diamond crystals. The faceted stones resemble natural yellow diamonds. A technology now being tried is the growth of diamond and diamondlike films over other materials, natural or synthetic.

The Russians also produce synthetic diamond in quantity. They have not claimed gem-quality synthetics in the past, but there was a persistent rumor that an impossible number of high-quality diamonds have been exported. More may be learned as political changes pave the way for better communication. Russia now says their laboratory has grown 2 kilograms of clear synthetic diamond for laser use. A Russian laboratory now has a contract with Chatham for the marketing of gem-quality synthetic diamonds.

Quartz

Several color varieties of fine synthetic quartz are used by lapidaries, and in many cases with more elegant results than the natural crystals. Amethyst, citrine, smoky quartz, blue quartz, and green quartz are among the lapidary choices. The amethyst and cobalt blue material from Russia have been exceptionally popular. Thousands of February Aquarians may be wearing synthetic amethyst without knowing it. Korea is said to be exporting large quantities of synthetic amethyst at present.

Colored quartz gems are also manufactured in Japan. The need for synthetic quartz was demonstrated during World War II when advanced technologies demanded clean, uniform, easy-to-use crystals.

Bell Labs of the United States perfected hydrothermally grown transparent quartz crystals using crushed natural crystalline quartz as feed. Excellent-quality crystals were grown in autoclaves using Brazilian seed crystals. An exceptionally large crystal weighed 40 pounds. Hydrothermal quartz is difficult to detect, since it is close to

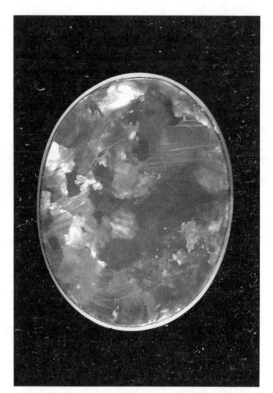

Gilson synthetic opal is both durable and beautiful.

Spinel

Doped with various elements to produce an artist's palette of colors, synthetic spinel was an early success for laboratory gems. Grown by the Verneuil method, the boules were red, pink, blue, blue-green, green, yellow, lavender, and orange. Colorless synthetic spinel was an early diamond substitute. Commercial producers manufactured 30 colors or more. Some of the colors were marketed as aquamarine-colored spinel, peridot-colored spinel, and other gem names. Trade names were Berylite, Emerada, Perigem, and Aquagem. The colors did not bear a very close resemblance to the natural gems, however, being too even, uniform, and intense.

Four-rayed star spinel and cat's-eye spinel were also developed, but found too much competition on the market. Another spinel had better success because it imitated alexandrite, a stone so little known by the public that many people thought they were getting natural alexandrite instead of an alexandrite-like spinel.

Another synthetic spinel was a lapis lazuli imitation with real gold substituting for "fool's gold" pyrite. Colorless synthetic spinel has also been used in doublets.

natural quartz in all respects. The largest producer of commercial-quality synthetic quartz is now Brush Wellman, Inc., of East Lake, Ohio.

Lapidaries like the synthetic amethyst and citrine because the colors are splendid, the flaws are few, and there is little waste. They also like the cobalt blue because this color is so rare in natural gemstones. Synthetic colorless quartz is used for doublets and triplets for opal and other delicate materials. Faceters have used synthetic quartz to create replicas of the world's most famous diamonds. Laboratory quartz can be cut and polished the same as natural quartz. Automated machines are used for some commercial synthetic quartz gems since the material is so predictable.

SYNTHETIC CABOCHON MATERIALS

Gilson Created Coral

Gilson Created Coral is a calcium carbonate with a specific gravity of 2.6 and a hardness of 3.5. Dr. Kurt Nassau calls the material a *near* synthetic, but not a true synthetic, since it contains materials other than natural coral, which is an organic material. The coral comes in an exquisite array of colors: angel skin, rose, oxblood, and that specific tint between red and orange that has given its name to the decorator color, coral.

The texture of the coral is grainy, but uniform, and the material takes a wonderful polish. It is sold as natural material or as finished cabochons of many shapes, and as beads and finished jewelry. Large cabochons appear flawless and are popular for jewelry because of the colors.

Jadeite

Synthetic jadeite was reported by the General Electric Company of the United States. The chosen colors were the most popular colors of natural jade, green and lavender. Experiments also resulted in white and black. The jadeite has the toughness of natural jade and the composition of interlocking crystals. However, it lacks the translucency of the best jades, for example, the imperial jade of Burma.

High pressure plus high temperature were required for the synthesis and also for another experiment at reconstruction of crushed material. Chromium was used for the green hues and manganese for the violet. The greens are not as saturated as the best natural jade, but the violets are more intense and darker than most lavender jade.

Although the General Electric experiments were deemed successful, the company has no intention, at present, of putting the material on the market. The Japanese are known to be working on a synthetic jadeite using a similar technique. To date, a Japanese company has marketed a glassy simulant of light green material, hardness 5½, which some have misleadingly called Siberian jade.

Lapis Lazuli

High-quality lapis lazuli is among the most desired and costly of the opaque gem materials, so it was natural to attempt to synthesize it. Thus far, only the Gilson laboratories have come up with a quality synthetic. Called Gilson Created Lapis Lazuli, the vivid blue to purplish blue can be had with or without pyrite inclusions.

High-quality lapis lazuli is a combination of several minerals, principally lazurite, and the Gilson lapis lazuli is very similar except that it is more porous and has a lower density. The best grade of natural lapis lazuli is subtranslucent while Gilson's is not. Large pieces make splendid cabochons for pendants, bracelets, earrings, and rings. Gilson lapis lazuli has been used for elegant small carvings.

Malachite

Gem-grade synthetic malachite is being manufactured in Russia where some of the largest deposits of high-quality natural malachite have been located. In most ways, the synthetic is identical to the natural. The banded green material looks like the natural product of Zaire. Spherulitic aggregates of hairlike or platy crystals produce a wavy banded texture. Typical eyelike patterns of malachite with silky chatoyance add to natural appearance.

Synthesized from an aqueous solution, the Russian material has the advantage for the cutter of being made in extremely large, compact, high-quality pieces. Botryoidal specimens are very attractive.

With contrasting light and dark greens, the highest-quality material has eyelike radial concentric patterns, referred to as *budlike*. This quality is being cut in Russia for jewelry. Carvings are also being made of the handsome material.

Opal

The Gilson Opal is the product of inter-molecular forces in hydrothermal suspensions of colloidal silica. It takes a year to produce the Gilson Created Opals with either black or blue-white ground colors, with flashes of pure hues of the spectrum. As in nature, every opal is different and many types of fire pattern can occur. Gilson Created Opals have pin fire, rolling flash fire, and rare harlequin patterns. Gilson has also replicated the Mexican fire opal.

These opals can be used for large cabochons, free-form shapes, beads, small carvings, and inlay. The price is about one-third that of natural opals of similar quality. Beads or pendants are the most spectacular use.

The spheres are closely controlled until they settle into a tightly packed uniform arrangement. Spaces between spheres must also be filled with a silica solution and the gel must harden without cracking, crazing, or losing its most valuable asset—those spectral colors.

The upper cabochon is synthetic quartz and the lower one is a jadelike material from Japan called Victoria Stone.

Pierre Gilson, Sr., began marketing his fine white opal in the mid-1970s. This was soon followed by the splendid black opal. Since then, the opal has been marketed as beads and cabochons. Gilson products are now being distributed by Japan.

An Australian company now has patents on synthetic opal. At one time the Australian company tried a soft plastic simulant but discontinued this research .

In the early 1980s the Inamori Division of Kycera introduced a synthetic opal with milky white body color or almost colorless highly translucent ground color similar to crystal opal. As in natural opal, the play of color varies widely.

Turquoise

Gilson has produced a beautiful blue synthetic turquoise similar in appearance to the best Persian turquoise. Both uniform blue and veined spiderweb material are available. The color is stable and the material is less porous and a little heavier than a lot of natural turquoise. The turquoise is produced from pure chemicals and not from inferior grades of turquoise.

Large flawless cabochons of Gilson turquoise are easily matched for jewelry that requires many cabochons. The large pieces are also excellent for carved pendants or small carvings. It has been reported that Russia now has a natural-appearing synthetic turquoise on the market.

SYNTHETIC LABORATORY ORIGINALS

Cubic Zirconia

The cubic form of zirconium oxide beat out all its antecedents as a diamond simulant for several reasons. It has a hardness of 8 to 8½;

the brilliance and fire make a convincing diamond simulant. It can be unusually pure, clean, and colorless, and can be produced in large quantities at a moderate cost.

The new technique for CZ, called *skull melting*, was developed in Russia. Ads for CZ rough began to appear in the *Lapidary Journal* and other magazines in the late 1970s, along with articles on how to cut it. Eminent jewelers as well as pawn shop operators were fooled by the new simulant and there was a rush to find ways to identify it, including the invention of several machines to verify true diamonds. Thermal conductivity of diamond is greater. Cubic zirconia is stabilized by variable percentages of yttrium oxide and several patents have been granted by other countries since the original Russian patent in 1972.

After the initial success with the colorless material, the market was dazzled with colored CZ—red, pink, lavender, blue, yellow, orange, and green. The colors are induced by cobalt, chromium, iron, manganese, copper, nickel, titanium, and other elements. Faceters get amazing results with CZ if it is cut in barion, trilliant, or other new generation cuts.

Among the names by which this manmade gem has been called are C-OX, Phianite, Diamonique, Diamonesque, Djevalite, and Diamonaire III. To most lapidaries it is just CZ.

The Ceres Corporation makes most of the CZ on the market and they also make the Diamond Probe, which will distinguish the real from the simulant.

Garnet

GGG (Gadolinium Gallium Garnet)

Synthetic garnet, used as a simulant for diamonds and colored stones, is gadolinium gallium garnet. Almost flawless material, very close to diamond in appearance, it failed to fill the diamond simulant market because of its hardness, which is only 7.

YAG (Yttrium Aluminum Garnet)

YAG was temporarily a prominent diamond simulant because of its hardness, which was superior to previous simulants. Pulled from a melt by the Czochralski technology, the synthetic garnets brought an end to the popularity of the more brilliant but less durable stones such as Titania and Fabulite. Many companies manufactured YAG and it was produced in a rainbow of colors. YAG stones were given many trade names, among them Gemonair, Linde Simulated Diamond, Replique, Triamond, Diamonique, and Di'Yag. Both YAG and GGG were more or less pushed out of the jewelry business by cubic zirconia, the reigning diamond simulant.

Rutile

For several years synthetic rutile was the diamond imitation of choice. It is a slightly yellowish transparent material of about 6½ in hardness, grown in boules that at that time were the diamond simulants most popular with amateur faceters. Marketed under the names of Titania, Kimberlite Gem, Kenya Gem, Kima Gem, and others, the stones were too brilliant to be realistic.

After its introduction, Titania became available in several intense colors that were faceted into sensational-appearing gems. Amateurs learned to change the color of the straw-colored Titania by heating it to shades and tints of blue and green.

Strontium Titanite

Strontium Titanite succeeded Titania in popularity as a diamond simulant. It did not have the yellow tint of Titania and was softer at 5, but somewhat tougher than Titania. Its refractive index of over 2.40 made it a convincing diamond look-alike. In addition to the colorless material, which had the greatest demand, there were other colors, such as blue, green, and yellow. Faceted stones were easily scratched when exposed to daily wear.

Some of the trade names for this material were Diamontina, Diagem, Dynagem, and Fabulite. Fabulite was the predecessor of synthetic garnet gemstones.

Silicon Carbide

Silicon carbide, the single most effective invention to cause the lapidary explosion of the mid-twentieth century, has also been used as a gem material. The 9½ hardness material developed as an industrial abrasive from inexpensive materials, such as sand and coke, and is grown as lustrous platy crystals, usually in shades of green and blue with a near metallic, highly iridescent appearance.

Small stones, with splendid dispersion, have been faceted. The crystals are thin, but their hardness, luster, and "fire" are exceptional.

SIMULANTS AND IMITATIONS

Amber

Amber is imitated by various resins, plastics, and sometimes glass. When celluloid beads were invented, beads were coated with melted amber. Composite material often has bits of amber or resin embedded in plastic. An early imitation amber was bakelite, a phenolic resin. It was used for jewelry, which has been handed down on occasion as heirloom amber. Polystyrene and other plastics have been made to simulate amber. Nonfossil resins are also true amber look-alikes. Copal and Kauri gum are miscalled amber.

The glass imitations are considerably heavier than natural amber. Even bakelite has greater density. (Bakelite will sink in saltwater while true amber will float.) A hot needle piercing amber smells like pine.

Besides plastic, glass, and other resins, natural amber has many treated versions for competition. For example, the amber may be melted and filled with exotic inclusions.

Coral

Coral imitations are made of glass, plastic, and dyed stone such as dolomite or marble. Imitation coral is used for beads, cabochons, pendants, and carvings.

Black plastic and glass have been used to simulate the handsome black coral of Hawaii. Recently some ceramic coral beads were marketed.

Emerald

Emerald look-alikes have been made of dyed beryl, beryl treated with green pigmented Opticon, or treated with green wax. A manufactured fluorite "emerald crystal" in matrix was examined by GIA. Emerald crystals have been fabricated from glass.

An Idar-Oberstein company sells emerald simulant triplets with the trade name *Smaryll*. The cabochons use clear Brazilian beryl for the cap, included Madagascar beryl for the base, and a layer of transparent green cement in between, according to the manufacturer, Kammerling. The faceted triplets have used synthetic spinel, rock crystal, and colorless beryl, also with green cement to provide color. Lapidaries experiment with green cement or green stones and colorless materials to make stones resembling emeralds. Emerald simulants have been made of quartz.

Glass and Steel Simulants

Alexandrium

A glassy lithium aluminum silicate of 6½ in hardness has a slight color change from blue to lavender and has been named to indicate a similarity to alexandrite. It has been used for faceted stones and cabochons.

Goldstone

Goldstone is an old and widely accepted imitation gemstone. It is glass with copper oxide, which has some similarities to natural aventurine sunstone. Goldstone has been manufactured so long that it has many legends and myths attached to it. It was said to have been discovered by Italian monks, and there are stories that a monastery in Europe still makes it. Tons of it have been exported from Czechoslovakia in the rough and as cut stones or finished souvenir-type jewelry.

A midnight blue variety is also available. Goldstone was very popular at the turn of the century and was often set in good gold mountings, so many heirs assume the sets are genuine gemstones. The spangled glass remains so much admired that there is now an imitation goldstone made of plastic.

Like all glass imitations, goldstone is brittle and heat sensitive and must be kept cool while grinding and sanding. Cerium oxide on leather will polish it.

Helenite

After the eruption of Mount St. Helens, Washington, in 1980, faceted stones, cabochons, and rough material began appearing on the market variously called Helenite, St. Helen's Emerald, Emerald Obsidianite, and Obsidianite. The green glass was purportedly made from Mt. St. Helens ash. High in silica, amorphous, and about 5 in hardness, the material was found to contain quartz, feldspar, and calcite.

Helenite did not actually contain much, if any, St. Helens ash, except possibly at first. Kurt Nassau, authority on manufactured gem materials, estimated after extensive testing that the actual amount of ash was probably less than 10 percent. The material was easy to work and took a good polish, but scratched easily.

Hematine

A dark steel composition called hematine is used for a hematite simulant for inexpensive jewelry, not that hematite itself is very expensive. The material looks like hematite and is used for beads and cabochons for costume jewelry. There is also an imitation of the simulant made of lightweight, shiny, metallic-appearing plastic. The plastic material is used for curio shop and souvenir store jewelry in the bottom price brackets.

Laserblue

Laserblue is a blue borosilicate glass, colored by copper. It comes in saturated tints and shades, often unbelievably bright. The more subdued tints may imitate blue sapphire. Laserblue has been used to simulate faceted lapis lazuli beads that are spectacular. About 6½ in hardness, this stone should be handled like glass.

Jade

White quartzite has been dyed to imitate jadeite. The colors may be similar to imperial jade or lavender jade, but in the case of beads, the dyed material may be spotted rather easily because every bead is a duplicate of the next.

Some new imitation lavender jade beads from the Orient have been found to be round glass shells filled with dyed lavender-orchid wax that rapidly fades.

Jade with pale grayish undesirable colors is dyed, or bleached and dyed, to make it look like a higher-grade material. Many green materials have had their color intensified to pass as jade. Customers should beware of a color that looks too good for its price. Dyes have a tendency to collect at drill holes of beads and in fractures. A commercial acetone tissue will remove a small spot of dye.

Jade has been imitated by plastic, glass, and ceramics. The Japanese Iimori stone is a glass jade simulant. Jade imitations are used for beads, cabochons, rings, pendants, and decorative items. Work glass imitations the same as obsidian.

Jet

Black glass is a much used jet simulant. Another jet substitute is the hardened rubber called *vulcanite*. A more realistic imitation is anthracite coal. Plastics are now the most used jet look-alikes. Jet is light in weight, soft, and tough. Most of the imitations are heavier and also harder, but not as tough.

A lustrous asphalt has been used for jet carvings and beads. Called *albertite*, the material has some jetlike qualities. It has recently been used for fancy carved beads from the Orient, which lack the gleaming polish of jet.

Lapis Lazuli

Vivid cobalt blue synthetic spinel has been used to imitate lapis lazuli. This was produced in the 1950s when natural lapis was not as readily available on the market as at present. The intense blue color was complemented by flecks of gold that appeared similar to the pyrite inclusions of natural lapis lazuli. Another imitation, cobalt blue glass from India, was more opaque and had a hint of violet as well as white crystallites resembling calcite.

Several materials have been dyed with analine dye to imitate lapis lazuli. Blue-dyed jasper has been called Swiss Lapis. Recently, imitation lapis beads have been made from dyed howlite, magnesite, quartzite, marble, and dolomite. While the color is good on some of these imitations, particularly the dolomite, it is not always stable.

Natural lapis lazuli itself is subject to various treatments, including heat treating, dyeing, waxing with blue wax, and oiling. An acetone-treated tissue, available commercially, will test the materials for dye.

Opal

A plastic-appearing—and feeling—imitation opal was being sold as opalite at a Tucson show in the 1980s. The plastic opal had believable change of color because its spherical composition imitated natural opal. It was manufactured in Japan but was not a success .

Fragments of natural or synthetic opal have also been encased in glass for unconvincing look-alikes. Foil-backed plastic has been used in another faux opal. Small glass glycerin-filled balls with scraps of opal have also been used for jewelry.

Slocum Stone (Opal Essence)

This glass imitation opal was on the market for a few years and became popular among amateur lapidaries because it was colorful, easy to cut, available in large sizes, and inexpensive. It was manufactured by John Slocum of Rochester, Michigan. It was made with several base colors including some that were quite realistic and some that spelled "fake" even from a distance.

The best of the Slocum Stones, as they were first called, had white or black ground colors with bright metallic flecks of variegated colors layered in the stones similar to color patterns of true opal. The play of color, however, was dead. The color was there all right, but it stayed in one place instead of mysteriously moving and changing as in a natural opal. Bubbles and swirl marks, typical of glass, were inclusions. Large well-cut stones of selected material did create a sensation though, because, at first glance, or from a little distance, they resembled fine black opal. Recently some dealers have advertised it.

Quartz

Agates, jasper, and other quartzes have now found the sincerest flattery. They are being widely imitated. Imitation agates, carnelian, black onyx, red jasper, and other quartzes are seen in upscale department stores and discount stores as beads, pendants, pins, bracelets, and earrings. The fakes are made of plastic. Examination shows they must be made in several places. While they may look good from a little distance, a close look and the heft test are dead giveaways. In spite of the fact that in some cases the real stones would be in the same price range, the plastic imitations seem to catch on with costume jewelry purchasers.

There are also numerous glass imitations of such materials as carnelian or onyx, and of such crystalline quartzes as rose quartz, aventurine, tigereye, amethyst, and citrine. Ceramic beads have been given agatelike patterns or given a color resembling rose quartz or amethyst. Common soft stones have been dyed to resemble the more expensive quartzes.

Turquoise

There are several imitations of turquoise on the market, some of them available only as finished jewelry. Howlite, calcite, dolomite, and magnesite have been dyed to imitate fine turquoise. Very often, the colors are too intense and the dye job is too uniform to make really credible imitations. Some of the imitation turquoise claims to be ground-up dyed chalk turquoise treated with resin. The source of the material is inconsequential, since all that makes the material usable are the manufacturer's additions, substitutes, and techniques.

The Colbaugh Company of Kingman, Arizona, markets stabilized turquoise that it makes in blocks. Not really a synthetic or an imitation, the turquoise is hardened with resin. The better grades have good natural color. Colbaugh material resembles what the family used to get from its Kingman mines.

A company called Syntho Gems made a simulated turquoise with either a white or a black matrix. The colors were a little lighter than Persian blue. The claim was that the material was neither plastic nor dyed and treated chalk-turquoise. It has been sold to California lapidaries as preforms.

Victoria Stone

A man-made lapidary material, said to be in some respects similar to nephrite, Victoria Stone is tough and compact with a hardness of near 6 and a density of 3. It has fibrous inclusions and is heat sensitive and brittle. The outstanding characteristic of Victoria Stone is its chatoyancy, which produces shimmering fan-shaped or aurora borealis swirls as the light moves across the stone.

This gold pendant is set with two pieces of synthetic turquoise.

The glasslike substance, made by Iimori of Japan, comes in many colors, light and dark, bright and muted. The colors are usually more intense than those of natural materials. The most popular colors are red, purple, and blue-green. Select pieces, if carefully cut, will yield handsome optical effects. Two of the variations of Iimori Stone are fair jade imitations. Both are chatoyant and about 6 in hardness.

RECOMMENDED READING

Anderson, B., *Gem Testing*, 10th ed. London: Butterworths, 1990.

Arem, J., *Color Encyclopedia of Gemstones*, 2d ed. New York: Van Nostrand Reinhold, 1987.

Elwell, D., *Man-made Gemstones.* New York: Wiley, 1979.

Nassau, K., *Gems Made by Man.* Radnor, PA: Chilton, 1980.

Vargas, G., and Vargas, M., *Faceting for Amateurs.* Thermal, CA: Private, 1969.

APPENDIX A

Refractive Index (RI) and Dispersion (DP) of Gemstones

Gem	DP	RI	Gem	DP	RI
Actinolite	—	1.62	Bone	—	1.54
Adamite	—	1.74	Boracite	.024	1.66
Albite	—	1.54	Bowenite	—	1.56
Almandine	0.27	1.81	Brazilianite	.014	1.60
Amber	—	1.54	Bustamite	—	1.67
Amblygonite	—	1.58	Bytownite	—	1.57
Analcime	—	1.48	Calcite	.020	1.48
Anatase	.213	2.50	Cancrinite	.010	1.51
Andalusite	0.16	1.64	Cassiterite	.071	2.10
Andradite	0.57	1.88	Catapleite	—	1.62
Anglesite	0.44	1.88	Celestite	.014	1.62
Anhydrite	0.13	1.57	Ceruleite	—	1.60
Apatite	0.13	1.64	Cerussite	.055	2.07
Apophyllite	—	1.53	Chalcedony	—	1.53
Aragonite	—	1.68	Chambersite	—	1.73
Augelite	—	1.58	Charoite	—	1.55
Axinite	—	1.68	Childrenite	—	1.63
Azurite	—	1.83	Chlorastrolite	—	1.70
Bayldonite	—	1.97	Chondrodite	—	1.64
Barite	.016	1.63	Chrysoberyl	.015	1.75
Benitoite	.046	1.76	Clinohumite	—	1.63
Beryl	0.14	1.59	Clinozoisite	—	1.75
Beryllonite	.010	1.55	Colemanite	—	1.59
Boleite	—	2.03	Coral	—	1.65

Gem	DP	RI	Gem	DP	RI
Corundum	.018	1.76	Hauyne	—	1.49
Covellite	—	1.45	Hematite	—	3.00
Crocoite	—	2.40	Hemimorphite	—	1.62
Danburite	.017	1.63	Herderite	—	1.61
Datolite	.016	1.62	Horn	—	1.54
Demantoid	.057	1.88	Howlite	—	1.59
Diamond	.044	2.41	Huebernite	—	2.20
Diaspore	—	1.72	Idocrase	.019	1.71
Diopside	—	1.69	Inderite	—	1.49
Dioptase	.036	1.66	Iolite	.017	1.57
Dolomite	—	1.68	Ivory	—	1.53
Durangite	—	1.67	Jadeite	—	1.67
Dumortierite	—	1.68	Jeremjevite	—	1.64
Ekanite	—	1.60	Jet	—	1.64
Enstatite	—	1.65	Kammererite	—	1.59
Eosphorite	—	1.63	Korite (Ammolite)	—	1.67
Epidote	.019	1.75	Kornerupine	.018	1.67
Euclase	.016	1.66	Kyanite	.020	1.72
Eudialyte	—	1.63	Labradorite	.012	1.56
Euxenite	—	2.06	Lazulite	—	1.63
Fibrolite	.015	1.64	Lazurite	—	1.50
Fluorapatite	—	1.64	Legrandite	—	1.71
Fluorite	.007	1.43	Lepidolite	—	1.55
Friedelite	—	1.66	Leucite	.101	1.51
Gadolinite	—	1.78	Linarite	—	1.83
Gahnite	—	1.82	Ludlamite	—	1.65
Grandidierite	—	1.60	Magnesite	—	1.70
Grossular	.027	1.75	Malachite	—	1.67
Gypsum	.033	1.52	Manganotantalite	—	2.30
Hambergite	.015	1.58	Meerschaum	—	1.53

Gem	DP	RI	Gem	DP	RI
Mellite	—	1.51	Sapphirine	—	1.72
Mesolite	—	1.50	Scapolite	.017	1.56
Microcline	—	1.52	Scheelite	.038	1.92
Microlite	—	1.93	Scorodite	—	1.79
Mimetite	—	2.12	Serandite	—	1.68
Natrolite	—	1.48	Serpentine	—	1.55
Nepheline	—	1.54	Shattuckite	—	1.75
Nephrite	—	1.65	Siderite	—	1.87
Obsidian	.010	1.60	Smithsonite	.037	1.68
Odontolite	—	1.57	Sodalite	.018	1.48
Opal	—	1.45	Spessartine	.027	1.81
Orthoclase	.012	1.52	Sphalerite	.156	2.39
Parisite	—	1.70	Sphene	.051	1.99
Peridot	.020	1.67	Spinel	.020	1.72
Perthite	—	1.53	Spodumene	.017	1.67
Petalite	—	1.50	Spurrite	—	1.67
Phenakite	.005	1.66	Staurolite	.023	1.74
Phosgenite	—	2.10	Stichtite	—	1.54
Phosphophyllite	—	1.60	Strontianite	.028	1.60
Prehnite	—	1.63	Sugilite	—	1.61
Proustite	—	3.00	Taaffeite	.019	1.70
Purpurite	—	1.86	Talc	—	1.58
Pyrope	.023	1.73	Tanzanite	—	1.69
Pryoxmangite	—	1.75	Thaumasite	—·	1.46
Quartz	.013	1.55	Thomonsite	—	1.53
Realgar	—	2.60	Thulite	—	1.70
Rhodochrosite	—	1.61	Topaz	.014	1.62
Rhodolite	.026	1.73	Tourmaline	.017	1.63
Rhodonite	—	1.74	Tugtupite	—	1.50
Rutile	.028	2.90	Turquoise	—	1.62

Gem	DP	RI	Gem	DP	RI
Ulexite	—	1.51	Willemite	.027	1.70
Vanadanite	—	2.41	Williamsite	—	1.57
Variscite	—	1.56	Witherite	—	1.60
Verdite	—	1.58	Wulfenite	.023	2.30
Vivianite	—	1.58	Zectzerite	—	1.58
Wardite	—	1.59	Zincite	.012	2.02
Wavellite	—	1.56	Zircon	.039	1.94
Whewellite	—	1.50	Zoisite	—	1.70

APPENDIX B

Educational Associations

Asian Institute of Gemological Sciences, 987 Silom Road, 4th floor, Bangkok, Thailand 10500

Canadian Gemological Association, Box ll06, Station Q, Toronto, Canada M4T 2P2

Gemmological Association of Australia, G.P.O. Box 2551 W., Melbourne, Australia 3001

Gemmological Association of Great Britian, 27 Grenville, Street, London, EC1N 8SU England

Gemological Institute of America, l660 Stewart Street, Santa Monica, CA 90404

German Gemmological Association, Schlossmacher Str 1, D-55743 Idar-Oberstein, Germany

GEM, MINERAL AND LAPIDARY FEDERATIONS

American Federation of Mineralogical Societies, P.O. Box 26532, Oklahoma City, OK 73126

Australian Federation of Lapidary & Allied Crafts Association, 59 Harvey Road, Elizabeth Grove, South Australia 5112

Central Canadian Federation of Mineral Societies, 400 Highland Avenue, Orillia, Ontario, Canada L324 37

Federation of South African Gem and Mineral Societies, 30 Van Wouw Street, Groenkloof, Pretoria, South Afrida 0181

Magazines with regular (R) or occasional (O) articles on gems and/or jewelry. Out-of print-files (OP) are available in some libraries.

Arizona Highways. 2039 W. Lewis Avenue, Phoenix, AZ 85009 (O).

Australian Gemmologist. Box 35, South Yarra, Victoria, 3141 Australia, (R).

Canadian Gemologist. Station F, Toronto, Ontario MAY 2N7 (R).

Colored Stone. Devon Office Center #201, 60 Chestnut Avenue, Devon PA 19333 (R).

Connoisseur. (OP) (O).

Gems and Gemology. Gemological Institute of America, 1660 Stewart Street, Santa Monica, CA 90404 (R).

Gems and Minerals. (OP) (R).

Jewelers Circular Keystone. Chilton Way, Radnor, PA (R).

Lapidary Journal. Devon Office Center #201, 60 Chestnut Avenue, Devon, PA 19333 (R).

Lapis. Orleanstrasse 69 D-81667 Munchen, Germany 80 (R).

Lizzadro Museum. 220 Cottage Hill, Elmhurst, IL 60126 (R).

Mineralogical Record. 7413 Mowry Place, Tucson, AZ 85741 (R).

Mineralogist. (OP) (R).

Modern Jeweler. P.O. Box 2939, Shawnee Mission, KS 66201 (R).

National Geographic. 17th and M Streets, NW, Washington, D.C. 20036 (O).

National Jeweler. 1515 Broadway, New York, NY 10036 (R).

Rock and Gem. 4880 Market Street, Ventura, CA 93003 (R).

Rocks and Minerals. 1319 18th Street, Washington, D.C. 20036 (R).

Smithsonian. 900 Jefferson Drive, Washington, D.C. 20560 (O).

BIBLIOGRAPHY

GENERAL

Anderson, B., Gem Testing. London: Butterworth-Heinemann, 10th edition, 1990.

Arem, J., Gems & Jewelry. Tucson: Geoscience Press, 2nd edition, 1992.

Arem, J., Color Encyclopedia of Gemstones. New York: Van Nostrand Reinhold, 2nd edition, 1987.

Axon, G., Wonderful World of Gems. New Jersey: Criterion, 1972.

Bancroft, P., Gems and Crystal Treasures. Fallbrook, Cal.: Western Enterprises, 1984.

Bauer, M., Precious Stones. Rutland, Vermont: Tuttle, 1969.

Becker, V., Antique and 20th Century Jewelry. London: N.A.G., 1980.

Bell, J., Old Jewelry. New York: Crown, 1983.

Cipriani, C., & Borelli, A., Simon and Schuster's Guide to Gems and Precious Stones. New York: Simon and Schuster, 1986.

Coles, J. & Budwig, R., The Book of Beads. New York: Simon and Schuster, 1990.

Core, H., et al., Wood Structure & Identification. Syracuse: Syracuse University Press, 1979.

Desautels, P., The Gem Kingdom. New York: Random House, 1970.

Desautels, P., The Mineral Kingdom. New York: Random House, 1968.

Desautels, P., Rocks and Minerals. New York: Grossett & Dunlap, 1975.

Dietrich, R., Stones; Their Collection, Identification and Uses. Tucson: Geoscience Press, 1989.

Dietrich, R., and Skinner, B., Gems, Granites and Gravels. Cambridge: Cambridge University Press, 1990.

Emmons, W., et al., Geology. Principles and Processes. New York: McGraw-Hill, 1955.

Fenton, C., & Fenton, M., The Rock Book. Garden City, N.Y.: Doubleday, 1976.

Frondel, C., The System of Mineralogy. The Silica Minerals. New York: Wiley, 1962.

Grigorietti, G., Jewelry Through the Ages. New York: American Heritage, 1969.

Gubelin, E., Internal World of Gemstones. Zurich: ABC, 1974.

Harlow, W., Inside Wood, Masterpiece of Nature. Washington, D.C.: American Forestry, 1978.

Heiniger, E., & Heiniger, J., The Great Book of Jewels. New York: Graphics Society, 1974.

Hurlbut, C., & Switzer, G., Gemology. New York: Wiley, 1979.

Keller, P., Gemstones and their Origins. New York: Van Nostrand Reinhold, 1990.

Kraus, E., & Slawson, C., Gems and Gem Materials. New York: McGraw-Hill, 1939.

Kuehn, L., The Guide to Colored Gems. Dallas, Texas: Private, 1977.

Kunz, G., Curious Lore of Precious Stones. New York: Dover, 1968, reprint 1989.

Kunz, G., Gems and Precious Stones of North America. New York: Dover, 1968, reprint 1989.

Liddicoat, R., A Handbook of Gem Identification. Santa Monica, Cal.: GIA, 12th edition, 1989.

Mac Fall, R., Gem Hunters Guide. New York: Crowell, 1975.

Mac Fall, R., Rock Hunters Guide. New York: Crowell, 1980.

Meen, V., & Tushingham, A., Crown Jewels of Iran. Toronto: University of Toronto, 1968.

Metz, R., Precious Stones. New York: Viking, 1964.

Michael, P., Crown Jewels of Europe. New York: Harper & Row, 1983.

Mielach, D., Ethnic Jewelry. New York: Crown, 1981.

Nassau, K., Gemstone Enhancement. London: Butterworth-Heinemann, 1984.

Nassau, K., Gems Made by Man. Radnor, Penn.: Chilton, 1980.

O'Donoghue, M., Gemstones. London: Chapman & Hall, 1988.

Palache, C., et al., The System of Mineralogy. New York: Wiley, 1951.

Parsons, C., Practical Gem Knowledge for the Amateur. San Diego: Lapidary Journal, 1969.

Pough, F., The Story of Gems and Precious Stones. New York: Harvey House, 1969.

Ramsey, J., & Ramsey, L., Collector/Investor Handbook of Gems. San Diego: Boa Vista, 1985.

Ransom, J., Gems and Minerals of America. New York: Harper & Row, 1975.

Ransom, J., Rock Hunter's Guide. New York: Harper & Row, 1963.

Read, P., Gemmology. London: Butterworth-Heinemann, 1991.

Roberts, W., et al., Encyclopedia of Minerals. New York: Van Nostrand Reinhold, 1989.

Sanborn, W., Oddities of the Mineral World. New York: Van Nostrand Reinhold, 1976.

Sauer, J., Brazil: Paradise of Gemstones. Rio de Janeiro: Private, 1982.

Scalisi, P., & Cook, D., Classic Mineral Localities of the World. New York: Van Nostrand Reinhold, 1982.

Schumann, W., Gemstones of the World. New York: Sterling, 1977.

Sinkankas, J., Gemstone and Mineral Data Book. Tucson: Geoscience Press, 1991.

Sinkankas, J., Gemstones of North America. New York: Van Nostrand Reinhold, 2nd edition, 1976.

Sinkankas, J., Mineralogy for Amateurs. New York: Van Nostrand Reinhold, 1964.

Smith, G., Gemstones. New York: Pitman, 1958.

Snowman, A., Carl Faberge Goldsmith to the Imperial Court of Russia. New York: Greenwich House, 1983.

Sofianides, A., & Harlow, G., Gems and Crystals. New York: Simon and Schuster, 1990.

Sperison, F., Art of the Lapidary. Milwaukee: Bruce, 1969.

Webster, R., Gems. Hamden, Conn.: Archon, 5th edition, 1994.

SPECIFIC GEMS

Bruton, Diamonds. Radnor, Penn.: Chilton, 1978.

Dake, H., The Agate Book. Portland: Mineralogist, 1957.

Dake, H., et al., Quartz Family Minerals. New York: Whittlesy, 1938.

Desautels, P., The Jade Kingdom. New York: Van Nostrand Reinhold, 1986.

Dickinson, J., The Book of Pearls. Philadelphia: Chilton, 1968.

Dietrich, R., The Tourmaline Group. New York: Van Nostrand Reinhold, 1985.

Downing, P., Opal Cutting Made Easy. Tallahassee: Majestic, 1989.

Downing, P., Opal Identification and Value. Tallahassee: Majestic, 1991.

Farn, A., Pearls. London: Butterworth-Heinemann, 1986.

Fraquet, H., Amber. London: Butterworth-Heinemann, 1987.

Hemrich, G., Handbook of Jade. Menton, Cal.: Gembooks, 1966.

Hunger, R., The Magic of Amber. Philadelphia: Chilton, 1977.

Hughes, R., Corudum. London: Butterworth-Heinemann, 1990.

Laufer, B., Jade. New York: Dover, 1974.

Leaming, S., Jade in Canada. Geological Survey of Canada, 1974.

Leechman, F., The Opal Book. Sidney: URE/Smith, 1973.

Leiper, H. (Ed.), Agates of North America. San Diego: Lapidary Journal, 1966.

Mac Fall, R., Wyoming Jade. San Diego: Lapidary Journal, 1980.

Muller, H., Jet. London: Butterworth-Heinemann, 1987.

Newman, R., The Ruby and Sapphire Buying Guide. Los Angeles: International Jewelry, 1991.

Nott, S., Chinese Jade. Rutland, Vermont: Tuttle, 1966.

O'Donoghue, M., Quartz. London: Butterworth-Heinemann, 1986.

Rice, P., Amber. The Golden Gem of the Ages. Tucson: Geoscience Press, 1989.

Rouse, J., Garnet. London: Butterworth-Heinemann, 1986.

Sinkankas, J., Emerald and other Beryls. Tucson: Geoscience Press, 1989.

Ward, F., Emeralds. Bethesda, Md.: Gem Book, 1993.

Ward, F., Rubies and Sapphires. Bethesda, Md.: Gem Book, 1991.

REGIONAL BOOKS OF GEM MATERIALS

Andrews, E., Georgia"s Fabulous Treasure Hoards. Hapville, GA: Private, 1966.

Anthony, J., et. al. Mineralogy of Arizona. Tucson, AZ: University of Arizona Press, 1977.

Ash, S., and May, D., Petrified Forest: The Story Behind the Scenery. Holbrook, AZ: Petrified Forest Museum, 1969.

Beckwith, J., Gem Minerals of Idaho. Caldwell, ID: Caxton, 1987.

Berry, R., Wyoming Collecting Localities, Wheatland, WY: Eloxite, 1965.

Bitner, F., Arizona Rock Trails. Scottsdale, AZ: private, 1957.

Blakemore, J., We Walk on Jewels. Rockland, ME: Seth Low, 1961.

Brown, V., and Allen, D., Rocks and Minerals of California and Their Stories. San Martin, CA: Naturgraph, 1957.

Burrow, D., Northern California Gem and Mineral Collecting Areas. Sonoma, CA: Studio Press, 1970.

Clarke, D., Copper Minerals of Keweenaw. MI: Private, 1974.

Conley, J., Mineral Localities of North Carolina. Raleigh, NC: Mineral Resources Division, 1958.

Dake, H., Northwest Gem Trails. Portland, OR: Mineralogist, 1956.

Dietrich, R., Virginia Mineral Localities. Virginia Polytech, 1960.

Dodson, D., and Dodson, D., Rockhounding in Arkansas. Little Rock, AR: Private, 1974.

Farfard, R., Cowee Valley Ruby Mining Story. Franklin: Ruby City Gems, 1966.

Girard, R., Texas Rock and Mineral Localities. Austin, TX: Bureau of Economic Geology, 1964.

Harshaw, R., Emeralds of North Carolina. Ashville, NC: Hexagon, 1974.

Heinrich, W., Minerals of Michigan. Ann Arbor: University of Michigan, Michigan, 1967.

Helton, W., Kentucky Rocks and Minerals. Lexington, KY: Geological Survey, 1964.

Hutchinson, B., and Hutchinson, J., Rockhounding and Beachcombing at Vancouver Island. Vancouver, B.C.: Private, 1971.

Johnson, P., Gems and Minerals of Mexico, Mentone, CA: Gembooks, 1965.

Kachlik, R., Gem Hunting in the Smokies. Private, 1966.

Keller, P., Gemstones of East Africa. New York: Van Nostrand Reinhold, 1990.

Kimbler, F., and Narsavage, R., New Mexico Rocks and Minerals. Santa Fe, NM: Sunstone, 1959.

Leadbeater, J., Maine: Minerals and Gems. Freybury, ME: Private, 1963.

Leaming, S., Rocks and Minerals of British Columbia. Ottowa: Geological Survey of Canada, 1973.

Macintosh, E., Rocks, Minerals and Gemstones of Southern Africa. Cape Town: Struik, 1976.

Mason, B., Trap Rocks of New Jersey. Trenton: New Jersay Geological Survey, 1960.

Miller, C., Minerals of Rhode Island. Kingston, RI: University of Rhode Island, 1972.

Mitchell, J., Gem Trails of Arizona. Pico Rivera, CA: Gem Guides Books, 1987.

Mitchell, J., Gem Trails of California. Pico Rivera, CA: Gem Guides Books, 1986.

Mitchell, J., Gem Trails of Nevada. Pico Rivera, CA: Gem Guides Books, 1991.

Mitchell, J., Gem Trails of New Mexico. Pico Rivera, CA: Gem Guides Books, 1987.

Mitchell, J., Gem Trails of Oregon. Pico Rivera, CA: Gem Guides Books, 1989.

Mitchell, J., Gem Trails of Texas. Pico Rivera, CA: Gem Guides Books, 1987.

Mitchell, J., Gem Trails of Utah. Pico Rivera, CA: Gem Guides Books, 1987.

Myatt, Bill, et. al., How and Where to Find Gemstones in Australia and New Zealand. Sidney: Summit, 1972.

Nicolay, H., and Stone, A., Rocks and Minerals. A Guide for Collectors of the Eastern United States. South Brunswick, N.J.: Barnes, 1967.

Northrup, S., Minerals of New Mexico. Albuquerque: University of New Mexico, 1959.

Oles, F., and Oles, H. Eastern Gem Trails. Mentone, CA: Gembooks, 1967.

Overstree, S., and Bell, H., Crystalline Rocks of South Carolina. U.S. Geological Survey, 1958.

Overstander, C., and Price, W., Minerals of Maryland. Baltimore: Baltimore Historical Society, 1940.

Pabian, R., Minerals and Gemstones of Nebraska. Lincoln: Geological Survey of Nebraska, 1971.

Panczer, W., Minerals of Mexico. New York: Van Nostrand Reinhold, 1987.

Pearl, R., Colorado Gem Trails. Denver: Sage, 1951.

Perry, B., and Perry, R., Australian Gemstones in Color. Sydney: Reed, 1967.

Ransom, J., Petrified Wood Trails. Portland, OR: Mineralogist, 1955.

Razmi, R., and Snee, L., Minerals of Pakistan. Pakistan Geological Survey, 1989.

Rapp, G., and Wallace, D., Mineral Collecting in Minnesota. Minneapolis: Geological Survey, 1979.

Roberts, W., and Rapp, G. R., Minerals of the Black Hills. Rapid City, SD: South Dakota School of Mines and Technology, 1976.

Sabina, A., Rocks and Minerals for the Collector. Bancroft: Geological Survey of Canada, 1963.

Sabina, A., Rocks and Minerals for the Collector: Sudbury to Winnipeg. Winnipeg: Geological Survey of Canada, 1963.

Sabina, A., Rock and Mineral Collecting in Canada: Ontario and Quebec. Quebec: Geological Survey of Canada, 1954.

Schwartz, G., and Thiel, G., Guide to Minerals and Rocks of Minnesota. Minneapolis: University of Minnesota, 1960.

Stevens, J., Maine Treasure Chest: Gems and Minerals of Oxford County. Trapp Corner: Perham, 1972.

Strong, M., Desert Gem Trails, Mentone: Gembooks, 1966.

Stuckey, J., North Carolina: Its Geology and Mineral Resources. Raleigh: Department of Commerce, 1965.

Thomas, W., et. al., Rocks and Minerals of Alabama. University of Alabama, 1975.

Tolsted, L., and Swinford, A., Kansas Rocks and Minerals. Lawrence: University of Kansas, 1948.

Umberger, J., and Umberger, A., Texas Mineral and Fossil Locations. Tyler, TX: Tyler Star, 1967.

Willman, L., Gem and Mineral Localities of the Southeast United States. Jacksonville, FL: Private, 1963.

Wilson, W., and Wilson, C., Mineral Collecting Sites in North Carolina. Raleigh: Geological Survey of North Carolina, 1978.

Zabriski, D., and Zabriski, C., Rockhounding in Eastern New York State and Nearby New England. Albany, NY: Many Facets, 1990.

Zeitner, J., Appalachian Mineral and Gem Trails. San Diego, CA: Lapidary Journal, 1968.

Zeitner, J., Midwest Gem, Fossil and Mineral Trails: Great Lakes States. Pico Rivera, CA: Gem Guides Books, 1989.

Zeitner, J. Midwest Gem, Fossil and Mineral Trails: Prairie States. Pico Rivera, CA: Gem Guides Books, 1989.

Zeitner, J., Southwest Mineral and Gem Trails. San Diego: Lapidary Journal, 1972.

GEM CUTTING BOOKS

Dake, H., Gem Cutting. Portland, OR: Mineralogist, 1954.

Hunt, H., Lapidary Carving for Creative Jewelry. Phoenix: Geoscience Press, 1993.

Kennedy, G., et. al., The Fundamentals of Gemstone Carving. San Diego: Lapidary Journal, 1967.

Kraus, P., Introduction to Lapidary. Radnor, PA: Chilton, 1987.

Leiper, H., et. al., Gem Cutting Shop Helps. San Diego: Lapidary Journal, 1964.

Quick, L., and Leiper, M., Gemcraft. Philadelphia: Chilton, 1977.

Sinkankas, J., Gem Cutting: A Lapidary's Manual. New York: Van Nostrand Reinhold, 1988.

Vargas, G., and Vargas, M., Faceting for Amateurs. Thermal, CA: Private, 1969.

Walter, M., Gem Cutting Is Easy. New York: Crown, 1972.

Zeitner, J., and Lee, H., How to Carve Jade and Gems. Aberdeen, SD: Northern, 1987.

SELECTED ARTICLES FROM PERIODICALS

Gems and Gemology

Note: W = Winter   Sp = Spring   Su = Summer   F = Fall

Bowersox, F., A status report on gemstones from Afganistan, W1985:192.
Epstein, D., Amethyst from Brazil, W1988:214–228.
Fritsch, E., and Misiorowski, E., The history of gemology of queen conch "pearl," W 1987:208.
Fryer, C., and Koivula, J., An examination of four important gems, Su1984:99.
Gubelin, E., Gemstones of Pakistan: Emerald, ruby and spinel, F1982:123.
Keller, P., Emeralds of Colombia, Su1981:80.
Keller, P., The rubies of Burma: A review of the Mogok stone tract, W1983:209.
Keller, P., and Wang, F., A survey of the gemstone resources of Chima, Sp1982:3.
Koivula, J.; Fryer, C.; and Keller, P., Opal from Queretaro, Mexico; Occurance and inclusions, Su1983:87.
Nassau, K., The early history of gemstone treatments, Sp1984:22–23.
Proctor, K., Chrysoberyl and alexandrite from the pegmatite districts of Minas Gerais, Sp1988:16.
Proctor, K., Gem pegmatites of Minas Gerais, Brazil: The tourmalines of the Araquai districts, Sp1985:3.
Proctor, K., Gem pegmatites of Minas Gerais, Brazil: The tourmalines of the Governador Valadares district, Su1985:86.
Shigley, J., and Koivula, J., Amethystine chalcedony, W1985:219.
Stockton, C., and Manson, D., Gem andradite garnets, W1983:202.
Stockton, C., A proposed new classification for gem quality garnets, W1985:205.

Lapidary Journal

Bancroft, P., Spectacular Spinel. February 1990, pg. 25.
Bastos, F., Gemstones of Brazil, February 1964, pg. 1136.
Courter, E., Michigan's Copper Country, May 1976, pg. 452.
Dahlberg, J., Thomsonite, April 1974, pg. 42.
Frazier, S., and Frazier, A., Discover Drusy. September 1993, pg. 24.
Frazier, S., and Frazier, A., Heavenly Peridot. February 1992, pg. 20.
Frazier, S., and Frazier, A., In the Light of Day. February 1992, pg. 20.
Frazier, S., and Frazier, A., Name That Agate. April 1988, pg. 65.
Frazier, S., and Frazier, A., Name That Jasper. April 1989, pg. 75.
Gosse, R., Hexagonite. January 1963, pg. 964.
Gosse, R., Rare and Unusual Gemstones of New England. May 1964, p. 336.
Gregory, G., Prehnite, A Beautiful Gemstone. August 1969, pg. 768.
Howard, D., Oklahoma. April 1962, pg. 154.
Hutchinson, B., and Hutchinson, J., Chrysanthemum Rocks from British Columbia. November 1967, pg. 1990.
Jones, R., Arizona, Heartland of Gems. April 1977, p. 90.
Jones, R., Chryscolla, Arizona's Premium Gem. April 1979, pg. 6.
Kennedy, M., Petrified Wood of Oklahoma. August 1964, pg. 558.
MacFall, R., Florida Coral, June 974, pg. 490.
MacFall, R., Historic Blue John and Other Fluorites. January 1982, pg. 1998.
McMackin, C., Memories of Ricolite Gulch. August 1979, pg. 184.
McMackin, C., Petrified Wood from East to West. February 1984, pg. 582.

Meen, V., Gem Hunting in Burma. October 1962, pg. 636, November 1962, pg. 746, December 1962, p. 816.

Musgrove, M., Pipestone. August 1980, pg. 1174.

Nassau, K., Mt. St. Helens Ash. July 1988, pg. 41.

Nassau, K., Amethyst and Citrine. 1982, pg. 1130.

Nassau, K., Synthetic Garnets. April 1971, pg. 100.

Nezelrod, E., Turquoise Inside Out. January 1984, pg. 1152, January 1985, pg. 1304.

Pabian, R., Lake Superior Agate. May 1980, pg. 462.

Pough, F., Alexandrite. November 1987, pg. 14.

Pough, F., Ammolite. January 1986, pg. 35.

Pough, F., Aquamarine. March 1986, pg. 62.

Pough, F., Azurite. Spetember 1980, pg. 16.

Pough, F., Bustamite. March 1989, pg. 16.

Pough, F., Calcite. April 1989, pg. 22.

Pough, F., Ceruleite. July 1989, pg. 18.

Pough, F., Covellite. May 1990, pg. 16.

Pough, F., Danburite. September 1990, pg. 16.

Pough, F., Garnet. January 1987, pg. 16.

Pough, F., Heliolite and Sunstone. January 1989, pg. 16.

Pough, F., Lapis Lazuli. April 1987, pg. 18.

Pough, F., Sacpolite. July 1987, pg. 14.

Pough, F., Spinel. March 1980, pg. 54.

Pough, F., Zircon. December 1986, pg. 15.

Ramsey, J., and Ramsey, L., Out of Africa. November 1991, pg. 38.

Rieman, H., Palms and Palm Wood. January 1977, pg. 2310.

Rothstein, J., The Gem Micas. June 1969, pg. 692.

Shaub, B., Genesis of Agates, Geodes, Septaria and Other Concretions of Sedimentary Origin. July 1980, pg. 860.

Shaub, B., Genesis of Thundereggs, Geodes and Agates of Igneous Origin. February 1979, pg. 2340, March 1979, pg. 2548.

Sinkankas, J., Strawberry Quartz. What Is It? February 1962, pg. 677.

Sinkankas, J., So-called Psilomelane Is Chalcedony. February 1962, pg. 677.

Sinkankas, J., What Do We Really Know about the Formation of Agate and Chalcedony? June 1961, pg. 242.

Smith, K., Arizona's Petrified Forest. July 1963, pg. 7420.

Smith, K., Turquoise of the Southwest. November 1962, pg. 1786.

Smith, W., Mozarkite, Missouri's Legendary Gem. April 1977, pg. 160.

Towner, J., Palm Wood of Texas. April 1975, pg. 494.

Vargas, G., and Vargas, M., Ametrine Comes Out of the Dark. April 1981, pg. 270.

Vargas, G., and Vargas, M., Every Color But Blue. Spetember 1990, pg. 75.

Webster, R., More Notes on Turquoise. November 1975, pg. 28.

Webster, R., Ornamental Serpentine. April 1967, pg. 88.

Wilson, M., Montana Moss Agate. October 1988, pg. 58.

Windisch, H., Polishing Materials in Southern Africa. April 1979, pg. 18.

Zeitner, J., Agates Around the World. March 1977, pg. 2668.

Zeitner, J., Colorful Chalcedony in America. July 1977, pg. 1026.

Zeitner, J., Gathering Garnets. September 1990, pg. 81.

Zeitner, J., Feathers, Flakes and Fans. February 1970, pg. 52, March 1970, pg. 1530, April 1970, page 4.

Zeitner, J., Gem Chrysocolla. Sepbember 1985, pg. 28.

Zeitner, J., Grunerite and Other Gems from Wyoming. December 1966, pg. 1094.

Zeitner, J., Jasper, Gem of Confusion. December 1964, pg. 980.
Zeitner, J., The Opals of Quertaro. July 1979, pg. 868.
Zeitner, J., Royal Cycads. July 1988, pg. 83.
Zeitner, J., Thunder Bay. November 1989, pg. 86.
Zeitner, J., Tourmaline of Pala. February 1987, pg. 34.

Rock and Gem

Jones, R., Quartz Family Minerals. July–November 1986.
Jones, R., Mexican Agate. October 1989, pg. 40.
Jones, R., Colorful Minerals of the Greater Southwest. May 1988, pg. 28.
Jones, R., Peridot. September 1983, pg. 52.
Jones, R., Iris Agate. June 1979, pg. 50.
Jones, R., Mines of Mexico. August 1992, pg. 12.
Jones, R., Garnet. March 1992, pg. 36.
Mitchell, J., Oregon's Petrified Wood. June 1992, pg. 28.
Voynick, S., Colorado's Mineral Belt. January 1993, pg. 44.

Rocks and Minerals

Campbell, T., and Roberts, W., Mineral Localities of South Dakota. May 1985, pg. 109.
Dietrich, R., Rhode Island's State Rock and Mineral: Cumberlandite and Bowenite. September 1986, pg. 251.
Hausel, W., Diamond Bearing Kimberlite Pipes in Wyoming and Colorado. September 1983, pg. 241.
Jacobson, M., The Proctor Collection. January 1988, pg. 40.
Jones, R., Ubiquitous Quartz. January 1987, pg. 6.
Jones, R., Opticon, Oh, Opticon! November 1986, pg. 60.
Marble, L., The Minerals of Mont Ste. Hilaire. January 1979, pg. 4.
Stallard, M., Florida Coral. April 1979, pg. 141.

Mineralogical Record (special one-subject or one-region issues)

Arizona, I, May 1980; II, July 1980; III, January 1988; IV, March 1983; V, September 1983.
Australia, November 1988.
Colorado, November 1976, November 1979, May 1985.
Greenland, March 1993.
Katanga, July 1989.
Michigan Copper Country, September 1992.
Mont Saint Hilaire, July 1990.
New Mexico, January 1989.
Nevada, January 1995.
Ontario, March 1982.
Tourmaline, September 1985.
Tsumeb, May 1977.

INDEX

Abalone, 260-261
Abrasives, 31-33, 318
Actinolite, 237
Adamite, 275-276
Adularescence, 236
Agate, **85-125**
  banded and fortification, 85-99
  brecciated, 99-100
  cutting, 87, 90
  defined, 87
  eye and dot, 100-103
  fire, 103-104
  heating, 90, 92
  iris, 104
  lace, 104-105
  moss, 105-108
  names, 90
  onyx, 90, 91, 97
  plume, 108-110
  pseudomorphs, **145-168**
  sagenitic, 110-112
  thundereggs, 112-14
Agatized bone, 147-148
Agatized coral, 145-146, 148
Agatized or jasperized wood, 146, 150-167
Alabaster, 207
"Albertite," 320
Albite, 241
Alexandrite, 24
  synthetic, 312
"Alexandrium," 319
Algodonite, 248
Allen, Susan, 79
Allochromatic, 186
Almandine, 33
Amazonite, 187
Amber, 260-261
  imitation, 318
Amblygonite, 45
American Museum, 20, 22, 28, 29, 42, 172, 177, 203

Amethyst, 66-68
Ametrine, 68
"Ammolite," 262
Analcime, 301
Anatase, 276
Andalusite, 46
Andradite, 34
  topazolite, 35
Anglesite, 276
Anhydrite, 34, 207-208
"Anyolite," 204
Apache tears, 194, 195
Apatite, 46
Apophyllite, 277
Aquamarine, 20
Aragonite, 278
Argillite, 208
Arizona Sonora Desert Museum, 55, 56, 118, 301
Ashley, George, 154
Asterism, 236
Augelite, 278
Australian Museum of Earch Sciences, 42, 196
Aventurescence, 236
Aventurine, 66, 69
Axinite, 47
Azurite, 187
Azurmalachite, 187

Bancroft, Peter, 61
Bank, Eberhard, 27, 61
Barite, 209
Basanite, 128
Bauxite, 210
Bayldonite, 248
Beads, 11
Becker, Gerhard, 62, 76, 79, 81
Bediasite, 60
Bell Labs, 313
Benitoite, 44, 47-48
Bernhardt, Ute, 62, 98, 180
Beryl, 19-24, 308

Beryl (continued)
  aquamarine, 19, 20
  emerald, 19, 21-23
  goshenite, 19
  heliodor, 19, 23
  maxixe, 20
  morganite, 19, 24
  red beryl, 19, 24
  synthetic, 308-310
Beryllonite, 279
Biggs, Jasper, 132-133
"Binghamite," 69-70
Black chalcedony, 115
Bloodstone, 101
Blue chalcedony, 115, 120
Blue quartz, 70
Bog, 162
Boleite, 279
Bone, 263
Boracite, 279
Bornite, 249
Bowenite, 228
"Bowesite," 210
Brazilianite, 48
Brecciated agate, 99-100
Breihauptite, 250
Bridges, Campbell, 35
British Museum, 26, 28, 38, 55, 77, 198
Bronzite, 239-240
Bruneau Jasper, 133
Burbankite, 277
Bustamite, 188

Cabochon materials, 10, **85-125**, **131-143**, **169-184**, **145-185**, **185-204**, 205-234, **235-246**, **247-258**, **259-272**
  how to select, 183
  synthetic, 314-316
Calcite, 210-215
  marble, 213-215
  onyx, 211-212
  petoskey stone, 214
California Academy of Science, 20, 56, 239, 253
"Californite," 192
Call, Jerry, 21, 23, 24, 26, 28, 41, 51, 54, 59, 297
"Campbellite," 217
Cancrinite, 188
Carey plume agate, 109
Carletonite, 280
Carnegie Museum, 171
Carnelian, 116
Carving, 11, 24, 58, 61, 124, 171, 177, 182, 187, 190, 192, 195, 206, 207, 208, 266

Carving (continued)
  soft stone, 206, 297, 211, 214, 233, 263
Cassiterite, 280
Catapleite, 280
Catlinite, 215
Cat's-eye stones, 25-26, 39, 41, 46, 236, 237, 239, 241-242, 244, 245, 246
  chrysoberyl, 25-26
  orientation, 26, 237
Cave Creek Jasper, 133-134
Celestite, 281
Ceruleite, 189
Cerussite, 281
Chalcedony, **85-125, 145-167**
  colored, 114-122
  pseudomorphs, **145-167**
Chalcopyrite, 250
Chalcosiderite, 184
Channel work, 216
Charoite, 41, 215-216
Chatham synthetics, 307, 308, 310, 311-312
  beryl, 308
  corundum, 307, 310, 311-312
Chatoyancy, 236
Chert, 128-131
  basanite, 128
  mozarkite, 129
  novaculite, 130
Chiastolite, 189
"Chicken-blood stone," 216
Chihuahua agate, 93-94, 105
Childrenite, 282
Chlorastrolite, 238
Chlorite, 74, 75, 78, 121
Chloromelanite, 172
Chondrodite, 282
Chrome chalcedony, 117
Chrome diopside, 48
Chromite, 251
Chromium clinochlore, 287-288
Chrysanthemum stone, 221
Chrysoberyl, 24-26
  alexandrite, 25
  cymophane (catseye), 25
  synthetic, 312
Chrysocolla quartz, 117-118
Chrysoprase, 118
Cinnabar, 120
Citrine, 70-71
Clinohumite, 282
Clinozoisite, 50
Coal, 263-264
  anthracite, 263

Coal (continued)
  cannel, 264
  jet, 264
Cobaltite, 251
Cobaltocalcite, 211
Colemanite, 283
Collectors' stones, **273-303**
Color, 13-15, 170, 186
Coloring, 90, 92, 184
  agate, 90, 92
  turquoise, 184
Columbite, 251
Conch "pearls," 265
Copper rocks, 217-219, 251-252
  copper in basalt, 252
  copper conglomerate, 251-252
  copper rhyolite, 252
Coquina, 212
Coral, 266
  imitation, 318
  synthetic, 314
Cordierite, 53
Corundum, 26-31, 310
  ruby, 26, 28
  sapphire, 28-31
  synthetic, 310
Covellite, 252
Cranbrook Institute, 48
Crandallite, 303
Crazy lace agate, 105
Cryptocrystalline quartz, **85-168**
Cubic Zirconia (CZ), 316-317
Cuprite, 253
Cycad, 162
Cymophane, 25
Cythodendron Texanum, 163
Czochralski synthetics, 306, 307, 312, 317

"Dallasite," 222
"Damsonite," 119
Danburite, 49
Datolite, 186, 190
Demantoid, 34
Deter, Bruce, 74, 238, 245
Diamond, 4, 31-33, 313
  G.E., 313
  Sumitomo, synthetic, 313
Diaspore, 50
Dinosaur bone, 147-148
Diopside, 239
Dioptase, 283-284
Dispersion, 323
Dolomite, 213

Domeykite, 248
Downing, Paul, 180
Dravite, 60
Dryhead agate, 95
Dyber, Michael, 79, 81

Eilat stone, 217
Ekanite, 284
"Elaeolite," 194
Elbaite, 60
Emerald, 4, 19, 21-23
  imitation, 318
  synthetic, 308-310
  trapiche, 22
Enhydros, 124
Enstatite, 239-240
Eosphorite, 282
Epidote, 50
Epstein, David, 67, 68
Etching, 12
Euclase, 51
Eudialyte, 284
Eye and dot agate, 100-103

Fabergé, Peter Carl, 77, 176
Faceting materials, **43-62**, 66-69, 70-71, 75-78, 78-80, 81, **273-303**, 305-314
Factory materials, 318-321
Fairburn agate, 95-96
Fantasy cuts, 13, 44, 68
Faustite, 184
Feldspar, 4, 52, 187, 193-194, 241-242, 243
  amazonstone, 187
  heliolite, 52
  labradorite, 52
  microcline, 193-194
  moonstone, 241-242
  orthoclase, 240
  perthite, 242
  spectrolite, 240
  sunstone, 242-243
Ferruginous quartz, 72
Fibrolite, 243
Field Museum, 20, 78
Fire agate, 103-104
Fire opal, 179, 180
Fishegg agate, 101
Flame fusion, 307, 314
Flexible shaft tool, 12
Flint, 128-130
Flowerstone, 221
Fluorescence, 203
Fluorite, 44, 190

Flux grown, 307, 308, 309, 310, 311, 312
Forsterite, 38
Fortification Agate, 85-94
Fossil ivory, 267
Franklinite, 203
Frazier, Sy and Ann, 49, 56, 303
Friedelite, 284
Frondel, Clifford, 88, 128
Fuchsite, 66, 69, 224, 232-233

Gadolinite, 303
Garnet, 33-38
   almadine, 33
   andradite, 34
   demantoid, 34
   grossular, 35
   hessonite, 35
   pyrope, 36
   rhodolite, 37
   spessartine, 37
   star, 34
   synthetic, 317
   tsavorite, 35
   uvarovite, 38
Gaudefroyite, 277
Gems of history, **17-42**
General Electric, 7, 313, 315
Geodes, 122-125
"Georgia Midnight," 219
Ghanite, 39
Gilson synthetics, 307, 308-310, 314, 315, 316
   coral, 314
   emerald, 307, 308-310
   lapis lazuli, 315
   opal, 316
   turquoise, 316
Gingko, 164
Glass simulants, 319
Goergyite, 277
Goethite, 253
Gold in quartz, 72
Goldstone, 319
Grandidierite, 285
Granite, 4, 219-222
   colored, 220
   graphic, 220
   larvikite, 220-221
   orbicular, 221
   porphyry, 221
   unakite, 222
Grant, Arthur, 23, 56, 190, 210, 268, 275, 276, 278, 279, 281, 284, 290, 293, 294, 295, 296, 301, 302

Graveyard plume agate, 109
Gray, Elvis, 40, 52, 211
Gray, Michael, 48, 51, 58, 71, 76, 190, 253
Green quartz, 73
Green slate, 209
Grossular, 35
Grunerite, 226
Gubelin, Edwin, 163, 311
Gypsum, 244

Hackmanite, 200
Hambergite, 285
Hanneman, Dr. W., 30
Haüyne, 285
"Helenite," 319
Heliodor, 19
Heliolite, 52
"Heliotrope bauxite," 210
"Hematine," 319
Hematite, 254
Hemimorphite, 286
Herderite, 286
Hermanophyton, 164
Hessonite, 35
Hexagonite, 245
Hiddenite, 57
Hodson, Keith, 181
Horn, 263
Horn coral, 148
Hornblende, 191
Houston Museum of Science, 58, 68
Howlite, 222
Huebernite, 191
Huereaulite, 286
Huett, Dale, 135, 143, 181
Hydrothermal, 307, 308, 309, 310, 313
Hypersthene, 240

Idar-Oberstein, 13, 25, 27, 34, 86, 91, 93, 118, 132, 284
Ideochromatic, 186
Idocrase, 192
"Imperialite dancer," 217
Inamori, 308
Inderite, 287
India moss agate, 106
Indicolite, 61
Inlay, 216
Intarsia, 12, 154
Iolite, 54
Iridescence, 194, 236
Iris agate, 104
Ivory, 266

Jade, 170-175
  cutting, 172
  imitation, 319-320
  synthetic, 315
Jadeite, 170-172
Jasper, 131-143
  algal, 132
  conglomerate, 137
  defined, 131-132
  morrisonite, 139
  orbicular, 140
Jaspilite, 254
Jeremjevite, 287
Jet, 264-265
  imitation, 320
Jewelry, 11, 154

Kainite, 277
Kammererite, 287-288
Kashan ruby, 310
Kaufman, Jim, 182
Kemp, Doris, 12, 265
Kindradite, 137
Klein, Herbert, 62
Kona dolomite, 213
Kornerupine, 288
Kroenkite, 277
Kunz, G. F., 57, 73, 129
Kunzite, 57
Kyanite, 289
Kyocera, 311

Laboratory materials, **305-318**
Labradorescence, 236
Labradorite, 240
Lace agate, 104-105
Lake Superior agate, 96-97
Lapidary materials, 1-16
  defined, 1-16
  how to acquire, 7
  minerals, 5
  organic, 6
  rocks, 4
  selecting, 7
  uses, 10-13
Lapidary projects, 11-12
Lapis Lazuli, 170, 175
  imitation, 320
  synthetic, 315
Lapis Nevada, 223
Larimar, 186, 195-196
Larimides, 97
Larvikite, 220-221

Laserblue, 319
Lazulite, 289
Lazurapatite, 47
Lazurite, 175
Lechleitner, 308, 311, 312
Lee, Hing Wa, 24, 58, 61, 124, 171, 177, 182, 266
Legrandite, 289-290
Lehrer, Glen, 41, 76
Leifite, 303
Lennix, 309
Lepidolite, 224
Leucite, 290
Leucophanite, 277
Leucosphenite, 277
Liddicoatite, 60
Limestone, 213
Linarite, 290
Linde emerald, 309
Linde sapphire, 312
Lintonite, 200
Lizzadro Museum, 20, 41, 58, 81, 171, 175
Lora Robins Gallery, 266
Los Angeles County Museum, 22, 26, 52, 58, 180, 211
Lowell, Jack, 67
Ludlamite, 290-291
Luna and Apache Creek agate, 97

Maine State Museum, 61
Malachite, 186, 92
  synthetic, 315
Mallas, Aris, 26, 282, 307, 311
Manganotantalite, 291
Mansfieldite, 303
Marble, 213-215
Marcasite, 256-257
"Mariposite," 224
Maw-sit-sit, 171
Meerschaum, 225
Mellite, 267-268
Mesolite, 301-302
Mettalic gem materials, **247-258**
Meteorites, 254
Mexican agate, 93-94, 99, 100
"Mexican onyx," 211-212
Mica, 66, 69, 224, 232-233
  fuchsite, 69, 224, 232-233
  lepidolite, 224
Microcline, 193
Microlite, 291
Milky quartz, 74
Miller, Robert, 195

Mimetite, 292
Minerals as lapidary materials, 5-6
Miniatures, 11, 153
Missouri lace agate, 105
Mohave stone, 218
Mohawkite, 248
Mohs's scale of hardness, 5
Moldavite, 59
Mookaite, 129
Moonstone, 241-242
Mordenite, 244
Morganite, 19
Morion, 81
Mosaics, 12
    Florentine, 12
    intarsia, 12
Mosandrite, 277
Moss agate, 105-108
Mother-of-pearl, 260
"Mozarkite," 129
Mueller, Eugene, 139
Munsteiner, Bernd, 13, 44, 59, 64, 79
"Myrickite," 45, 120
Narsarsukite, 277
Nassau, Kurt, 68, 314
National Museum of Melbourne, 76
Natrolite, 302
Natural mosaic, 218
Nepheline, 194
Nephrite, 172-175
New York State Museum, 210
Niccolite, 255
Novaculite, 130
"Nuummite," 226

Obsidian, 186, 194
Ocean Picture Rock, 225
Odontolite, 268
Oil Shale, 225-226
Olivine, 38
OMF faceting machine, 44
Onyx, 90, 91, 97-98, 211-212
    agate, 97-98
    calcite, 211-212
Opal, 21, 170, 177-181
    common, 178
    Gilson, 316
    imitation, 320
    precious, 178-181
    synthetic, 316
    terminology, 179
Opalescence, 236
Opaque Quartz, **128-143**

Orbicular granite, 221
Orbicular jasper, 140, 141
Orbicular rhyolite, 227
Orchid Star quartz, 78
Organic lapidary materials, **259-272**
Ornamental materials, **205-233**
Orthoamphibolite, 226
Orthoclase, 240
Osmundites, 164
Ostrich eggshell, 269
Owyhee jasper, 139

Padparadscha (sapphire), 29, 312
Painite, 292
Palm wood (petrified), 165
Paragonite, 303
Parisite, 293
"Pastelite," 130-131
"Patricianite," 218
Paua shell, 260-261
Pauley, Erwin, 76
Pearls, 269-270
Pectolite, 195-196
Peridot, 38
Peristerite, 241
Perthite, 242
Petalite, 293
Petoskey stone, 214
Petrified wood, 150-167
    defined, 150-151
    forests, 157-161
    identification, 154-157
    specific kinds, 162-167
    uses, 153-154
Phantom quartz, 75
Phenakite, 293
Phenomenal gemstones, **235-258**
Phosgenite, 294
Phosphophyllite, 294
Piemontite, 50
"Pietersite," 83
Pinite, 303
Pink chalcedony, 120
Plasma, 121
Plume agate, 108-110
Polka dot agate, 102
Pollucite, 302
Polyhedroids, 124
Pom Pom and Thistle agate, 111-112
Poppy jasper, 140
Porphyry, 221
Pough, Frederick 48, 52, 103
Prase, 121

Precious, 4
Prehnite, 196
Prikazchikov, Leonid, 41, 216
Proctor, Keith, 20, 61
Prospite, 184
Proustite, 255
Pseudomorphic jade, 173
Pseudomorphs, quartz, **145-168**
    animal, 146-149
    mineral, 149-150
    plant, 150-168
Psilomelane, 256
    in chalcedony, 122
Pumpellyite, 238
Purpurite, 196-197
Pyrite, 256-257
Pyrope, 36
Pyroxmangite, 294
Pyrrhotite, 257

Quartz, 41, **63-167**
    blue quartz, 70
    crystalline, **63-84**
    cryptocrystalline, **85-167**
    defined, 63-65
    dumortierite quartz, 71-72
    ferruginous, 72
    gold in quartz, 72
    green quartz, 73
    imitation, 321
    lapidary treatment, 65-66
    opaque, **127-144**
    phantom, 75
    pseudomorphs, **145-167**
    rock crystal, 75
    rose, 77
    rutilated, 78-79
    sagenitic, 78-80
    smoky, 80
    strawberry, 81
    synthetic, 313-314
    treatment, 65-66
    white, 74
Quartzite, 66, 80
    aventurine, 66
    Sioux quartzite, 80
Qualities of lapidary materials, 2-7

Ramsey, John, 58
Ramaura, 311
Rare gem materials, **273-303**
Realgar, 295
Red beryl, 24

Refraction, 6
Rhodochrosite, 197
Rhodolite, 37
Rhodonite, 186, 197-198
Rhyolite, 226
Ribbonstone, 140
Ricolite, 229
Rio Grande agate, 188
Rock crystal, 75
Rocks as lapidary materials, 4-5
"Rodingite," 228
Rose quartz, 77
Royal Ontario Museum, 24, 58, 66
Rubellite, 61
Ruby, 4, 26-27, 310-311
    in zoisite, 27
    locations, 26-27
    synthetic, 310-311
Russian synthetics, 310, 312, 313, 315, 317
Rutilated quartz, 78-79
Rutile, 257-258
    synthetic, 317

Sabina, Anna, 200, 245
Sagenite, 78
Sagenitic agate, 110-112
Sagenitic quartz, 78-80
San Diego Museum, 40, 58, 61
Sand blasting, 12
Sanidine, 241
Sapphire, 4, 28-31, 311-312
    locations, 28-31
    star, 28, 30
    synthetic, 311-312
Sapphirine, 295
Sard, 122
Sardonyx, 122
Satelite, 229
Satin spar, 244
Scapolite, 244-245
Schaub, Benjamin, 88, 112
Scheelite, 54
Schiller, 236
Scorodite, 295
Scrimshaw, 266
Selection of material, 7-8, 44, 186
Selenite, 244
"Selwynite," 228
Semi-precious, 4
Sequoia, 166-167
Serandite, 296
Serpentine, 227
    bowenite, 228

Serpentine (continued)
 ricolite, 229
 satelite, 229
 verde antique, 232-233
 williamsite, 228
 "yalakonite," 230
Shattuckite, 198
Shell, 260-261
Siderite, 55
Silicon carbide, 318
Simulants and imitations, **318-321**
 alexandrium, 318
 coral, 318
 emerald, 318
 goldstone, 319
 helenite, 319
 hematine, 319
 jade, 319-320
 jet, 320
 lapis lazuli, 320
 laserblue, 319
 opal, 320
 quartz, 321
 turquoise, 321
 Victoria stone, 321
Sinhalite, 55
Sinkankas, John, 23, 56, 58, 76, 81, 88, 89, 294, 302
Sioux quartzite, 80
Slabs, 10, 11, 186
Slate, 208
Slocum stone, 321
Smith, Kevin, 76, 181
Smith, Mark, 55, 245, 295, 297
Smith, Rob, 79
Smithsonian Institution, 20, 22, 28, 40, 46, 47, 48, 53, 59, 71, 76, 171, 176, 182, 197, 285, 294, 302, 313
Smithsonite, 199
Smoky quartz, 80-81
Soapstone, 232
Sodalite, 199-200
Spectrolite, 240
Specularite, 254
Spessartine, 37
Sphalerite, 56
Sphene, 56
Spinel, 39
 synthetic, 314
Spodumene, 44, 57-58
 hiddenite, 57
 kunzite, 57
 triphane, 58
Spurrite, 230

Star stones, 28, 35, 54, 181, 236, 239, 245
State stone agates, 87
Staurolite, 230-231
Steatite, 232
Stichtite, 231
Stillwellite, 277
Stoller, Lawrence, 41, 76, 209
Strawberry quartz, 81
Strontianite, 296
Strontium titanite, 317
Sturmanite, 297
Sugilite, 41, 170, 182
Sunstone, 242-243
Synthetic gem materials, 7, **305-318**
Synthetic laboratory originals, 316-318

Taaffeite, 197
Talc, 232
Tantalite, 251
"Tanundaite," 219
Tanzanite, 41, 58, 203
Tektite, 59
 moldavite, 59
Tempskya, 167
Tepee canyon agate, 99
Teredo wood, 167
Thaumasite, 232
Thomsonite, 200
Thulite, 201
Thundereggs, 112-114, 181
Tigereye, 66, 82-83
Tiles, 153
"Titania," 314
Titanite, 56
Topaz, 39-41
Topazolite, 34
Tortoise shell, 270
Tourmaline, 60-62
 cat's-eye, 60
 chrome dravite, 60
 cutting, 62
 elbaite, 60
 indicolite, 60
 liddicoatite, 60
 Paraiba, 60
 rubellite, 61
 watermelon, 60
Tremolite, 245
"Trilliumite," 46
Triphane, 58
Triphylite, 298
Tsavorite, 35
Tucson show, 24, 25, 35, 39, 47, 50, 60, 79, 81,

Tucson show (continued)
    93, 120, 188, 208, 209, 218, 243, 245, 253,
    260, 279, 286, 289, 290, 302
Tufa, 215
Tugtupite, 201
Tumbled stones, 10, 66
Tunnelite, 277
Turquoise, 182-184
    Gilson synthetic, 316
    imitation, 321
    treatments, 184
Turritella agate, 148-149

Ulexite, 246
Unakite, 222
University of Alaska Museum, 51, 173
University of Pennsylvania Museum, 76
Uses of lapidary materials, 10-13, 153, 154
Uses of petrified wood, 153-154
Uvarovite, 38

Van Pelt, Harold & Erica, 76, 79
Vargas, Glen & Martha, 68, 276
Variscite, 202
Variquoise, 203
Vayrynenite, 277
Vegetable ivory, 271
Verde antique, 229
Verdite, 232-233
Verneuil, 305, 314
Vesuvianite, 192
Victoria and Albert Museum, 263
"Victoria stone," 321
Villiaumite, 303
Violane, 239

Virgilite, 277
Vivianite, 298
Wardite, 299
Wavellite, 299
Whewellite, 300
Willemite, 203
Williamsite, 228
Windisch, Horst, 82, 83, 231
Witherite, 300
Wollastonite, 246
Wonderstone, 226, 277
Wood, 271
Wood pseudomorphs, 150-167
Woodward plume agage, 110
Wulfenite, 300-301

Xenotime, 277

"Yalakomite," 230
"Youngite," 100
Yugwaralite, 277

Zebra stone, 209
Zectzerite, 301
Zeolites, 301-302
    analcime, 301
    mesolite, 301-302
    mordenite, 244
    natrolite, 302
    pollucite, 302
Zincite, 203
Zircon, 41-42
Zoisite, 203
Zunyite, 203

Rock, Gem and Mineral Classics from
GEOSCIENCE PRESS

GEMSTONES OF AFGHANISTAN. By Gary W. Bowersox and Bonita E. Chamberlin. A superbly illustrated survey of the gems of Afghanistan, their locations, and their impact on that nation's economy and society. $60.00, hardcover, 240 pages, 100 illustrations (40 in color), ISBN 0-945005-19-9.

GEMSTONES OF EAST AFRICA. By Peter C. Keller. The comprehensive chronicle of the richest gemstone deposits in the world, replete with maps and superb color photographs. $50.00, hardcover, 160 pages, 70 illustrations, ISBN 0-945005-08-3.

STANDARD CATALOG OF GEM VALUES. Second edition. By Anna Miller and John Sinkankas. The standard reference for both rough and cut gems. $24.00, paperback, 286 pages, 50 illustrations, ISBN 0-945005-16-4

PHOTOGRAPHING MINERALS, FOSSILS, AND LAPIDARY ARTS. By Jeffrey Scovil. A complete how-to for photographing minerals, gems, and fossils. $40.00, hardcover, 240 pages, 230 illustrations (37 in color), ISBN 0-945005-21-0.

ROCKS AND MINERALS. By Joel E. Arem. This invaluable color guide by the author of *Gems and Jewelry*, 2nd Edition, provides basic information in one easy-to-understand and easy-to-carry volume. $12.00, paperback, 160 pages, 230 illustrations, ISBN 0-945005-06-7.

STONES: THEIR COLLECTION, IDENTIFICATION AND USES. Second edition. By R. V. Dietrich. A practical guide for collectors, full of recommendations on where to find particular stones and information on how they are formed. $8.95, paperback, 208 pages, 79 illustrations, ISBN 0-945005-04-0.

FIELD COLLECTING GEMSTONES AND MINERALS. By John Sinkankas. The primer on how to extract, preserve, store, and exhibit specimens. $23.00, paperback, 397 pages, 133 illustrations, ISBN 0-945005-00-8.

Please ask your local bookseller to order our books for you or order them directly from one of the following distributors: (U.S. and Canada) Mountain Press, P.O. Box 2399, Missoula, MT 59806 or (rest of world) Melia Publishing Services, P.O. Box 1639, Maidenhead, Berkshire SL6 6YZ, England.